THE
EDITOR

THE EDITOR

HOW PUBLISHING LEGEND JUDITH JONES SHAPED CULTURE IN AMERICA

SARA B. FRANKLIN

ATRIA BOOKS

NEW YORK   LONDON   TORONTO   SYDNEY   NEW DELHI

ATRIA
BOOKS

An Imprint of Simon & Schuster, LLC
1230 Avenue of the Americas
New York, NY 10020

First Atria Books hardcover edition May 2024

ATRIA BOOKS and colophon are trademarks of Simon & Schuster, LLC

Simon & Schuster: Celebrating 100 Years of Publishing in 2024

For information about special discounts for bulk purchases,
please contact Simon & Schuster Special Sales at 1-866-506-1949 or
business@simonandschuster.com.

The Simon & Schuster Speakers Bureau can bring authors
to your live event. For more information or to book an event,
contact the Simon & Schuster Speakers Bureau at 1-866-248-3049 or
visit our website at www.simonspeakers.com.

Interior design by Lexy East

Manufactured in the United States of America

1   3   5   7   9   10   8   6   4   2

Library of Congress Cataloging-in-Publication Data

Names: Franklin, Sara B., author.
Title: The editor : how publishing legend Judith Jones shaped
culture in America / Sara B Franklin.
Description: First hardcover edition. | New York : Atria Books, 2024. |
Includes bibliographical references and index.
Identifiers: LCCN 2023057173 (print) | LCCN 2023057174 (ebook) |
ISBN 9781982134341 (hardcover) | ISBN 9781982134389 (ebook)
Subjects: LCSH: Jones, Judith, 1924-2017. | Book editors—United States—Biography. |
Women editors—United States—Biography. | Publishers and publishing—
United States—History—20th century. | American literature—20th century—
History and criticism. | BISAC: BIOGRAPHY & AUTOBIOGRAPHY / Women |
BIOGRAPHY & AUTOBIOGRAPHY / Culinary
Classification: LCC PN149.9.J65 F73 2024 (print) | LCC PN149.9.J65 (ebook) |
DDC 070.5092—dc23/eng/20240221
LC record available at https://lccn.loc.gov/2023057173
LC ebook record available at https://lccn.loc.gov/2023057174

ISBN 978-1-9821-3434-1
ISBN 978-1-9821-3438-9 (ebook)

*To my children, C & E—for helping me unlearn
so much and teaching me anew;
for grounding me in daily practices of care;
and for tethering me to this world*

and to Judith, in loving memory, for everything.

I like the unpath best.
—Nan Shepherd, *The Living Mountain*

CONTENTS

INTRODUCTION

On the morning of August 22, 1961, an assistant editor at the illustrious New York publishing house Alfred A. Knopf went to work. It was quiet when she arrived. The publishing industry ground nearly to a halt in those dog days of summer. The senior editors were all away, in the countryside or at the beach. They'd given their secretaries leave, too, and all those typewriters, which usually filled the office with their relentless clacking, for once stood silent. The air was still and thick.

The editor made her way to her desk, the one she'd been assigned amid the typing pool; she was always getting lumped in with "the girls" at Knopf. Piles of marked-up manuscript pages and neat stacks of interoffice memos stood like sentinels on either side of her typewriter. She had loads of work to do. She hung her purse on the back of her chair, sat down, smoothed her skirt, and began to type: "Dear Miss Plath: Sylvia, We have only just received from England the signed contract from Heinemann's for their *Colossus* and other poems—incredible how official wheels seem to grind so slowly sometimes! So I am hastening to write you now to let you know that we are scheduling the book for Spring, April '62 and are ready to put it into production. . . . I am delighted to see that we are finally under way."

In March of that year, the editor had turned thirty-seven. It wasn't a notable birthday, per se, but it was shaping up to be a very big year, one that would herald her arrival as a literary tastemaker and foretell a legendary career.

The editor had fought to acquire the American rights to Sylvia Plath's debut poetry collection, *The Colossus*. Plath was then twenty-seven, and balancing a baby on her hip. Few poets ever grow famous, but the editor sensed in Plath a level of ambition and discipline, and an originality of voice, that suggested she might prove an exception.

The editor had also recently begun working with John Updike. The thirty-year-old writer was astonishingly prolific; he put out his first books of poems and short stories, as well as his debut novel, all within the space of two years. Updike had requested to work with her himself. He wasn't the only one vying for her attention. In February 1960, the Pulitzer Prize–winning poet Theodore Roethke had written her, asking if she would help facilitate Knopf's publication of his 1959 National Book Award–winning collection, *Words for the Wind*, in paperback.

And then there was a cookbook, one written by two French women, Simone Beck and Louisette Bertholle, and an American named Julia Child. All three were entirely unknown. Knopf didn't publish cookbooks often; they weren't seen as literary enough in subject or form. But the editor, an enthusiastic eater and cook herself, had convinced her bosses to take a chance on this one in the spring of 1960. She believed the French cookbook had the potential to revolutionize home cooking in America. The editor had been working on the manuscript for more than a year by then. Knopf would publish it that fall.

The editor was Judith Jones, and though you may not know her name, you know her work: *The Diary of Anne Frank. Mastering the Art of French Cooking.* The entire oeuvre of John Updike and decades' worth of work by Anne Tyler. The work of John Hersey and William Maxwell, longtime *New Yorker* editor and author in his own right. The poems of Thomas Kinsella and Langston Hughes; William Meredith, Sylvia Plath, and Sharon Olds. A roster of cookbook authors that reads like a veritable culinary hall of fame—Claudia Roden; Edna Lewis; Marion Cunningham; Irene Kuo; Marcella Hazan; Madhur Jaffrey; Joan Nathan; M. F. K. Fisher; Lidia Bastianich; James Beard; and, most famously, Julia Child. Judith's career was astonishingly wide-ranging and long; she was an editor at Alfred A. Knopf for more than fifty years. Commenting on Judith's career in 1986, John Hersey said Judith was "one of the few remaining editors who fulfill the whole range of the editor's function rather than merely a packager of books." Knopf's longtime editor in chief Sonny Mehta called Judith's "body of work as an editor . . . unrivaled in the industry."

Judith Jones began at Knopf in 1957, in the midst of a transformative era in American culture at large and in American womanhood, more specifically. In the 1940s, women had been called into public service on behalf of the war effort, but when World War II drew to a close, they were sent back into the domestic realm again. Dominant postwar rhetoric suggested that women's patriotic duty was to relinquish the paid work outside the home they'd taken on. Returning male soldiers, the thinking went, needed their jobs back. Some women were relieved by the return to more traditional gendered roles, while others resented the postwar conservative turn. Regardless, many women felt they had no choice but to give themselves over to marriage, motherhood, and keeping house. Then, in 1960, the Food and Drug Administration approved the birth control pill. The ability to separate sex from childbearing offered women unprecedented control over their bodies and lives. The notion of modern womanhood was up for grabs. While the emergent second wave feminist movement squared off against media-driven notions that women should settle for the role of mother and housewife, Judith fashioned an unorthodox womanhood—in both her career and larger life—all her own.

Judith rose through the ranks of publishing when it was an industry still dominated by men. Her editorial oeuvre is a reflection of her perspicacity. Judith's books embody the cultural tensions of her times, illuminating the friction between women's private and public lives, and explore both the expectations foisted on them and their desires for themselves. Several of those books are today considered part of the feminist canon: the homoerotic fiction of Elizabeth Bowen; Florida Scott-Maxwell's writing on women and aging; a theoretical monograph on androgyny by Carolyn Heilbrun; and the searingly honest explorations of motherhood, marital strife, and mental illness in Sylvia Plath's verse. The dozens of cookbooks Judith published—the majority penned by women—blurred the lines between embodied knowledge, caregiving, and art. And while she may not have had explicitly feminist aims, Judith's work had major political impact. It changed the possibilities Americans—especially American women—saw for themselves.

Judith Jones left an indelible imprint on American letters and culture, but the story of her remarkable life and career is largely unknown. This is, in part, deliberate. The work of editors is inconspicuous by design, their labor playing out behind the curtain. Editors work in the service of their authors, not themselves, and their touch is meant to be difficult, if not impossible, for readers to see. The novelist Anne Tyler called Judith's style "very delicate and graceful, almost weightless."

To read Judith's authors is to encounter "the invisible hand of an extraordinary editor," said journalist Laura Shapiro. "Of course you don't see her. That's why she was great."

The scope of editors' role is little understood, even by the most avid readers. Editors' work extends far beyond moving words around on a page. They are shepherds of individual authors' careers, and responsible for the literary landscape as a whole. They must, at once, remain laser focused on their writers' specific needs, while keeping abreast of shifts in the culture at large. They are alternately called upon to be confidants and careful readers, patient coaches, and taskmasters. The role requires a business mind and a capacity for intimacy. A good editor is agile enough to navigate between these demands and sensitive enough to understand which to inhabit, and when. To possess such a wide array of skills is rare; to choose to spend one's life in service of the role is an act of devotion. Editing is more vocation than job. Judith spent her life answering the call.

Judith's invisibility, though, cannot entirely be chalked up to her position behind the scenes. Her veiled historical import owes much to the fact that she is a woman; misogyny shaped the arc of her life and career and continues to diminish her legacy today. Judith's impact on American culture and literature has been further muted due to the genre with which, to the extent she is known at all, she is associated: cookbooks.

While, in twenty-first century America, food is firmly ensconced at the center of our culture, books *about* food were (and to some extent still are) treated with an air of condescension by the literary world. Despite their popularity, cookbooks are often viewed as technical manuals rather than vessels of story, memory, and voice; and their authors are often seen as artisans rather than artists. Making cookbooks demands tremendous precision, creativity, expertise, and huge quantities of labor and time. Like the day in and day out labor of cooking itself, most books about food are written and edited by women. And like that quotidian work and those who perform it, writing *about* food is not only undervalued but often completely unnoticed. It is unsurprising, then, if no less troubling, that writers who choose food as their subject are often met with disregard, and that cookbooks' most famous editor was similarly patronized throughout her lifetime. "For a long time, the women—and they were usually women—who wrote about food were treated as second-class citizens," Judith said in a 2015 interview. "All because they cook!"

To Judith, all forms of writing had a place. She believed cookbooks deserved the same careful attention and editorial rigor as fiction, memoir, essay, and poetry. She was "imaginative, versatile, fascinated with stories, curious about people and places, a deft wordsmith and above all insatiable for the pleasures of . . . cooking," wrote Kim Severson in Judith's *New York Times* obituary. "[S]he built her reputation on finding well-educated, underappreciated cooks like [Marion] Cunningham, Marcella Hazan and Madhur Jaffrey, turning them into stars." With her deft editorial hand and keen cultural sensibility, Judith shepherded into print cookbooks that redefined the form, books threaded through with quiet but fierce political resistance. "Food started getting serious respect largely because of her," said Ruth Reichl, former restaurant critic for the *New York Times* and the final editor of *Gourmet.* "When you talk about the cookbook revolution, she *was* the revolution," Reichl said. Yet even as Judith's reputation as a cookbook editor grew, she was wary of being pigeonholed. "I never wanted to be identified as just this or just that," she told me.

While Judith was a brilliant editor with worldly, catholic tastes, she, like everyone, contained biases that shaped her worldview. History has revealed her blind spots: She passed on Sylvia Plath's *The Bell Jar,* cautioned her Knopf editor in chief not to take on *The Collected Poems of Frank O'Hara,* and twice rejected the stories of Alice Munro, who went on to win a Nobel Prize. In cookbooks, especially early in her career, Judith was prone to flattening the perspectives of her authors of color. In her desire to make the "exotic" more appealing to an audience largely assumed to be white, she too often excised nuances of her authors' identities, especially elements of race and class. Judith wasn't perfect. There were paradoxes in her work and in her presentation of self.

Those close to Judith experienced her as sensuous and playful, even mischievous. She was tender of heart, a romantic in many ways; deeply spiritual and highly spirited. But at work, she projected reserve. Her public persona was a product of her discipline, rigor, and commitment to her work. A practiced restraint. Judith learned early on to be judicious in how, and to whom, she directed her attention and energy. To mete out her resources with care. But when Judith gave of herself, it was with her whole self, so fully that she was sometimes left with diminished reserves for those in her personal life. For all these reasons, both systematic and specific, Judith has remained a liminal figure in history.

· · · · · · · ·

In 2007, when Judith was eighty-three years old, she published a memoir called *The Tenth Muse: My Life in Food.* I was in college when I stumbled upon the book in a shop one day. I'd never heard of Judith Jones before, but I was interested in food, and *The Tenth Muse*'s subtitle caught my eye. I bought the book on a whim.

The Tenth Muse is fun—a sunny romp through postwar Paris and the greatest hits of twentieth century American food culture—but it lacks interiority. In telling her own story, Judith glossed over her larger literary life. She also elided her dis-appointments, hard choices, mistakes, and pain. I had a hunch Judith had lived a more complicated life than the one she broadcast to the world, but it wasn't until I was given an opportunity to spend several months interviewing her about her life and work in food that I would begin to understand.

Judith was eighty-eight years old and newly retired when first we met. She was tiny—no more than five feet tall, and slim as a green bean. Her white hair was cut in a girlish bob. She wore her age like a fact: Neither good nor bad. Just true. In-tractable. Our work together took place across six months in 2013, first at Judith's apartment on Manhattan's Upper East Side, and later that summer at her second home in northern Vermont. We always cooked and ate. Working in the kitchen and sharing in the pleasures of the table laid the foundation for our rapport. We sniffed and squeezed, chopped and stirred. We licked our fingers. We didn't use recipes but were guided instead by instinct, experience, and one another's input. We came to know and trust each other that way. Only after the dishes were done and the coffee poured did we begin our interviews. On some matters, Judith was forthcoming, barely needing my prompting. On others, she remained guarded and reticent. Our conversations were hours long and full of digressions, intimate de-tails, and active reflection on past events. Many of Judith's revelations surprised me. Judith told me they surprised her, too.

After the project was complete and I'd sent the interviews off to be archived, we remained in each other's lives. We'd become confidants. Friends.

In 2015, after more than nine decades of robustness, Judith's health took a sharp turn. And in 2017, at ninety-three years old, Judith succumbed to Alz-heimer's. At Judith's memorial service for family and friends in Vermont, her stepdaughter, Bronwyn Dunne, pulled me aside. She asked if I'd like to come to Judith's apartment to have a look at her personal papers. I'd written a bit about Judith, Bronwyn knew, and thought I might be interested. There was a lot of ma-terial, she told me. Two rooms full.

I missed Judith, and I saw Bronwyn's offering as both an opportunity and a gift: More time to think about Judith. To be with her. To look for clues to ques-tions about her that still lingered in my mind, the ones she hadn't answered or I hadn't yet known to ask when she was alive. And so I said yes.

It took more than a year for me to make a first pass through the material; it went all the way back to the 1930s, when Judith was a girl. I read through correspondence with family members and friends, former lovers and longtime authors. Her photographs, notebooks, and papers deepened my understanding of who she'd been as both a person and an editor. I gained insight not only into how Judith worked but into her motivations and preferences as well. The more I learned, the more I realized Judith had a much more complex story than the one she'd written about herself.

I began reading everything I could get my hands on about Judith, but there was precious little of substance. She shows up in fleeting moments in biographies of some of her authors and former colleagues. In the late 1990s, when *The Diary of Anne Frank* was adapted for the stage, her role in the book's publication was finally made public, and a short-lived flurry of publicity celebrated her foresight in regard to that book. When she published *The Tenth Muse*, food publications buzzed for a while, acknowledging the huge mark she'd left on the field. Most often, when Judith's name surfaced, it was in concert with Julia Child's. There, Judith was portrayed as something of a sidekick rather than a decades-long collaborator and major player in the formation of Julia's career. Nowhere could I find a depiction of Judith that even suggested the reaches of her curiosity and sophistication, her complexity and acumen, her savvy and her guile; the extent of her effect on our lives—what we cook and eat, the stories we read and the ones we tell—and the literary and publishing communities at large. This book is my attempt to give the editor, the *woman*, her due.

· · · · · · ·

Judith's personal papers go back to her girlhood, beginning with journals and correspondence from the 1930s. I've read hundreds of Judith's handwritten letters, and they've given me invaluable insight into her earlier life. The Knopf archive at the Ransom Center at the University of Texas at Austin holds a great deal of Judith's professional correspondence from her first two decades working at the publishing house. When Judith began there in the 1950s, all official Knopf correspondence was typed in triplicate, with a carbon copy for the writer, the recipient, and the archive. Those years of fastidious paper-based communication and systematic filing of records at Knopf make up the most thoroughly illuminated period of Judith's working life. With the advent of the fax machine, publishing's day-to-day functioning changed significantly, as did the volume of paper in the archive. Later, email—which Judith never got the hang of, relying on assistants and friends for help—supplanted faxing, and the record of written communications on paper thins further still. Much from Judith's later decades at the house is scattered; and the editorial files for some of her authors are incomplete, or missing altogether. Where possible, I helped fill in the gaps by speaking with Judith's colleagues, authors, family, and friends. But some I couldn't track down, while others declined to be interviewed or go on record. And many of those who knew Judith, especially in her younger years, were long gone by the time I began work on this book.

Even the most complete archives can't tell the entire story of a life. Intimacies Judith exchanged with lovers and friends, small talk made around the office and conversations over meals, telephone calls, trips taken, and walks in the park and along Vermont's quiet dirt roads. Desires and disappointments never named. Secrets kept. Most of what constitutes any life goes undocumented, and Judith's was no exception to that rule. All of which is to say, absences have shaped this book as much as the materials available to me.

Judith worked with well over a hundred writers in her lifetime. To try to tell the story of her relationship to all of them would result in an unreadably long and dense book. Rather than exhaustive, I've been selective in attempting to show the full arc of Judith's life from her childhood until her final days. I've given priority to those authors who played a particularly important role in Judith's life's trajectory, and those that mark important moments in the evolution of her taste over time. The Judith Jones we encounter in these pages is an amalgam of what I learned of Judith through the materials she left behind and how I experienced her in real time. Which is to say, the story of Judith told here is not the only one possible, but rather a particular telling, cast through the lens of a lived relationship, one that unfolded at a time in which Judith was looking back on her life as it neared its end. This book not a definitive biography but an intimate portrait, one that aims to highlight Judith's prescience and outsize influence on American culture and to humanize her—from girlhood through old age—as well.

A note on names: I refer to Judith by her first name throughout this book. *Judith* was the name by which I called her when she was alive, and the name that everyone I spoke to about her used as well. For all others who appear in these pages, I've taken a more flexible approach, using full or last names when referencing published work, public life, or professional roles, and first names when showcasing Judith's more familiar correspondence and closer relationships, including the many she cultivated with her authors over time.

And one final note: everyone has a right to tell their own story, and to have their experience accepted as their truth. I've hewn as close to the essence of Judith, as I knew her, as I could in rendering her in this work. She was a woman preoccupied with voice. In keeping with that spirit, I've let Judith speak for herself wherever possible, in her own words.

CHAPTER 1

In January 1942, Judith showed up at 14 West 49th Street for her first day of work at Doubleday, Doran & Company. She was seventeen years old. As she crossed the street to the office's entrance, she tipped her face skyward. The building before her soared into the sky, light glinting off its windows. The publishing house's offices were in Rockefeller Center, into which oil tycoon John D. Rockefeller had driven the final rivet in November 1939. More than forty thousand people had been employed in the development's construction; it was the largest private building project of its time. Stars studded the marquee at Radio City Music Hall; *King Kong* premiered there. *National Velvet* did, too. There was a sunken skating rink and the Rainbow Room restaurant; high on the sixty-fifth floor, where the dance floor rotated and a big band played. Joan Crawford, Bette Davis, Marlene Dietrich, and Laurence Olivier all dined there. It was a place to see and be seen. A modern New York City sensation. The building was terribly imposing. Judith pushed eagerly through the glass doors and into the soaring lobby.

Just a month earlier, on December 7, 1941, Japan had launched an attack on Pearl Harbor. President Franklin Delano Roosevelt declared it "a date which will live in infamy." Suddenly, the United States was at war. Anticipating the country's being drawn into the global conflict, FDR had instituted a peacetime draft in September 1940. Swarms of men enlisted voluntarily. By the end of 1941, the U.S. military was 2.2 million strong. Initiatives sprung up to support the war effort on the home front, too. Sacrifices had to be made, and jobs, abandoned overnight by American men, needed filling. Everyone was expected to do their part. Everything was changing, and fast.

Judith wasn't one to sit idly by. She wanted a way to make sense of what was happening around her and was hungry to contribute in some way; Judith had always been hungry. But for a young woman of genteel means, that path wasn't immediately clear. So Judith began with what she knew: stories and words. She understood their power and potential. All her life, they had moved her. Shaped her. Judith thought that maybe, just maybe, she could make her mark in that world, the world of books. She wasn't sure just how, but she was young, a quick study, and full of gumption. And she was determined to try. Judith couldn't wait to get inside.

· · · · · · · ·

Judith Fifield Bailey was born on March 10, 1924. She was the second daughter of Charles "Monty" Bailey, a lawyer from Montpelier, Vermont; and Phyllis Hedley Bailey, the youngest of three sisters whose family had moved to New York to chase opportunities in the pharmaceutical industry. The Bailey family lived at 139 East 66th Street, an unremarkable nine-story brick apartment building between Third and Lexington Avenues on Manhattan's Upper East Side. Phyllis's two sisters, Hilda and Helen, also lived in the building with their respective husbands and children, and the three family factions owned and managed the building cooperatively. They raised their children that way, too. Judith; her older sister, Susan; and their cousins all shared a nanny. And it was she, not the children's parents, who did most of the day-to-day caregiving work.

Judith's mother, Phyllis, and her sisters had been groomed their whole lives to climb the social ladder and become ladies of society. And though 139 East 66th Street wasn't the ultimate Manhattan address, it was the most the Hedley sisters and their respective husbands had been able to afford. They hitched their fate to the belief that their real estate investment would appreciate over time and that the property's proximity to the limestone mansions of Park Avenue and Millionaires' Row on Fifth Avenue would both symbolize and secure the extended family's class ascent.

Phyllis aspired to an image of flawlessness, and raised her daughters to follow in her image, expecting them to be impeccable in every way. But from an early age, Judith didn't conform. As a girl, she was often sickly, and, as such, she spent a great deal of time in bed, alone save for the family's dog and a book propped against her knees. She read children's picture books in her younger years, and later, poetry and Scripture; the Baileys were practicing Christians. Judith was drawn to the beautiful language she discovered in books. Stories and verse of all kinds helped Judith envision a life richer and deeper than the one she was being raised to lead. Books provided Judith some solace and escape, but only in mind. The more she read, the more she longed to know and feel firsthand that which existed outside of her cloistered childhood milieu.

The building at 139 East 66th was a world of formality, prescribed roles, and high expectations. The fathers went to work, while the mothers focused on socializing and running their households. Judith's mother was markedly disciplined in her management of hers. Though she never worked outside the home, Phyllis wielded her organizational skills nonetheless. She designed and sewed the family's drapery, bedspreads, and her daughters' clothes. She orchestrated her family's social lives and planned all of their meals, ordering produce from the local greengrocer, and the neighborhood butcher by phone. "My mother," Judith would later say, "was an expert." What Phyllis was not was nurturing or warm. For that, there was the kitchen, and in it, Edie.

Phyllis hardly set foot in the family's kitchen; a woman of standing, she believed, didn't dirty her hands with household work unnecessarily. It was Edie, the Baileys' domestic employee, who cooked. Judith was drawn to the kitchen, and spent all the time there with Edie that she could. She felt alive and at ease amid the pots and pans and the sounds of dough slapping on the countertop, the plop-plop of cake batter being mixed in a big ceramic bowl. Sometimes, Judith helped grate blocks of cheddar for macaroni and cheese, or melt butter for dipping artichoke leaves. While she worked, Edie often told Judith about her childhood in Barbados; she spoke of the island's red dirt, the fruit that grew in wild abundance there, and local dishes seasoned with hot peppers. Edie's stories lit up Judith's imagination; they were the girl's first exposure to a culture other than her own. "I just loved her," Judith told me, "because I saw a world beyond, somehow."

At mealtime, though, Judith had to tuck away her curiosity and interest in all things food. She and her sister were expected to eat quietly and to be well-mannered, pretty, and neat. "I was told never to mention the food at the table," Judith told me. "You didn't talk about mundane things like that." Phyllis considered food as vulgar a subject of conversation as sex. A lady didn't take pleasure in eating, nor did she give voice to her hungers. But "I was a little rebel!" Judith told me. "I think that's when you learn. It's that wonderful sense of growing up, of freeing yourself and finding your own world."

Judith wished for even more distance from Phyllis's reign than her afternoons with Edie could provide. From her youngest years, she'd wished her family lived in Vermont, Monty's home state, and the place where he and Phyllis had met and courted. Judith's father's branch of the family was utterly unlike uptight Phyllis and the Hedley sisters' side. The Baileys were engaged, hearty, pragmatic people, especially the women. They worked hard and relished fun, and Judith loved to be around them. When Phyllis packed up the girls to head back home from their long stays in the Green Mountain State each summer, Judith rued having to return to New York. She felt far more at ease in Vermont than she did in the big city. "I used to stamp my feet as a little girl and say, 'I'm not a New Yorker, I'm a Vermonter!'" she told me.

In 1935, when she was eleven years old, Judith talked her parents into letting her spend a year living with her paternal grandmother, Fannie Hubbard Bailey, in Montpelier. Judith mounted a convincing argument. Earlier that spring, she had flunked the entry exam for the elite Brearley School, where Phyllis insisted her girls attend high school. Judith would have to repeat eighth grade. Judith proposed that instead she attend public school in Vermont for a year, get her grades up, and then retake the admissions test. She made a point of emphasizing that Monty and Phyllis would save a year's worth of expensive private school tuition. It was a crafty maneuver on Judith's part: the family was feeling the strain of the Great Depression, and while they still lived in comfort and privilege, they were struggling to pay the mortgage on the building and to keep up appearances. After hemming and hawing, Judith's parents agreed to let her go. And so, at the end of August 1935, when the rest of the Bailey family headed home to Manhattan after their annual holiday in Greensboro, Judith took the train thirty miles southwest to Montpelier instead. "I was going to Vermont to grow up," she later said.

Fannie Bailey—"Nanny" to Judith—was a force. Since her husband's death in 1925, she'd lived alone in the big clapboard house at a bend in the Winooski River where Judith's father grew up. The house stood at the corner of State Street and the eponymous Bailey Avenue; the Baileys were that kind of family in Vermont. They'd been one of the earliest white families to settle the state, and Bailey kin were everywhere, with their hands in everything from state politics to infrastructure, medicine to manufacturing. Fannie's late husband, Burnside B. Bailey, had worked for the Central Vermont Railway and later became deputy secretary of Vermont.

Fannie took the obligations of prominence seriously; all her life, she served on boards and worked in service of those less fortunate than she. As a young child, Judith had discovered her grandmother fed hoboes, carving a special symbol in an elm tree in the yard to signal that her house was a safe haven, a place where one could warm up and get a free meal. Fannie was upstanding, but also had a "deliciously mischievous" streak. Most days, after school, Judith did her homework while Fannie sipped sherry by the fire. But every Monday, Judith and her grandmother walked arm in arm to the cinema downtown. Afterward, they went to Jackson's pharmacy for ice cream sodas.

Fannie fostered Judith's independence, offering her granddaughter a chance to explore and develop on her own. She sent Judith horseback riding on golden autumn days, and in winter, out to play in the deep snow. Judith rode her bicycle all over Montpelier, and had sleepovers with friends at her aunt Marian's, just down the street from Fannie's house. Marian was a marvelous cook, and though she could've afforded to hire someone to do the work for her—her husband was a prominent general practitioner in town—Marian preferred to prepare meals herself. "Cooking with love was such an expression of her feelings for her household and her family," Judith later said. "That got to me." When Judith stayed the night at her aunt's house, she'd wake to the smell of breakfast. Sometimes there were popovers "a mile high," which Judith slathered with "thick layers of jam and cream." Marian relished the pleasure her niece took in her cooking, and, unlike Phyllis, she encouraged Judith to indulge her appetite.

Judith kept her word to her parents, making the honor roll at school in Montpelier amid all the fun. She handily passed Brearley's entrance exam on her second go, and began high school there in the fall of 1936. Judith's classmates recognized something remarkable in her—in the yearbook, they called her "lovable" and "magnetic," "a rare individual with a great attraction for all kinds of people"—but Judith did not return their high regard. On the contrary; she found her classmates as dull and colorless as the East River that coursed beside the school.

Privately, she mocked them. In a notebook, she wrote:

Oh, sing a song of Brearley
A school house full of bores
Full of fat and thin girls working on their chores.
Oh the typical Brearley girl is a worthy dame
But just like her friends she's exactly the same.

As graduation neared, Judith's classmates split into two groups: those already engaged and headed for the altar, and those who intended to enroll in college. The latter wasn't so much a different path as a way of delaying arrival at the same eventual outcome: women's colleges at the time were seen as holding pens for young ladies while they awaited a suitable proposal of marriage. All that education was but further grooming for future wives and meant, it was implied, to be tucked away once a woman wed. Judith, who had aspirations beyond becoming a mother and wife (and, as of yet, no real prospect for a husband anyway), wanted a place that would act as more than an advanced finishing school, somewhere that would challenge her and broaden her worldview. While many of her Brearley peers eagerly applied to the prestigious Seven Sisters colleges—Vassar, Wellesley, Barnard, Mount Holyoke, Smith, Radcliffe, and Bryn Mawr—Judith had eyes only for Bennington College.

Bennington, which had enrolled its first class in 1932, was at the vanguard of liberal arts education. The college regarded "education as a sensual and ethical, no less than an intellectual, process," and strove to nurture its students' whole person, in body, mind, and spirit. The curriculum emphasized hands-on experience and self-directed learning. Plus, it was in Vermont, and Judith was dying to put some distance between herself and New York.

Judith had long found her mother's snobbish class consciousness distasteful, but as Judith grew older, it had become downright suffocating. Phyllis kept a copy of the social register—an index of phone numbers and addresses of the who's who of New York society—by the telephone, a constant reminder to her daughters of who she believed they were and who she expected them to be. So when Judith received a letter of acceptance from Bennington in the spring of 1941, she didn't have to think twice. It felt like her ticket out.

Judith chose Bennington for its progressive ethos, but when she applied, she hadn't realized just how high the caliber of teaching was at the school, nor how much it would affect what she would be exposed to and how she would learn. The college prized the literary and performing arts especially, and recruited those at the cutting edge of their crafts in an attempt to prepare young women students for a changing world. When Judith started her first term in the autumn of 1941, the faculty included the poet Léonie Adams, who would be appointed seventh Consultant in Poetry to the Library of Congress (the role that, since 1986, has been known as Poet Laureate Consultant of Poetry, and, colloquially, as Poet Laureate of the United States) in 1948, and her husband, the critic William Troy. Catharine "Kit" Osgood Foster was both a well-regarded literary scholar and a beloved teacher. The economist Lewis Webster Jones, one of Bennington's founders and, as of 1941, the college's new president, still taught classes. Peter F. Drucker, a sociologist and philosophy-minded economist, was known to be especially tough in the classroom. He became a favorite of Judith's. "You'd make some broad statement, as you do when you're young, and think you have all the answers," Judith told me. "But he would get you out on that limb and keep pushing with questions until soon you were left having made yourself quite foolish. It was brilliant! I never saw such good teaching."

Each winter, Bennington dismissed its students for an extended recess during which they were expected to travel or work, and to seek "the educational advantages of metropolitan life." The message was clear: Bennington believed a woman could be more than a wife and mother. She could have a career.

Judith had started college with an interest in literature. When it came time to choose a place for her winter work placement, Judith perused Bennington's list of places that hosted student workers and noted Doubleday was on it. Working in publishing seemed a good way to get closer to the world of books, to understand how they came into being, and associate with the people who wrote and made them. A family friend of the Baileys who knew someone at the publishing company wrote Judith a nice letter of recommendation. And with that, she was in.

By the time Judith began at Doubleday, American book publishing had evolved from a decentralized niche business to a cultural powerhouse industry. The book business had arrived in the current day United States with early European settlers, but for centuries, its reach was limited due to the high cost of printing and shipping and low literacy rates. In the late nineteenth century, the industry expanded rapidly on the heels of wartime innovations in technology and the expansion of the nation's railroads. And by the turn of the twentieth century, New York City had become the firmly established center of American publishing.

Publishing houses, known as shops, or "houses" in book business parlance, grew in number; and with the industry's growth came changes to its structure. Literary agents began to play an important role, acting as middlemen between writers and publishing houses. Payment to authors and their agents—who then, as now, worked on commission—began to come in the form of book advances, a form of payment rendered after a contract between author and publisher is brokered. And the royalty system—by which publishers paid out a percentage of the sale of each book if and when its total earnings exceed the amount paid at signing—was introduced. The boomtime 1920s brought an unprecedented influx of capital and entrepreneurial spirit into American publishing; in 1927, Doubleday merged with George H. Doran Company, becoming the largest publishing company in the English-speaking world. Many publishers didn't survive the Depression. But

Doubleday—with its diverse array of revenue streams including retail bookstores, a huge mail-order business, and the largest book club operation in the country—came through alive.

A place as big as Doubleday relied on a huge fleet of employees from mailroom workers to secretaries all the way to the upper ranks. Most publishers were in it for the money, not an interest in literature. There were exceptions; the house of Alfred A. Knopf, founded in 1915, was known for its commitment to authors and the literary world. But for the most part, the attitude among publishing's top brass was, "I sell books, I don't read them," as Frank Doubleday, Jr. famously said.

In those days, Alfred A. Knopf later said, "things were quite simple. The books came in. We published them as written." But by the 1940s, the editors' role had begun to enlarge. When a manuscript came in, it was an editor's job to assess a writer's talent and to try to gauge their future potential as well. Editors began to collaborate more closely with writers, helping hone their voices and finesse the work they'd submitted into publication shape, "working together with their authors," as the writer and publisher Keith Jennison put it, "to ask more of the book." Increasingly, editors played a role in nurturing "to the fullest extent the craft of each writer they deal with," the writer John Hersey said, building a relationship over time. It was a role that, in the winter of 1942, with no experience at all, Judith took on with gusto.

On her first day on the job, Doubleday's newly appointed editor in chief, Ken McCormick, put Judith right to work. He was swamped. Doubleday was short on staff that winter; many editors had enlisted and gone overseas. Where previously women had been relegated to the secretarial pool, the war brought unprecedented opportunities for them to make their mark on books. That first week, McCormick gave Judith an array of work: a health pamphlet for Lenox Hill Hospital that needed to be copyedited and proofread and a stack of submissions he asked her to read. He wanted her opinion on each: Should Doubleday make an offer or pass? And he handed her a novel, *Hotel Berlin* by the Viennese-Jewish writer Vicki Baum, to edit.

Baum, born in 1888, didn't begin writing professionally until she was thirty-one, well after the birth of her first child. By then, she'd married, divorced, and married again; she published her first story under her first husband's name. In the 1920s, as a mother of two living in Berlin, Baum began to box; the Turkish prizefighter, Sabri Mahir, taught her "a pretty mean straight left, a quick one-two." There were few "tough enough to go through with it," only a handful of women—including Marlene Dietrich—entered Mahir's ring.

Baum prized toughness and grit; the work ethic she learned in the ring she later said helped her to write. "I don't know how the feminine element sneaked into those masculine realms," Baum later said in her memoir. But Baum was a New Woman, determined to make a life of her own. In 1929, when her novel *Grand Hotel* became a bestseller, Baum was forty-one years old. And when, in 1932, the book was made into an Academy Award–winning film, Baum rocketed to international fame. She'd go on to publish more than fifty books—more than ten of which became movies—as well as scripts for both the stage and the screen.

When McCormick handed Baum's manuscript to Judith, it was without specific instruction for what to do. "He said, 'She needs work,' but he didn't say what *kind* of work," Judith told me. "So I decided to trust my own instinct." Judith began making her way through the novel, cutting extraneous prose and moving pieces around to ease narrative flow. "I was editing! At seventeen!" Judith told me, still a bit incredulous even after so many years. She stayed at Doubleday only a short time, that winter of 1942, but it was long enough for Judith to develop a taste for the trade. Judith became indispensable, but remained invisible; she never did meet Vicki Baum. At Doubleday, "They never showed me to the authors," Judith told me. For a young woman still emerging out of her shell, editing this way, behind the scenes, was ideal. "I loved it. And I thought I was pretty good at it, too," Judith told me.

McCormick agreed. He recognized Judith as an astute reader who maintained her perspective as she "waded through thousands of words of mediocre manuscripts." "I do want to compliment you on the way you kept your balance," McCormick wrote Judith in March, when her time at Doubleday came to an end. "You blended your own excellent ideas with our suggestions skillfully rather than superimposing them on what we assigned to you." McCormick continued: "We regret you had to go back to school. I hope we will have the pleasure of seeing you at work with us again." Judith clung to the praise, calling it her "absolute pride and joy."

. . . .

Judith smoothed her bedspread and pulled aside the starched white curtains to let in the warm breeze; finally, spring had arrived in southern Vermont. Mathilde, a classmate and friend, put on a jazz record, while another, Laura, fussed over the appetizers. Sarah Moore, Judith's best friend from New York and roommate at Bennington, filled five glasses with Haig & Haig Scotch. It had taken some doing to find the booze—all the most delicious things, it seemed, were being rationed due to the war raging overseas—but Judith hoped their efforts would pay off. The poet Theodore Roethke had just been hired by Bennington, and was set to teach an advanced poetry seminar the following fall. Judith and her friends all wanted in. Having had a taste of publishing in New York, Judith was determined to get as close to the literary scene on campus as she could before graduating. So she'd orchestrated a little party in her and Sarah's dorm room that evening.

It wasn't unusual, at Bennington, for students to fraternize with faculty. Freedoms, including sexual ones, were baked into the Bennington ethos of liberation: "We wanted a college where a girl could hang upside down from a tree in her bloomers if she felt like it," one of the college's founders said. The college's permission of such liberal behavior quickly earned it the nickname "the little red whorehouse on the hill." There were no house mothers, no curfews, and no prohibitions on socializing in the dorms. And with many men away at war, "You were sort of starved for that kind of attention. So we had to seduce the professors," Judith said. The young women planned to put their charms to use to win entry to Roethke's invitation-only course.

Roethke had made waves in the literary scene with his 1941 collection, *Open House*. The verse was deeply personal; the lines "My secrets cry aloud. / I have no need for tongue" opened the title poem. The volume, published by Knopf, was a slim collection built from ten years of work. Knopf printed a thousand copies of the first edition, a publishing feat for a poetic debut. The *New York Times* called Roethke "a scrupulous craftsman," "even the most delicate poems have the ribs of technique." W. H. Auden said *Open House* was "completely successful," and in the *Atlantic*, Elizabeth Drew wrote, "his poems have a controlled grace of movement, and his images the utmost precision . . . an austerity of contemplation and a pared, spare strictness of language very unusual in poets of today." Roethke's work rocked Judith, who'd long been drawn to poetry's transcendent power.

Roethke had a reputation as an unconventional teacher. In a lecture on physical action, he once crawled out a classroom window and onto the roof. He sometimes held class in a local bar. Roethke was demanding, too. He'd chant, "Motion is equal to emotion" like a mantra and say, "Don't be so guarded—let your mind buzz around!" He was intent on his pupils mastering rhythm in verse and attuning themselves to voice. Before analyzing, Roethke implored his students, "Listen, listen, listen." It would become one of the most enduring lessons of Judith's life.

The poet, whom his friend the poet Stanley Kunitz described as "perfectly tremendous" and "a shambling giant," took advantage of all the attention that night; after they'd eaten, he invited all four young women back to his house. "But," Judith said, "we all decided (he, too) that, progressive as Bennington was, that might be stretching things too far." But the young women's hostess skills did the trick. Before the night was over, Judith and her cohort had all been invited to participate in Roethke's course.

Judith was relieved to return to Bennington in the fall of 1943, after a summer of vapid cocktail parties surrounded by her mother's friends. There was the Roethke class to look forward to. There was also Kenneth "Papa" Burke. "We have a new teacher up here this term. Kenneth Burke. Have you heard of him?" Judith wrote home excitedly at the semester's start. "He is quite a well-known critic and he's giving a marvelous course in literary criticism which I'm taking," she said. Like Roethke, Burke was at the cutting edge of the literary scene. For Burke, the scope of literature's impact wasn't relegated to the page; he believed it could change lives. He put forth the notion that words could "form attitudes or induce actions," an idea Judith found enlivening. When Burke announced his "maximum course" on Eliot, Judith signed right up.

Burke often taught class in the farm fields that year, his students set to weeding while he lectured. "There's nothing better than to have your feet firmly in the earth while your mind soars," Judith remembered him saying. But Burke also brought his students to the farm to help them meet their mandated work quotas there.

In 1942, after the United States joined the war, all Americans were urged to grow more of their own food. American rations were needed overseas, and local gardens offset the victuals sent to Europe. The U.S. government urged citizens to grow food at home, in community spaces, and also in schools. "Vitamins for Victory!" went the slogan. Bennington, whose campus had once been farmland, took the call seriously. By spring 1942, the students had planted fourteen thousand seedlings in a greenhouse and put more than fifteen acres into vegetables. They tended livestock, too. In 1943, Bennington students preserved more than two tons of pork from pigs they'd raised, and froze more than three thousand tons of chicken from birds they'd slaughtered and processed themselves. Between 1943 and 1944, the extensive garden became a full-blown farm of more than one hundred acres.

The farm fed Bennington well, but morale toward it was often low. Most of the students hailed from wealthy families—Bennington was then the most expensive college in the country—and had never lifted a finger in pursuit of a meal. The shift toward producing their own food amused some but irked many more. Students complained and traded shifts for cash. Judith openly rued farmwork. Her peers accused her of lacking "community spirit" and being "uncooperative at the farm," Judith wrote in a letter home to her father, "because I flatly refused to kill chickens." "I can't," she wrote to her parents, "manage to summon forth any patriotic energy toward it." Judith maneuvered out of the heavy lifting as best she could. "Dearest Mums," she wrote to Phyllis in early fall of 1943, "With the coming of the cold I decided that I definitely couldn't stand the fields so I've now become a vegetable preparation girl. I'm learning all the tricks of canning from cutting and peeling to working a powerful electric pressure cooker. I must admit that I had to pretend I was allergic to rag-weed in September to get where I am but I'm being so diligent now that before you know it I'll be promoted to the role of squad leader." Judith wanted, instead, to give her time and attention to poetry, and to the poet Roethke himself. As his student, she'd quickly fallen under his spell.

Roethke became one of Judith's greatest teachers, and her first love. He was thirty-five, she was nineteen. Judith was smitten with everything about the poet: the workings of his intellect and his big, hulking frame. The serious set of his jaw, even his tendency toward dark moods and drink intrigued her. Roethke's whole affect suggested an emotional rawness and vulnerability Judith was unaccustomed to in men. She found him irresistibly alluring.

Under Roethke's sway, Judith's writing became more disciplined and mature. In a "minor thesis" she wrote for him on Wordsworth and Vaughan, she commented boldly on those poets' work, engaging with the idea of pantheism, "the belief that everything in the finite world is a manifestation of God." She tried her hand at writing poems of her own, too:

> Listen how
> Circling other skies
> That will soon sweep
> Down over tops of trees
> And scatter the last of the rain.
> Even the oak
> The huge, the ancient oak
> Sunk deep in earth's depths
> Unbends, and boughs
> Now spineless
> Heave to the ways of the wind.

She titled it, simply, "Poem," and signed it "Judith Bailey." Roethke kept her poem with him for the rest of his years.

Judith loved Roethke, in part, because he took her seriously; in a first edition of *Open House*—copy number 669 of the original run—he wrote: "To Judy, a good writer, still not bold enough." It was at once a recognition of Judith's uncommon mind and a sharp criticism. Roethke, a rogue in his own right, urged Judith to cut her own path. He saw her raw potential and dared her to live up to it. No one had done that for her before.

Judith devoted herself to Roethke, despite his unreliable affection and mercurial moods. While one month, he'd be animated by a swell of excitement and creative energy; the next, he'd grow glum, prone to self-flagellation, and unmotivated to write. Manic depression, or bipolar disorder, had plagued Roethke all his life. The disease wasn't well understood then, nor had safe, successful treatments for it been established at the time. Roethke's swings had grown both more intense and more frequent since his first breakdown in 1935, when he was teaching at Lafayette College. It's unlikely Roethke mentioned that incident to Judith, and the depth of his dark moods confused her. How, she wondered, could someone so gifted be prone to such paralysis and insecurity? But she was already in the poet's thrall, too enamored of him to pull away in order to protect herself.

Her final year at Bennington, Judith was overcome; her love affair with Roethke was pained and she was overwhelmed academically. She'd been made head editor of *Silo*, Bennington's literary magazine, and put in long hours on nights and weekends. Her mind was alight, but her body wouldn't keep pace; she was plagued by insomnia and dogged by painful menstrual periods that sent her to bed for days at a time. She wrote to Phyllis to report that a certain Dr. Lewis's course of treatment was bringing no relief. "You can tell our worthless friend . . . that my condition is not in the least improved." Judith's symptoms were more than vexing; monthly, her body derailed her ability to study, think, and work.

Still, she had a thesis to finish under Burke's tutelage. She'd chosen to write on the Victorian poet and Jesuit priest Gerard Manley Hopkins, who'd found his pathway to God in the wonders of nature. It was a conception of spirituality that struck Judith as both beautiful and true. Her thesis began: "One thing that distinguishes the poetry of Gerard Manley . . . is the assertion of a positive doctrine of faith. . . . What concerned him was not simply the individual and his expression, but the individual soul, its meaning in terms of a greater whole, its life and its salvation. . . . The mystical experience is accompanied by a reveling in the physical beauties of the world."

As her time at Bennington neared its end, Judith watched as her classmates "popp[ed] off one by one." Wartime accelerated courtships, and many of Judith's friends interrupted their studies or dropped out to marry, as Judith's sister, Susan, did in November 1942. Phyllis gloated publicly about her elder daughter's match, announcing both the couple's engagement and wedding in the *New York Times*. Judith had no interest in following suit. She was in love with Roethke but had no intention of making their bond official or settling down so soon. "I should think you'd be a bit nervous, Mrs. Bennet," Judith wrote home, alluding to the protagonist's mother in Jane Austen's *Pride and Prejudice*. Judith implied, but did not say, that she was Elizabeth Bennet, the novel's fickle heroine, who refuses to marry on anyone's timeline but her own. Judith delighted in flaunting Phyllis's expectations, even more so in rubbing them in.

As Judith listened to Supreme Court Justice Frank Murphy give the commencement address at Bennington in June 1945, what came next for her was yet unclear. She knew, though, that she wasn't heading for the grooves of the well-worn path. If Bennington had taught her anything, Judith would later say, it had been "to live an audacious life."

CHAPTER 2

Judith hurried to keep pace with Ken McCormick's long stride as he led her through the labyrinth of office hallways. He looked dapper, if a bit offbeat, in his loose brown slacks, brightly colored shirt, and plaid blazer. He'd aged quickly, Judith thought, in the past few years; his time in the air force had added lines to his face and a deeper furrow to his brow. But McCormick remained warm, chatting casually with Judith as they walked, calling her "baby" and "sweetie," as he did with every woman at work.

McCormick showed Judith to a small office with two desks; one telephone line; and an office mate, Betty Arnoff. The editor in chief introduced the two young women, patted Judith on the shoulder, and left them to get acquainted. The publishing house hummed around them. It was 1947, and Judith was back at Doubleday.

The return had taken Judith some time and casting about. With no husband, job, or money of her own, she had, after graduation, reluctantly returned to living back with her parents. She needed a job if she was going to escape from under her mother's thumb. But for women, paid work—so easy to come by during the war years—had grown scarce. "The boys" were coming back from overseas, and American women were being sent back home. And men were making more than ever before. When the war ended in September 1945, the median income for wage earners in the United States was $1,400 per year; by 1952, it had risen to $2,300. Meanwhile, women's progress stagnated: By 1947, women's employment had returned to its prewar rate. Many who wanted to work were regularly refused jobs. Judith experienced it firsthand.

Several months after graduation, Judith wrote to Roethke. The two were still involved, though it had become complicated by distance since Judith's graduation from Bennington. Things had grown even more strained when the poet suffered a second mental health breakdown in early 1946. Early in that spring term, Roethke had locked himself in his faculty house in a fit of mania, declaring he'd only emerge if his friend, the poet Stanley Kunitz, was brought in to replace him at Bennington. Kunitz, who had just completed his military tour, had never taught a lick in his life. Nonetheless, Bennington hired him on the spot, and Roethke went home to Saginaw, Michigan, to rest.

"Dear Ted," Judith wrote him there in April 1946. "All winter I have been going through the motions of job hunting, prompted only by the fact that I assure you that it makes you rather gloomy and tied to the famille to have your pockets constantly empty." She'd tried everywhere she could think of, save newspapers. After spending a winter work stint at the *New York Post*, Judith had decided she'd never go back into a newsroom again. "We were all called 'boy.' They'd literally call you, 'Hey, boy, need you to take this to . . .' But all those boys were girls!" Judith told me. Judith contacted publishing houses and magazines throughout the city, but no one offered her a job. She "tried to sell" herself to Barbara Lawrence, the features editor at *Harper's Junior Bazaar*, by offering pitches for story ideas, but to no avail. She was called in for a meeting at the *New Yorker*, in which William Shawn, then assistant editor at the magazine, was "much too nice—and I finally had to force a confession [from him] that there was really nothing for me at least until the fall," Judith wrote Roethke, chagrined. "But perhaps it is out of kindness that everyone seems to send me on my way. For there is always that horror at the last moment that someone might hire me and that overnight I should become a $30-a-week girl, bound to New York and some grubby little desk," she said.

Finally, in the fall of 1946, she was offered an assistant position in the promotion department at E. P. Dutton. In her internship at Doubleday, Judith had been in editorial, working directly on authors' manuscripts. The work of promotion was different. Editorial departments gestate authors and their books; promotion helps deliver them into the world. In her role, Judith helped craft short, attention-grabbing descriptions of books for catalogs and sales materials, with the aim of convincing booksellers to order and stock Dutton's titles. She also wrote copy for both advertising campaigns and the jackets of books, meant to encourage consumers—readers, that is—to buy them. Judith's time at Dutton showed her that books' audiences don't spontaneously emerge. Publishers have to create them.

One of Dutton's new associate editors when Judith came on at the house was Gore Vidal. He was a year and a half Judith's junior, and fresh out of the army. His job as editor gave him an in to the literary scene and helped support him financially, though not well, while he tried to write. At $35 a week, Vidal's job paid him well below the national average of $3,000 per year. It wasn't much, and certainly not enough to live on, but "it kept me in cocktails," Vidal said. Publishing was a gentleman's industry—"They paid us a pittance!" Judith told me—and only the privileged could afford to work in its ranks.

Judith took a shine to Vidal right away. She admired his wit and thought he was gorgeous, with his tawny hair; slim build; and brooding, gold-flecked eyes. She flirted with him relentlessly. "We used to go out to dinner sometimes," Judith told me. "And I wondered why he never put his hand on my shoulder or anything like that. Then he came by once at the office and said, 'I've fallen in love,' and I said, 'Oh, who is she?'" Judith knew of Vidal's promiscuity, but had no idea he slept with both women and men. She'd had no exposure to queer culture, and what she couldn't see, she couldn't yet square. Judith laughed at the memory, and at her youthful naïveté. "That was my first encounter with a whole different world," she told me.

Vidal published his first novel, *Williwaw*, with Dutton in 1946 when he was twenty-one. When Judith started at the house in fall of that year, Dutton was preparing to publish Vidal's second novel, *In a Yellow Wood*. Judith was tasked with writing the short summary meant to hook readers that appears on the inside jacket flap of hardcover books. Vidal introduced Judith to his friends—young, glamorous bohemians all. It gave Judith a taste of a different New York. "He helped me a lot," she told me. "And we became great friends."

Judith's time at Dutton didn't last long. "They expected me to write all the minutes of the meetings, but I'd never learned shorthand," she told me. "I just couldn't keep up with the job." It wasn't for lack of motivation, though. Quite the opposite. "I didn't want to go to shorthand school," Judith said. By refusing to train in secretarial skills, Judith was rejecting her relegation to what was then the only readily available role for women in publishing. "So," she said, "I was gently urged to quit." Out of a job again, Judith circled back to her former boss, Ken McCormick. This time, she had a copy of *Williwaw* tucked under her arm, and ties to literary scenesters including Vidal, Roethke, and her Bennington adviser, Kenneth

Burke. She also mentioned the name John W. Vandercook, or Jack, as she'd known him personally, a reporter, host, and rising star at the National Broadcasting Company (NBC), whom her cousin Jane H. T. Perry, alongside whom Judith grew up at 139 East 66th Street, had married in 1938. Impressed by her apparent savvy and growing network of connections, McCormick offered Judith a job.

Since Judith had last worked at Doubleday, the company had grown. By 1947, the house had nearly five thousand employees, and was the largest publisher in the United States. Its diversity, however, was still lacking; there were only two Black employees on its payroll, and almost no Jews or women. In Judith's memory, she and Betty Arnoff were two out of only three women outside the secretarial pool at the enormous house. The third, Clara Clausson, worked on cookbooks, a genre that, at the time, Judith knew nothing about. As two junior editors in a sea of men, there was no question Betty and Judith would be put together at Doubleday. An ambitious, and somewhat anomalous, alliance of two.

In their cramped space, Judith and Betty worked together side by side. In Betty and Judith's capacity as readers, their job was to lighten the load of more senior editors by taking a first look at the manuscripts that had been submitted to Doubleday. The two would take weeks to read a manuscript, then weigh in on whether it seemed promising or, instead, if they thought the house should pass. "It was a leisurely process," Betty told me, "nothing like the breakneck pace of contemporary publishing." Throughout, Judith maintained a sort of "private distance," always waiting until Betty had left the room before making phone calls, which only contributed to Judith's "mysterious air." "I always had the impression," Betty said to me, "that anything she told me about herself went through some kind of censorship. It never came out half-baked, and it was always self-edited." Judith struck Betty as out of step with their generation somehow, especially in the way she spoke. "She used words that seemed to come out of a novel by Brontë or Austen," Betty said. "She seemed almost prim." Still, it wasn't long before the two became friendly and developed a shared ritual for their days.

The two would both arrive around nine, then immediately go downstairs to one of the restaurants on the building's ground level for breakfast. Then it was back upstairs for a little reading, maybe a few phone calls, then out again for lunch. French restaurants had popped up throughout the West 40s; it was there that Judith tasted her first celery remoulade and pâté de campagne. Sometimes Judith was invited out by the more senior editors, who held working lunches with the literary agents who hoped to sell them books. "They'd have two or three martinis," Judith recalled, "and smoked their way through lunch." Nothing about the job or industry was cutthroat or head down. "It wasn't a lot of work," Betty recalled. "It just seemed like so much socializing." Every day, the young women quit by five. Then the parties began.

· · · · · · ·

Judith checked her lipstick in the mirror and tucked a loose pin back into her hair. In her reflection, she saw a waiter come into view carrying a tray of Manhattans. She whirled around to grab one before he passed her by. Turning to face the room, Judith nibbled one of the cherries from her drink. The apartment's windows were thrown open to the hot night. The laughter and clinking of glasses from the party floated out over Central Park.

It was June 1947, and Betty's parents were away for the summer. They'd left her with some extra cash in case she needed anything while they were away, and Betty had known immediately just what to do with it. Betty set a date and told Judith and the rest of the recent college graduates they'd met in publishing to invite anyone who was anyone to come. Betty, Judith, and their friends were young and hungry, all angling to find a foothold in publishing as new opportunities came down the pike.

The war had ended on September 2, 1945, and, in its wake, publishing boomed. Many of the GIs filtering home had developed a reading habit while overseas, fed on cheap paperback editions of bestsellers distributed for free by the Council on Books in Wartime (CBW). In 1943, the CBW began printing Armed Services Editions on a mass scale. By the end of the war, when its operations ceased, CBW had put almost 123 million books into circulation. The CBW kept publishers and magazine presses afloat during the war, and democratized reading as well.

The G.I. Bill of 1944, the most ambitious educational experiment in history, sent American vets to college, and lots of them: 2,232,000. Higher education meant higher wages; and with the growth of the middle class, consumer spending soared. With literacy and leisure time on the rise, Americans began buying books in droves. America's Golden Age of Capitalism had begun. So had its golden age of publishing. "Print was king," wrote Al Silverman, longtime president of the Book-of-the-Month Club and later, at Viking, editor of T. C. Boyle, William Kennedy, and Saul Bellow, "and literature was at the center of American culture."

Judith, Betty, and their friends began the evening of the party nervously clustered by the bar, knocking back their drinks too fast, wondering if anyone would show. But by the time the high summer sun melted over the West Side, the Arnoff apartment was packed with writers and their friends, as well as agents, editors, and the young people aspiring to join their ranks.

Judith had invited the Vandercooks and Gore Vidal; the couple and the writer had both showed up flanked by big-name friends. Roethke, who was briefly in town, came as her date. Betty was stunned at the star power surrounding her office mate and friend. "There were so many authors Judith knew and was involved with. Anything she was doing with her contemporaries was kind of incidental," Betty said to me. A year into her time at Doubleday, Betty had just begun to try to cultivate relationships with authors she admired. But Judith, she saw when they went out on the town, was way ahead in the game. At parties like hers, Betty began to see another side of Judith personally as well. "She'd have a drink or two and be entirely different," Betty told me. "Much looser. And less careful." Betty began to realize Judith's austere office persona was a deliberate and controlled public presentation of self. "It never occurred to me what a spicy life she was leading," Betty recalled.

It didn't feel that way to Judith. No sooner had she moved home after graduation than 139 East 66th had become a revolving door of potential suitors whom Phyllis invited for cocktails or dinner, impatient for her daughter to choose a husband and finally settle down. "I was *supposed* to find a nice man, preferably on Wall Street so he had a lot of money," Judith told me, "and supposed to be well educated and social. Maybe join a club. Be in the social register. It was that kind of insidious snobbery." There was mockery in her voice. "That was what I was *supposed* to be. What I *wanted* to be was free." So in the spring of 1947, when Sarah Moore told Judith her parents would be away on Long Island all summer and invited Judith to move into the family's apartment on Riverside Drive while they were gone, Judith jumped at the chance. She needed breathing room and space to sort things out for herself. It had been a confusing year.

Out on the town with her work friends and her cousin Jane, Judith met plenty of men. At Doubleday, "There was no one around. Or else they were married, and wanted just a quick jump in bed." She went on dates, but no one held her attention. "American men," Judith told me, "were kind of boring." Roethke remained the only man who made Judith's heart flip, but she wasn't sure she saw their relationship going anywhere.

In the spring of 1947, after coming down from his manic break, Roethke began searching for a new teaching post. He wanted to be in New York, but no offer came. Instead, he ended up nearly 250 miles west at Penn State. Bored and isolated, he pawed at Judith for attention. "Well I'm here and it's as grim as hell," Roethke wrote in a letter to her in February 1947. "It would be so nice (as you'd say) to hear that low-pitched 'hello' over the phone. Love, T." The distance and Roethke's dark moods were hard on Judith's heart, but when the poet swung a visit to the city, she pushed her doubt aside. The two sipped cocktails and went to jazz clubs with friends. Back at Roethke's hotel, they'd tangle in the sheets until Judith had to go home. Even when they were together, she was always anticipating his departure. It made her feel needy and insecure. The weekend after Betty's party, Judith wrote, "Please forgive me my more trying moments. I like you to remember the nicer me. I like you too much—and for that you, after all, are to blame. Much love, Judy."

Roethke remained unpredictable, often canceling plans at the eleventh hour. Judith found being jerked around like that both exhausting and humiliating. After the poet stood her up in the city in early July, she was angry and hurt. He plied her with letters from Saratoga Springs, where he'd just started a residency at Yaddo for the months of July and August. But for several weeks, Judith didn't respond at all. "Dearest Ted," she wrote at last, "I imagine your silence has been in answer to mine. All right, but remember, dear, that I have always been the one to be indulgent with you in distracted moments and generally hectic states of mind." Despite her increasing wariness, she couldn't bear to cut him off completely or to end on a curt note. "I miss all of you too much. Goodnight darling, and please try to think nicely of your 'blondest Baby,'" she wrote.

The contact roused Roethke, and he wrote, begging Judith to come see him upstate. She didn't respond. Mid-August, the poet wrote again in a fit of disquiet. "Dear Puss: I waited around: got no call from you (Somehow I got the notion you didn't give a damn whether I got in touch or not—maybe a childish pique; or a mixed fear; but not indifference. Here's the point: Are you coming by? But if you're mad I suppose that's that.)." He had big news to report: he'd accepted a job at the University of Washington in Seattle that began that fall. "I'm in a strange state. Funny and lively and maybe naughty. But I've been drinking too much: it's like in the old days—as if I don't give a damn. Maybe you'd like me; maybe you wouldn't. You wouldn't be bored, though." He went on, "I had wished for a tender missive of some sort when I got back even though I didn't deserve it. I think of you with love and intensity. Goodnight, pet." Roethke wrote a second letter that same day, saying, "I do miss you very much. And I seem vaguely irked that you don't seem to be missing me." Two days later, unnerved, he scribbled. "Darling: This is just a last shot in the dark—a last try—" He listed a number of ways their paths could cross. "Something? Please think." It was clear to Judith that Roethke was unstable again. She was unsure what to do. So she remained silent, maintaining a cautious distance.

Later that month, Judith sat beside her cousin Jane on the edge of the bed. Below, in Washington Square Park, children skipped rope and called out in glee. The two women were in Jane's little flat, the one she'd just moved into. Having finally had enough of her husband's booze-fueled fits of rage, Jane had left him. The apartment was a temporary sublet, a place to land while she collected herself and figured out how to file for a divorce. But it wasn't Jane who was in pieces that day; it was her cousin.

Judith wiped her tears from her cheeks, as Jane tried to convince Judith to end things with Roethke. "Dreadful as it seems to even mention it," Jane wrote to Judith soon thereafter, reiterating her stance, "I do really think an enforced separation is probably the best solution." Jane placed a gentle hand on her cousin's shoulder. Overheated and emotionally wrung out, Judith crumpled into sobs.

Roethke's acceptance of the job in Seattle made it clear to Judith that their romantic relationship was, at last, destined to end. But she couldn't find a way to make a clean break. In March, Roethke had left Knopf and sold his second collection of poems to Doubleday. Judith's presence at the house had, in large part, motivated his switch; having an in with a publisher as powerful as Doubleday was a major boon. McCormick, knowing of Judith's deep ties to the poet, had made her Roethke's handler in-house. Just as she'd been almost ready to sever ties, the two had become professionally enmeshed.

Once settled out West, Roethke became obsessed with the publication of his book. He wrote to Judith at work almost daily with questions, reminders, and requests. Judith began to second-guess herself; perhaps she'd been wrong to jump to the conclusion over the summer months that their romance was doomed. He did need her, after all. But rather than attending to Judith's tender feelings and the heartache he'd caused her, Roethke wrote brusquely, making demands of her time and labor. "I am going to devote some effort to your jacket copy this weekend, dear," Judith responded, annoyed. "You aren't nagging but it really isn't due until the middle of December." The lines between romance and business had become terribly blurred. And the power dynamic in their relationship had shifted. Whereas, at their start, Roethke had represented the literary world Judith wanted so badly to be a part of, now it was she who had access to the publishing establishment and a foothold in New York, while Roethke was farther and farther from the center of things. It made the poet uncomfortable to cede his upper hand. Judith yielded to his bluster and ego. "Forgive me, dear," she wrote, "you are probably distressed by thinking you've overburdened me. But I love doing it, truly—and am doing a good job." In another letter that fall, she was even more plaintive. "Love me please and miss me—you don't know how much I need you." Judith was slipping back into old habits, further muddling the boundaries within her relationship to Roethke.

· · · · · · · ·

In September, Judith returned to 139 East 66th Street. Now in her childhood home, she'd realized she was in a rut. She'd hoped her job at Doubleday would bring her back into "the world of thoughts and people" from which, "since Bennington, [I] feel so cut off," she wrote Roethke. But she'd been disappointed to discover that New York was "frightfully glum at times," and the atmosphere of the publishing world in New York was "really unliterary" instead. After she and Betty were pulled into an editorial pitch meeting one afternoon, Judith reported to Roethke on the "viciousness" and "contempt for the ones who run the show [that] came out of some of those more uneasy people at Doubleday." She was relieved to feel less alone in her disappointment with the way things worked at the house. "It was a very nice feeling to have everyone else as angry and disgusted with that set-up as I so often feel," she wrote.

In Doubleday's stultifying atmosphere, Judith began to doubt herself. "I know I am lazy, or to be more honest, it springs from a sort of defeatism at the start, a lack of confidence, which is worse. The foolish thing is that I do have a lot of integrity," she wrote Roethke. Judith could feel cynicism starting to eat away at her earnest passion. She knew she needed to nip it in the bud. She began toying with leaving her job, and the city entirely. "I have been trying to think of all possible alternatives to spending the winter at Doubleday," she wrote Roethke. She reported that she and Sarah Moore were thinking of moving into Sarah's parents' house on Long Island for the winter, to try to make a go of it writing on their own. "Do you think that's a good or completely senseless idea?" she asked. Roethke suggested she ask McCormick for temporary leave, "or use it for a chance to get more money." Judith fed off his validation and encouragement. "Thank you for your thoughts upon the Long Island venture," she responded. "At least you weren't so dubious as to laugh the whole thing off. I really don't think it could be a total loss as far as general studying and worthwhile reading goes, though I have no assurance of what might come out creatively. But unfortunately I can't afford to live that way long and I'd certainly be no farther ahead in the publishing game. As for a leave, I'm afraid I'm not important enough yet to pull that. To Ken anyway I'm going to talk about the general prospects of this winter."

For the first time in months, Roethke communicated steadily with Judith. He was attentive, acting supportive and almost warm. Judith wrote him proudly that she'd made good on his advice, finagling a little bump in her salary by voicing that she was considering leaving the house. "Darling, I got the raise—am now a $40 a week girl which is somewhat better and also promises far more varied and interesting work. So my small show of agressiveness was something of a success." "I'm delighted about the raise," Roethke wrote in response. "From now on I want you to 'agressive' [sic] with two g's 'aggressive.'"

"Dearest Ted," she wrote a couple of weeks later, "I have been in a completely frenzied state the last several days. Perhaps it is good to be aggressive but I am paying for it heavily. For all of a sudden there has descended upon me via Ken such an abundance of work that I am truly snowed under. I had a meeting last Friday with the doctors (the authors of a repulsive little baby book I'm editing) plus the fact that Ken threw the latest Vicki Baum monstrosity at me, the size of a *War and Peace*, to please, please cut. We pulled in none too early last night and I had all of Vicki still before me. It certainly felt like old Bennington days too as I brewed up a pot of bitter coffee and settled down for an all-night session." Her tone turned melancholy then. "The fall is a particularly upsetting time, with a kind of urgency in that first cold air that brings things back so sharply. There is one thing—and this I haven't even dared approach for fear you might be beginning to waver a bit in your promise—and that is, you are coming for Christmas, aren't you?" Judith needed something to look forward to. For all his mercurial tendencies, Roethke still seemed, to Judith, the only bright spot amid so much drab. "All I can think of is thank god for you—but I can't bear not being with you, darling," she wrote him.

In November, Roethke wrote that he would, indeed, be coming East for Christmas, "though not for long," he said. Judith splashed out for tickets to *A Streetcar Named Desire* on Broadway; Marlon Brando played Stanley and Jessica Tandy was Blanche. Judith presented the poet to her family as the man she loved. For a few days, it was wonderful amid all that holiday cheer. But then Roethke left, as he always did. And Judith fell apart. "Darling," she wrote, "this is the second night I've been trying to get you—lurking about until the family is well retired, moving the telephone into the kitchen and then squatting there on the cold kitchen floor, only to have a persistent buzzing sound on your end which no one bothers to pick up. My God, I wish that Seattle would just blow up so you wouldn't have to ever go back." Roethke offered no response. When, finally he surfaced, again ignoring her personal pleas and asking only for her help with the promotion of his book—"Look, it just might be I could get back for the date of the book. Are there any reading possibilities that might defray expenses; or any such stunts?"—this time, Judith didn't back down. She fired back a sharp retort. "Really, Ted . . . get off your own letter."

. . . .

It was April 1948. Winter had been long and dark, and Judith was low. "It's been dismal here—a terribly let-down feeling I've had. I've been working much too hard for those Doubleday bastards, it's cold and blizzardy, and I miss you," she'd written Roethke. "I've just had a dreadful weekend—out in Long Island with

some very distant cousins who married well," she reported. "It threw me into a terrible fit of rage to see how ignorant and appallingly dull the young well-bred could
be. In fact, what is the matter that everyone should be so unutterably dreary?" But
finally, spring had come, and the forsythia was in bloom. "It is getting warmer and
Monty and I walk pleasantly to work in the morning. I've also been bringing lunch
(to save money) and eat a soggy sandwich with beer bought from the zoo in the
park on sunny days," Judith wrote Roethke. "I think Burke is back, was supposed
to be by the end of March. I must write him too. Much love, J."

Judith did write Kenneth Burke. And he, in response, invited her to join him
at a literary party. She accepted with delight. On a balmy evening, Judith walked
with Burke to the bar, a new lightness in her step. He ordered himself a whiskey,
and asked what she was drinking. Champagne, Judith said. She was jubilant, too
excited to sleep. She'd managed to keep her news to herself until they were together in person, not wanting to spoil the surprise. She wanted to see Burke's face
when she told him she was going to Europe for the summer.

Judith had had enough. She'd grown weary of Doubleday, and of doing other people's bidding rather than signing (or "acquiring") authors of her own. She was sick
of being Roethke's part-time girlfriend, too; the pattern had gone on long enough
for her to see, once and for all, that he paid her any mind only when it suited his
needs. "I am very tired of being mournful and melancholy. It is time I did something about it," she wrote Roethke, giving voice to her discontent. Judith felt both
unburdened at the admission and adrift; now that she'd made a declaration of
intent, she would have to figure out what to do next. It wasn't until the spring of
1948 that Judith had realized what her move should be.

By the time Judith's cousin Jane's divorce was signed in late 1947, she was already
engaged to be married again to John Gunther, a foreign correspondent at NBC.
He and Jane's first husband, Jack Vandercook, worked together as broadcasters,
which is how he and Jane met. The new couple made plans to elope to Chicago
in March 1948, and invited Judith as their only guest. After that, they'd sail for
Europe. It would be a working honeymoon; Gunther needed to get back into the
field.

Judith saw her opening: she would go to Europe, too. With Jane and John on
the continent at the same time, surely her parents couldn't object. Before she lost
her nerve, Judith requested leave from Doubleday. McCormick granted her two
months, unpaid. Then she broke the news to Roethke. "It will be very good for
me—to be off on my own, to get out of this terrible in-a-rut feeling for a while,
and above all to see a little something of the world," she wrote. Judith convinced

her father to give her a loan, then applied for her first passport. She talked Sarah Moore into coming along, too. They bought tickets to steam across the Atlantic on the *Vulcania*; the trip would take ten days in each direction. In between, they'd spend several weeks touring the continent.

By April, Judith was brimming with anticipation. Kenneth Burke could see why; with the war finally over, the European cultural scene had come roaring back. As they stood discussing all Judith hoped to see, Burke spotted an acquaintance across the room, and waved him over. It was Arthur Koestler, the Hungarian writer renowned for his 1940 novel *Darkness at Noon*. Koestler took a shine to Judith at once. (Koestler took a shine to many women, whether they wanted him to or not; he later was connected to multiple incidents of sexual humiliation and rape.) Judith told him she was sailing for Europe in June. She wanted to see it all, she said. Florence and Rome, London and Paris, too. Koestler had lived in Paris, and started in with advice. He told Judith of his favorite bistros, and gushed about the city's nightlife, food, and wine. "Now, don't be afraid to go to a restaurant by yourself," Judith remembered him saying. "They'll treat you very well. But you have to be comfortable," he said to her. He had friends there, Koestler told her. He was sure they'd show Judith the town. He offered to write her letters of introduction to André Malraux, Albert Camus, and Jean-Paul Sartre. "All three!" Judith told me. "How could you resist?" Judith felt the tide was finally beginning to turn in her favor.

CHAPTER 3

I n the early summer night, Judith and Sarah rolled the taxi's windows down as they pulled out of the Gare du Nord and out onto the city streets. The two young women stared wide-eyed as they passed the manicured gardens and fountain of Jardin du Palais Royal and the vast, statue-studded Jardin des Tuileries. Stray cabbage leaves and onion skins dotted the streets around Les Halles, a few crates and baskets errantly left behind. In the morning, the centuries-old market would bustle again, but just then, it was at rest. They whizzed past the ornate facade of the Louvre Museum, then crossed over the Seine on a narrow bridge. The taxi pulled up in front of the Hôtel du Palais d'Orsay, with its two clock towers facing the Seine.

Judith paid the driver with a tourist's clumsy *"Merci!"* Inside, chandeliers dangled over the columned grand staircase and lit the marble walls. The lobby was abuzz with porters and doormen, necktied men and silk-draped women who laughed and flirted, drinks in hand. Judith felt as though she'd been shot through with an arrow. It was June 16, 1948, and it was midnight in Paris.

. . . .

Paris had been freed in August 1944, but times remained taut; liberation brought an end to the city's Nazi occupation, but it hadn't turned on the heat or put meat back on French tables or bones. "Parisians, who expected to fill up on something more than freedom are still underfed," the American writer Janet Flanner wrote, reporting from France. After the war's end, rationing continued for years. Bombings had ravaged the city, and its infrastructure was in shambles.

Paris, as it had been before the war, would never return. Still, after so many tense years, there was relief and, among the young, a sense of wild abandon. Alcohol flowed freely, and French women rode bicycles in patchwork skirts made so short by the scarcity of fabric they "generously uncovered pink thighs." In February 1947, Christian Dior premiered his "New Look" on the city's streets, all nipped waists and accentuated curves, wrought from bolt upon bolt of the finest fabrics. Many gawked, aghast; after years of scrimping, haute couture seemed a thumb in the eye of patriotic thrift. It seemed antifeminist, too. "Fashion is a veneer foisted on naive women by despots," quipped one Rive Gauche critic. "Give me sincere blue jeans!" At the market Rue Lepic, war-ravaged women ripped a dress from the body of one of Dior's models in protest. To Judith, French femininity—contested as it may have been—seemed refreshingly open, irreverent, and free. "I admired the French enormously," Judith told me. "And I loved the women."

In May 1948, for the first time since before the war, the cathedral of Notre-Dame, Sainte-Chapelle, and the Place de la Concorde were once again alight, restoring the city's signature glow. That summer, when Judith and Sarah arrived, saw more American tourists in Paris than any year since 1929, an estimated hundred thousand in all. They brought with them the strength of the U.S. dollar and the American inclination to spend. It was as essential to the French economy as building materials were to the Marshall Plan. "We were welcomed with open arms," Judith told me. For Paris, it was a season of hope. Supply chains dragged, but new ideas flowed freely forth, especially from the headwaters of Saint-Germain-des-Prés.

After their first night at the luxe Hôtel Palais d'Orsay, Judith and Sarah moved to the more modest Hôtel Montalembert on the city's Left Bank, and the two made haste to find seats at the tables of Boulevard Saint-Germain. Café de Flore and Les Deux Magots thrummed with writers with pens in hand. A young Simone de Beauvoir had been working on Flore's second floor every morning for years; she'd brought her lover, Jean-Paul Sartre, there with her in 1941, after he'd been released from a German prison camp. The two became fixtures of the place, while Maurice Merleau-Ponty and Camus anchored the first floor. The publishing houses Gallimard and Seuil were just down the street. Saint-Germain was the beating heart of Paris's postwar literary scene, and Judith wanted to experience it for herself.

Armed with Koestler's letters of introduction, she tried to reach Sartre first. He didn't answer, though. And "Camus," Judith said, "was out of town." But she wasn't discouraged; Judith tracked down Stuart Gilbert, a British scholar who was the first to translate Camus's *L'Étranger* into English, and went to lunch with him instead. Before long, her dance card was full, though mostly with American writers, not French. After the war, American artists, many of whom had fled or avoided the city during the occupation, had come flooding back in. Judith had cocktails with Robert Lowry, a Cincinnati-born veteran and literary wunderkind, and Jack Vandercook, her cousin Jane's ex, who was passing through on a reporting trip. Ken McCormick came to Paris that summer. So did Gore Vidal. He'd gone to Europe to escape the controversy that arose with the publication of his latest novel, *The City and the Pillar*, in which he exposed himself as gay. Vidal went first to Rome, where he'd heard men could flirt more openly. There he met Tennessee Williams. The two hit it off. By July 1948, both had posted up in Paris.

Judith bumped into Vidal on the street, and he promptly introduced her to Williams, whose *Streetcar* she'd so loved. Williams was a social magnet, and around him that summer were clustered not only Vidal but also the writer Christopher Isherwood and the composer and writer Paul Bowles. Vidal's British publisher, John Lehmann, had crossed the Channel to network and pick up new American talent which, that summer, was easier to do in Paris than in New York. Truman Capote blew in, flaunting an amethyst ring he claimed he'd been given by André Gide, the French writer who'd won the Nobel Prize in 1947. Capote and Williams lunched at Les Deux Magots with their mutual friend Johnny Nicholson; they introduced Nicholson to Vidal. No wonder New York's literary scene seemed so dull, Judith thought; everyone interesting was in France. The men kept Judith amused, socially connected, well-fed, and in drinks. But it was a young French woman who proved most influential of all.

With Koestler's letter in hand, Judith called on Malraux. But the French novelist, freedom fighter, and former minister of information was busy working on *The Voices of Silence*, his three-volume meditation on art. So he passed Judith off to his press aide, Brigitte Friang. Friang was headed to dinner with friends, and invited Judith to tag along.

Friang had been an active member of the French Résistance. She'd been seized by the gestapo; fired upon while trying to escape; tortured in Fresnes, France's second largest prison; and then sent to the north to Ravensbrück, a German concentration camp, the only one exclusively for women. After the Liberation, she returned to Paris and began working for Malraux. Friang still met up regularly with her political compatriots. "They used to get together every Friday at this bar," Judith told me, "to remember and exchange stories."

That evening, Friang introduced Judith around. One fellow in particular caught Judith's eye. His name was Pierre Ceria. In Judith's broken French, they made small talk. She commented on the delicious food, and he told her about his days at the news outlet Gaumont Actualités, where he'd worked since the war's end. These people, Judith saw right away, were different from those she knew back home. Friang, Ceria, and their friends were clear-eyed about the world. Their ideals remained intact, but the war had scrubbed them of any naïveté. They were curious. They read. They argued. Their hunger for ideas seemed endless. They seemed so *alive*. Judith knew she'd been right to come to Paris. "Well," she told me decades later, "a world opened up!"

· · · · · · ·

It was a heady summer, awash in writers and lovers. Judith spent her days with the literati, and, most of her evenings and weekends with Pierre Ceria. On their first date, he'd picked Judith up in his quatre-chevaux Simca with a picnic of bread, cheese, fruit, and wine. Then he'd driven her out of the city to see the Palace of Versailles. That night, he took her to dinner in Montmartre, then to the underground *cave à musique*, Jimmy's Bar in Saint-Germain. The Left Bank's clubs drew the best in rhumba, bebop, and jazz. Miles Davis, Charlie Parker, and Duke Ellington all came through, playing to packed crowds of "the young, rootless, and vaguely politicized." Judith and Pierre danced until their legs gave out. A few days later, Judith and Sarah took a train to Normandy to see Mont-Saint-Michel. The next day, while Sarah returned to Paris on the train, Pierre met Judith in the Loire Valley where she had, he insisted, to see Château de Chenonceau. He took her to lunch in a little auberge, where Judith tasted her first sole meunière. A few days later, Pierre prepared the dish for her in his apartment. Judith had never had a man cook for her before; indeed, she'd never known a man who cooked at home at all.

Pierre's Paris kitchen was tiny, hardly big enough for two to fit, and far more basic than Judith's parents' back home in New York. But Pierre was a marvelous cook—spontaneous, confident, and deft—and Judith learned a great deal just by watching and asking questions. Pierre showed her how to heat the butter to just the right temperature, its nutty aroma filling the air, how to scale and fillet the delicate fish, and how to add a squeeze of *citron* at the very end. (Pierre didn't speak a lick of English, and while Judith, having studied the language in high school, read French with relative ease, much of her practical education in colloquial, spoken French took place in, and revolved around, the lexicon of *la cuisine*.) Their meals were long and sensuous. There was always wine. It was all so seductive, Judith discovered, the ultimate form of foreplay.

· · · · · · ·

Judith felt her life taking on an expansive new direction. "Paris is such a won-derful city," Judith wrote home. "In the evenings one sits around in cafés, eats in small and always good little restaurants, then dances, perhaps. Nobody has much money; nobody drinks much, except wine. It is the first place, and don't let this frighten you, where I'd really like to settle down and work." Judith hadn't been in the City of Light two full months, but she could feel how much she'd changed in her time there. In Paris, everything felt possible and new. As the date of her return to New York drew near, Judith wished she could stay.

One warm August afternoon, Judith wandered through the Jardin des Tuileries. The sun and the wine she'd had with lunch made her sleepy. She found an empty bench, hung her purse on its back, and set her book on her lap. Judith sat awhile, reading and looking up every so often to take in the beauty of the scene. Before leaving the Tuileries, she turned her face up to the sun and closed her eyes in its warmth, easing out of her reverie. Then she stood up, tucked her book under her arm, and strolled off. It wasn't until several blocks later that she realized she'd left her purse behind. She hurried back to where she'd been sitting, but by then, the bag and its contents—her travelers checks, her passport, and her ticket home—were gone. "Something snapped, then," Judith told me. "I just saw the world differently."

Three weeks later, Judith sat in the lobby of the shabby Hôtel Lenox at 9 Rue de l'Université, where she'd been staying since Sarah steamed home to New York. Her parents had wired her money after she'd lost her purse, just enough to get by until her new passport came through. "Dearest ones," Judith began in a letter home, "The question is one that has, I'm sure you've suspected, been brewing in my mind a long time, and that is whether I should stay here all year." The slow work-ings of the embassy had given her time to think. What if the loss of her passport and return ticket hadn't been an accident but an omen? "Perhaps it was all an act of fate," Judith wrote, and "I was destined to stay."

· · · · · · ·

Judith hurried to keep up alongside Pierre as he strode among the market stalls. He'd picked her up at 6 a.m.; they needed to get to the market early before the best was gone. Judith watched, riveted, as Pierre pressed a finger into the flank of a fish; it if sprung back, he instructed Judith, "*ça va bien*"; but if an impression remained, the fish was tired. Pierre selected several pounds of *rascasse*, *grondin*, *dorade*, *turbot*, and *merlan*, each fish carefully wrapped in newspaper. Would fish, Judith asked, be the evening's main course? *Non, non, non*, Pierre scoffed, it was just for the soup. Rabbits, still cloaked in their fur and dangling from hooks, were next, and then the aromatics—savory, shallots, fennel, and leeks, all still novel to Judith's palate. They were shopping for the debut dinner, that evening, of a pop-up supper club for which Judith would act as sous-chef. It had been planned on a whim, a result of the sense of unrestrained possibility and whimsy that postwar Paris seemed to inspire in the young. But Judith still wasn't sure what was on the menu.

It had all started earlier that summer when Judith bumped into Paul Chapin, an acquaintance from New York, at the American Express office on Rue Scribe, a popular gathering place for young Americans overseas. Judith and Paul had first met the previous year, when Paul interned at Doubleday while on break from Bard College. He, like Judith, had come to Paris for vacation, and had decided to stay on to do his junior year at the Sorbonne. He'd asked her to lunch, then, wanting more of her, invited Judith for dinner at his aunt's flat, where he lived.

Paul's aunt was the Princess Marguerite Caetani, Princess of Bassiano, Duchess of Sermoneta. Born Marguerite Chapin in a well-to-do Connecticut family, she'd been orphaned as a child As a young woman, she'd sailed for Paris to study opera, and ended up marrying into the Italian aristocracy. The Caetanis bought a lavish apartment at 4 Rue du Cirque, and often hosted artists and writers there. In addition to a patron of the arts, the princess was a publisher. In 1948, she founded the avant-garde literary journal *Botteghe Oscure*, which ran work by the likes of E. E. Cummings, Marianne Moore, Malraux, and Sartre. By the time Paul took up residence in their apartment, the Caetanis had swapped Paris for the prince's castle in his native Italy. They'd left their flat sitting empty save for a reclusive modernist painter, Balthus, to whom the princess had rented one of the many rooms.

In the Caetanis' well-appointed French kitchen, Paul cooked Judith spaghetti. The gesture struck Judith as sweet but sophomoric and incongruous. All that gorgeous gleaming copper cookware hanging from the rafters, and only noodles to show for it. Neither the meal nor Paul himself held a candle to Pierre and his *cuisine française*. She began to dine there frequently, though, Paul inviting different groups of friends. Sometimes Judith put what she'd learned from Pierre to use, and prepared dinner herself.

Judith enjoyed Paul's company but wasn't romantically interested in him the way he was in her. But after Judith had lost her purse, Paul made Judith a proposal she couldn't resist: Why not move in with him and live rent-free?

Before making her decision, Judith wrote home about the "Bard Boy" and his cohabitation idea. A nice group of friends often gathered at 4 Rue du Cirque, Judith explained, and "I am asked, usually, as cook. Last night, for instance, I produced a rather elegant meal." "The important thing really is that I am extraordinarily happy here," Judith continued. "And somehow I do not find much to look forward to in New York. [It is] so rushed, and it is so easy to be lost. Here things are so much more easy and less self-conscious and one can have an identity. And I do love the French; they know how to live so wonderfully." She'd begun looking for a job, she wrote, but "if all else failed," perhaps she'd "open a small restaurant there."

An *identity*, a *restaurant*, a *cook*! Phyllis was appalled. Monty and Phyllis cabled, frantically urging Judith to come home at once. Judith responded, but this time only to Monty, who she hoped would sympathize. "I have so many irons in the fire now that I can't see how I can fail. I won't starve for I can always file at the Embassy—of that I have been assured," she wrote. "Perhaps I am taking a chance and won't end up with as happy a position as I had at Doubleday, but one has to take chances and there are many advantages to be had. Anyway, I am an adventurous girl. Don't worry, and much, much love." On Saturday, October 2, Judith packed her bags and crossed the Seine from the Left Bank to the Right, moving into 4 Rue de Cirque.

Judith settled in easily, and set her mind to finding work. Since August, she'd done odd jobs for Ludwig Bemelmans, the writer and illustrator of *Madeline*, and a few days here and there for various writers and publishers. The pay wasn't much, but Judith thought such connections would be very good for her "prestige." She'd even cold-called the offices of *Vogue*, thinking, perhaps, she'd give modeling a try. With her housing covered, she didn't need to earn all that much.

The idea for the Cercle Rue du Cirque began as a caper. Judith and Paul felt the Caetanis' apartment wasn't being used to its full potential. There were "so many rooms, such a big kitchen, and a living room so high-ceilinged and gracefully designed it seemed a shame not to use it for some real entertaining," Judith later wrote. Perhaps, Judith and Paul thought, they could pay to feed themselves by feeding others, turning the flat into something of a restaurant-cum-salon; it was illegal to run such a business out of one's home, but neither Judith nor Paul was dissuaded by the finitudes of the law. They already had the venue and enough money to cover the cost of food. All they needed was a chef. Judith knew just who to ask. Which is how she ended up with Pierre on the morning of Wednesday, October 6, protesting as he picked out an expensive Burgundy not even to drink but in which to marinate the evening's meat. The martinis, Judith thought to herself, had better sell well. She and Paul would need to charge extra for drinks if they hoped to break even that night.

Back at the apartment, Pierre gave Judith and Paul instructions to peel and chop, then left for work. As the piles of vegetables grew higher, Judith grew overwhelmed. But Pierre returned on his lunch break as promised, tied on an apron, and got right to work. He expertly disjointed the rabbits and set an enormous kettle of water and herbs on the stove to poach the fish. Once cooked, Pierre showed his pupils how to force the seafood through a cloth-lined sieve. Then, once again, the chef took off, leaving his apprentices to finish the job.

Paul spent the afternoon arranging little tables in the salon and practicing carrying a serving tray while Judith soldiered on in the kitchen. Her fingers were sore from French-cutting haricots verts and her arms, covered up to the elbows in fish pulp, ached. It was far more work than Judith had anticipated, but the excitement of learning as she went and the sensual richness of the labor carried her along. Her cheeks were flushed from effort and flecked with bits of green herbs, and she was having a ball. There was no shred of the resentment she'd felt toward the work of growing and processing food on the Bennington farm. In that kitchen in Paris, she was all lit up.

Pierre returned after work, tied an apron tightly around his waist, and began finishing the dishes whose component parts Judith and Paul had been preparing all afternoon. When the doorbell buzzed at seven that evening, 4 Rue du Cirque was awash in candlelight. Paul bounded to greet the first guests; an American singer who performed at the Left Bank Hôtel L'Aiglon, and five of her friends who all worked for the Marshall Plan. John and Jane Gunther, back in town, took a table near the fire. Before long, Judith heard the clinking of martini glasses and the swell of laughter. More guests arrived, then more.

It was well after nine when, at last, Paul carried out trays of soup. As Pierre finished preparing the rabbit, Judith sneaked down the hall and peered into the dining room just long enough to catch exclamations of delight over the evening's fare. Bolstered, she returned to the kitchen to beat the egg yolks, marsala, and sugar for a zabaglione while Pierre retired to the salon with a drink in his hand.

Several hours later, as those in the salon lingered over their wine and cigarettes, Judith went out to, at last, greet her guests. John Gunther, who'd been dozing while Jane talked politics with Pierre, opened his eyes and asked Judith, "So, when are you going to open in New York?"

Judith and Paul collapsed into their beds that night, ignoring the mounds of dishes awaiting them. They awoke the following morning to the telephone ringing. "Our instant regulars," Judith later wrote, "were trying to make reservations for the next night."

Judith booked a full house, then went about her day. But when she called Pierre that evening to tell him about Rue du Cirque's encore and discuss what they might serve, he told her he was headed out of town on assignment. Judith was not deterred: "Tant pis," she later said of learning she and Paul had lost their head chef. "I would cook."

The singer from L'Aiglon returned, this time with a cadre of adoring men for whom, Judith wrote, "1,000 francs for dinner was peanuts" trailing behind her. The women working for the Marshall Plan were there again, as was Paul's Scottish cousin. Judith had settled on an ambitious menu: "An hors d'oeuvre of lobster, crab, and a white fish all in a rich, warm sauce, with soft-boiled eggs and shrimps in their shells all around the dish; then chicken in a cream, mushroom, and wine sauce; nice thin beans; an artichoke-heart salad; and for dessert, a wonderful discovery that Paul and I made one night when the larder was a bit depressing, of apples, crushed black grapes, sugar, lemon, and rum all baked with a foamy sauce on top." She later admitted that the martini hour had had to be extended—in the kitchen, she'd discovered that the poultry vendor had misunderstood her request for broiling chickens as *boiling* chickens. The tougher birds required an extra hour cooking in cream. After dinner, Judith served mulled wine made sizzling with a hot poker. With little more than her instinct, pluck, and will, Judith pulled it off. The next day, she wrote home, giddily recounting every detail. "I know you didn't send me to an expensive college for me to become a cook. But you must understand: Here in France cooking is not regarded as demeaning. Here it is an art."

The run at 4 Rue du Cirque didn't last long: The princess caught wind of the goings-on at her flat, and promptly gave Judith, Balthus, and even her nephew the boot. On December 7, Judith reluctantly moved back into the Hôtel Lenox, determined to find work in order to remain in Paris. The following afternoon, after a fruitless day of calling on the Gunthers' contacts in search of a job, Judith returned to the hotel lobby awash in exhaustion and feelings of defeat. A woman stood at the front desk, talking on the telephone. "Hello? Is this *Weekend* magazine?" she said. On the bottom of the list of names John Gunther had handed Judith the week before was the name Dick Jones at *Weekend* magazine, but Judith hadn't been able to find an address or number. At hearing the magazine's name, Judith moved closer to the woman, who was saying something about the art department. Then, just as the mademoiselle was about to hang up, Judith reached over with a *"Pardonnez-moi,"* and snatched the phone from her hand. Only later did Judith give any thought to her own boldness. "It surprised me, but you do it when you want it enough," she told me.

The man on the other end of the line was Sterling Lord, *Weekend*'s managing editor. "Is there a Mr. Jones there?" Judith later told me she'd asked. "Oh yes, he's our editor and publisher," Lord said. Judith explained her situation, trying not to sound too desperate. The magazine, Lord conceded, was overwhelmed—putting out a weekly was no small task. He thought the fellows could use someone to help out with secretarial duties, and invited Judith to come into the office the next day.

CHAPTER 4

Judith felt the hum of industry before she even set foot in the room. The men crowded around paper-strewn desks, pored over images and copy, and debated the layout for the magazine's next issue; thirty-two pages of stories written for an audience of U.S. troops and English-speaking Europeans. They wore shirtsleeves and loosened neckties. Cigarette smoke clouded the air, blurring the cover images and centerfolds pinned to the walls.

Weekend, a glossy offshoot of the U.S. military's newspaper, *Stars and Stripes*, had made a splash earlier that fall with its story, "Is Hitler Still Alive?," a photo of the führer's face emblazoned on the cover. German authorities hadn't yet lifted their prohibition on displaying Hitler's image in domestic publications, and so the arrival of *Weekend* on German newsstands—the first glimpse of Hitler's likeness Germans had had since V-E Day—caused a frenzy. The issue sold out overnight.

In the summer of 1948, *Weekend* moved its offices from Frankfurt to Paris; printing and distribution had become markedly more affordable in France in the wake of Germany's currency reform. When Judith arrived for her interview, the office was still only half unpacked, with piles of boxes teetering against the walls and bare bulbs strung from the ceiling for light. Standing in the doorway at 416 Rue Saint-Honoré with an issue of *Silo*, the Bennington literary journal she'd edited, clutched to her breast, Judith felt anxious. She had no experience in magazines. Still, she was prepared to convince the magazine's editors she could be of use.

Sterling Lord greeted Judith, and led her through to a small office, where he introduced her to the magazine's editor, Richard Evan Jones. Jones, who went by the name Dick, was strapping, broad-shouldered and sturdily built, with dark hair and piercing blue eyes. He reached out to shake Judith's hand, then offered her a seat.

Judith handed Dick her copy of *Silo*, and waited quietly while he flipped through its pages. She was surprised, she later told me, when he actually began to read. Nervously, she glanced up at the wall. Dick had a series of photographs of two young girls tacked beside his desk. Dick paused, looked up, and smiled wryly. "You can type, right?" she later recalled he'd asked. Judith fumbled—the answer, really, was no; not quickly or well, anyway, and she couldn't take dictation for anything. But she badly needed a job. Yes, she said, of course. The lie slipped out easily. Dick closed the journal with a snap. He told her to come in at nine the next morning, Friday, to make a start. There was, Dick said, certainly no shortage of work to do around the place.

When Judith arrived the next morning, the *Weekend* staffers were already hunched over their work. Cigarettes dangled from the corners of their lips as they tapped furiously at their typewriter keys. Dick seemed in no hurry as he introduced Judith around the office to the serious young men. It was a stable of remarkable talent. The journalists Andy Rooney and Dick's brother Russ Jones were there, as well as photographers Hanns Hubmann and Tony Vaccaro. Dick gave Judith a rundown of the magazine's systems and the various tasks that would become hers. There was a genuine warmth about Dick that made Judith want to oblige him. She was distracted by thoughts of him that Friday evening, while out with Pierre, and again at lunch with Paul the following day after her morning at the office; everyone at *Weekend* worked Saturdays. Sunday dragged; Judith couldn't wait to be near Dick Jones again.

At *Weekend* on Monday morning, Dick set up a little table for Judith in his office. She made phone calls and handled proofs of promotional posters, and tried not to let her abysmal typing show. "I used to wait for him to leave to fix all my mistakes and start over," she told me, laughing. That day, Dick invited Judith to lunch.

At a little bistro tucked away on a side street, Dick ordered wine. Together, they looked at the menu, and Dick asked a server about the boudin blanc. The waiter described the dish as a seasonal holiday sausage infused with cream and black truffle. Dick ordered a portion for two. "I mean, a *man* that's interested in food! And finding out all these tiny restaurants and asking questions in his stumbling French," Judith told me. She was impressed.

Dick was a talker. Over lunch, he told Judith of his upbringing in a middle-class newspaper family in Minnesota. Both his parents worked. His father, Lewis, was impenetrable and serious. His mother, Elizabeth, had been disabled by polio as a child, but hadn't let it slow her down. She was endlessly industrious, both at the paper and at home. Newspapers were more than work, they were the Jones family's way of life. Dick grew up under the relentless demands of a weekly publication schedule. He chased stories, sold advertisements, and set type. He delivered papers, too, even through the deep freeze of Minnesota winters. Every Thursday night, Dick and his three younger siblings worked into the wee hours, putting the forthcoming issue to bed.

Dick told Judith that when the market crashed in 1929, he'd lost his meager savings, and with them his hopes of attending college. He fell back on what he knew instead. "He was a natural journalist who always asked questions," Judith told me. But for Dick, inquisitiveness was more than a tool of the trade. The loss of his hard-earned money, Judith quickly saw, "had made him determined to educate himself." Dick learned by doing, and seemed impelled to work doubly hard to prove himself. Judith found his openness, curiosity, and roll-up-your-sleeves work ethic refreshingly earnest and endearing. "There was already something brewing in me that didn't like this emphasis on social caste," she told me. "And he was completely clear of that."

Dick told Judith of his and his two brothers' time serving in the war. His brother Mac had died when his plane was shot down in battle. Dick spoke, too, of his wife, Barbara, and their daughters, Pamela and Bronwyn. When the family was still stationed in Germany, Barbara had begun an affair with John Sharnik, a colleague of Dick's. Barbara had left Dick and taken the girls with her back to the States. Judith realized those were Dick and Barbara's daughters in the photos on his office wall. She could see on Dick's face that their absence was a painful gap in his life. The world seemed to shrink around the two of them as they talked and ate. Judith was, in short order, smitten.

Dick and Judith's courtship moved quickly. Judith had realized she and Pierre "were worlds apart from each other." His attention was always divided—"He had about three women at one time," she told me. "Sometimes he'd call one of them when I was right there in his apartment." Judith craved devotion. "I wanted to find a nice man that I really loved and respected," she said. She found it in Dick.

He was, Judith observed in a letter to Sarah Moore, "A curious person. He has so much native intelligence, a wonderfully aware mind and a capable one. . . . What he has particularly that I admire is a warmth, a humanity, a caring." She saw, too, that he lacked confidence and "suffers too sometimes from a sense of personal failure—partly as a result of his first marriage, partly because of a lack of ease among the brash and successful." She found these qualities a little sad, but mostly tender and dear. "I just wanted to spend my life with this person! It was pretty quick that I felt that," Judith told me, still radiant, so many years later, as she spoke.

Before long, Judith and Dick were spending all their time together, at work and outside of it, too. But sharing an office didn't last. Soon after Judith started at *Weekend*, the magazine ran aground financially. Dick and Sterling were good editors, but they weren't shrewd businessmen, and the demands of running a weekly while trying to sell advertisements proved too much. By the end of 1948, the *Weekend* team couldn't afford to pay their printer anymore. In mid-February 1949, Judith typed an official-looking letter, posing as "Chief of Personnel," that released editors Richard Jones and Sterling Lord from duty "due to the suspension of operations." *Weekend*'s entire staff was out of a job.

Dick and Judith took their rather sudden unemployment as an opportunity to move their relationship ahead a major step. In February 1949, Judith moved in with Dick and Sterling at 80 Rue Lauriston. She was one of three new additions to the flat, the others being Dick's brother and *Weekend* reporter Russ Jones, and their mutual friend Max. Becoming roommates was as pragmatic as it was romantic: split five ways, the rent was cheap, and none had money to spare.

Judith knew the arrangement would appear scandalous in her parents' eyes. "I know it is hard for you," Judith wrote home, "to accept the idea of gents and ladies all under one roof, but practically in terms of expense, it is not possible for me to live alone." The men also employed a maid who cooked. "Which means," Judith added, anticipating Phyllis's fears, "I shan't be cooking for the boys." Judith conveniently omitted that she'd fallen in love with one of her new flatmates, and that Dick was thirty-three to her twenty-four, a father already, and still a married man. Though she hid the cause, she made her newly buoyant spirits plain. "Spring in Paris is unbelievably wonderful," Judith wrote. She'd become emotionally bound to Dick, and he had no plans to leave France. But if Judith was to stay in Paris, she'd have to secure steady work.

. . . .

The low slant of late afternoon light cut through the naked branches of the Bois de Boulogne and through the leaded glass windows at 35 Rue de la Faisanderie, casting the silk-papered walls in gold. Judith was at her desk. It was a hulking thing, elegant but old. The morning's tasks had been light, as usual: managing her boss's calendar, helping him plan parties, and such. He'd left early for a full day of meetings. Left alone, she'd taken a long lunch break, then sipped a Dubonnet in front of the fire. The day was wintry and cold. It was early 1950.

In March 1949, Ken McCormick had written to Judith to say Doubleday was considering establishing a European office, and that Paris seemed like the place. The editor in chief had watched carefully as American readers' appetites expanded across the Atlantic, and he was keen to get a foothold on the continent. He would come back to France that summer, he told Judith, and wanted to see her and hear her thoughts.

On July 1, McCormick took Judith to dinner. It was, by then, official: the house was opening an outpost in Paris. McCormick told Judith he'd deputized Francis K. Price as editor and head scout. The two men signed a lease on a large apartment in the 16th arrondissement to serve as both headquarters and company housing for Price. He was given an allowance to hire someone to cook and clean, and funds to pay a secretary, too. Given her experience at Doubleday and the fact that she was already established in Paris, McCormick felt Judith was the obvious pick. In late October, after he'd had a chance to settle in, Price asked Judith to meet him. He needed a right hand and Judith needed work. It was an easy match. Price hired her on the spot.

"My job is an easy, undemanding one (mostly social secretary)," Judith wrote to Sarah Moore. Price, Judith wrote, was "an arrogant s.o.b.," but "I do manage to get along with him." Tolerating Price seemed a small price to pay for steady wages. Plus, the job had other perks. Judith clearly saw the advantage of having access to resources and the literary world. With "just a slight amount of dishonest effort," as Judith put it herself, she used the Doubleday offices to establish Judith Bailey and Associates, a literary agency of her own.

Judith spent the mornings fulfilling her Doubleday duties, and afternoons for work of her own. She took advantage of the office's phone line and typewriter, and helped herself to the ready supply of ink and paper to conduct her own correspondence. "This agency business, which I'm just beginning to make a going thing of," Judith wrote to Phoebe Pierce, an editor at the short-lived literary magazine *Flair*, the same month she started at Doubleday, "is actually an attempt to ferret out some of the work being done by American writers over here and when good enough, to try to sell it both here and to stateside markets." John Gunther had given Judith the rights to *Inside U.S.A.*; it had become a bestseller stateside when it came out in 1947. Judith was trying to get a publisher in France to bite on the book. Judith was also hoping to sell one of Roethke's poems to Pierce at *Flair*. With a continent and the Atlantic between them, Judith felt she could keep professional involvement with the poet compartmentalized and clear.

· · · · · · ·

Though it had only been a few short months since Doubleday had set up shop in Paris, the office quickly was awash in submissions. One day, before heading out for a string of meetings, Price heaped a pile of books and manuscripts on Judith's desk and told her to write a rejection letter for each. The titles comprised the slush pile, the unsolicited manuscripts that had been sent in by hopeful agents and foreign publishers. Price had determined those in the stack on Judith's desk weren't good fits for Doubleday, and so Judith went to work on the polite pass letters.

Judith sighed and began to flip aimlessly through the heap. She stopped when she came to a book with a photograph of a young girl on its cover. The image was striking—she had a pronounced nose, a crop of dark, wavy hair, and thick eyebrows to match. The girl's gaze was cast slightly upward, giving her a searching air. It was an advance copy of a book due out in French later that spring from Parisian publisher, Calmann-Lévy. It had been submitted to Doubleday to be considered for translation and publication in English. Judith was intrigued. Price wouldn't be back for hours. Judith knew she had time. She gathered the book into her arms, carried it over to the armchair by the fire, tucked her feet under her, and began to read.

The book was a first-person account written by a Jewish girl born in Germany and raised in the Netherlands. In 1942, when she was thirteen, two families—the girl's and another—moved into a series of secret rooms behind her father's office in Amsterdam. There they lived for two years, hiding from the Nazis. On the girl's thirteenth birthday, June 12, 1942, she'd received a red-and-white plaid notebook as a gift, and started to write. Outside the walls, the war raged. But in the annex, life unfolded with all its quotidian drama. So did the girl's adolescence. She addressed her diary entries to "Kitty," an imaginary reader and friend, and told of her family's daily happenings; their gestures, both tender and mean; and the events of her own coming of age. Her entries were, at turns, insightful and serious, playful and strong-willed.

On March 28, 1944, the girl listened as Gerrit Bolkestein, Dutch minister of education, arts and sciences, came on air on Radio Orange, the London-based broadcast service of the Dutch government-in-exile. When the war was over, Bolkestein announced, the government planned to collect, edit, and publish "all historical materials relating to these years." If the Jewish people didn't tell the story of the war themselves, someone else would later do it for them. "History cannot be written solely on the basis of official records and archives. If posterity is to fully understand what we as a people have endured and overcome in these years, we must collect an enormous amount of material relating to daily life. Only then can this struggle for freedom be depicted in its full depth." He called upon all listeners to contribute. The girl began to revise her diary, imagining it might one day be published. How funny it would be, she wrote, if, years later, "we Jews were to tell how we lived and what we ate and talked about here."

In August 1944, the girl and her family were discovered. The girl's mother died at Auschwitz in January 1945; and the girl and her sister, who'd been transferred to Bergen-Belsen, died of typhus that March, just before the camp's liberation. Only the girl's father survived. Six million people were murdered in the Holocaust. Anne Frank, the girl in the photograph and the book's author, was one of them.

Judith knew very little then about the extent of the atrocities carried out against Jews during the war. But Frank's writing, so intimate and clear, rendered the horror of the Holocaust more wretched and more real. The book was historically important; Judith recognized that right away. But it was Anne Frank's singular voice that so captivated Judith. She thought Price was crazy to pass up a chance to publish the book.

That afternoon, Judith read and read, immersed in Frank's world. When she heard the key turning in the apartment door's lock late that afternoon, she jumped. Judith rose from her chair, discombobulated and stiff. With Frank's book still clutched in her hands, she told Price he should send it to Doubleday's headquarters in New York.

"We have to publish this book," she said.

Price, who'd been surprised to find Judith still at work so late, asked incredulously, "What, that book by that kid?"

Judith stuck to her guns, imploring him to change his mind. As she later told me, "Frank Price liked my ideas, but he wasn't giving me *too* much license. He had asked me to reject it, but I couldn't. He'd wanted a little girl Friday secretary. And I was too independent." Price was irritated and amused. He conceded and gave Anne Frank's diary a second look, rereading it with new eyes, and decided to send it to his colleagues at Doubleday in New York. In the letter of support he wrote and forwarded along with the book, he made no mention of Judith at all.

Anne Frank's book already had a story and a life before Judith encountered it. After the Franks were discovered, Miep Gies and Bep Voskuijl, two of those who'd helped sustain the families in hiding, found Anne's diary and held on to it. When Miep Gies caught word that Anne Frank had died, she gave the book to Otto Frank. "Here is your daughter Anne's legacy to you."

Otto was blown away. "The Anne that appeared before me was very different from the daughter I had lost. I had had no idea of the depth of her thoughts and feelings," he said. He began exploring possibilities for the diary's publication. It wasn't an easy sell; the war was over, and publishers believed no one wanted to be reminded of it. But the doubters, it turned out, were wrong. Otto found a publisher; and in 1947, Anne Frank's diary was published in Holland. It was a modest first run, just over three thousand copies. By the time Judith got her hands on the book in early 1950, it had been translated into French and German, and hit shelves in those countries later that same year.

It was an article by American writer Meyer Levin, which came out almost simultaneously as the arrival of Price's letter endorsing publication of Anne Frank's diary in New York, that convinced Doubleday to make an offer on the book. Levin was then living on France's Côte d'Azur. His wife, Tereska Torres, had heard stirrings about the diary, and bought her husband a copy of the French edition upon its publication in the summer of 1950. In response, Meyer wrote an article about the diary for *Congress Weekly* magazine about "the attitude of American publishers toward books of Jewish content." In it, he praised Frank's writing as "delicate" and "pure in candor," and made a strong case for publishing the book in the United States.

In early March 1951, after much negotiation, Doubleday agreed to Otto Frank's terms, guaranteeing him protection of dramatic rights to the diary. Anne Frank's father had been insistent upon that condition, and it had cost him deals with other American publishers. Frank Price and Otto Frank signed the contract for the diary's publication in April 1951.

In Doubleday's New York office, the diary was handed off to Barbara Zimmerman, a young Jewish woman and one of the house's most junior editors. Eleanor Roosevelt gave her name to the book's foreword. It read: "Written by a young girl—and the young are not afraid of telling the truth—it is one of the wisest and most moving commentaries on war and its impact on human beings that I have ever read." The First Lady's name provided a boost, but many believe that it was actually Barbara Zimmerman who ghostwrote *Anne Frank*'s introduction.

On June 12, 1952, Anne's birthday, Doubleday published *Anne Frank: The Diary of a Young Girl*. It was a cautious first run of five thousand copies. On June 15, Meyer Levin reviewed the Doubleday edition in the *New York Times*. He declared Frank "a born writer" and the diary "a classic." The review catapulted the Doubleday edition to immediate success: Just days after Levin's review ran, the book was in a second printing. Anne Frank's diary, eventually translated into more than seventy languages, has never stopped selling since. More than thirty million copies have sold in all, making it "the most popular secular book in history," according to the *New York Times*, and a publishing phenomenon. Judith had been right.

Anne Frank's widespread resonance proved the power of individual voices within larger political events, and played a pivotal part in humanizing the lived experience of the Holocaust. Doubleday capitalized on Judith's shrewdness and temerity but didn't bring her along with the book's rewards; Judith and her actions were erased from the historicization of the diary's publication and success. Until many years later, when *Anne Frank* was adapted for the stage and Judith righted the record herself, she received no credit at all for the crucial part she'd played.

At the time she convinced Price to reconsider his rejection of *Anne Frank*, Judith had priorities other than the book's future fate. It was her own endeavors, not Doubleday's, that concerned her most. By late 1950, she'd gained some ground, selling a few of Dick's articles and short stories. Judith also brokered the deal for Dick and her, together, to coedit a new edition of Doubleday's *How to Save Money in Paris* (though when it published, the book bore only his name, not hers). That volume led to one the couple wrote on their own. Dick did most of the writing, while Judith handled the rights. They called the book *How to Live in Paris on Practically Nothing*, which Judith sold stateside. She also acquired and sold the foreign rights to *Vivez Jeune, Vivez Longtemps* by American nutritionist and whole-foods proponent, Gayelord Hauser. Before long, Hauser's book was everywhere in the windows of Parisian shops; it appealed, Judith believed, to French women's particular insistence on remaining slender.

Price had begun to pay a bit more attention to Judith by the time she'd been working for him a full year. He extended her hours and gave her a raise of 10,000 francs, or $25, more per month. (Judith needed the money more than she let on; since January 1950, Dick hadn't been earning a steady paycheck.) "I tell you it's really just because F-boy needs company and didn't like my running around, you know, doing things in competition with him so he wants to keep me here all day," Judith wrote home. If the increase in pay was intended to dampen Judith's independent pursuits, it had the opposite effect: Judith grew bolder instead.

Price went "away a good deal," Judith wrote to Sarah Moore in April 1951, "and I am on my own there." She began using Doubleday's office to throw fetes for her friends and clients she hoped to land for herself. "I can give a very tony dinner with two servants to take care of all while I just order the fine wines and arrange the flowers (and Doubleday pays for it)," she bragged. To her parents, Judith wrote, "I am playing politics at both ends (you've always claimed I was a little diplomat!)," flaunting her shrewdness and moxie. Judith delighted in working the system on the job, but her adventures at home pleased her more still. "I must confess," she wrote to Sarah Moore in April 1951, "I have more fun in my own two-by-four kitchen, and we've gotten pretty good ourselves at French menus. We live," Judith said, "an awfully nice life."

· · · · · · ·

It was just after five in the afternoon when Judith stepped off the bus from Paris and started the walk uphill. It was only ten minutes, but the climb was steep. She passed a block of newly constructed apartment buildings. One, which looked to her like a prison, seemed so enormous and overefficient it lacked any characteristic identity at all. Judith found it depressing. But her mood didn't dip for long. A few minutes more and she found Dick, waiting, as he'd done each afternoon since spring arrived, at their favorite sidewalk café. Dick rose to kiss her, then pulled out her chair and ordered them each a beer. They sat together in the warmth, Judith so glad to be home with her love in Saint-Cloud.

The flat at Rue Lauriston had disbanded soon after *Weekend* folded in the spring of 1949. Sterling had married his girlfriend, Dodie; Russ hit the road to work as a freelance reporter; and Judith and Dick set about looking for somewhere to live. They'd found a cheap room on the Boulevard Pereire with a Greek landlady, Madame Damianos, who took in tenants to keep herself afloat. She liked Dick and Judith, and so permitted them to use her kitchen to cook. The amenities were minimal: only two burners and no oven. There was no refrigeration, either; but below the window was a metal box, a garde-manger, where food would stay cool, provided the day itself wasn't overly hot. Dick and Judith learned to do as the French did, marketing twice or more each day, making the rounds of "the *charcuterie*, the *boucherie* or *poissonnière*, the *épicerie*, to say nothing of the *fromagerie*, and the *marchand du vin*," Judith later wrote.

By spring 1950, after years of scarcity, French markets were full to overflowing again. Any sausage, truffle, bird, fish, salad green, or leek a Parisian might want could be had from the stalls and storefronts of the Rue du Faubourg-Saint-Denis. One morning, waiting in line at the neighborhood *boulangerie*, Judith heard a cry go up. "*Hourra! Hourra!*" customers around her began to shout, passing a baguette from hand to hand. Judith turned to a bystander, confused. "The *flour* is white! It's pure!" the woman told her, relieved. The wheat harvest in 1948 had been a strong one, and white flour, gone all the years of the war, was finally back. What a thing, Judith thought, to be so overjoyed by one's daily bread.

For the couple, cooking at home became a shared adventure. It was also a means of stretching their francs. Dick didn't earn much as a freelancer, and until Judith got her raise a year into her time at Doubleday, they scraped by. They learned to be humbly curious at the shops. From the butcher, Judith learned how to cook entrecôte; from the *poissonnière*, she gleaned tips for sautéing dourade. She and Dick practiced economy and inventiveness in the kitchen, learning how to prepare offal and other cheap cuts of meat. Bones and the trimmings of herbs became soup. Most evenings, the couple ate together, perched on the edge of their bed. Those were salad days. In Judith's mind, they remained forever halcyon.

Dick and Judith were content but yearned for a place of their own, somewhere they could host. And in late fall of 1950, once Judith felt her position at Doubleday was secure, they began their hunt. Apartments in Paris proper were scarce, and outrageously expensive at that. So Dick and Judith began to look farther afield. They caught wind of a flat across the Seine in Saint-Cloud, a suburb perched atop a hill with old world architecture and a large, stately park. The apartment at 7 Rue Alexandre Coutureau was fully furnished and the kitchen was well equipped. Linens and hot water were included in the rent of thirty U.S. dollars a month. Best of all was the roof—enormous, open, and seven floors up—which boasted a sweeping view of Paris. "You're allowed to have deck chairs up there," Judith wrote home, giddy. "I visualize myself drying my hair in the sun or serving Tom Collins to dinner guests there. Isn't that the nuts!"

Judith and Dick had hardly been able to fit together in the tiny borrowed kitchen of their previous flat. But in Saint-Cloud, they cooked side by side, albeit with very different styles. Dick was experimental in the kitchen and, cooking with him, Judith grew more so, too. "I think men very often have less anxiety," Judith told me. "They're not so uptight about making a mistake. I like that." Judith was inclined to coax and correct, though she quickly realized it rankled Dick. "Well, you do it, then!" she told me he'd say if she tried to intervene. "I'd be biting my tongue as he threw something into a pan that was so hot the flames went up! I was trying very hard, very consciously, not to be bossy," Judith said. Instead, she learned to make suggestions so subtly that Dick would think her ideas were his own. It was an artfully diplomatic tack that would inform her approach at home and at work for many years to come.

For Christmas that year, 1950, Judith and Dick invited their closest friends, the Roths, to help them christen their new home. Judith had met Bettina in the spring of 1949 at a job she held briefly after *Weekend* folded and before getting hired at Doubleday, where she had worked for a "rather fabulous American" named Rodgers, "an angle worker, with a finger in every pie." One evening, when Judith and Dick were still living in their shared flat, Judith invited Bettina and her husband, Jacques—Holocaust survivors, both—to dinner. The two couples had hit it off.

For their Christmas meal, Judith and Dick decided to cook a goose. Short on cash, they went to the open-air market and bargained for a bird, then lugged it home by Métro and bus. When they went to pluck it, though, they were astonished how stubbornly its feathers held on. It reminded Judith of the dismal days of plucking chickens at Bennington, but this time, she was game. She and Dick filled their bathtub with kettles full of boiling water from the stove, and scalded the bird until the skin released its plumage. At last, they slid the bird into the oven, surrounded by chestnuts cheap as cabbage, to roast. The meal was a rousing success. Even after the four feasted, there was still plenty of goose fat and meat left over, with which they made cassoulet the next day.

Judith relished her home life with Dick. And by early 1951, it felt as though her work, too, was humming along. But the situation in Paris was growing tense. Stalin was still vying for power, and Germany remained contested ground. Since May 1949, when Germany had been cleaved in half—the West, a democracy; the East, under Soviet rule—France, Germany's neighbor to the west, had felt the strain.

In late 1950, Judith's parents had written that they feared Russia would declare war on Western Europe any day. Phyllis and Monty fretfully urged their daughter to come home to New York. Just before Christmas, Judith responded. "I would be willing to consider this if there were nothing particular holding me here at the moment. However, for the next several months, I am going to have the entire responsibility of Doubleday's Paris office on my shoulders. As long as I'm here working for them, they will in a sense be responsible for me. If any drastic action had to be taken to get me out fast, there isn't a doubt in this world that their influence would bring results." Judith pleaded with her parents to support her decision to stick it out. "Maybe it will turn out that the gods are against us, but please you be with us," she wrote.

In truth, though, Dick and Judith had already decided to return to the States. Dick missed his girls; he'd lost so much time with them already, and wanted to be a part of their lives. What's more, anti-American sentiment was on the rise, a response to U.S. propaganda—financial involvement dressed up as aid—aimed at expanding the nation's capitalist project into postwar France. When Judith arrived in Paris in 1948, she told me, there had been a banner on the Rue Saint-Claude that read "Welcome, Americans." But by the spring of 1951, it said "Americans, go home." All signs indicated it was time to go. Only one obstacle stood in their way: Judith, who had shirked so many conventions in Paris, refused to return to the States with Dick, unwed. Before the two could tie the knot, Dick needed to get divorced.

Dick's wife, Barbara, consented. In early 1950, both she and Dick had filed the necessary paperwork. But on the Parisian side, the process was painfully slow. Judith's parents offered money and assistance to help things along. By then, they knew all about Dick (though they hadn't a clue the couple shared a bed and an address). In June 1949, Phyllis had traveled to Paris with her sister-in-law to check up on her daughter. Judith introduced Phyllis and Dick at a restaurant, and later that day, Dick sent a bouquet of flowers to Phyllis's hotel with a card: "From the man who's going to marry your daughter." Dick wasn't Phyllis's cup of tea; "I think he was a little too much for her," Judith told me. Disapproving though Phyllis may have been, when push came to shove, her priority was her daughter's safety. The Baileys wanted to fly Judith directly home, and Dick to the Virgin Islands where he could file for a faster, and more discreet, divorce, like Judith's cousin Jane had done. But Judith worried that if she and Dick accepted Monty and Phyllis's help, he'd feel indebted to her parents. Judith thought it would be a terrible way for the next chapter of their life as a couple to begin.

At last, in mid-July, word arrived that the divorce decree was imminent. The papers would clear that fall. Official documents arrived on October 8, but still the couple was not free to wed: France's courts demanded a nine-month waiting period before any party could remarry in order to ensure no woman or gestating child's reputation was ruined. So Dick and Judith eloped to Vienna instead.

Dick's brother Russ and his sister Gwen, both working as journalists in the Austrian capital, acted as witnesses. The date was October 22, 1951. Judith was poised and stunning in a black velvet dress with a cinched waist and low neckline, a custom-made knockoff of a Dior. She wore long black gloves, a smart black hat, black pumps, and a black cape over her shoulders. Her long hair was pinned up in a twist. A string of pearls and a delicate white orchid at her breast completed the look. Dick wore a suit and tie and trench coat.

On the train back to France, Judith wrote home with the happy news. "Dearest ones. Am writing this as we're riding the air on our way back to Paris. We had a very charming little matrimonial service this morning all in German. J.B. (now J.B.J.). . . . We were already celebrating with a bottle of champagne. I do wish you could have been with us and we can't wait to be all together. All our love. Judith." Three days later, Dick left Paris aboard an Air France flight. Stateside, he would be greeted by his parents, who were traveling from Minnesota to meet him in Boston; together, they would go to visit Dick's daughters and ex-wife at their home in Cambridge. Judith followed, by sea, on the steamer *Mauretania*. She had no idea what awaited her, as she hadn't been in the States in more than three years. Regardless, with all she'd gotten from her time in Paris in tow, Judith was ready to face the unknown.

CHAPTER 5

The car sped northward, with Judith at the wheel. The back seat was stacked with suitcases with the couple's warmest clothes inside, their big, bulky coats flung over the top. Dick's typewriter was positioned carefully on the floor. A ream of paper stabilized it on one side, Judith's camera, in its scuffed leather case, on the other. The towers of Manhattan had receded into the rearview mirror hours ago. The city had given way first to small towns, then broad sweeps of farmland and long stretches of dense woods.

Dick sat in the passenger seat, fiddling with the radio dial as a station faded into static. He stilled his fingers as the chords of "The Saga of Jenny," a forties tune with Gershwin lyrics, came in clear over the airwaves. Judith looked over at her husband, his left hand resting on the tiny ball of golden fur curled on the seat between them. The puppy had been Dick's idea. He'd located the litter amid their preparations to leave the city, and Judith and Dick had stopped on their way north the city that morning, November 1, 1953, to make their pick. "Jenny!" Judith called out over the chorus. "Let's call her Jenny."

Several hours later, Judith pulled into the driveway of the peculiar little house in Alstead, New Hampshire, that she and Dick had leased. The tires crunched on the frozen gravel. She, Dick, and the puppy all tumbled, stiff legged, out of the car. Judith stood still, breathing in the sharp air and listening to the hush. She was so relieved to be out of New York.

The couple's return to the States from Paris had been a bumpy one. Without jobs, they'd moved in with the Baileys at 139 East 66th. Monty welcomed the couple warmly, but Phyllis was prickly and stiff. Dick, Judith could tell, was ill at ease, too, working hard to perform for his new in-laws, hoping to win their favor. Judith acted as the buffer, trying to absorb the tension between them. It exhausted her. Judith tried to focus on the future; Dick wanted to sell his novel and work as a journalist. Judith wanted children badly, and she and Dick, now wed, had just begun to try. While she waited to get pregnant, she decided, she'd work.

Just days after the *Mauritania* delivered her safely ashore on the first of November 1951, she set about reconnecting with her New York circle: Sarah Moore and her parents; Jane and John Gunther; and her former office mate, Betty Arnoff, now married and going by Prashker. Judith worked her connections, asking everyone she saw about possible job leads. She met with Ken McCormick at Doubleday the week after arriving home, and William Shawn at the *New Yorker* the Monday after Thanksgiving. Both said they had nothing for her. On a Sunday in mid-December, Judith and Dick had dinner with Sterling Lord and his wife, Dodie; the Lords had returned to New York just a few months ahead of the Joneses. Sterling told Dick and Judith he'd just moved into a tiny basement office on East 36th Street off Park Avenue. He was starting a literary agency of his own.

The next day, Judith went to see a fertility specialist named Dr. Jackson. The debilitating pain, vomiting, and heavy bleeding that had begun with her first periods had never ceased. She'd endured myriad attempts at alleviating the symptoms, including a series of "large jabs in the fanny of I don't know what" from a doctor who specialized in helping couples conceive. Each month, she sat alongside "anxious brides waiting, often with their embarrassed husbands," Judith had written Roethke in 1947. But the treatments hadn't worked.

At her appointment in December of 1951, Dr. Jackson told Judith there was little he could do to help. At nearly twenty-eight, Judith was already on the older side to start having children, he said. At the time, most American mothers had borne their first child by twenty-three. He didn't tell Judith she and Dick shouldn't try, but made it clear that he believed her hopes of conceiving were in vain. When Dick and Judith boarded a train early the following weekend for Boston—a chance for Dick to introduce his new wife to his daughters—Judith's heart ached.

Cambridge had been Dick's first stop on his return to the United States. He'd headed straight to Walker Street, just up the hill from Harvard Square, where Barbara had settled with their two elementary school–aged girls. She and John Sharnik, the man she'd left Dick for, had just had a baby together, a boy named John, after his father, who went by the nickname Pete. Barbara's mother, Mrs. Busse, had moved to Cambridge to help, while Sharnik commuted back and forth to New York for work.

On December 22, 1951, when Dick and Judith arrived at the house together, it was Barbara's mother who answered the door. The girls rushed to their father, while Barbara stood with the baby on her hip at a safe remove. Judith wore a fetching suit and a silk scarf tied about her neck. Her blond hair was swept into a chignon, and moonstone studs sparkled on her earlobes. Bronwyn later told me that, upon seeing her new stepmother, she gasped out loud; how *beautiful* Judith was. "I fell in love with her in an instant," Bronwyn told me.

Dick and Judith took the girls to dinner at Le Gourmet in downtown Cambridge. The Joneses drank wine, while the girls, with their perfect posture and legs crossed at the ankles, sipped water. Judith asked Pamela and Bronwyn what they liked to do, and they talked about drawing and playing the piano, school and poetry. Judith listened and watched as her husband turned childlike himself in the presence of his girls, delighting in the children's wit and charm.

The next day, Judith and Dick returned to Walker Street to exchange gifts and help decorate the Christmas tree. With the smell of spruce in the air and the twinkling lights reflecting against the windowpanes in the dark, the whole blended family sat down to eat. Late that evening, Judith and Dick said their farewells, promising to visit again soon. As the Joneses made their way through the frozen streets to the station, Judith felt another tug at her gut. Dick's girls were lovely, so lovely. But they were already half-grown and had a mother who loved them and with whom they lived. They would never be Judith's own.

By May 1952, Judith and Dick had moved into a railroad flat in a brownstone on East 48th Street in Manhattan's Turtle Bay neighborhood. Dick had a few story leads and an idea for an historical book framed around the Minnesota River, which ran through his home state. (Dick would publish that book, *The Minnesota: Forgotten River*, under the name Evan Jones. There was another Dick Jones publishing work in similar spaces, so Dick began to use his middle name professionally. He would write under the name Evan Jones for the rest of his life and increasingly go by it personally as well.) In January, he'd taken a reporting trip to Vietnam (then Indochina), stopping in Paris on the way. Dick had been gone only two days when Judith wrote to him: "I miss you horribly and have absolutely decided that no matter what, even if we starve to death, you shall never take a job that will keep you away even 10% of the time. It's not worth it." In his absence, Judith continued to look for work. She applied for a position at a law library. "I'd be able to close up my desk at 5 o'clock and forget the whole business," she wrote Dick. "And would be so much more cheerful in the long run to you." But Judith was passed up for the job.

For distraction, Judith left town for Princeton, New Jersey. Her sister, Susan, lived there, and was pregnant with her fourth child. She was experiencing complications and her husband, Jon, was out of town for several weeks. Judith went to lend a hand. "I am after all free," Judith wrote Dick, "and it seems really piggish not to help out. I hope nothing really drastic happens though for if you must know, I don't even know how to change a diaper." Two days into the visit, she wrote Dick again. "I'm really quite expert now at changing diapers, calming a weeping, teething infant at the same time that I'm playing the Lone Ranger with Jody and fighting off Sally who seems to have an endless passion for biting me." The relentlessness of children's needs was entirely new to Judith. But "it is," she noted, "a pleasant kind of fatigue, not that awful mental, discouraged kind of weariness that's come over me lately as a result of the eternal job hunt. So it's been rather good for me." Time spent with Susan's children only made Judith want her own more. "I do think children are an endless delight," she wrote to Dick. But each month, Judith's period arrived, and with it a new wash of disappointment and a lessening of hope.

Mid-April, Judith finally landed work, "not for Doubleday thank heaven," Judith wrote to Roethke, but for Harold Ober Associates, a literary agency. "It's an unbelievably pleasant sort of work. I've a small office and a comfortable chair where I can sit curled up all day reading manuscripts, and for an unambitious girl it couldn't be better." She wrote of herself under pretenses that were only partially true. The job at Ober was merely a placeholder while she waited, with increasing desperation, to become pregnant—"I was *dying* for children," Judith told me—and kept other professional irons in the fire. While Judith tried to come off as contented and self-effacing, in truth, she craved more.

In the summer of 1952, when *Anne Frank* became a runaway success upon its publication in the States, Judith decided it was time to speak up about her role in the book. She hoped it would help her get her foot back in the door of the publishing world. She went to Doubleday and "let [them] know that I was entirely responsible," she wrote Dick, who was off in Minnesota doing research for his book at the time. "It's really an incredible book, though I'm gritting my teeth at the translation occasionally and wish to hell I could have edited it." A higher-up, she wrote, had told her, "I've heard Price never does any work and I assumed you must have been practically running that office," the one in Paris, that is. Still, the house didn't offer Judith a job. She turned her back on Doubleday for good after that.

Judith was growing restless and bored. "I must confess that I find New York pretty gloomy after Europe," she wrote Roethke in November 1952. Conservative senator Joseph McCarthy's communist witch hunt was on at full tilt, and anyone considered remotely creative or intellectual was suspected. It was a precarious time to be working in journalism, or in any field even tangential to the arts. Judith and Dick watched as so many Americans faced the indignity of blacklisting, losing their jobs, and losing face. No one knew how long the hysteria would continue, but it seemed a good time to wait in the wings. "I think I must give all this up and retire to domesticity soon myself, before it gets the better of me," Judith wrote.

It was hard to be in New York, surrounded by so much political unease and their friends' success, too. Dick's colleagues from *Weekend* all seemed to be thriving. Sterling Lord had his agency; Hanns Hubmann and Tony Vaccaro, both photographers, were much in demand; and Andy Rooney had been hired as a staff writer by the Columbia Broadcasting System (CBS). Dick couldn't help but rake himself over the coals, feeling like a failure next to his peers. He wasn't the only one for whom such comparison stung.

Judith knew her family was watching her, sizing up her trajectory against Susan's and her cousin Jane's. Susan was settled in Princeton, well wed and mother of a small brood. And Jane and John Gunther were on a run of success; Gunther's 1949 book, *Behind the Curtain*, had been a hit, and they had used the proceeds to buy a brownstone at 216 East 62nd. They'd also adopted a child. Jane, who'd worked until she married "Big John G.," channeled all her ambition into supporting her husband's success and raising her son. Outwardly, Judith disdained the wifely conventions to which Jane and Susan had caved. But she envied them, too, for how easily—or at least, so it seemed—things had fallen into place in their lives. Judith needed some space from it all.

It wasn't the first time she and Dick had considered alternatives to New York. While still in Paris, they'd discussed settling outside New York, perhaps in a college town in New England. Judith wanted to be somewhere quiet and cheaper to live. "The thought of the Radio City rat race, of the fantastic cost of living in New York, and all the social demands of magazine and publishing jobs, plus the difficulty of bringing up a family in New York, depresses us profoundly," Judith had written her parents in early 1951. Dick wanted to write for a living, and Judith believed in him. "Do you know what these magazines pay? $750 is standard for the first story, and then it goes up with each successive one," Judith wrote to her disapproving mother. "I am telling you all this," Judith added, "only because I am trying to prove to you that the writing business does make the most sense—in fact, seems the only answer."

By summer 1953, the Joneses had settled on Alstead, New Hampshire.

Through friends, they'd found a furnished house close to the headquarters of *Yankee* magazine. Dick would freelance and continue to try to sell his novel. Judith planned to pick up odd jobs, maybe even do a little writing herself. But her chief ambition was motherhood. Though medical intervention had failed to help, Judith hoped a less stressful life in the country might prove the miracle fix.

Dick settled into his writing—he'd managed to place a few features in big glossies, *Cosmopolitan* and the like. Judith, too, wrote a couple of pieces for *Yankee*; all puff, concerning the latest fashion trend for girls. She signed up to be a substitute teacher at the local school and worked as a truck dispatcher just over the border in Vermont. In her free time, she played around with photography, hanging curtains for a makeshift darkroom in the storage shed out back.

One afternoon in April 1954, with patches of snow still dotting the yard and a few days after Judith had subbed in for a few days for a sick teacher, their neighbor, a plumber and member of the school board, stopped by. He rapped loudly at the door. When Judith answered and invited him in, he refused, staying in the doorway instead.

He said, "I'd like to talk to you," Judith told me, recounting the scene. "And he said, 'What's this you told the children about the Allies, and the Russians being our friends?'" Judith responded, "Well, I was just telling them how the word 'ally' was used that way during the Second World War, and . . ." The man's expression was severe. "He said, 'Well, a funny thing to call them our *friends*!' And then he said, 'What's that, why are there always shades on the window there?'" He gestured at the shed, its windows obscured from the inside by the blankets Judith had hung. "Well, I take photographs and I do darkroom work." But still the man shook his head. Judith told me he asked, "Why is your hair so long for a married woman?" The questions were ridiculous. But Judith was flummoxed nonetheless.

McCarthy's Senate Committee on Government Operations had reached the boiling point that month when the senator's hearings were broadcast live on TV. "Any man who has been named . . . as dangerous to the welfare of this nation, his name should be submitted to the various intelligence units, and they should conduct a complete check upon him. It's not too much to ask," McCarthy said in 1953. Communist infiltrators were everywhere, McCarthy believed, hidden among Americans in plain sight. Dick and Judith stood out in rural New England, and the plumber thought he smelled a rat.

Judith knew she and Dick had done nothing wrong, but the encounter left her rattled. It was time, Judith knew, to take a hard look at what they were doing out in the sticks. The life she'd imagined for herself and her husband there had been pegged to the arrival of children and with them, full absorption in domesticity. "I was convinced I'd have all these little babies and have a good life," Judith told me. But she hadn't been able to twist the arm of fate in her favor. "Never had the babies. Never got pregnant," she said, laughing sadly. She mourned the disintegration of the dream. But she also realized she and Dick were misfits in small-town New Hampshire. After the encounter with the suspicious neighbor, and "when the birthday parties started for the second year, the same [people], and everybody started drinking at 4 o'clock when the sun went down," Judith told me, "we began to think, '[We] want to get out of this atmosphere. This is not for us!'" It was time to return to New York. And this time, Judith was determined, they'd find a way to stay.

CHAPTER 6

Judith stood before her boss, Blanche Knopf, and cleared her throat. The translation that had just come in of Albert Camus's *Exile and the Kingdom* needed fine-tuning; Knopf was set to publish it in 1958, the following year. Blanche had asked Judith to read it and craft a full report with a turnaround time of less than a day. Judith took it home that night and stayed up reading through the night; "I wanted to prove myself," Judith told me. The following day, Judith told Mrs. Knopf she felt the translation "was far too stiff and academic, and needed to be brought into balance with nuanced, idiomatic language." Blanche, who'd newly been made president of the house, sat with her lips tight. Judith could tell she was displeased. Blanche Knopf was often displeased. "Then get rid of him!" Blanche cried. "I felt awful," Judith told me. "Here's somebody who had worked for Knopf for years." But once Mrs. Knopf had made up her mind, there was no changing it. Judith would have to give the poor translator the boot.

In late 1956, Judith had heard through the grapevine that Blanche Knopf was looking for an assistant. Alfred A. Knopf was then considered the most prestigious literary house in the United States, and among the most esteemed in the world. Knopf published its first hit, W. H. Hudson's *Green Mansions*, in 1916, and earned its first Pulitzer for Willa Cather's 1922 novel, *One of Ours*, in 1923. It published Thomas Mann, Raymond Chandler, Maxim Gorky, and Nikolai Gogol; Dashiell Hammett, Kahlil Gibran, H. L. Mencken, and John Hersey; D. H. Lawrence, Franz Kafka, E. M. Forster, Wallace Stevens, and the debut poetry collection of Judith's former beau, Theodore Roethke. As Knopf declared in an *Atlantic Monthly* advertisement in 1957, they operated with a love and understanding of books, and loyal service to their authors at the fore. They did not aspire to be popular—the book business, Alfred Knopf said, was not "Madison Avenue ballyhoo"—they aspired to be the *best*. An opening at Knopf was rare, and Judith eagerly threw her hat in the ring.

Blanche Knopf hadn't set out to hire a lady editor; outside the secretarial pool, she'd always been the only woman at the house. But Judith, Blanche saw, was qualified, so she called the young woman in. Blanche was notoriously persnickety, but when Judith told her about her role in the publication of *Anne Frank*, Mrs. Knopf perked up. Blanche had pushed for Knopf to acquire Anne Frank's diary; she, like Judith, had been moved by the girl's candor and voice. It also made *sense* for Knopf to publish the book: they were, at the time, the only Jewish-run publishing house in town. But Blanche's colleagues—among them Harold Strauss; William Koshland; and Blanche's husband and the house's cofounder, Alfred Knopf—didn't agree; they thought Frank's book wouldn't sell. When the diary became a runaway success, not for Knopf but for Doubleday, Blanche fumed. The day of her interview, Judith recalled, Mrs. Knopf "reached into a drawer beside her, and in it was a file about her editors who turned down Anne Frank." Blanche offered Judith the job. The young woman's role in Doubleday's decision to publish the diary is "what sealed it, no question," Judith told me.

Blanche Knopf (née Wolf) and Alfred Knopf founded Alfred A. Knopf together in 1915. Blanche was promised full partnership. Any other arrangement had been, for her, a nonstarter; she refused to marry Alfred until he gave her his word. Mrs. Knopf helped build the company from the ground up and brought in many of the house's most illustrious authors. It was she who signed James Baldwin—Knopf published *Go Tell It on the Mountain* in 1953—and she who brought in Langston Hughes. Knopf published his first book of poetry, *The Weary Blues*, in 1926, and his first novel, *Not Without Laughter*, which won the Harmon gold medal for literature, in 1930. Hughes remained loyal to the house until the end of his life.

Most of Blanche Knopf's best-known authors were men; indeed, the vast majority of published writers then were, too. But the women writers she worked with were a standout bunch. Her list included Edith Sitwell, Katherine Mansfield, and Elizabeth Bowen. Blanche first published the Norwegian writer Sigrid Undset in 1921. In 1928, Undset won the Nobel Prize in Literature. She was only the third woman to ever do so.

Blanche Knopf was known especially for her impressive stable of foreign writers. She'd convinced Sigmund Freud to let Knopf publish his *Moses and Monotheism*, and nabbed Brazilian writers Jorge Amado and Gilberto Freyre for the house. She became the American publisher of the French existentialist gods from Judith's Saint-Germain days: Sartre, Camus, Gide, and Simone de Beauvoir. Knopf published de Beauvoir's *The Blood of Others* in 1948 and *The Second Sex* in 1953. The house was among the first American publishers to have a boots-on-the-ground presence scouting for talent abroad, and Blanche Knopf did it all in heels, resisting gawking and gendered tropes all the while. "I don't think a lady publisher is any different than a man publisher," she once told an interviewer. "And I don't see anything interesting about her. I'll talk about my books and my authors, yes. But me? I should say not."

In her heyday, Blanche Knopf was known as sharp-witted and fiercely independent. With her dark, red-tinged hair, oversize jewelry, and designer clothes, she drew attention wherever she went. Her irreverence helped her build Knopf's remarkable list. John Hersey said that with Mrs. Knopf's "courage went a kind of stubbornness," Elizabeth Bowen noted the "effrontery" of her publisher's literary taste, and Thomas Mann called Blanche Knopf "the soul of the firm." But her outsize impact didn't earn her recognition as a true equal, not within the Knopfs' marriage and not at the office, either.

All those years of working against the current, the demands and challenges of working motherhood, and a publicly volatile marriage to Alfred, hardened Blanche. By the time Judith began at Knopf in February 1957, the house's co-founder had grown impetuous and impatient. If Judith had been hoping for a sense of solidarity between her and her boss, as the only two women in editorial at Knopf, she was sorely let down. "I don't think she liked me," Judith later said. "I don't think she liked women." But Blanche needed Judith more than she would readily admit.

From a young age, Blanche had suffered from body dysmorphia. She used cigarettes and later diet pills to curb her appetite. Between the world wars, she began taking what she called her "magic" pills, which contained 2,4-dinitrophenol, or DNP, a chemical the French used in World War I for manufacturing dynamite. By 1935, more than one hundred thousand Americans were using such diet drugs to slim down, but in 1939, its chief active ingredient was banned in the States. There had been a wave of user deaths, and a high incidence of cataracts among those who lived. By the time Judith began at Knopf, Mrs. Knopf was sixty-two years old and going blind. More, even, than a savvy assistant, Blanche needed someone to be her eyes. Judith learned to read everything aloud. She told me, "Very delicately I'd say, 'Would you like to hear how this sounds?'" For Blanche, whose identity was pegged to text, losing her eyesight was a humiliating blow. With discretion and tact Judith helped Blanche preserve her dignity.

Judith hoped the job at Knopf would give her a sense of purpose and a chance to engage with a society that was changing fast and in which writers played a pivotal role. American literature had exploded in the postwar years, with fresh new voices representing various poles striking a chord. The year Judith began at Knopf, Allen Ginsberg, a leader of the antiestablishment Beat generation, was tried for obscenity after the publication of his book *Howl and Other Poems* by City Lights Books in San Francisco. Ayn Rand's *Atlas Shrugged* celebrated capitalism and the rights of the individual, and Mary McCarthy's controversial *Memories of a Catholic Girlhood* won praise as "one of the most brilliant and disturbing memoirs ever written by an American." Jack Kerouac's *On the Road* was published that same year; Sterling Lord had sold the book to Malcolm Cowley at the Viking Press. It had taken Dick and Judith's old friend four years to find a publisher for the then-unknown writer who'd wandered into his office off the street. *On the Road* launched the author's and agent's careers at once.

Publishing itself was changing, too. In 1953, a young Jason Epstein—then freshly out of Columbia and an editorial trainee at Doubleday—kick-started Anchor Books, America's first trade paperback imprint. Anchor reprinted many of Doubleday's higher-brow and classic titles, building upon the makeover of paperbacks' bad rep that, during World War II, the Council on Books in Wartime had begun. Paperbacks were markedly less expensive for publishers to produce than hardcovers and lowered the price tag for consumers as well. For the first time, building a home library was within range for the American middle class.

Alfred A. "Pat" Knopf Jr., Blanche and Alfred's only child, saw Anchor as an ingenious move for Doubleday, and thought Knopf should follow suit. The house launched Vintage Books, their own paperback line, in 1954.

From the start, Judith wanted to join the vanguard by acquiring talent on her own. In June 1957, she reached out to Roethke in Seattle. They'd been out of touch since the Joneses' return from New Alstead to New York. "Dearest Ted," she began, "I have been meaning to write you ever since I became a lady editor at Knopf. Our New Hampshire phase is over and we are now settled back in New York where I am putting all that good Bennington training to excellent use." She continued: "I feel sure you must have a source of burgeoning young writers who would like to be read with a sympathetic eye. Or perhaps you might have some stimulating ideas for the Vintage series—one of our recent acquisitions being *The Philosophy of Literary Form* by our own Papa Burke. Do let me hear from you." It was a quiet exploratory move toward Judith eventually building a list of her own. For the most part, though, she did Mrs. Knopf's bidding and edited under her boss's name. "You didn't just go on your instinct and fight for something," Judith told me. If securing her place at the house required her to keep her head down, then that's what she would try to do.

At first, the duties Mrs. Knopf heaped on her new assistant were menial, but as the publisher grew to trust Judith, she gave her more editorial work. Elizabeth Bowen was first. Bowen was an Irish writer who'd steadily climbed in prominence and popularity since she'd begun publishing in 1923. Bowen was known for detailing the lack of fulfillment in intimate relationships among the bourgeois and for her controversial descriptions of homoerotic love between women. The writer was often compared to Katherine Mansfield and Virginia Woolf. Blanche Knopf and Bowen had grown very close over the years, but "[Blanche] really needed somebody" to work with the writer on the page. "Blanche asked if I would be the house editor on *A Time in Rome*," Bowen's next book, Judith said. "I said 'Sure,' and Blanche said, 'Well, if you have some comments to make, show them to me and I'll get them off to her.'" Judith read the manuscript and shared her feedback with Mrs. Knopf. Since Judith took her boss's dictation and did her typing for her anyway, Blanche had Judith weave her own suggestions into the editorial response letter to Bowen written under Blanche Knopf's name.

Bowen came to New York for her book's launch in 1959, and Knopf threw a luncheon to celebrate. "Elizabeth Bowen was observing everything, and talking fast; she had a terrific stutter," Judith recalled. At the end of the party, Judith told me, she and Bowen both "went into the coat room and put our boots on. And she said, 'You! You, you're the one, aren't you!' I said, 'What?' I thought I'd done something horrible. So she said, 'You're the one who's been editing my books, haven't you?'" Judith laughed. "She knew Blanche pretty well, and she just knew! She had that novelist's eye, and she saw all the pieces when finally we were all together." Rather than being angry at having been handed off to Blanche's young desk editor, Bowen was impressed. She invited Judith to lunch. "She was a great woman," Judith said.

After Bowen, Blanche gave Judith Langston Hughes; Judith edited his *Selected Poems*, which Knopf published in 1959. Judith inherited William Maxwell, writer and fiction editor at the *New Yorker*, and longtime friend of the Knopfs, too. Maxwell's first book with the house was his 1961 novel, *The Château*. From then on, Judith edited everything Bill Maxwell published with Knopf. Working with him gave Judith a direct line to talent at the *New Yorker*, where Maxwell edited the likes of Eudora Welty, Vladimir Nabokov, Shirley Hazzard, Mary McCarthy, John Cheever, and a young John Updike.

John Updike came to Knopf in 1959 to publish his second and third books; he'd done his first, a collection of poems called *The Carpentered Hen and Other Tame Creatures*, with Harper Brothers in 1958. Stewart "Sandy" Richardson, an editor at Knopf, had courted Updike and brought him over to the house. In 1959, Knopf published Updike's debut short story collection, *The Same Door*, and his first novel, *The Poorhouse Fair*. "I can remember Sandy reading me parts of it in his office, and I just loved it!" Judith told me. "I guess I said something to Alfred, so he knew I liked Updike," she said.

In the summer of 1959, Judith and John Updike met for the first time in the hallway at Knopf. Updike was struck by Judith's poise. And he liked how much younger she was than most editors he knew. Sandy Richardson had readied Updike's two books for publication. But when Updike came into the office that summer, Alfred Knopf told him that they'd fired Sandy; Updike would need a new editor at the house. Updike told Mr. Knopf he thought Judith, the woman he'd met in the hall, would suit him well. Alfred Knopf took Judith and Updike out to lunch, like a setup on a first date. The publisher could tell immediately that the two were a fit, and that Judith would make "a proper editor for John," she later told me. Judith began working on Updike's books immediately, though "[Alfred] didn't tell John right away," she said. On paper, Alfred Knopf would remain Updike's editor for several years to come; but behind the scenes, Judith was the one editing his work.

In the fall of 1960, Knopf published Updike's second novel, *Rabbit, Run*. The book chronicled a chapter in the life of twenty-six-year-old Harry "Rabbit" Angstrom, an "American everyman saddled with wife, child, and uninspiring job, the trappings of mid-century white middle-class woe." *Rabbit* was Updike's attempt to depict "what happens when a young American family man goes on the road and the people left behind get hurt." It was a response to Kerouac's *On the Road*, Updike said. The *Times* called *Rabbit* "moving and brilliant," and praised Updike for his sensitivity and "perfectly pitched" prose. In the autumn of its publication, *Rabbit, Run* was named a finalist for the National Book Award. The book marked Updike as a writer to watch. Judith's pride swelled.

Not long after, Alfred approached Judith about working with John Hersey, an important author for the house. Hersey's 1944 novel, *A Bell for Adano*, won the Pulitzer Prize for Fiction; the writer was only thirty years old. Hersey wrote fiction on the side; his bread and butter was reporting. His 1946 *Hiroshima*, which first appeared as a thirty-thousand-word article in the August 31, 1946, issue of the *New Yorker*, exposed the horrific aftermath of the atomic bomb in Japan by way of profiling six survivors. It is considered a pioneering work of New Journalism, a style in which the narrative techniques used in fiction writing are adopted for nonfiction reportage. All three hundred thousand copies of that issue of the *New Yorker* sold out almost immediately. Knopf published the long-form article as a book late that same year.

Blanche had been the one to bring Hersey to Knopf, but she didn't edit him herself. Instead, she'd passed the writer off to another editor who was, Judith recalled, "afraid to touch anything because [Hersey] belonged to Blanche. Hersey hadn't really been edited." Alfred Knopf saw that Hersey, one of the house's luminaries, wasn't getting the attention he deserved. He needed a close reader, someone unafraid to get involved. "[Alfred] thought we would be a good match," Judith told me. "But he said, 'I have to be sure that you like each other. You're going to have to spend a lot of time together!' That was what mattered to [Alfred]," Judith explained, "that you kept Hersey happy." Alfred Knopf arranged a luncheon in Connecticut; him and Judith, Hersey and his wife. Judith wasted no time feeling the writer out and trying to earn his trust. "I said to him, 'How much do you really want me to participate? Because, I'd love to, but I don't want to be intrusive.' And he said, '*Please.* I *need* that first reader, that response.'" That settled it. Judith became Hersey's editor. She'd continue to work with him for the rest of his career.

Judith was elated; being entrusted with Hersey was a triumph. "But Blanche was kind of mad when Alfred started stealing me," Judith told me. The Knopfs were always vying with each other for power. Emotions ran high. "It was a family, you can't even call it a business. And if [people] goofed, out they went. There was a lot of firing," Judith said to me. From the first day of her job at Knopf, Judith feared she'd be shown the door. ("When I get fired from Knopf," they'd plan a trip to Spain, Judith wrote Dick in the summer of 1957 when he was out of town reporting.) Blanche and Alfred loved to "play their staff one against one another," Judith told me, forcing them to pick sides. And Judith was caught in between. She worried that if Mrs. Knopf sensed any disloyalty in her, it would cost her her job. "I liked Alfred as a person much better, I have to admit," Judith told me. "I think he liked me, too."

· · · · · · ·

It was early the week of Thanksgiving 1959, and there was a restless, distracted energy at Knopf. Judith was trying to tie up loose ends before making the long drive north to Vermont where her family would convene. It had been a busy fall season, and Judith was looking forward to a few days out of the office, taking long walks with the dog in the cold, the smell of woodsmoke in the air. She was deep in work when Bill Koshland stopped by her desk.

Koshland had been at Knopf since 1934. He'd become a trusted adviser to both Alfred and Blanche, and had a hand in nearly every one of the house's books. "I always saw him as the grand vizier in the court. The diplomat who makes the pieces come together," Judith told me. In an office often rife with tension, Koshland was warm and playful. "A lovely man," Judith said.

Koshland handed a thick, unwieldy stack of paper over to Judith. It was a cookbook, he said, that had just come in from Avis DeVoto, a writer, editor, book critic, and avid cook who lived in Cambridge, Massachusetts, and scouted talent for Knopf. Koshland, who hadn't a clue about cookbooks, asked Judith if she'd weigh in. "Everybody knew that I had spent that time in Paris and that I did like to cook," Judith told me. Koshland plunked the hulking thing on her desk, "probably," Judith said, "because they thought it would amuse me, and then I'd probably reject it." Judith eyed the manuscript. The book was huge—750 pages long. *French Recipes for American Cooks* by Louisette Bertholle, Simone Beck, and Julia Child, the cover read. Judith didn't recognize any of the authors' names. Still, she was intrigued; unbeknownst to Koshland, Judith had been searching for a good French cookbook for years.

Ever since Judith and Dick had returned from France, Judith had been pining for *la cuisine française*. The couple had done their best to re-create the dishes they'd eaten in Paris, but most of their attempts fell short. The American foodscape had shifted radically in the postwar years, with small grocers and specialty shops giving way to supermarkets that kept food in boxes, cans, and behind glass. "Everything was going into packages so the 'poor little woman' wouldn't soil herself with cooking, the *ignominy* of cooking," Judith told me. "It was a whole emphasis; everything was done for you. It was really sort of pathetic!" How, Judith wondered, was one to judge a fish's freshness without poking it, or the ripeness of a melon without giving it a sniff or squeeze?

Judith tried to make do. But even with a begrudging acceptance of products far below the standard she'd grown accustomed to in France, Judith lacked the instruction she needed to guide her to success. She'd tried cookbook after cookbook, finding each one lifeless and uninspired. What rankled her most, though, was that the books didn't *work*. At the time, most cookbooks relied on cursory instructions and assumed a great deal of skill and knowledge among home cooks. All that brevity and vagueness left ample room for improvisation (and error). Not one of the French cookbooks Judith tried offered the precision, detail, or depth of explanation she sought. She told Koshland she'd have a look at *French Recipes for Home Cooks*. Koshland, in turn, wrote to Avis DeVoto, "Thanks for letting us take our time with the book. Judith Jones is already experimenting at home and I shall start in, I trust, next week."

Julia Child moved to Paris in late 1948 with her husband, Paul, who worked for the State Department as an exhibits officer. Paul already knew and loved Paris and had a feeling his new wife, Julia, who'd never been to France before, would, too. He was right. With her first bite of sole meunière, Child, who loved to eat and had tried and failed to teach herself to cook as a newlywed living in Washington, DC, fell head over heels with French cuisine. Shortly after their arrival in France, Child enrolled in Le Cordon Bleu to learn how to cook it herself.

Not long after completing her course, Julia Child met Simone "Simca" Beck at Le Cercle des Gourmandes, a Parisian club for gutsy food-loving women. Beck and her friend, Louisette Bertholle, had been working on a French cookbook for Americans for years by then, but had been unable to get it into print. They'd been advised by someone in publishing to find an American to offer the "inside" perspective they needed to get through to home cooks in the States. Beck had picked Child out of the crowd. (It wasn't hard to do; Julia was 6 foot 2.) The two French women asked Child if she'd join their writing team to help revise and re-pitch the book. Child enthusiastically agreed.

Having learned to cook French food as an outsider, Child understood the book's intended audience in a way Beck and Bertholle could not. In order to work, she insisted, the book would have to be so detailed and clear that even Americans who knew nothing at all about French cuisine—or even how to cook—could successfully prepare the dishes therein. At Julia's behest, the three stripped the book down to its studs and, recipe by recipe, began to retest and rewrite the entire thing. They explained everything with a granular, step-by-step approach, from how to shop for the right cuts of meat to how to simmer, sauté, and salt. To further support the project, the three began teaching cooking classes for American women abroad, naming the setup L'École des Trois Gourmandes.

The book was all-consuming, and reworking it took years. As it progressed, Child sent sections of the manuscript to Avis DeVoto. The two had first connected when Child wrote Bernard DeVoto, Avis's husband, a letter in response to a magazine article he'd published on kitchen knives. Avis DeVoto handled all her husband's correspondence, so it was she who read Child's letter first. Avis was so struck by Child's excitement, conviction, and verve that she fired off a reply herself. DeVoto and Child recognized in each other a shared sense of irreverent vivacity, spunk, and drive, and they bonded over their common love of food. Though they hadn't met in the flesh, they quickly became fast friends.

DeVoto, a serious home cook herself, thought the book had real promise.

"You really have got something here that could be a classic and make your fortune and go on selling forever," she wrote to Julia on Christmas Day, 1952. Avis told Julia that she thought *les trois gourmandes* ought to submit the work they'd done so far to Dorothy de Santillana, a top editor at Houghton Mifflin, the Boston house that published Avis's husband. The trio heeded Avis's advice. Houghton bit, and signed a contract in 1953 to publish the book. Five years later, in early 1958, Child, Beck, and Bertholle finally turned in a complete manuscript. But De Santillana said it was far "more complex and difficult to handle" than what she felt she'd been promised. She gave the authors a choice: kill the project altogether or revise the whole book again.

Beck and Bertholle were crestfallen, but Child refused to give up. She decided they'd simplify the book as their editor had asked, and finally get it into print. But in November 1959, after Child and her team had overhauled the whole thing and cut the book nearly in half, Houghton balked again. The book was too long, and thus too big an investment on the publisher's part, Paul Brooks, Houghton's editor in chief, wrote them. "Believe me, I know how much work has gone into this manuscript," but "I suggest you try this book on some other publisher." Child was devastated. This time, she was certain they'd come to the end of the road. But Avis didn't agree. Without waiting for *les trois gourmandes'* permission, she had Houghton forward the manuscript into the hands of her influential friend Bill Koshland at Knopf. Koshland, Avis knew, wasn't bad in the kitchen himself, and he loved to eat and drink. "Do not despair," Avis wrote Julia, "we have only begun to fight."

French Recipes for American Cooks was different from all the other French cookbooks. Judith saw that right away. "I *knew* from the tone, from the writing," Judith told me, "that I was going to learn things." Judith took the book home in pieces to cook from it with Dick; cooking together remained the anchor of their domestic life. They started with the boeuf bourguignon. "First [Julia] told what kind of meat to use, which is so important," Judith recalled. "And what kind of fat to use—if you brown the meat just in the butter, the butter burns. She told you not to crowd the pan, because you steam rather than brown the meat, and doing the mushrooms and the little onions separately. It just went on and on, these suggestions. I couldn't believe it! Well, it was the best boeuf bourguignon we'd ever had!" Judith said. *French Recipes* actually *taught* readers how to cook. Judith thought it was revolutionary. The very book she'd been looking for had fallen right into her lap. But Knopf's editorial board, Judith knew, was unlikely to be as enthused as she about such a project. Judith would have to channel her excitement into a convincing argument and a workable strategy if she wanted a chance at the book.

CHAPTER 7

J udith tried to focus. There were pages to mark up, memos to write, and correspondence to attend to. Usually, she could block out the world at work, lost
in authors' pages, green pen in hand. She puzzled over structure and word
choice, attended to cadence and tone. But that morning in April 1960, her attention had strayed, and she couldn't rein it back in. Behind closed doors, the Knopf
bigwigs were in a meeting, discussing the fate of *French Recipes for American Cooks*.

Judith had, by then, read every word of the book and cooked through a good
portion of it at home. In an impassioned memo to her colleagues, she wrote: "I
don't know of another book that succeeds so well in defining and translating for
Americans the secrets of French cuisine. Reading and studying this book seems to
me as good as taking a basic course at the Cordon Bleu." Judith thought Houghton had made a major misstep, turning down the book. She knew *les trois gourmandes* were onto something. Something big. Judith told me, "I thought, if I love
this so much and want to learn, there are other people like me." Judith believed
Knopf should publish the book, and she wanted it to be hers. But someone else
would have to make the pitch on her behalf.

Though Judith had been at Knopf more than three years, she still hadn't been invited to discuss submissions or acquire on her own. "I didn't even go to our editorial meetings," she told me, "I wasn't enough of a"—she paused, searching for the right phrase—"'matured editor.' I wasn't that young then, but people just perceived me as more of a secretary. That's the word they would use." So Judith sat helplessly at her desk, waiting to hear what her bosses' verdict on *French Recipes* would be.

Judith understood what she was up against with the cookbook. It wasn't only that she was considered so junior or that she was a woman, though she knew her sex certainly didn't help; as a woman in publishing, Judith told me, "you were kept down." It was that Knopf had no real interest in cookbooks. None of the major publishing houses did. Though Judith experienced the kitchen as a place of pleasure, experimentation, creative engagement, and play, much like the day in, day out work of home cooking itself, cookbooks as a genre were patronized, written off, or altogether ignored. Their authors weren't seen as *real* writers, and cookbooks were considered decidedly unliterary in subject and form.

Despite the bias against cookbooks, Judith saw potential: Alfred Knopf was a bon vivant, and fancied himself a gourmet. He was founding director of the Wine and Food Society of New York, and threw legendary dinner parties at his country home in Purchase, New York. His interest in food occasionally showed up in his work, too. In 1930, he'd published André Simon's *The Art of Good Living*, a hedonistic book on food and drink. Knopf had done a few books on wine making as well. Blanche Knopf, on the other hand, hardly ate, and she certainly didn't cook. Cookbooks, and food as a subject more broadly, were of little interest to her (though she made an exception in publishing the British food writer Elizabeth David's *Italian Food*, which, like *French Recipes*, came to Knopf by way of Avis DeVoto).

French Recipes was a risk all around. It was technically complex and very long. It would be expensive to print, which would mean its price point would have to be high—three knocks against it right out of the gate. But sticking her neck out for a cookbook was also dicey for Judith's reputation at Knopf. She risked angering Blanche by openly appealing to Alfred's sensibilities and, what's more, being pigeonholed as unserious and unduly interested in "women's stuff." Judith needed an in-house ally, someone to advocate passionately on both her and the book's behalf if *French Recipes* was to stand a chance. Someone trusted, senior, and male.

Angus Cameron arrived at Knopf in 1959, already a veteran of the publishing industry. He'd been at Bobbs-Merrill, then Little, Brown, where he published J. D. Salinger, Lillian Hellman, and Evelyn Waugh. He became Little, Brown's editor in chief in 1943. Cameron was known for taking risks on the right books;

he'd once been called "the foremost United States book editor." His pot stirring had earned him a reputation in publishing as a man to watch, but it caught the attention of the Cold War communist witch hunt, too. In 1947, Cameron was accused of supporting anti-American causes. Thirty-one of his authors got dragged into the mess alongside. He was told he'd need to clear all his outside activities by the company from then on if he wanted to keep his job. Instead of complying, he resigned. He took his wife and children first to the Adirondacks and then, flying with a bush pilot, on to Alaska to lie low while the Red Scare cooled. From spring to September 1952, the family lived in the isolated Brooks Range. Cameron called upon his skill as a fisherman, hunter, and cook; he caught and sold whitefish to Indigenous people of the region, and fed his family like royalty. Cameron's return to publishing in the mid 1950s was heralded as a victory for publishing and a testament to the triumph of free speech over censorship. For Knopf, landing Angus Cameron was a coup.

Judith watched how Angus Cameron handled the senior editors. She particularly admired his ability to get through to Alfred when the publisher was in a mood. "Angus knew so much and was so interested," Judith told me. "He was a brilliant person, and a true Renaissance man."

Judith and Angus became friendly and often went to lunch, talking about books, food, and wine. But Angus didn't just love to eat and cook. He knew cookbooks, too. At Bobbs-Merrill, Cameron had helped debut the first commercial edition of Irma S. Rombauer's *Joy of Cooking* in 1936; to date, it remains one of the best-selling cookbooks of all time. At Little, Brown, he'd published Dione Lucas, a restaurateur who, in 1942, founded the Cordon Bleu in Manhattan. For many years, Lucas was considered the most prominent American teacher of French cooking, and Lucas herself the hub of New York's niche food scene. So when Judith realized what gold she had in *les trois gourmandes'* book, she knew Angus Cameron was the one to go to for help.

Judith gave Cameron *French Recipes* and asked him for his honest opinion. She braced herself for disappointment, but as it turned out, she needn't have worried at all. Angus was as blown away by the book as Judith had been. "Both as aspirant cook and editor," Cameron wrote in his reader's report, "this seems to me, short of actually trying the recipes, the best working French cookbook I have ever looked at. To my knowledge what these authors have done has never been done before. . . . I am convinced that a path will be beaten to the door of this book." Page after page, Cameron detailed his faith in the book, going to bat for its cause.

In the editorial meeting that April day while Judith waited anxiously at her desk, Cameron gave an impassioned pitch to echo his gung ho report. The book was an astonishing achievement. There was simply nothing else like it, he said. As far as money was concerned, Cameron didn't think the high cost of production and, thus, the book's high retail price, would hinder its sales. Knopf should take the book, Cameron urged, and put Judith at its helm.

Blanche Knopf fidgeted grumpily as Cameron went on. Judith was *hers*, and the last thing Blanche needed was some silly cookbook competing for her desk editor's time. Finally, Blanche had had enough; she pushed back her chair and huffed out of the conference room. There was a beat of silence, then Alfred Knopf spoke. "Well," he said gruffly, a smile turning up the corners of his mustache, "let's give Mrs. Jones her chance!"

Judith was jubilant when Cameron told her the news. She wrote to Julia Child right away. "Our publication proposal for the Child, Beck, and Bertholle has just been approved." Knopf offered $1,500 for the book, twice what Houghton had paid. Judith reiterated the book's brilliance, but emphasized in her letter that it was nowhere near ready to go to press. The team had a massive undertaking ahead.

Julia, acting as chief correspondent on behalf of *les trois gourmandes*, wrote that she was overjoyed at Knopf taking the book and noted her surprise that Judith had cooked from it. "It means that we can have truly meaningful communication," Child said. It was clear, though, that Child didn't quite see the scope of revision their new editor had in mind. "The final manuscript can be ready for you certainly within a month," Child wrote in May 1960. "I shall start right in on it now."

. . . .

By 1960, American consumer culture was attempting to dissuade American women—especially those who were white and in the rapidly expanding middle class—away from cooking from scratch. "Mom gets damned tired of preparing and planning three meals a day," quipped *Esquire* in 1953. Postwar consumerist culture promised an unprecedented era of leisure, made possible by prepackaged and heat-to-serve foods. New appliances were marketed as further help. "The prevailing message was that the poor little woman didn't have time to cook," Judith told me, "and moreover that it was beneath her dignity." Advertisers framed meal prep as a chore to be minimized and mechanized so ladies could get out of the kitchen, put their feet up, and have a drink. Cookbooks, too, were part of the scheme.

In 1950, McGraw-Hill and General Mills jointly published *Betty Crocker's Picture Cook Book*. It hit the bestseller list right away (and, at more than sixty-five million copies sold to date, no other cookbook has ever come close to matching its commercial success). It offered American women lessons on feeding children and hosting; labor-saving tips for the kitchen; and advice on how to design, build, and outfit a new one, too. *Betty Crocker* promised that General Mills products and "the latest short cuts, equipment, and prepared foods," would bring "more fun in cooking and deeper joy in your homemaking."

It was all part of a marketing ploy; the intent behind cookbooks like *Betty Crocker* wasn't to teach women to cook, it was to get them to shop. And it worked. American wives did the lion's share of the buying; spending on appliances and furniture increased by 240 percent in the postwar years. It wasn't a vision accessible to all; America's farmers, craftsmen, and working poor, as well as most people of color, didn't benefit from the same upward mobility as the G.I. Bill–boosted white middle class. But for those with extra money to spend, the new era of consumerism was, as *Betty Crocker* proclaimed, a "dream come true." For those overwhelmed or exhausted by cooking from scratch, the message offered relief. But not everyone was on board.

After the war, American women had been pushed from the public realm when they were ousted en masse from paid jobs. Now, with their culinary skills recast as old-fashioned and obsolete, they were being edged out of the private space of their kitchens, too. It was almost as though women themselves were falling into disuse. Judith wanted to resist, and she understood that Julia Child did, too. While living in Paris, both women had come to see the kitchen as a place of purpose and sensual pleasure, and one of power as well. In their view, cooking wasn't drudgery (though it certainly was work), and it wasn't a gendered trap to be escaped. Rather, they saw the culinary arts as a gateway to the wider world and a richer, more autonomous life. Through food, Judith and Julia had found something of a shared politics, a way to express a femininity unfettered by what they saw as conservative American norms. "Food was our rebellion," Judith told me. "It gave us the courage to see things, make things happen." The time was ripe, Judith thought, to get their message through. But if *French Recipes* was to change American attitudes toward cooking, as she believed it could, it would have to be perfect.

· · · · · · ·

On the Saturday of the Decoration Day (now known as Memorial Day) weekend in 1960—the kickoff of summer in New York—Judith sat at her desk, with hundreds of marked-up manuscript pages beside her, writing to Julia Child. "Dear Mrs. Child," Judith began, "I'd like to suggest two areas that you might be thinking about expanding. I felt that there was a lack of certain hearty peasant dishes," the sort "that anyone who has lived in France remembers with such delight." Judith thought the book could use a bit more on beef; it was, after all, the most readily available meat in the States. "You might offer even more variety for its use than you have given."

Julia Child received the letter in Oslo, Norway, where Paul had recently been reposted. Child, Beck, and Bertholle were continuing their collaboration by international post. Child was eager at Judith's invitation to expand upon certain topics, especially after Houghton's condemnation of the cookbook's complexity and length. She agreed with Judith's suggestion to enlarge the section on beef, but pushed back on the "peasanty" dishes bit. "Perhaps Americans think French peasants are more 'peasanty' than they are?? Real peasants boil everything," Child sassed.

Judith's editorial involvement with *les trois gourmandes*' cookbook was multifold from the start. She knew the book needed to be well organized, and the recipes' instructions crystal clear on the page. But she was also assessing the book as the book's target readers would, as an aspiring cook herself. She became proxy for *les trois gourmandes*' audience. "[Julia] used me as a guinea pig," Judith told me. "She'd say, 'See if the supermarket has mushrooms,' or something like that. And so I'd scurry around and go to some supermarkets, and of course they *didn't*. It was a sorry picture." Judith reported her findings, and then Child adjusted the recipes, tailoring them to "the foods you could get." "I felt that she appreciated me because I was so enthusiastic," Judith told me.

Author and editor didn't see eye to eye on everything, but Judith's deep involvement and hands-on participation did wonders for building Child's trust and their collective rapport. So when Judith did levy a critique, Child took note. In June, Judith wrote to Child with a quip about the book's recipe for cassoulet. "I have read through carefully, though I've not had time to experiment (and indeed it would take time!)," Judith wrote. "Two things bother me. It seems to me that the recipe calls for a great deal of meat—about seven pounds in all. But more worrisome was the fact that you have to cook a whole pork roast separately and a lamb stew before you put everything together. . . . I wonder if in this one case, your directions are not unnecessarily complicated."

Judith saw her role as to help her authors organize, clarify, and finesse their work, not control or impinge on their vision or voice. A less forceful approach, Judith learned early on, often succeeded in lessening her authors' resistance and brought about the editor's intended result. "You have to get the writer to see what I might think is wrong, to try to get them to see it as though, 'Oh! This isn't working,'" Judith told me. "And then it comes from them instead of writing little dots along the margin and 'Don't like this word here.'" "Of course," Judith continued in her letter to Child, "you are the final authorities, but you did ask for my comments on it." Child responded, "A good cassoulet is a time-consuming process, which is why you don't often get one which tastes as it should." Still, she saw her editor's point; "I am going to re-do that recipe."

All year long, Judith and Child volleyed multipage letters and marked-up chapters back and forth across the Atlantic. They shared an eye for detail and a penchant for hard work; it was a pairing of grit and will. In the fall of 1960, they spent weeks exchanging new title ideas for the book. Child sent Judith a long, typed list of suggestions, with "Mastering the Art of French Cuisine/Cooking/Cookery" scribbled at the end. "We have all liked the idea of playing around with the word 'master' or 'mastery,'" Judith reported on behalf of Knopf. "But I told you the objection to the idea of 'the mastery of.' However, I think we have now found the solution by calling it: 'Mastering the Art of French Cooking.' 'Mastering' becomes an active verb now and it gives us everything we need to work with in terms of copy. Furthermore, a buyer will look at all the other books (including the S. and S. twenty-five-dollar job) and think that he must buy *Mastering the Art* before he can possibly tackle any of the others. What do you and [the] two other 'gourmands' think?"

When it came to elements of the book that would affect cover art, marketing, and sales, Judith ran things by her colleagues at Knopf. But for the most part, no one paid any attention to the editor as she toiled tirelessly over the book. For the first time, Judith was free to work as she pleased, calling the shots on her own. And with no house style for cookbooks at Knopf, Judith relied on her intuition, making it up as she went along. She may have been improvising, but her acuity shone through. In September 1960, as editor and authors shifted from making major revisions to fine-tuning the manuscript, Child wrote, "I have made all the corrections you have suggested specifically," and though "I am not so naive as to suppose that we shall get all the rough spots, you have certainly picked up some dillies. Thank heaven that you are such a perceptive editor." Judith, for her part, was equally impressed. "I had tremendous admiration for [Julia]," Judith told me, "because she knew what she was doing and why." Julia Child was a workhorse and moreover, precise and clear. Most important of all, Judith told me many decades after the book's completion, "she was a wonderful teacher." "I think you are a wonder," Judith wrote Child in April 1961." I don't know what we'd do without your efficiency and your patience."

More than a year had passed since Knopf had acquired *Mastering*, and still, the book wasn't done. Child wrote to Judith that she and her husband were packing up to return to the States. Paul Child had handed in his resignation; he'd had enough of the foreign service and wanted to focus on his own artistic pursuits, photography and painting. The Childs were coming home, this time for good.

They'd bought a house in Cambridge, Massachusetts, just a few blocks from Avis DeVoto. It would be a long, complicated move. "I hope you're not getting too discouraged at the magnitude of this job," Judith wrote Child in April 1961, worried that *Mastering* might get lost in the mix. Before setting sail, Child wrote to reassure her editor. She'd be finishing the book's index at sea, she said, and had already made plans to come to New York upon docking so the two of them could finalize *Mastering*'s manuscript together in person. Knopf had slated the book's publication for fall 1961, and it had to be at the printer's well before that. Child told her editor not to worry, she wouldn't lose her stride; "The book," she wrote Judith, "is more important than anything."

. . . .

While Julia Child focused all her energy and attention on *Mastering*, Judith was juggling a number of projects at once; "I was doing ten, twelve books a year," she said. While Judith awaited the Childs' arrival in New York, she gave herself over to Blanche Knopf's ceaseless demands and to another author and project she'd claimed for her own.

In November 1960, almost a year to date after Bill Koshland delivered *les trois gourmandes*' cookbook to Judith, he stopped by her desk with another book in hand. This one was slim—a collection of poetry, Koshland said. Judith's love of verse was almost as well-known around the office as her interest in food. Koshland said the volume was the poet's debut. It had just been published in the UK by Heinemann; it wanted to know if Knopf would be interested in purchasing the American rights and publishing the book in the States. Koshland asked Judith if she'd give it a look.

Judith set aside the work she'd been doing, opened to the first poem, and read: *Perhaps you consider yourself an oracle / Mouthpiece of the dead, or of some god or other. / Thirty years now I have labored / To dredge the silt from your throat. / I am none the wiser.* The collection was called *The Colossus and Other Poems*. Its author was Sylvia Plath.

Knopf had had their eye on Plath since 1953, when she'd done a stint as a guest editor at *Mademoiselle* during her summer break from Smith College (whence Julia Child had graduated two decades before). Plath, who'd been placing her stories and poems in national publications since she was a teen, had won her place at the magazine "for smart young women" by submitting a work of short fiction the year before. That piece, which Plath had entered in *Mademoiselle*'s annual Guest Editor contest and which won first prize and was published therein, had caught the attention of Harold Strauss, at the time, Knopf's editor in chief.

He'd written to Plath, asking her to keep him abreast of her future work. He said he hoped that one day she would pen a novel Knopf could publish. Plath was flattered but said that, as a student on scholarship, she worked summers to help pay her way, and was "not in the position to concentrate on any sustained writing project as yet." She thanked Strauss for his confidence in her writing and assured him that, if and when the time came, she would happily submit her novel to Knopf. "I hope within the next few years," Plath wrote.

Mademoiselle's annual college issue of August 1953 contained three pieces by twenty-year-old Sylvia Plath: an article about notable poets teaching on college campuses; an interview she'd conducted with Knopf author, Elizabeth Bowen; and an original poem titled "Mad Girl's Love Song": *I shut my eyes and all the world drops dead; / I lift my lids and all is born again. / (I think I made you up inside my head.).*

Plath had suffered from depression and wrestled with mental illness all her life. In her journals and letters, she described that summer of 1953 as one of "pain, parties, and work." Plath was thrilled to be in the thick of things; she was also overwhelmed. In August, she attempted to take her own life, swallowing a large dose of her mother's sleeping pills. "I blissfully succumbed to the whirling blackness that I honestly believed was eternal oblivion," she later wrote. But having taken too many pills, she "vomited them, and came to consciousness in the dark hell."

After her attempted suicide, Plath underwent "therapeutic" treatments of the talk, electroconvulsive, and insulin-shock kinds. Then she returned to Smith for spring term of 1954. She put on a good face, writing an honors thesis on Dostoyevsky and graduating summa cum laude in June 1955. Before graduating, she learned she'd been awarded a Fulbright to study literature at Cambridge starting that fall. There, at a launch party for a student magazine in which she'd published some of her poems, Plath met Ted Hughes. Plath described their first encounter as "cataclysmic." The couple married in June 1956, less than four months after meeting.

Plath and Hughes were both ambitious poets, but in their marriage, Hughes's work as an artist was prioritized. In addition to writing, Plath also kept house: "chicken & squash ready in the oven for her husband's return from the library, back achey," she noted in her journal. Plath enjoyed cooking but resented the scarce time it left her with to write. "Whoa, I said to myself. You will escape into domesticity & stifle yourself by falling headfirst into a bowl of cookie batter," Plath wrote soon after she and Hughes wed. But in spite of her "disease of doldrums," and the couple's geographic upheaval—they moved to the States in 1957 and returned to the UK two years later—Plath kept the plates spinning and muscled on, determined to write.

In April 1959, Plath completed her first book of poems and began looking for a publisher, "A much more difficult job for a poetrywriter than a novelist or a children's book writer," she wrote in a letter to a friend. That June, she submitted it to Knopf, making good on her word to editor Harold Strauss. Strauss knew little about poetry, and the manuscript was promptly given to Judith. Judith passed on Plath's collection but was "impressed enough," Judith later wrote, "to write her, although I did not think she was ready for a collection—at least one that we could do." That summer, Plath and Hughes moved back to the UK and settled in London's Chalcot Square. From overseas, following Knopf's rejection, Plath submitted her collection to the Viking Press and Farrar, Straus and Cudahy in October 1959. Neither house bit. Plath switched tack to focus on finding a British publisher for her book, while preparing for the arrival of her first child. The writer was twenty-seven when Frieda Rebecca Hughes was born in April 1960.

On Halloween of that year, with Frieda just seven months old, Heinemann published Plath's Colossus. When the house sent a copy of the British edition to Knopf for consideration, Koshland promptly handed the collection off to Judith, who he knew had seen the poet's earlier submission, to assess.

Judith spent a month with Plath's poems, letting the verse sink in. She took it home and shared portions of it with Dick. Poetry, like food, was a shared passion of theirs. Often, after dinner, the two would read poems aloud. In December 1960, Judith wrote a report to her colleagues at Knopf about Plath's book: "This girl is a poet, there is no question about it," she said. "I think one of the most exciting ones that has emerged in a long time." Judith was inclined to endorse Knopf's acquisition of The Colossus, but thought they ought to try to get hold of some of Plath's recent short stories, too. "It would be a sounder investment to launch her if we felt we were getting a potential fiction writer as well." Publishing poetry was always a risky investment; the form had literary clout, but rarely sold well.

Judith did have one reservation about The Colossus. She felt that "Poem for a Birthday" hewed dangerously close to Theodore Roethke's "The Lost Son." "The birthday poem" seemed "so deliberately stolen," Judith wrote, "that I would almost fear the charge of plagiarism." The editor, still gaining confidence at Knopf, suggested that "a pro," in the field of poetry, "someone like Stanley Kunitz," be asked to weigh in. Kunitz, who'd won a Pulitzer for his Selected Poems, 1928–1958 the previous year, knew his friend Roethke's body of work intimately. Judith wanted to know if Kunitz saw the "imitativeness" in Plath's poem that she did.

In January 1961, Judith sent The Colossus to Kunitz along with a note: "'Poem for a Birthday' at the end of the book is the one I am so uneasy about." It took Kunitz two months to reply, but when he did, he agreed with Judith both about the collection's promise and the trouble with the particular poem. With that, Judith felt she had what she needed, and got her superiors' go-ahead to move on the book. In March 1961, she wrote to Plath. "I feel I have lied [*sic*] with these poems for a long time now," she said. "I am convinced that they are remarkably fresh and exciting and vigorous. In fact, I cannot remember when I have been as impressed by any collection of a young poet." She included her concern about "Poem for a Birthday," too. "The feeling," Judith explained, "is that both in terms of imagery and rhyming structure it is so close to Theodore Roethke's 'Lost Son' that people would be likely to pounce on you." She would hate, Judith said, "to see your book reviewed and have almost all the critics use this as an opening wedge." She urged Plath to consider cutting the poem for the American edition, and wondered whether she might want to "weed out some of the more uneven poems" while she was at it. "If so, I would be glad to discuss which ones we might sacrifice." Judith signed off: "I shall be looking forward to hearing from you very anxiously indeed."

Plath was surprised at Judith's willingness to reconsider her work, and over the moon at the prestigious house of Knopf's offer on her book. To her mother, Aurelia, Plath wrote, "GOOD NEWS GOOD NEWS GOOD NEWS . . . ALFRED KNOPF will publish *The Colossus* in America! It is an immense joy to have what I consider THE publisher accept my book for America with such enthusiasm." When she responded to Judith, Plath conceded, without a whiff of defensiveness, that Judith was right about "Poem for a Birthday." It was, she admitted, "written under the undiluted influence of Roethke, and I now feel it is too obviously influenced. There are, however," she added, "two sections of the poem I wonder if you would reconsider and perhaps be willing to publish on their own— 'Flute Notes from a Reedy Pond' and 'The Stones.'" Those poems, the poet wrote, had been "written separately and much later than the other five . . . and have been published as separate poems in America where the others have not." As for cuts, Plath included a list of the poems she was inclined to cull; it would bring the collection down from the fifty poems in the British edition to forty for the American one, "a good and reasonable number," she wrote. "I'm eager to hear what you think of these suggestions. As for the rest, I couldn't be more in agreement with you. Sincerely yours, Sylvia Plath."

Judith concurred with most of Plath's proposed cuts, although on two, she suggested alternatives instead. "Do think about it," Judith wrote, "the final decision must, of course, be yours." Judith wrote that she liked Plath's idea of printing a trimmed version of "Poem for a Birthday," too. "I am pleased that our opinions seem to coincide so closely," Plath responded in May 1961. Their back-and-forth had helped her be more objective about her own work, Plath said, "and will result, I think, in a much stronger and shorter book in America." So pleased was Plath with her "lady editor"—as she referred to Judith in a letter home, and her astute handling of her work—that she called the collection's British edition "a trial run." In August, when *The Colossus*'s contracts were, at last, fully executed, Judith wrote to Plath, "hastening . . . to let you know that we are scheduling the book for Spring, April 1962 and are ready to put it into production. . . . I am delighted that we are finally underway." Judith felt the satisfaction of things beginning to click into place. At last, her editorial instincts were coalescing into something real, a work she would be able to hold in her hands and rightfully claim as her own.

Judith was still working largely at the Knopfs' behest, helping support authors given her by Blanche and Alfred and editing under their names. But, quietly and off to the side, Judith was nurturing her own ambitions as well; with Sylvia Plath and Julia Child, she had begun to build her list. The two writers were strategic choices on Judith's part: low-profile authors whose work, in poetry and food, respectively, existed outside the literary mainstream. As such, Judith was able to work with Plath and Child as she saw fit, with very little oversight from Knopf's higher-ups. As long as she fulfilled her obligations to Blanche and Alfred, no one at the house questioned what Judith did with the rest of her time. "I was allowed to do [my] own thing," Judith told me. Still, she was keenly aware that the reception of Plath's *Colossus* and *les trois gourmandes'* cookbook would largely determine her ability to pursue more authors independently. The future of her career at Knopf hinged on her books' success. And so Judith committed to doing everything in her power to help those books, those authors—and, thus, herself along with them—get ahead.

CHAPTER 8

n July 1961, after Judith and Julia had finally met in person and spent a few days working intensely together to put finishing touches on the book, *Mastering*'s revision was at last complete. Julia and Paul Child headed for a couple weeks to recharge with family on Mount Desert Island in Maine, and to await the shipment of their furniture from overseas. Julia was relieved for a break from the book. It had been years since she had cooked and eaten just for fun, without the pressure of perfecting a recipe or a deadline hanging over her head. On the rocky Down East coast, the Childs picked wild blueberries, gathered mussels, and swam in the frigid Atlantic. But for Judith, there would be no rest. No sooner was the book off to the printer than she began trying to drum up some buzz on behalf of *Mastering*. She started with Craig Claiborne at the *New York Times*.

In 1957, Claiborne had been made food editor at the *Times*. There, all things culinary were then housed in the women's pages alongside fashion, family, and furnishings. Food sections had long been the rare space in American print media for which women were hired and where they held sway; Claiborne became the first man at a major American paper to hold such a job. Four years Judith's senior and a Mississippian by birth, Claiborne had earned a degree in journalism before enlisting in the navy and serving in World War II. Afterward, he put his G.I. Bill benefits toward enrolling at the École hôtelière de Lausanne in Switzerland. It was the first, and, at the time, still premier, hotel management and hospitality school in the world. It was there that Claiborne trained in French cuisine. But it was back in the States that he began to apply his journalistic training to gastronomy. When, in 1955, *Gourmet* editor Ann Seranne assigned Claiborne his first piece on food, he knew he'd found his niche.

Since Claiborne had taken the helm of the food pages at the *Times*, Judith had been following closely along. He treated food as a subject as worthy of study and appreciation as any other form of culture or artistry. "I think he saw his job as to unearth wonderful people and their relationship to food and the past," Judith said to me, "and see how it was done here." She thought perhaps Claiborne could help get the word out about *Mastering the Art of French Cooking*.

Judith didn't know Claiborne, and neither did any of her colleagues at Knopf. But that didn't stop her from tracking him down and reaching out to him, cold. The number of the *New York Times* was listed in the telephone book; Judith simply picked up the phone, dialed the paper, and asked to be patched through. She introduced herself to Claiborne, and said she wanted to tell him about "a really remarkable book" she had coming out that fall. She asked if he would meet and suggested a restaurant. Claiborne agreed.

Judith struggled to hold Claiborne's attention over lunch. "He didn't buy things easily," she later told me. "He could be difficult, and he drank a lot." At one point, to keep the conversation moving along, Judith told Claiborne about how she and Dick lived and cooked. She explained that they'd moved back into the building where she'd grown up, and cobbled together a penthouse apartment out of maids' rooms, which no one in the building had anymore. When the weather was fine, Judith said, she and Dick climbed through their window onto the building's roof and cooked outdoors on a barbecue grill. "That wouldn't be a story today!" But at the time, there were "people leaning out their windows," Judith told me, "saying, 'Those people, they're gonna set the place on fire!'" Claiborne didn't seem all that interested in Knopf's big new French cookbook, but Judith and Dick's outdoor cooking caught his attention as a potential story. He thought it might make for decent copy to help fill in during the summer season's slack. Claiborne made Judith an offer he saw as mutually beneficial: He'd take a look at *Mastering* if she'd let him do a story about her and Dick. Judith readily agreed.

On a sweltering 93-degree day in July, Claiborne met Judith and Dick on the rooftop of 139 East 66th St. The Joneses served Claiborne steamed mussels with fresh thyme they'd grown in boxes on their ledge. Dick spit-roasted a lamb, and

Judith made a green mayonnaise from homegrown herbs to go alongside. (Judith had gotten her green thumb tips and tricks from Philip Truex, a Broadway actor who'd started a small gardening shop on 34th Street. She would publish his *The City Gardener*, one of the first books on urban agri- and horticulture, in 1964.) Claiborne's piece, titled "The Joneses Delight in Keeping Up with Cuisine," headlined the *Times*'s food section on August 3, 1961. "They live by the dictum that food is fun and that cooking is a prime pleasure," Claiborne wrote. Accompanying the article were several recipes adapted from the meal and a photo of Judith and Dick. She wore a form-hugging sheath dress; he, a shirt and tie. They looked ravishing, despite the heat. Judith just hoped Claiborne would keep up his end of the deal.

· · · · · · ·

Heels click-clacked across the tile and the air grew thick with the scent of hair spray, lipstick, and wool. Women streamed through the entryway and crowded inside the lobby of Bloomingdale's on East 59th Street and Lexington Avenue. Early that morning, Judith had met Julia Child and Simca Beck to help them set up for a cooking demonstration at the department store. The authors thought such a performance stood to increase *Mastering*'s visibility and boost sales of the book. Simca Beck had come to join forces with Julia, while Louisette Bertholle had stayed in France.

That morning, at Bloomingdale's, *Mastering* had been out for less than a week. Julia and Simca hoped to draw a few dozen curious shoppers to their demo and display and sell half as many books at best. But hundreds were pouring into the store. Judith stood on tiptoe amid the rush, trying to locate Julia's towering form. Judith hadn't been expecting this. In fact, she'd never seen anything like it before.

Knopf released *Mastering the Art of French Cooking* on October 16, 1961. Two days later, Craig Claiborne's review of the book ran in the *Times*. He called *Mastering* "probably the most comprehensive, laudable, and monumental work on the subject" of French cooking. The recipes are "all painstakingly edited and written as if each were a masterpiece, and most of them are," Claiborne wrote. The authors used "the simplest terms possible and without compromise or condescension." *Mastering*, he noted, "is not a book for those with a superficial interest in food," but "for those who take fundamental delight in the pleasures of cuisine." It was an important distinction: *French Recipes* had been rejected by Houghton for being too difficult and complex, but Judith knew the book's very appeal lay in its intricacy and sophistication. *Mastering* was an invitation to get seriously involved.

All that year, America was being seduced by French cuisine. John F. Kennedy took office as president in January 1961. His glamorous wife, Jacqueline "Jackie" Bouvier Kennedy, and the couple's two young children were part of the package deal. After eight years of conservative Ike, the Kennedys felt like so much fresh air. They were worldly, progressive, and suave. While President Kennedy got down to business running the country, Jackie set to work making the White House their own. She'd lived in Paris for a year during college, and spoke beautiful French. At the First Lady's urging, the Kennedys hired René Verdon, a Frenchman, as White House chef in the spring of 1961. It became front page news. Immediately, interest in *la belle cuisine* soared, with so many Americans aspiring to do as the Kennedys did. *Mastering* arrived on the scene just months later. The timing couldn't have been more opportune.

The *Times* review got *Mastering* off to a strong start, but it was television that really spread the word. On the eve of publication, Child and Beck had been invited to go on NBC's *Today Show* to do a spot plugging the book. It would air, live, just days after *Mastering*'s launch. Neither woman owned a television, but they understood the medium was changing the game. The first household television sets had been displayed at the 1939 World's Fair in New York City; there was only one station at the time. But that had changed fast. By 1945, there were close to ten thousand television sets in American homes, and at the decade's end, nearly a hundred commercial stations in major cities in the United States. By 1960, there were fifty-two million TV sets in the country; almost nine out of ten Americans had one. In 1961, when *Mastering* launched, nearly four million households turned on the *Today Show* each day.

Julia Child understood that the TV appearance was a huge opportunity to promote the book, to be seen; she and Simca couldn't just *sit* there, Julia knew. But she worried that her and Simca's middle-aged appearances—Julia was forty-nine, Simca fifty-seven—might lead viewers to dismiss them as washed-up and old. Julia knew they needed to demonstrate, to viewers, their youthful vigor and pluck. She decided they ought to cook. They'd bring their own hot plate, pan, eggs, and butter. A simple French omelet, Julia thought, would be just the thing. Julia and Simca practiced doggedly the day before they were scheduled to appear on set, preparing *les oeufs* over and over again. When the cameras rolled, Julia Child lit up the screen with her skill, her enthusiasm, and her dip-and-swoop voice. The next morning, at Bloomingdale's, Julia and Simca were inundated by women who'd seen them on TV.

Judith had managed her expectations for the book; steady sales over time had been her goal. With any luck, *Mastering* might be considered a classic. But the book had already outdone itself. After the *Times* review, the *Today Show*, and Bloomingdale's, copies of *Mastering* began flying off the shelves. Julia wrote her sister, Dorothy: "Our publishers are beginning to think they have a modest best seller on their hands." By the end of *Mastering*'s first week in the world, Knopf had ordered a second printing of ten thousand copies more, doubling the book's run, and had made plans for a third round of the same. "That was just remarkable," Judith recalled.

Judith worked fervidly to keep up the momentum of the book's initial success. In late October, she wrote to William Hogan, book review editor at the *San Francisco Chronicle.* "I hope by now you have received your *Mastering the Art of French Cooking*," Judith wrote, "and have, maybe, even sampled some of its delights." Julia Child and Simca Beck, she said, were "going to be making a trip across the country to help promote the book." The pair had mapped a route across the Northeast, Midwest, all the way out to the West Coast, helped along by their vast network of contacts and friends. They'd be in San Francisco before Thanksgiving. Judith wondered if the paper's "women's page editor" might be interested in interviewing the two authors and writing a feature on them and *Mastering.* "The book has gotten off to a roaring start here—beyond my greatest expectations, and you know I had high hopes for it," Judith wrote.

In early November, Julia and Simca hit the road in support of the book. Knopf had sent a publicity person along with them, and Paul Child had tagged along, too. The day after Thanksgiving he wrote to Judith: "The girls are going good: being real troopers." Their cooking demonstrations were having the desired effect, "with eager potential customers storming the book-store ramparts." But Paul was frustrated on *les dames'* behalf. "Awful dearth of books everywhere," he wrote. Demand for *Mastering* had quickly outpaced Knopf's initial printing and distribution efforts. "Though I know it's unavoidable it still is frustrating to continue blowing the publicity trumpet under these circumstances." He signed off perfunctorily—"Chins up!" he said.

Judith wanted to be a part of the excitement and to do what she could to help the book along. So she flew to California to join her authors for a few days. "It was *simply* exhausting work! You were running from one place to the next, and had to keep your schedules," Judith said to me. "I was biting my nails, but Julia was perfectly relaxed! She was just so good at making that contact with the public. And they adored her." Americans were smitten with French cuisine, and with its newest ambassador, Julia Child, too.

Julia and Simca carried on tirelessly along their route, but Judith had to return to New York and continue acting as the book's evangelist. "There wasn't much of a food world," Judith told me, "and I certainly didn't know anybody." But with a cookbook to promote, she'd made a point of seeking out the tastemakers in its ranks. "There were some very forceful people," Judith said. "And Jim Beard knew them all." James Beard was a widely syndicated and beloved American food writer. Known as "the Dean of American Cooking," he operated a cooking school out of his Greenwich Village row house, which also served as the informal hub of New York's emergent food scene. Judith had never met Beard, but she'd come to know him by reputation. His name was in the phone book, and "so," Judith told me, "I picked up the telephone, and I said, 'I have a remarkable manuscript, and you've got to look at it.'" She laughed. "I mean, he may have known who I was—I'm not even sure about that. And, he said, 'Oh, I will, send it down.'"

Beard called Judith back two days later. "I mean, he just devoured it," Judith said. "He said why it was remarkable, and so on and so forth. Then, at the end of this conversation, he said, 'I wish I had written it.'" Then Beard asked her, "'What should we do? What are you—what are you planning? I'll do anything to help.'" Judith responded honestly: "I don't know! I've never done a cookbook like this before!" But Beard had a plan. "He said, 'Well, the first thing you must do is get them over here so we can give a party,'" Judith recalled. "So he got this little French restaurant on 57th Street." The restaurant was the Egg Basket, and it belonged to Dione Lucas, also a power player in New York's culinary circle. Lucas, who'd been Angus Cameron's author at Little, Brown and had founded the American Cordon Bleu cooking school, had been an early adopter of television as a promotional tool. Her first program, *To the Queen's Taste*, was shot on site at the Egg Basket and aired on CBS from 1947 to 1949. Its later iteration, *The Dione Lucas Cooking Show*, ran until 1956. Beard talked Lucas into offering her restaurant to host *Mastering*'s fete. The venue settled, Beard promised Judith that he would invite all his food-loving friends and would act as the evening's MC. "He was wonderful, and so generous," Judith said. "And he was *always* throwing the party. He was quite good at that."

In California, *Mastering*'s authors and editor alike were beginning to register the magnitude of the book's reach. Every event was flooded with fans who buzzed around Julia and Simca with the ardor of disciples, all atwitter with talk of how the cookbook was changing their cooking and their lives. "I mean, this book was in *many* people's homes," Judith told me. "There were people who'd been married and never cooked a meal. I had friends like that. And they suddenly started doing a whole French dinner, and spending the whole day doing it. It's as though you suddenly released something that had been suppressed since the Puritan age. It just was like a contagion." It had only been a few weeks, but already *Mastering* was taking on a life of its own. Judith felt buoyed by triumph. She bid her authors farewell; they would all reconvene in New York in December for the party at the Egg Basket. Judith would have liked to stay on the road with Julia and Simca longer, but she had other books on her docket, and they needed her attention, too.

. . . .

Judith hadn't heard from Sylvia Plath since August, when the editor had written that *The Colossus* was ready to go into production. In October, Judith had nudged again. Plath replied quickly, apologizing, "I've been up to my ears in moving our household from London to Devon or I would have answered sooner." She responded concisely to Judith's requests for updates on copyright permissions for her poems, her phrasing cordial but stiff.

Judith didn't know it, but Plath was in distress. Ted Hughes was frequently trotting off to mingle with London's literati, and Plath was left with their child, a household to manage on her own, and precious little time to write. In late 1960, soon after *The Colossus*'s release in the UK, Plath discovered she was pregnant again. But in February 1961, Hughes assaulted her, and two days later, she miscarried. Judith knew none of this, but she perceived the shift in Plath's tone; the warmth and intimacy of the poet's spring letters was gone. Plath seemed, to Judith, distant and out of reach.

In late November 1961, after returning from her *Mastering* trip out West, Judith wrote Plath again. Judith had read the news in the *New York Times* that the poet had been awarded a prestigious Eugene Saxton Fellowship to support a novel she had in the works. Judith wrote, offering her congratulations. "Having seen some short stories of yours, I had hoped you might someday tackle a novel, and this is very good news indeed. I won't ask you how far along you are, but I do want you to know that we shall be looking forward to seeing the manuscript just as soon as you feel it is ready to show."

Plath replied to Judith two weeks before Christmas saying she, too, was delighted about the award. The money couldn't have come at a better time. "It enables me to go on writing to schedule in spite of the obligations of our recently acquired pre-Domesday farmhouse and orchard, and the prospect of a second infant around New Year's. If all goes according to plan, as I think it will, the novel should be finished by early next fall and I imagine Heinemann will send a copy along to you." Judith was heartened to hear the news of Plath's pregnancy and pleased at the writer's lighter tone. And though she tried to ignore it, Judith found herself a bit jealous, too. Plath had a literary marriage, her writing, babies, and a quiet house in the country. It was so much like the life Judith had imagined for herself when she and Dick left for New Hampshire in fall of 1953. From the outside, Plath and Hughes seemed to have it all. Judith didn't know that Plath was suffering and overwhelmed.

In mid-January, Judith wrote Plath that she'd amended *The Colossus*'s biographical note; it now listed Plath as having two children rather than one.

"I suspect that by now that may well be a fact. Do keep me informed," Judith wrote. "I do hope, what with all your activities, you will manage to finish the novel this year, and I shall certainly be looking forward to seeing it."

"Thanks very much for your letter, and for the proofs of *The Colossus* which arrived today," Plath replied in early February. "Our daughter, Frieda, by the way, was joined by our first son, Nicholas, two weeks ago. Now all is peaceful again, I am back at my novel," she wrote.

Judith couldn't see that the chipper report was just a sunny facade. The editor took Plath at her word, and responded in kind. In April, Judith wrote to say that printed copies of *The Colossus* had arrived at Knopf. The book would launch in May. She'd already sent several off to the "opinion makers" in the world of poetry, Judith said. "I feel certain I am going to get some enthusiastic comments. I hope all goes well with you, that son, Nicholas, is settling down and letting you work." Judith had no understanding of the monstrous responsibility of caring for a home, books, and babies all at once. At the time, few mother-artists were speaking openly about their experience of attempting that juggle, and Judith had none of her own from which to draw. But that was about to change.

· · · · · · ·

The hills dipped into one another in every shade of green. It was high summer in the Catskills, 1962. Dick and Judith were quiet as they walked up the lane from the bus stop, a muted tension between them. Just days earlier, Jack Vandercook—ex-husband of Judith's cousin, Jane—had called the Joneses with a startling request: he wanted Dick and Judith to look after his two children, aged thirteen and ten. For good.

Vandercook's third marriage, to a woman named Iris Flynn, had been troubled from the start. By the time the couple wed, Vandercook had been traveling nonstop and living hard for two decades; he was ready to slow down. He moved the family from their East 19th Street apartment to Delhi, a village in the Catskills where he'd grown up, soon after his and Flynn's children, Chris and Audrey, were born. Upstate, the couple fought openly. Flynn, who'd wanted to paint or be an actress, was dissatisfied with life in rural New York. Her complaints irritated Vandercook, stoking his already alcohol-fueled temper.

Unhappy as Vandercook and Flynn's marriage had been, its end was tragic. In early 1961, Vandercook suffered a stroke that forced his retirement, leaving him ornery and in a great deal of pain. In September of that year, Flynn was found dead at the bottom of their home's basement stairs. Chris, the elder of the couple's two children, discovered her there. Publicly, it was recorded as an accident, but privately family members speculated that Flynn had been pushed in the heat of an argument, or may have taken her own life.

After that, Vandercook succumbed to his bed and his malaise. "He just sort of gave up on his career and his life," Chris Vandercook told me. "He never went back on the air." Audrey became her father's caretaker, administering injections of morphine to help manage his pain. Jack Vandercook had sense left enough to realize that something had to give. So he asked Judith, with whom he'd remained friendly despite his cold separation from her cousin, Jane, fifteen years before, if she and Dick would finish raising Chris and Audrey on his behalf.

Judith's yearning for children had never abated, and Vandercook's request touched right into the painful void. The Vandercook children needed a family and a home. It wasn't the sort of parenthood Judith had imagined for herself, but then, nothing in her life had unfolded as planned. Why not accept this unconventional path to motherhood as well? Before she and Dick traveled north from the city to Delhi that summer day, Judith had already made up her mind.

While Dick stayed with Jack Vandercook in his office, discussing particulars— Vandercook would, of course, offer money to help, he'd said when first he called to make his request—Judith went to find Chris. The Vandercook children barely knew the Joneses; they'd only met Dick and Judith a handful of times as their parents' dinner guests. Judith and Chris set out on a walk. Judith outlined what would happen as gently as she could. Chris idly kicked at chunks of gravel, then stopped and looked Judith in the eye. Chris knew he and his sister had heavy baggage to bear. "Judy," Chris later told me he'd said that day, "one of the things you need to know about us is that we are going to ruin your life."

"If I were her," Chris told me, "I would have called a taxi right there." But Judith stood firm. She wasn't so easily put off. Judith didn't know what their family would look like or exactly how it would take shape or function in the day-to-day. But she trusted that together she and Dick would find their way.

CHAPTER 9

The kitchen was bursting with industry and fragrant smells. Music from the record player mingled with the dull thwack of a knife against a cutting board and the clatter of a pan settling onto a burner on the stove. Dick and Judith were in the kitchen. One seared pieces of chicken in a pan of foaming butter. The other sliced onions, minced garlic, and measured out tinned tomatoes and paprika; they'd get added once the meat was browned. It was a work night, a school night, smack in the middle of the week, and it was nearly seven o'clock. But dinner preparations had only just begun.

As a twosome, Judith and Dick had long since developed an easy rhythm that suited their needs: They spent the workdays apart, Judith at Knopf, Dick off reporting sometimes or in his office at home. They spent their evenings and weekends together, cooking, often hosting and spending time with family and friends. When Chris and Audrey first came to live with Dick and Judith, the foursome acclimated to life together in the Vandercooks' apartment on East 19th Street, just south of Gramercy Park. It was a place familiar to the children, and there was no space to spare in Dick and Judith's little penthouse flat. By the start of the new school year in the fall of 1962, the Joneses and their new charges had moved into an apartment on East 86th Street between Lexington and Park, a mile north of Judith's childhood home.

There, the couple continued in their routines as best they could, assuming the children would fold right into the mix. Every morning, Judith walked to work on 52nd and Madison while the children went off to school. Dick settled in at his office on the first floor of their apartment building to write. In the afternoons, Chris and Audrey let themselves back into the apartment. It was quiet when they arrived; Dick stayed in his office downstairs. The kids watched *Rocky and Bullwinkle*; by then, the Joneses had bought a TV. Dick had a drink or two toward day's end, then came up around five. For the most part, he kept to himself, letting the kids carry on as they were.

At a few minutes to six, the phone would ring. It was Judith, calling from the office. She and Dick would start discussing what they'd have for dinner that night. "Judith didn't take part in the literary social rules," Chris told me. "She didn't go to industry parties or meet colleagues for drinks. She came home from work and that was it." After they'd hung up the phone, Judith would leave the office and Dick would leash up the dog to meet her halfway. Together, they shopped for ingredients for the evening's meal. When Chris and Audrey heard the keys jangling at the door, they'd run off to their bedrooms, as though they'd been doing homework the whole time. "It was like a folie à deux," Audrey's stepdaughter, Alexis Bierman, told me. "Dick pretending he didn't know they were watching TV. And the kids pretending they didn't know he'd been drinking."

Back home at the apartment, Judith would tie an apron over her work clothes, and she and Dick would begin to cook. It was how the couple reconnected at the end of each day, and a part of their new family life in which they easily shared responsibility. "We very definitely divided things like that," Judith told me. "Dick did at least half the work." In fact, after Chris and Audrey moved in, it was Dick, who worked primarily from home and had a flexible schedule, who took on more of the day-to-day. It was he who brought the children to school or picked them up when necessary and kept the laundry going, he who started cooking during the day if he and Judith were preparing a meal that required more time than the evening hours allowed. Some may have seen jumping into the kitchen after a long day at work as a chore, but not Judith. "By then," she told me, "I found cooking relaxing." It went like this every day, Chris told me, and dinner was served late, 7:30 or 8.

Dick and Judith cooked lavishly and to their own tastes, not catering to the preferences of the kids. When Chris and Audrey first moved in, the Joneses tried to make their views clear. "We told the children, 'We're a little crazy. We love food.

We love to experiment and try new things,'" Judith told me. She and Dick, Judith said, told the kids, "All of a sudden, we're a family. We have to get to know each other. So, you're going have dinner with us every night, and we'll try to be at home as much as we can. Just one thing: I don't want you criticizing the food! If you don't like it, put it aside. But don't say anything."

The children did their best to comply. Chris hated onions; in the Vandercook home, they'd never been used. For the first several months, he discreetly pushed them off to the side of his plate from every dish Judith and Dick served. For the children, who'd been fed on bland nursery food and eaten early with their nannies all their lives, mealtime with the Joneses was strange and new. "The children took it in stride," Judith told me, "well, until I fed them tripe. That was mean of me."

There may not have been room at the table for dissent over the food. But in conversation, Chris and Audrey were encouraged to formulate and express ideas of their own. "Dinner every night was a discussion in which we, as kids, were expected to participate," Chris told me. "We would go smoothly from current events to literature to poetry to how you liked the food." For Judith, it was a retort to the restraint she'd felt at her parents' dinner table as a girl. Chris found it exciting, the richness of the Joneses' life together, and their welcoming of the children into their sophisticated world. They often had guests for dinner. Among the regulars was their dear friend, the film and theater critic Stanley Kauffmann. When he came, Dick and Judith always made cassoulet. "Sometimes, they had a couple glasses of wine and they would read poetry to each other and dance in the living room," Chris recalled. "They had the whole romance of having gone through the war, that background of pain and yet of deep love." Chris, who was sharp-witted, sociable, and a born performer, bloomed in the Joneses' care. But Audrey struggled. "Sometimes, I'd try to get her to help me in the kitchen," Judith told me, "but she said I scared her."

Motherhood wasn't coming as easily to Judith as she'd hoped and imagined it would. "It was a transition," she told me. Judith wasn't sure how to *be* with the children, or how to meet their adolescent needs. "They could *do* everything. But it's hard to make that breakthrough and get really, really close," she said. "I think Audrey was the one that got the worst of it. Because she needed so much. I worried about that, I thought I should be giving them more time."

Judith was spread thin. The children needed her attention. Dick wanted it, too. And then there was her Knopf work, unrelenting, where Judith was still trying to prove her worth.

. . . .

Knopf published Sylvia Plath's *The Colossus* late in the spring of 1962. The poet had been out of touch in the months leading up to the launch. But in the first week of May, she surfaced. She had, Plath wrote Judith, been "almost flattened," by the babies, her writing, and the planting of a large garden intended to supply the family with vegetables for the rest of the year. She wrote that she was "perfectly delighted" with Knopf's production of *The Colossus*. "I am so happy with what you have done with it," the poet said. She asked Judith to send along any reviews that might come in. "I thrive on criticism of all sorts," Plath said, "especially the adverse sort."

Coverage of *The Colossus* was meager and lukewarm. It was Judith's first lesson in the challenges of publishing poetry successfully. Spring turned to summer, and still the editor had sent Plath no news of the book's reception at all. But by the end of August, Judith felt she could hold her silence no more. On August 30, two days before the Labor Day holiday weekend began, Judith finally wrote. "I'm sure you must be feeling terribly neglected, but the truth is I have been waiting to write you until I had a substantial collection of reviews on *The Colossus* to send along to you," Judith began. "I have come to accept the fact that papers and magazines are dreadfully slow about reviewing a poet. But I had hoped a few months after publication that notices would begin to appear in some of the 'little magazines.'" (For the "more important ones," Judith said, "we will just have to keep waiting.") Judith said she regretted that she didn't have better news to share. "I must confess that I feel discouraged not just by the review situation but by the fact that fellow poets seem so self-involved and, I might add, ungrateful that they can't even respond to a complimentary pre-publication copy of a first collection as good as yours." Judith had sent copies of *The Colossus* to the who's who of American poetry, each with a personalized note. But of all the collection's recipients, only Marianne Moore had been "gracious enough to answer."

Moore's words, though, hadn't been kind. She criticized what she saw as Plath's fixation on emotional pain. It was a shame, Moore wrote Judith, that *The Colossus* wasn't a more pleasurable read, given Plath's undeniable talent. Judith had received Moore's note back in April, before the book launched, but she hadn't forwarded the critique to Plath, as she'd "hoped I would have more letters that were a little more enthusiastic." Judith knew, though, that it was time. She enclosed a copy of Moore's letter with her own. To Plath, Judith wrote, "There's nothing here I want to withhold from you." Then the editor turned her attention to the future. "I'm very anxious to hear about how you're coming along with your novel. Wasn't September supposed to be your target date?"

Plath responded quickly, thanking Judith for her transparency. "I am sorry Miss Moore eschews the dark side of life to the extent that she feels neither good nor enjoyable poetry can be made out of it." Still, "I do like to see everything,"

Plath said before pivoting to news of her fiction. "The novel," she wrote, "is as good as done. Heinemann will be publishing it over here. I'll get on to them to send you a copy in a few weeks when it's ready. I hope a few things in it make you laugh."

Plath's novel was personal, and she worried it would cause upset and scandal if she published it under her own name. She wanted to remain anonymous as the book's author, and chose Victoria Lucas as her nom de plume. In her communications with Judith, she failed to mention this important fact. "Thanks very much for your kind concern," Plath wrote. Her words were measured. Terseness rippled from the page.

Earlier that summer, as Plath was nearing the end of work on her book, she'd discovered Hughes was having an affair with Assia Wevill. Wevill, too, was married; her husband, David Wevill, was a poet. The two couples had met when the Wevills applied to sublet Hughes and Plath's London flat. Hughes visited his lover often, coming and going from his and Plath's family home throughout the summer of 1962. The couple briefly tried to reconcile that September, traveling together to Ireland to visit their friend, the poet Richard Murphy. But after Hughes left abruptly one morning, telling Plath he was going to visit a painter friend but instead, she soon learned, running off to Spain with Wevill, Plath knew their marriage was over for good. Back at home in England, Plath worked through the fall in a prolonged manic sprint, rising daily at 4 a.m. to write before her children woke at 8. "I have managed a poem a day before breakfast. All book poems. Terrific Stuff, as if domesticity had choked me," Plath wrote in her journal. On October 27, she turned thirty years old.

In early December, Plath took Nicholas and Frieda and returned to London, moving into a flat where Yeats had once lived. She had two babies, her debut poetry collection out in the world, a fast-growing body of new work, and a novel she was determined to complete. And she was on her own.

In November 1962, Heinemann's sent a copy of *The Bell Jar* to Knopf. They wrote of the author's true identity in a note they posted separate from the book. *The Bell Jar* arrived in New York first. It was addressed to Bill Koshland, not Judith Jones. Koshland gave the novel a quick read, and decided to pass. He was unsure how, or why, the novel had been sent to him; he'd never heard of a writer named Victoria Lucas before. When, several days later, Heinemann's letter explaining that *The Bell Jar* was, in fact, the long-awaited novel by Sylvia Plath, Koshland was "knocked galley west." He handed the book to Judith and asked her to weigh in. After reading *The Bell Jar*, Judith, disappointed, agreed that Knopf should pass. "Re-reading the book in the light of this knowledge does make a difference," Koshland wrote to Heinemann when the author's identity had been made clear. "But we still cannot warm up to this as a novel. It seems to us as though this is a book that she had to get out of her system before coming to grips with a novel that

she can treat, as it were, in a novelistic way. This reads as if it were autobiographical, almost flagrantly so." Koshland's letter was a nearly verbatim lift of Judith's
damning reader's report on the book.

It was a resounding rejection. But still, Koshland went on. Knopf would pre-
fer, he wrote, if Heinemann withheld *The Bell Jar* from the American market entirely and didn't try to sell it to another publisher in the States. Though he knew
full well that Plath would have the final word, he wanted to make Knopf's wishes
clear. He took care to remind Heinemann's that if *The Bell Jar* remained unpublished in the United States, "obviously" Knopf would remain "entitled to a first
look at her next work."

Heinemann responded quickly and curtly. Plath did, indeed, they said, want to
explore other publishing options for *The Bell Jar* in the States. Judith had kept quiet,
allowing Koshland to communicate with Plath's British publisher on her behalf.
Judith had no weight to throw around in business negotiations; to Heinemann, she
was a nobody. But Judith knew she couldn't leave Plath hanging, not after the relationship they'd formed. During the Christmas holiday week, Judith wrote Plath
to offer an explanation of her own. Judith's letter, dated December 28, 1962, read:

> Dear Sylvia Plath:
> I know that you have heard now from Heinemann that we decided we
> would have to let your novel go. I'm sorry about it because, having re-
> spected so much your lovely use of language and your sharp eye for un-
> usual and vivid detail, I had looked forward greatly to seeing your talents
> put to use in a novel, if only because it is such a special group that reads
> poetry and I wanted you to be more accessible to more readers. But al-
> though these qualities were indeed apparent in *The Bell Jar*, to be quite
> honest with you we didn't feel that you had managed to use your mate-
> rials successfully in a novelistic way. I particularly felt that though the
> separate happenings made in themselves good stories, you as the author
> had not succeeded in establishing a viewpoint. Up to the point of her
> breakdown the attitude of your young girl had seemed a perfectly normal
> combination of brashness and disgust with the world, but I was not at
> all prepared as a reader to accept the extent of her illness and the suicide
> attempt. I had the feeling that you were not letting us in close enough so
> that we could share in and thereby understand the whole complex of this
> girl's feelings and attitudes and as a result the novel never really took hold
> for me. As you well know, it becomes increasingly hard to put a first novel
> across over here, particularly your kind of novel. Had we thought it really
> successful in its own terms, nothing else would have mattered and we

would have given it all the backing we are capable of. But I am afraid that with the reservations we feel, we could not have given it a fair shake. Perhaps another publisher will feel quite differently. But if not, I hope you will continue to consider us your publishers here, as we have a great deal of faith in your future. I enclose a couple reviews of *The Colossus* which I don't believe you have seen yet. All good wishes to you and your family.

Sincerely, Judith B. Jones

Heinemann published *The Bell Jar* on January 14, 1963. On February 11, just weeks after the book's launch and shortly after Judith's letter had arrived, Plath carefully sealed up her kitchen windows with towels while her children slept in their room. She put out bread and milk for when they awoke. Then she closed the kitchen door, stuffed cloth around its edges, and turned up the gas on the stove.

Within days of Plath's suicide, her lionization began. In his eulogy in the *Observer*, British critic Al Alvarez, wrote, "it was only recently that the peculiar intensity of her genius found its perfect expression." His words ran alongside four of Plath's previously unpublished poems, among them "Edge." Its lines were chillingly apropos: *The woman is perfected. / Her dead / Body wears the smile of accomplishment.* Alvarez called Plath's most recent work "a totally new breakthrough in modern verse" that established her "as the most gifted woman poet of our time."

With the news of Plath's death, Judith recognized the magnitude of her error on *The Bell Jar*. Every word of the novel, she understood, had been vitally and urgently true. But if there was any backpedaling or repairing to be done in regard to Plath's work, Judith knew her Knopf superiors would have to do it on her behalf. It was Blanche Knopf who circled back, asking Heinemann for another chance if *The Bell Jar* hadn't already otherwise sold. The British publisher agreed. The Knopf editors read Plath's novel again. Again, they turned it down. "It is a tragedy that Sylvia Plath died because she did have a talent and might have continued writing and doing very fine work," Mrs. Knopf wrote Heinemann coolly in April 1963. "But again I am afraid the answer is the same, that we cannot undertake it and would not have a chance in the world of finding a market for it." It was the last in a string of cold condemnations of Plath's book. The senior-most editors at Knopf had made their final call. Judith had no choice but to drop the cause.

· · · · · · ·

Privately, the loss of *The Bell Jar* gutted Judith, but she couldn't let the miss impede her professional momentum or bleed into her other work. So she masked her disappointment, switched gears, and moved on. *Mastering* was continuing to steadily gain prominence, as was Julia Child, herself. On February 20, 1962, Child appeared as a guest on *I've Been Reading*, a program on WGBH, Boston's nascent public television channel; she brought a copy of *Mastering* and her hot plate, as well as a few eggs, butter, and a small copper pan. On screen, she repeated the omelet performance she'd done on the *Today Show* the previous fall, albeit solo this time. "Have no idea how much it pulled, and know only 4 friends, plus Avis and our butcher who saw the program!" Julia wrote Judith after the fact. As it turned out, more viewers than Child imagined had tuned in. WGBH received twenty-seven letters about Julia's spot. "Get that tall, loud woman back on television. We want to see more cooking!" the fans said.

WGBH realized they'd hit on something, and approached Child to gauge her interest in making a series of cooking programs for them. Child would have to come up with the show's concept, WGBH's producers said, and foot the bill for all the ingredients to cook on set. The budget for the station was already strained. "They have no mazuma," Julia wrote Judith, "so have to find a sponsor like the Gas or Electric supermarket people." Still, Julia said, she'd "gladly appear" as long as the station would "loudly display the book." It was a boost to Julia's spirits, and came at just the right time.

In January 1962, Child had been featured on the cover of *Vogue*. It served as a stylish cap to *Mastering*'s busy autumn launch. But as the book continued to generate buzz publicly, its author was, privately, recovering at home from a hysterectomy. Like Judith, Julia had wanted children badly. In Paris, she and Paul had tried hard to conceive. When it began to seem that motherhood wasn't in the cards, Julia made food, which had been her hobby while she tried to get pregnant, her full-time pursuit. (Later, Julia admitted she couldn't have imagined having both children and a career at once; "I would have been the complete mother," she said.)

When the Childs returned to the States, a Boston doctor recommended a radical hysterectomy—a surgery that induces menopause—for Julia. She scheduled the procedure for early January 1962.

In the American mid-century, "the change" had earned a bad rap. "The unpalatable truth must be faced that all postmenopausal women are castrates," wrote Dr. Robert Wilson and his wife, Thelma, a nurse. To stave off menopause, the Wilsons publicly endorsed the use of hormone replacement therapy (HRT) that substituted synthetic hormones for decreasing natural estrogens. Hormone replacement therapy was a means, the Wilsons wrote, by which to keep women "fully-sexed," to save them from "nature's defeminization," and the "supreme tragedy" of their hormonal lives. In the wake of her surgery, Julia was prescribed, and began, HRT. She was determined to let neither childlessness nor middle age define her identity or fate. As soon as she was pain free and moving about, Julia turned all her attention right back to work.

In April 1962, Child sent WGBH her pitch: "An interesting, adult series of half-hour TV programs on French cooking addressed to an intelligent, reasonably sophisticated audience which likes good food and cooking," she wrote. In late May, the station gave the program the green light. Child would tape four half-hour shows beginning in July 1962. They'd air that summer as a trial run. If the program drew an audience, they'd tape more episodes in the fall. There was even a possibility, WGBH said, that the show might be syndicated; New York's channel 13 had shown interest in picking it up.

In August, Julia wrote Bill Koshland at Knopf, giving him the play-by-play. So far, in taping the pilot episodes, she'd made an omelet, coq au vin, and a soufflé on screen. "TV is certainly a much more difficult medium than I had supposed," Julia reported. "What with looking into one camera, showing into another, keeping all the pots and pans either hot or cold, and having to talk besides." All the while, *Mastering* continued to pick up speed. "The sales may not be spectacular," Koshland had written Julia earlier that summer, "but I have complete confidence that word of mouth will keep this going forever." In August, *Mastering* received another terrific boost: The Book-of-the-Month Club named it as a selection.

The club, founded in 1926, had helped launch the careers of writers like Margaret Mitchell, Ernest Hemingway, and J. D. Salinger. It relied on subscribers to purchase a minimum of four of their curated selection of books per year. Its reach was huge: By the mid-fifties, the club was selling close to five million books a year. Book-of-the-Month promptly distributed twelve thousand copies of *Mastering* and put publicity materials advertising it in the mailboxes of hundreds of thousands more. *Mastering* was the first cookbook Book-of-the-Month had ever selected as one of their picks.

In October, James Beard asked Child to come teach at his cooking school, which led to her meeting Craig Claiborne at last. At the holidays, Claiborne doubled down on his previous year's praise, calling *Mastering* the "most lucid volume on French cuisine since Gutenberg invented movable type" in the *Saturday Evening Post*. "Don't look now," Koshland wrote Child in January, "but the phone rang today and my friend Allan Ullman at the Book-of-the-Month Club called to say (are you sitting down?) that the total orders received thus far from the mail order campaign are somewhat in excess of 35,000 copies. I haven't recovered yet! At the moment they are some 18,000 behind in unfilled orders and the end is not yet in sight."

The months of promotional efforts were paying off; *Mastering*'s publicity had developed a momentum of its own. Just before the New Year, Julia wrote Judith with the news that WGBH wanted to go forward with her show. "26 programs in all, each of a half hour, doing 2 to 4 a week. (Busy!)," she said. It would be called *The French Chef.* On February 2, 1963, WGBH aired the first episode of the show, in which Child prepared her boeuf bourguignon. Within weeks, Julia Child was drawing a viewership unprecedented for WGBH, and drove *Mastering*'s sales through the roof. Julia was elated. Judith was, too. "I am flabbergasted at the way you seem to have catapulted into fame overnight as the cooking star of Boston," Judith wrote Julia in early May. "I wish to heaven that I could watch you perform." At fifty years old, Julia Child's career in food was taking off, and she was becoming a star. But not everyone was so keen to hop aboard her cooking train.

Just as Julia Child was inviting American women into the kitchen, a writer named Betty Friedan began publicly arguing that they should leave it behind. In her book *The Feminine Mystique*, which came out in February 1963, Friedan framed the domestic realm as a site of women's oppression, and their relegation to it as the foremost source of their discontent. Friedan—once a boots-on-the-ground reporter turned married suburban mother of three—dubbed the ambient malaise of mid-century American womanhood "the problem that has no name." Friedan's book gave voice to many women's secret longings for more than their husbands, children, and homes. And for the "mistaken ideas . . . incomplete truths and false choices" presented to them, Friedan laid blame at the feet of "the system," calling out the media and dominant culture at large. (Friedan paid little attention to the circumstances of poor, nonwhite, queer, and disabled women whose "discontent" was compounded by multiple levels of systemic inequality and prejudice, a narrowness of frame for which many BIPOC and lesbian activists criticized *The Feminine Mystique* and Friedan's message at large.) *The Feminine Mystique* touched a nerve, selling more than three million copies in its first three years in print. For the first time since the suffragettes' fight for the vote in the nineteen teens, white, middle-class American women galvanized behind a feminist cause.

The French Chef, in Friedan's view, only exacerbated the problem at hand. A female TV star smiling as she peeled, simmered, and chopped, Friedan thought, suggested not only that women should be happy with their role at home but that the work of feeding others was their burden to bear. Looking back on the moment, Betty Fussell, a food writer who in the 1960s was one of the many affluent, well-educated women who fell under Julia Child's spell, wrote, "It was work in the guise of leisure. The solution to the drudge problem was to make cooking an art, or at the very least a craft. A lady could become extremely accomplished, as long as no one took her work seriously or paid money for it, which was pretty much the same thing." Judith told me, "Some people resisted it because it was too demanding." Fussell's critique, though, was about more than the hard work required to prepare *Mastering*'s intricate dishes; Fussell began to see the Child-inspired cooking craze as a kind of widespread duping, a powerful isolation and diversion of women's resources and time away from the public realm. Adopting serious cooking as a lifestyle served to further sequester women in their homes, relegating the reach of their aspirations and skills to the household. Those who followed Julia Child's siren song to the stove were complicit, Friedan and her ilk believed, in undermining their own ambitions while further upholding those of men. They saw it as proof of women's internalization of patriarchy and the system's pervasive hold.

Despite the cultural tension shadowing Julia Child's rise, *The French Chef* was a hit, and other public TV stations wanted in. Within months, Americans were watching Child in their homes in San Francisco, Pittsburgh, upstate New York, Philadelphia, south Florida, and Maine, and it only grew from there. No one, not even Judith, had imagined the phenomenal successes that, by spring 1963, both *Mastering* and Julia Child were proving to be. Even decades later, Judith was still somewhat surprised. "Who would have thought?" she said to me.

Judith's colleagues at Knopf took note. The French cookbook they'd been skeptical of, the one in which they'd put so little stock, had become one of the house's best-selling books. Judith's take on *Mastering*'s potential had proved discerning and spot-on. She'd anticipated a stirring in the culture at large, filling a gap in the book market that others in publishing hadn't even noticed was there. Most of the team at Knopf didn't care a whit about food, nor did they understand what cookbooks needed to be in order to succeed. But clearly, Judith did. Others at Knopf began to see Judith as a true editor in her own right, one far savvier and more resourceful than at first they'd believed her to be. But Judith still wasn't considered an equal among the editorial staff.

When Knopf moved their offices to a new floor, the higher-ups announced that everyone's office had a window except Judith's. And when Judith wrote the Knopfs a formal letter saying she "didn't think she was getting quite enough money," she told me, Alfred Knopf himself could not be bothered to reply. Instead, he had his assistant answer her note. "He said that they had talked and, yes, they would give me—they didn't *say* a small raise—but it was," Judith recalled. They added, "We wish that you would try to have more little dinner parties and entertain more of your authors." It was a condescending, sexist dig. "That was very strange to me. And I really resented it because it was like being treated as the cook," Judith said. Though she was overworked and underpaid, Judith saw that she was gaining ground at Knopf. It gave her the confidence she needed to step farther out on her own.

· · · · · · ·

Judith had a hit cookbook on her hands but harbored "a little fear of getting too categorized," she told me. She hoped her next acquisition would help put "a little distance" between her and food. For years, she'd been waiting for the right novel to cross her path; fiction, she knew, was the form publishing held in highest regard. Judith had hoped such a book would come from Sylvia Plath, but *The Bell Jar* had been a miss and Plath was gone. So Judith kept her eyes open for a writer with potential but who was as yet unknown, someone with whom she could get in on the ground floor.

Early in the summer of 1963, Judith received a manuscript from heavy-hitting literary agent Diarmuid Russell. He represented writers including Eudora Welty and P. L. Travers; Nadine Gordimer; May Sarton; and George Plimpton, founding editor of the *Paris Review*. It was a debut novel, Russell told Judith, by a young writer named Anne Tyler. Judith was the first editor to whom he was showing the book. Judith took Anne's *If Morning Ever Comes* home with her, and read it in one gulp. The story was of a man's search for love and belonging, and explored themes of aging, family, and loss rendered in prose singular in voice and style. Judith knew immediately that she'd struck gold.

Later that summer, after the contracts for *If Morning Ever Comes* had been signed and publication slated for fall 1964, Judith and Anne Tyler met for the first time. While on their annual summer vacation in Greensboro, Vermont, Dick and Judith drove a couple hours northwest to visit the writer in Montreal; Tyler's husband, Taghi Modarressi, was completing his training in psychiatry there. "I was immediately impressed by her," Judith later said. "There was an interior sureness combined with a lovely modesty." Tyler was exceptionally talented, of that there was no doubt. She was also, Judith learned, something of a prodigy.

Tyler had gone to Duke on a full scholarship, enrolling at only sixteen years old. There she studied under the esteemed writer Reynolds Price, who Tyler later said "turned out to be the only person I ever knew who could actually teach writing." Price recognized Anne Tyler's talent at once. He said she was "wide-eyed," "an outsider," and "frighteningly mature." He showed Tyler's stories to his agent, Diarmuid Russell, in hopes that Russell could help sell her work. Before long, Tyler's stories were appearing in *Harper's*, the *New Yorker*, and the *Saturday Evening Post*. When Judith acquired Tyler's first novel, the writer was only twenty-one years old.

Judith surmised that Tyler was just getting started with *If Morning Ever Comes*. She could feel in her gut that the writer had a long and promising career ahead. "Somehow," Judith later said, "one knew immediately that she was a writer who loved writing above all and would continue to write no matter what." As she landed Anne Tyler, Judith felt that, after six years at Knopf, she was finally finding her feet.

CHAPTER 10

Judith lay on the couch, willing herself not to nod off. It was a Saturday night. She looked at the stack of manuscripts on the coffee table, then checked her watch; it was after midnight, later than she'd hoped. But she was nowhere near done. She'd promised to go over Chris's history paper for school and, Judith realized with a jolt, she'd forgotten to call Audrey's teacher before the school week's end. She had authors to get back to by Monday and memos to write for Blanche. She took a long breath, then turned back to her work; she wouldn't get much sleep. And it had already been a trying night.

Audrey had gone off to bed soon after dinner and Chris, who was in high school by then, had gone out to the movies with friends. Dick and Judith had settled on the couch to go over some pages of Dick's. Dick often asked Judith to read his work, but the conversations that followed were tough on both of them. When Chris arrived home around ten that night, he saw that the two were working and that Dick's face was strained. So Chris had said a quick good night and headed to his room. Once Judith and Dick heard the click of Chris's door, they resumed their work.

It was a familiar pattern: When Judith pointed out what she saw as the weaker points in her husband's writing, Dick rose up in defense, his voice growing loud. He was prone to dark moods and anger. His drinking only made it worse. Judith turned deferential, trying to calm Dick down. Chris heard it all through the wall. "Dick didn't take criticism well," Judith told me. "And I thought it awkward to play the two roles," editor and wife at once, "so I just shut up. I would have liked more back and forth, but people have their hang-ups." Eventually, Dick grew frustrated and called it a night. Since the children had come to live with them, the Joneses rarely went to bed at the same time anymore. Their marriage was showing the strain.

Judith had been caught off guard by how overwhelmed she'd become by family life, and the perpetual juggle of working motherhood. Keeping up with the demands of her career while remaining attentive and available to Dick and the children, Judith found, was an almost impossible balancing act, with "so much," she remarked, "dumped on the woman." With no models to look to, Judith was flying blind. "I hadn't really thought about it," she told me. "It just seemed natural. I knew you had to work hard if you had a good job. On the other hand, I thought, 'This is life. I wanted to do this.'" But Dick, who'd been less enthused about bringing two adolescents into the fold, resented the disruption to his and Judith's life as a couple. "I think he felt sort of deserted, that I didn't have enough time for him," Judith told me. "They weren't easy years."

Work became Judith's refuge: "It was my little cocoon, my escape hatch. My world, where life goes on," she told me. She was determined to keep up the momentum she'd finally started to build at Knopf. She was equally determined to do the best she could by Chris and Audrey, and to keep her marriage intact. Doing it all demanded sacrifice. So Judith stayed up late almost every night, snatching time to work while her family slept.

· · · · · · ·

In the years immediately following Sylvia Plath's death, her literary legacy ballooned. Going through his estranged wife's things, Ted Hughes had discovered the cache of poems Plath had written after their separation. He recognized right away that they were remarkable. And he took the liberty of editing them and getting them published. Within months of her death, Plath's previously unseen poems began running in prominent literary magazines in the UK and abroad. Stateside, the *New Yorker* and the *Atlantic* published her work, as did the *New York Review of Books*, which launched on February 1, 1963, less than two weeks before Plath's death.

The *New York Review of Books* was cofounded by a team of four: *Harper's* associate editor Robert Silvers; the writer Elizabeth Hardwick; A. Whitney Ellsworth;

and Barbara Epstein, formerly Zimmerman, who had edited *Anne Frank*. (Zimmerman was by that time married to Jason Epstein of Random House; the couple had met at Doubleday and wed in 1953, the year Epstein founded Anchor Books. Jason Epstein helped hatch the idea for the *NYRB* alongside his wife and Elizabeth Hardwick and her husband, the poet Robert Lowell.) The *NYRB* was intended to be a one-off, but its first run of one hundred thousand copies quickly sold out. The *Review* instantly became a must-read for the literati, and they wanted more. It lined up well for Ted Hughes. He was eager to capitalize on Plath's work, and the *Review* needed "literary-intellectual" material to fill its pages.

Judith read Plath's new poems hungrily and with a sharp pang of regret; she was deeply moved by their power and style. In March 1964, she wrote directly to Ted Hughes. "As you probably know, I was your wife's editor here at Knopf and have been enthusiastic about her work for a long time." Judith addressed Hughes as Plath's widower, as the fate of their marriage was not yet widely known. "I have been particularly struck by the poems I have seen which she wrote after the publication of *The Colossus*. I was very pleased to hear from Heinemann that you were getting together a posthumous collection of her poetry. I want to write you directly as well to tell you how strongly I feel that you should do the book and how grateful I would be to see it." It was a careful, strategic spin, one Judith hoped would help her land Plath's final crop of poems for Knopf.

Hughes didn't respond to Judith's letter, but she was not easily deterred. In August, she followed up. "We understand from Faber and Faber that they now have a manuscript from you of your wife Sylvia Plath's poems and that they have already got the book in the works. Would it be possible for you to air mail the copy of the manuscript to us right away?" Again, Judith was met with silence. So she found a workaround, writing to Faber directly requesting a copy of Plath's forthcoming collection, titled *Ariel*. They promptly sent one along.

Ariel laid bare Plath's thoughts of death, vengeance, rage, and her persistent belief in her own creative power as well. *Out of the ash / I rise with my red hair / And I eat men like air*, Plath wrote in "Lady Lazarus"; it would become her best-known poem. Whereas *The Colossus* showcased Plath's command over structure and poetic tradition, in *Ariel*, she broke the rules. In content and form, the collection highlighted the tension between expectations of women and their true ambitions and wants. Plath's verse resonated deeply with Judith, each poem landing like a punch to the gut. After reading through *Ariel*, Judith reached out to Hughes once more. "Dear Mr. Hughes, I was reasonably certain that we would want the book of your wife's poems," she wrote, "but I was not really prepared for the impact of that book. It is really an extraordinary collection, and, needless to say, we are very anxious to publish it." Though Judith hadn't yet heard a single word back from Hughes, she offered on *Ariel*.

That got Hughes's attention. He replied to Judith within days, listing the demands Knopf would have to meet if they wanted to publish *Ariel*. Hughes wanted a larger advance than the $200 Judith had offered and for Knopf to match Faber's 15 percent royalty rate as well. Though, after Plath's funeral, Ted Hughes had publicly declared that "everybody hated" Plath, to Judith, he laid claim to her "extraordinary talent" and reminded the editor grimly that the book was to be his late wife's "last and major work." Knopf had assumed they'd get the collection "without a hitch," but Hughes wasn't going to give it without a fight.

Judith and Hughes went back and forth all winter and into the spring of 1965. The British edition of *Ariel* was published in March, and Judith waited eagerly to see how it would be received. While both *The Colossus* and *The Bell Jar* had been met with middling reviews, *Ariel* took critics by storm. "Something amazing has happened," Robert Lowell declared. The collection sold fifteen thousand copies in ten months, an unprecedented success for a book of poems. *Ariel* was more than a book; it was a cultural event.

The hubbub overseas only made Judith want *Ariel* more. But those who held Knopf's purse strings weren't willing to markedly increase their offer. Judith had only so much leeway with which to work. She was granted permission to raise the book's advance by $300 and to offer slightly higher royalty rates. But Hughes refused to meet her halfway, and in mid-March 1965, he stopped responding to Judith altogether.

Judith, who'd hopefully held a spot for *Ariel* on Knopf's 1965 fall list, grew agitated and began to despair. Finally, in October, Hughes wrote: Harper's had made a stronger offer, and if Knopf couldn't match their terms, he'd go with the other house. Deflated, Judith replied the same day she received Hughes's note. She couldn't meet Harper's royalty rate; it was, she insisted, much too high. "The publishing of poetry would become prohibitive if we did so. So I guess that is that. I am sorry. Sincerely, (Mrs.) Judith B. Jones." No sooner had Judith begun to build up her sense of self and autonomy at work than she'd run aground yet again. Her inability to make a major move on a book she so believed in left her grappling with feelings of powerlessness and defeat. Her leash at Knopf was beginning to feel stultifyingly short.

· · · · · · ·

Just a week after Judith received the final blow on *Ariel*, Knopf published Anne Tyler's debut. Orville Prescott, then chief book critic for the *New York Times*, called *If Morning Ever Comes* "a brilliant first novel," and Tyler a "rarely talented" novelist who seemed to have been "born knowing how" to write. "Her touch is deft, her perceptions are keen, her ear of the rhythms and wild irrelevancies of colloquial speech is phenomenal. Her people are triumphantly alive." The novel was "so mature, so gently wise and so brightly amusing" that the critic said he'd been stunned to learn its author was only twenty-two years old. Prescott's review "gave [Anne's] book the send-off," Judith later said. "His reviews had a lot of influence, and it was clear that he recognized in Anne Tyler a genuine new voice. It was easier, then, for a quiet novel to make a small ripple," Judith said. She was over the moon.

Tyler wrote with dizzying speed. Before *If Morning Ever Comes* hit the shelves, Judith had another complete manuscript from the writer in her hands. Judith "made suggestions here and there," but she quickly learned to use a light touch with Tyler and to mostly leave her alone while she worked. "I feel that she becomes so totally immersed in the world of the fiction she is creating," Judith told me, "that once she's finished and walked out of the room—left it behind—it is hard for her to get back into it." When Judith did make suggestions, "although [Anne] might give it a try," Judith told me, "chances are she wouldn't succeed in making someone else's idea work." When, at one point, Judith suggested Tyler might want to consider cutting the final chapter of a novel she'd just sent in, Tyler became so distraught that she took up smoking again. "Dear Anne, I am terribly sorry that my suggestion . . . threw you into such a state," Judith responded, trying to quell Tyler's anxiety. Judith backed off, and reiterated her ultimate stance: "I've always felt that you and only you could be the final judge of what would work," Judith wrote. In the end, Tyler decided to keep that chapter in the book.

Tyler's manuscripts didn't require major editorial interventions—"She edited herself critically as she wrote," Judith told me. Rather, what the writer needed from her editor was faith and understanding; a quieter, though no less vital, sort of support. Judith learned this by trial and error, and by paying close attention to Tyler's disposition and tendencies. "The most important quality for an editor, a *sensitive* editor," Judith told me, "is diplomacy. Adapting your style to each situation. I think women have a talent for this." She continued: "I think women bring qualities that are feminine, which are—or can be—being persuasive, and winning through wiles sometimes." To one of her male superiors at Knopf: "I once said I think women make good editors because we're more nurturing," Judith told me. "I really hit a nerve!" She continued: "I realized—this came upon me gradually—that we had something. There were certain women that I didn't like in the business that just, you know, had to be aggressive and rude and slangy, and 'Oh, fuck this,'" she explained. "And I don't think that's the way, for publishing anyway. What we need is that feminine instinct." Judith was well aware that her stance was a provocative one. "I know that's not very popular today," she told me.

Still, Judith would do whatever it took to nurture Anne Tyler's writing life, and felt that her self-described feminine proclivities worked in service of understanding what, exactly, that was. Judith's attentive, individualized approach worked. From early on, she felt she and Tyler were in the process of building an exceptionally "good writer-editor relationship," one "based on trust and respect and knowing one another instinctively," Judith said. And though they'd only been working together for a couple of years, Tyler was already fully committed to Judith as her editor and to Knopf as her publishing house.

Tyler's second novel, *The Tin Can Tree*, came out only a year after her first. "Writers are rare who can swiftly generate a story with instantly distinguishable characters and the prospect of development. Rarer still is the fiction artist who controls his material with such subtle dexterity that his presence is barely felt," the *Times* cooed. "The dramatist's craft," the critic went on to say, is "normally mastered in middle age . . . when he is ripe in his understanding of the inherent mechanism of things." Tyler was way ahead, having "selected material slight enough to be controlled completely, and squeezed more emotional power from it than one would have thought it contained."

Judith had sent a copy of *The Tin Can Tree* to John Updike. Since 1963, she'd been working with him more openly, corresponding with him directly about his work, and bit by bit becoming his editor in full. Judith liked to have her authors connected; she often sent them one another's books. Updike responded enthusiastically to Judith, saying he felt that, as a writer, Anne Tyler was "not merely good, but wickedly good." Reynolds Price had recognized that Tyler was a once-in-a-generation talent when he taught her as a teen. Judith had seen it for herself, too, the very first time she read Tyler's prose. Now others with influence in the literary world were putting into words what Judith had sensed from the start: Anne Tyler was a literary wunderkind.

· · · · · · ·

Judith took a deep breath and dashed into the rain. At the newsstand closest to Knopf, she huddled under its awning and snatched a copy of the brand-new issue of *Life* magazine. On its cover, President Lyndon B. Johnson patted a smiling American soldier on the shoulder; the shot had been taken in South Vietnam's Cam Ranh Bay. Judith handed the clerk 35 cents, tucked the magazine under her coat, and ran back to the office's front door. In the lobby, she wiped her feet on the mat, opened to the magazine's table of contents, then flipped to page 74. There it was, a full-page spread of John Updike lying bare-chested on the beach, beside a portrait of him in a dress shirt surrounded by his smiling wife, Mary, and their four children. "John Updike has vast talent, charm—and a new book out, but Can a Nice Novelist Finish First?" the head-line read. It was November 2, 1966.

Knopf had published Updike's latest, *The Music School*, in August. The writer was then thirty-four years old, and the book, a collection of short stories, was his tenth. His 1963 novel, *The Centaur*, won the National Book Award, and *The Music School* had earned a rave in the *Times*; it was "beautifully written, an exquisitely artful book," the paper said. In that *Life* profile, Jane Howard said that Updike's writing is "dazzling—so dazzling, some critics think, that it blinds." There seemed to be no genre Updike couldn't master. Both writer and editor relished the praise.

Judith adored working with John Updike. She was drawn to the sensitive intimacy with which he rendered scenes of family life, desire, ambition, and disappointment; what critics called the restlessness and "unquiet adulthood" of mid-century middle-class life. Judith was moved by the way the writer captured both the high drama and mundane beauty of it all. She delighted, too, in his un-flinching treatment of sex, which was explicit enough, the *Times* said, to "shock the prudish." Updike's candor appealed to Judith's sensual nature, her mischievous side, and her reluctance to play it safe. Updike welcomed his editor's deep involve-ment; for him, the more hands-on her approach, the better. As such, Updike took up a great deal of Judith's time.

Back in 1963, when Knopf had been readying Updike's second book of poems, *Telephone Poles*, for publication, he'd plied Judith with details and made clear how he preferred things to go. "John knew *everything* that he wanted," Judith told me. "He chose the colors for his covers. He knew the quality of the paper, the size type. He wanted to be able to run his hand across a page so that you could really feel the print." Judith's work with Updike far exceeded tending to his words on the page; she became his chief cheerleader and also his sounding board. "Even if it was some little thing, he always wanted to hear my response, and then he'd decide," Judith told me. When at one point, Judith tried to arrange an interview with *Vogue* for him, Updike took a tone in response. Wasn't a fashion glossy such as *Vogue*, Updike griped, just the sort of thing of which Henry Bech would be suspicious? (Bech was Updike's character who first appeared in his story "The Bulgarian Poetess," originally published in *The New Yorker* in March of 1965; the story was collected in *The Music School* the following year.) But Updike had learned early on to trust Judith's judgment, and so often went along anyway. Begrudgingly, he let her set up the magazine interview.

Updike was aware his endless requests might test Judith's patience, but that didn't mean he let up. He'd make up his mind about some production detail for one of his books, then circle back with second, even third rounds of additional notes and revised ideas. Especially when his manuscripts were being readied for the printer, Updike often wrote or called his editor daily. Some of the others at Knopf got "a little annoyed," Judith told me. But she was quick to come to his defense: "'This is important to him!'" she'd say. Updike had become tremendously profitable to Knopf, and, Judith reminded her impatient colleagues, "He's already left one publisher" and did so because Harper had "tried to tell him what to do and he wasn't happy." Judith knew other houses would jump at the chance to lure Updike away if he made any noises of discontent about his experience with Knopf.

Judith understood that Updike's continued loyalty to Knopf fell largely upon her. So she patiently heard him out and did her best to meet his every demand. "I don't mean I just kowtowed," Judith told me; she could usually nudge the writer along or get him to rethink something if she really saw fit. Like when Updike submitted his short story collection, *The Music School*, in the fall of 1966, and Judith thought certain portions still needed work before the book went to the printer. "We are delighted to have *The Music School*," Judith began, kicking off half a page of praise. "The only story that bothers me—and I've gone back to read it a second time now," Judith was careful to note, "is 'Harv is Plowing Now.' . . . 'The Music School,' in which you used much the same kind of associative technique, seemed to me to demand a sort of imaginative leap on the part of the reader, but I felt you carried us right over the hurdle. But with Harv and Ur I didn't make it." Usually, when Judith offered a pointed critique like that, she was able to get Updike to come around. "He wouldn't have liked it if I had said 'you gotta,'" Judith had learned early on. "He wouldn't tolerate that. And so I was right for somebody like John," she said to me.

Once they'd grown accustomed to each other and Judith felt secure that Updike was sticking with Knopf, she began to respond to his requests with an air of cheeky play. Judith began one letter, "As for the jacket for which you are panting (and you must be out of breath by now)," before launching into a list of detailed answers to questions Updike had asked. "That doesn't mean you aren't perfectly free to howl about anything you don't like," Judith wrote, capping off her note. By then, Judith was signing all her letters to Updike, "Love, Judith." "We became very good friends," she told me.

Though they'd blurred the lines between the personal and professional, Judith was careful never to let their chummy rapport get in the way of the work. Instead, she cannily used their close relationship to grease the wheels. "Dear John, I think it would be grand if you were to deliver in person," Judith wrote when Updike told her he had a new manuscript ready for her eyes. She added, "Perhaps I could add that 'personal touch' by giving you a lunch or a drink or tea (I brew it in my office these days)." There was a spark between Judith and John Updike; everyone at Knopf saw it plainly. Kathy Zuckerman, who became Judith's assistant later in

her career, recalled a day when Updike came into the office and Judith sent her to
fetch something for him. When Zuckerman returned, Judith "leaned over to give
it to him, and she kicked her foot back up oh so coquettishly," Zuckerman recalled.
"Part of me thought, 'there's a crush here.'" Zuckerman knew Judith was "madly in
love" with Dick, but saw that she openly cultivated Updike's attention nonetheless.
"I do think she really enjoyed occasionally being naughty," Zuckerman said. "She
was also kind of a flirt."

Updike delighted in working with Judith every bit as much as she did him,
and readily made it known. After a lunch meeting with *Atlantic* editor Peter Davison one day, Updike wrote Judith recounting Davison's grumblings about some
award given out to editors he thought pointless and silly. Davison had one exception; if Judith Jones were honored in such a way, he told Updike, it wouldn't be a
bad thing. Judith, Updike wrote her affectionately, had admirers far and wide. He
signed the letter "Love, John." It was more than empty praise. After they'd been
working together for a decade, John wrote his editor to tell her he'd just drawn up
a revised will, naming her as his literary executor. He hoped she'd be flattered, or
at least mildly pleased. Though Judith received the anointment stoically, she was
chuffed; Updike's literary ascent was a major point of pride. "I think you came
out rather nobly, particularly for such an extensive exposé," she wrote him shortly
after the 1966 *Life* issue hit the stands. "This seems to be a big season for Knopf."

It was indeed a big season at the house, and specifically for Judith's authors, in
what had already been a momentous year. On May 22, 1966, Julia Child became
the first recipient of an Emmy for individual achievement in educational television by the National Academy of Television Arts and Sciences. Child and *The
French Chef* were honored alongside TV superstars including Bob Hope, Dick Van
Dyke, and Mary Tyler Moore. Then, in early fall, word came from *Time* magazine:
Child would be their November cover girl. By then, *The French Chef* had gone
national; it was running on 104 stations across the United States, and Julia Child
was well on her way to becoming a household name. But *Time* "catapulted her into
a whole other stratosphere," her producer at WGBH, Russ Morash, said. *Time*
called Child "Our Lady of the Ladle" and "the most influential cooking teacher in
the U.S.," leader of "a cult from coast to coast." Nineteen sixty-six, *Time* said, was
the "year everyone seems to be cooking in the kitchen with Julia."

By then it had become irrefutably clear to Knopf's senior editorial staff that
Judith was a true asset to the house. But Blanche Knopf didn't live to see the
young editor she'd brought to the house come fully into her own. On June 4,
1966, after two years of quietly battling cancer, Blanche Wolf Knopf died. The
Times memorialized her foremost as wife of "the publisher" Alfred A. Knopf,
and only secondarily as "a figure in the publishing field in her own right."

"[Alfred] and Blanche are like Jupiter and Juno. He is the ultimate, she the pen-ultimate," Robert Nathan, a novelist and friend of the Knopfs said. The sexist condescension didn't stop there. The obituary called out Blanche's beauty and fashion sense. It remarked on her weight, too. The lines most extolling Blanche's visionary work were buried several paragraphs down. "Book publishing, for the most part, is a man's world. But in this world, Blanche Wolf Knopf was a fem-inine presence that commanded respect." Only toward the article's very end did the *Times* note Blanche's unceasing devotion to the house; even when she was very ill and could hardly see, "she went regularly to the office and put in a workday that appalled her associates . . . refus[ing] medication most of the time lest it dull her mental acuity," the *Times* said.

Blanche's death was a turning point for Knopf; the house had lost one of its guiding lights. And in the immediate wake of her boss's passing, Judith's editorial load ballooned. But Blanche's death also brought a kind of autonomy Judith had grown restlessly eager for. As long as Blanche had been around, Judith had been unable to outgrow the status of underling. For the first time in nearly ten years of working at Knopf, she was finally standing on her own. William Maxwell once told Judith that patience was paramount, perhaps the single "most important pre-requisite for an editor" to have. He was right, she'd come to see. And hers was just beginning to pay off. She was ready to surge forth, unencumbered, to take her new independence and run.

CHAPTER 11

Judith pushed back the covers and eased out of bed slowly; she didn't want to wake Dick. It was early morning, but she couldn't wait. She had to check to see if the paper had come. Judith tiptoed out of their bedroom and down the hall, past Chris's empty bedroom—he was off at college—and his sister's closed door. Audrey, Judith knew, wouldn't be up for hours. Judith opened the front door as quietly as she could. There, on the welcome mat, was the fat Sunday *Times*. Judith scooped it up and stood in the doorway, riffling through the thin pages of gray on gray, in search of the *Book Review*. She found the review of John Updike's *Couples* on page 1 under the headline "Play in Tarbox." It was April 7, 1968. Knopf had published *Couples* two weeks before.

Judith read: "rumor has it that 'Couples' is a dirty book. But although Updike does call all the parts and attachments by name . . . if this is a dirty book, I don't see how sex can be written about at all." *Times* critic Wilfrid Sheed wrote, "This is an authentically decadent community," and called *Couples* "scorching" and "Ingenious . . . possibly too ingenious." Judith snapped the paper shut and went back inside to start coffee. She brimmed with satisfaction and pride.

In February 1967, Judith quietly celebrated a decade at Knopf. After Blanche Knopf's death, Judith had at last been given an office with a window of her own. She finally had a secretary (albeit one she shared with her colleague Ashbel Green), too. She certainly needed the help. Julia Child's television success had only fueled her fans' hunger for more of her books. Work on a second volume of *Mastering* was well underway. And in a mad dash, Judith helped Julia edit the recipes from her TV series for a cookbook due out in spring 1968. At the same time, John Updike had written Judith that he was nearly done with his next book. From his tone, Judith could tell John thought he was onto something big. But she was still surprised when she received his manuscript and saw just what he'd had up his sleeve.

In *Couples*, Updike chronicled a group of married but entangled small-town pairs. They flirted and screwed, fell in love with one another and fell out. *Couples'* characters were surfing a wave of cultural change. By the late 1960s, the sexual revolution, which had been brewing for years, was fully underway. The era of sexual liberation came on the heels of the 1960 FDA approval of birth control pills. For the first time, especially for women, the rewards of sexual pleasure began to outweigh its risk. It hadn't just been a buildup to more freely *having* sex. Since the end of World War II, Americans had demonstrated how much they wanted to read about it, too.

When W. B. Saunders published Alfred Kinsey, Wardell B. Pomeroy, and Clyde E. Martin's *Sexual Behavior in the Human Male* in 1948, it sold more than two hundred copies in its first two months. *Playboy* debuted in 1953, and the success of Hugh Hefner's magazine, with its risqué photos, further revealed readers' intrigue. In 1961, Grove Press reissued Henry Miller's *Tropic of Cancer*. Since the book's initial publication in France in 1934, it had been banned in the United States; conservative factions had charged Grove with violating obscenity laws. The case went all the way to the Supreme Court. In the meantime, other publishers seized on the opening *Cancer*'s publication made. Helen Gurley Brown's *Sex and the Single Girl* was published in 1962. Brown was then an advertising copywriter; three years later, she'd become *Cosmopolitan*'s editor in chief. In her book, Brown urged women to go after "love, sex, and money." Women, Brown believed, ought to explore their own pleasure and pursue financial autonomy before they married. She also supported women's choice not to marry at all. *Sex and the Single Girl* hit big: It sold two million copies in three weeks. A year later, in the summer of 1963, Mary McCarthy published *The Group*, a novel that included depictions of women losing their virginity out of wedlock and enjoying sex. *The Group*, the *Times* said, could not only "make you see but make you jump." But the book was not so much celebrated as a sign of women's sexual liberation as pooh-poohed as "trivial" ladies' stuff. Norman Mailer wrote that *The Group*'s heroines were "nice girls" living through "a near (or let us say quasi-) revolutionary period in American life" whose "Upper-Middle Class" Christian milieu was redolent of "a cross between *Ma Griffe* and contraceptive jelly." Regardless whether they liked it or not, everyone read McCarthy's book. Within six weeks, *The Group* was the number one *Times* bestseller, and it remained on the list just shy of two years. In 1964, the Supreme Court ruled in Grove Press's favor with regard to *Tropic of Cancer*. It was a watershed moment for freedom of the press. But no American novel that came before treated sex quite as John Updike's *Couples* did.

"Welcome to the post-pill paradise," one of the novel's characters proclaimed to another. It was a bold statement inspired, in no small part, by the writer's own escapades. Since the early sixties, he and his wife, Mary, had both been carrying on affairs (and in 1974, they would separate for good). Updike didn't oversimplify the new era; he was precise and sensitive about the emotional complexity and toll of it all. Nor did he stick to the surface when it came to descriptions of sex itself: "His tongue searched her sour labia until it found them sweet. She pulled his hair, *Come up.* 'Come inside me?' . . . He stroked and smoothed the outflowing corona of her hair. 'Your cunt is heavenly.'"

Couples was undeniably sexy; Judith knew that alone was enough to help it sell. But even in a moment of loosening mores around sex, *Couples* pushed the envelope. Judith understood that the book had the potential to move the needle on American literature's treatment of sex. Publishing it gave Judith a thrill. But whether or not the novel crossed a line was a source of some debate.

Couples was set in the fictional village of Tarbox. Updike had based it on Ipswich, Massachusetts, where he and his family lived. But the depiction of the town and its inhabitants hewed so closely and obviously to the lives of Updike and his neighbors that Judith feared Knopf could end up on the hook for libel or invasion of privacy. She gave Updike's book to Alfred Knopf for a second opinion. The house's founder agreed it was too risky to print *Couples* as written. In August 1967, during San Francisco's famous Summer of Love, Knopf wrote to Updike to tell him so himself. Updike grumbled; he wanted to be able to do as he pleased. But under Judith's guidance, he made the requested revisions, more carefully veiling his neighbors' identities in order to protect their privacy and to minimize Knopf's legal risk. Once both Judith and Alfred signed off on a final draft of *Couples* in the fall of 1967, Judith sent the pages for copyediting and set a pub date for March 1968. But before the first copies of *Couples* arrived at Knopf, the second major transition in as many years jolted the publishing house.

In 1960, Random House had purchased Knopf. And for some time, Bennett Cerf and Robert Bernstein, Random House's board chairman and publisher, respectively, had been worried that Knopf was losing its flair. Blanche was gone, and Alfred, though still present, was aging; in September 1967, he turned seventy-five. Cerf and Bernstein knew Knopf needed a succession plan and a new editor in chief to take the helm, someone who would bring the house up to speed with the changing times. Random House's executives thought Robert Gottlieb, then Simon & Schuster's young editor in chief, was the perfect man for the job.

Gottlieb had been at Simon & Schuster since 1955. He'd started as an editorial assistant to Jack Goodman, then the house's editor in chief. Within ten years of arriving, Goodman had died and Bob Gottlieb had taken his place. But when Cerf and Bernstein came calling, Gottlieb, who was thirty-six years old at the time, didn't hesitate. "Knopf was the publishing house of my dreams," he told me. He accepted on one condition: His two closest colleagues at S&S, advertising whiz Nina Bourne and associate publisher Tony Schulte, would have to be brought over, too. It wasn't a tough call for Random House's execs. The Gottlieb-Schulte-Bourne trio had proven themselves a crackerjack team, most notably with the success they'd made of Joseph Heller's 1961 *Catch-22*. "To have gotten even one of them would have been a coup," Cerf later wrote; all three, he said, were "almost a publishing business in themselves." In January 1968, the changing of the guard at Knopf took place, and Gottlieb became vice president and editor in chief of the house.

Judith wasn't sure what Knopf's new leadership would mean for her, but she intended to ride out the transition with stability and grace. Some things changed for the better immediately, like Gottlieb doing away with many of Knopf's outdated, rigid ways. "It was ridiculous," Katherine Hourigan, Knopf's longtime managing editor (until her retirement in 2023), said of the house's archaic protocols. "Bob had a systems destruction meeting and got rid of everything," she told me. Under Gottlieb, Knopf became a more casual, collegial place. Editors began leaving their office doors open, and at the end of the day, the staff often sat on the office floor and played "the Game," which was, Judith told me, a bit like charades. It was all part of Gottlieb's plan to boost morale at the house. "When I got there, everybody had been ground down, beaten regularly as gongs first by Blanche, then by Alfred," Gottlieb told me. "I saw these were zombies. Smart, funny, charming, nice. But they had no guts left. It was totally desultory." But though he brought a new laid-backness to Knopf, Judith and her new boss didn't connect easily. In both personality and editorial approach, the two were misaligned.

"That triumvirate from Simon and Schuster—Bob, Nina Bourne, and Tony Schulte—were all 'you gotta' kind of people," Judith told me. "They were, 'You do it our way, we're gonna make this book,'" she said. "I was not." Gottlieb's strong hand wasn't Judith's style at all. For his part, Gottlieb saw Judith as retiring to the point of "passive-aggressive." He told me, "She was a lady, and I was not used to ladies. I don't know whether it was her nature or being a woman in those days, but whatever it was, Judith did not want to show off or reveal what she really wanted. She was not going to be assertive." As for his understanding of her as an editor? "You never know what other editors do. Most of them do nothing," Gottlieb said. He did know, however, that Judith had a cache of important Knopf writers devoted to her, including Updike. Even with all his upstart energy, Gottlieb knew better than to interfere. So he stood back, prepared to watch the response to *Couples* unfold.

In the spring of 1968, critics pounced on the book. While some weighed in with a moral take—*Kirkus* called *Couples* "a commentary on America in the 1960s, gravid with a sense of loss, of isolation, of devaluation"—nearly all of the book's reviews focused on its depictions of sex. The *Atlantic* wrote *Couples* off as "fancied-up pornography," while the *Los Angeles Times* celebrated the novel's boldness; Updike's latest was "America's Most Explicitly Sexual Novel Ever," they said. In *Psychology Today*, Ludwig B. Lefebre, a practicing psychologist on the West Coast, lauded Updike for his realistic treatment of emotional and physical intimacy, albeit only among those in heterosexual relationships. "He describes the sexual experiences of both men and women with sensitivity that must be all but unmatched. . . . Updike's portrayals stress that sex is central rather than basic. It may be about time that the clinician starts learning from him." The book got its biggest boost in late April when Updike appeared on the cover of *Time* magazine with the words "The Adulterous Society" emblazoned across his portrait.

Couples hit the bestseller list upon publication and remained there for nearly a year. In September 1968 the book went into a sixth printing, and a seventh by July of the following year. *Couples* went on to sell more than two hundred thousand copies in its first three years in print. The combination of widespread coverage, controversy, and sex had proved irresistible and cemented John Updike's literary fame. And though Judith had done all the hard work before he arrived, Gottlieb counted the book as his first win as Knopf's editor in chief.

· · · · · · ·

In October 1969, Judith met Diarmuid Russell, Anne Tyler's agent, for lunch. The editor had just returned to New York from Provence, France, and began by telling Russell tales of her trip. Since Audrey had left for college in the fall of 1968, Judith had begun to reclaim time for herself. She took up playing the recorder and started practicing yoga. She and Dick began to travel more. Over dessert, Russell told Judith he, too, had news: A new novel from Tyler had just come in. Since *The*

Tin Can Tree's release four years earlier, Judith had been awaiting the writer's third novel.

In 1965, Anne Tyler gave birth to her first child. Another followed two years after that. During the blur of endless diapers and middle-of-the-night feeds, Tyler and her family moved twice, following opportunities in Anne's husband, Taghi's, psychiatric career. He eventually found a posting in Baltimore, and the family settled there for good. But the repeated uprootings piled atop the demands of early motherhood robbed Tyler of her focus and time. As she later wrote, "Everything I wanted to write was somehow coagulating in my veins." Tyler compared the experience to "living in a very small commune . . . one member was the liaison with the outside world, bringing in money; another was the caretaker, reading the Little Bear books to the children and repairing the electrical switches." Though Tyler's hands were full and she was distracted, her mind was far from still. She wrote book reviews to remain intellectually engaged and to help pay the family's bills; "I was trying to convince myself that I really did pull my own weight," Tyler later said. She also wrote and published a couple of short stories during that period of her life but lacked the unbroken chunks of solitude and quiet she needed to sustain the concentration a new novel required. Once both girls were in preschool, Tyler began to return in earnest to her work.

Russell had Tyler's new novel couriered over to Judith, who read it right away. As she turned the pages of *A Slipping-Down Life*, a coming-of-age tale set in the South, Judith noted with pleasure the changes in Tyler's writing since her last book. Her voice had grown sharper and even more distinct. The "special kind of detachment" the editor so loved about Tyler's perspective seemed to have bloomed. As Judith finished reading the novel's last lines, it was clear to her that Tyler had not backslid while ensconced in domesticity. Rather the writer was "very much continuing to go her own way, and growing," Judith remarked. Tyler resisted the trope that domesticity destroys women's creativity and ability to make art. Rather, she felt the fullness of family life had intensified and strengthened her work; "It seems to me that since I've had children, I've grown richer and deeper," Tyler wrote. "They may have slowed down my writing for a while, but when I did write, I had more of a self to speak from. . . . My life seems more intricate. Also more dangerous."

Judith understood, by then, how child-rearing can upend and remake one's sense of self, and she wanted *A Slipping-Down Life* to herald not only Anne Tyler's return to the literary world but to reflect her evolution as an artist as well. "This is a more mature book and tougher," Judith wrote to Knopf's art department after seeing the first mock-up of the book's cover design. "I think something starker than floral borders would be better."

Knopf published *A Slipping-Down Life* in the spring of 1970. Judith put it into the hands of everyone from Truman Capote to folk musician Arlo Guthrie, from the actor Paul Newman to women writers of note including Harper Lee, Eudora Welty, Nora Ephron, and Joyce Carol Oates. But the critics didn't all share Judith's level of enthusiasm for Tyler's newly fiercer voice. *A Slipping-Down Life* was met with mixed reviews. *Kirkus* called it less delicate than Tyler's previous two novels, but conceded, "Miss Tyler still exhibits a major talent, and this has a bleak, raw power." The writer saw the book's imperfections herself, calling it "flawed." Still, it "represented, for me, a certain brave step forward," Tyler would later say.

Two years after *A Slipping-Down Life*, Knopf published Tyler's *The Clock Winder*. The book's sales were slow, which Judith chalked up to the cacophony of glitzier novels that came out in 1972. ("I'm afraid it is a novel that is not getting its due amid so many noisier books," Judith wrote to journalist Nora Ephron, asking her, "if you find you do love it," to "make a little noise about it or perhaps nudge someone else.") Judith took a long view; she believed Tyler was gaining momentum as a writer and was convinced readers were discovering the author, albeit in their own time. "Dear Anne," Judith wrote Tyler in June 1972, "We are into a third printing of *The Clock Winder*. We went rather slowly because fiction in general seems to have fallen off so and returns have been bad, but you do have readers who love you I'm happy to see." Judith didn't want Anne to be discouraged. Regardless of its level of commercial success, the editor felt *A Slipping-Down Life* represented "a really good step forward for you," she wrote to her author. "It seems to me you have confronted a lot more here. You have a way of making a reader give himself over to you utterly, to accept your premises, enter the world you create, and take even the most unexpected turn of events quite as a matter of course. All of which is the mark of a true novelist. And there aren't many around today."

Anne Tyler's *Celestial Navigation* came out in 1974; by then both her children were in full days of school. Judith found the book remarkable. "Dear Anne," she'd written upon first reading the manuscript, "I feel so good about this novel that I want to make almost everyone I know sit down and read it. I wonder if you know how beautiful it is?" That book, Tyler later said, was the one that taught her to "rework and rework the drafts" to discover what her characters "really meant." Another novel, *Searching for Caleb*, followed in 1976, and *Earthly Possessions*—a book Tyler called "the work of somebody entering middle age"—came out in 1977. With each book, public recognition of Tyler's talent grew: In 1977, she received a citation from the American Academy of Arts and Letters "for literary excellence and promise of important work to come."

Anne Tyler was reclusive, and rarely left Baltimore, so Judith had to find a way to stay connected from afar. The editor knew that cultivating intimacy with her authors required a hallowed confidence essential to supporting their work and their trust in her. So she wrote to Anne frequently and often at length. The episto-lary mode suited the writer perfectly, and she reciprocated in kind. One June, after Anne wrote to Judith complaining that whiteflies were eating her basil, Judith sent the writer a book on herbs she'd just published. "This honest author," Judith wrote, "offers no surefire solution but she does make some useful suggestions, see p. 32–33. Love, Judith." Anne responded immediately, "I have been having a won-derful time" with the book, she said. "I don't know why this herb urge hits me every spring—it's like being at the mercy of hormones or something." The writer added how irked she was that one of her daughters was refusing to go to camp and thus would remain underfoot for the months school was out. "Summer is already looking very long," Tyler wrote, resigned.

Judith was invested not only in her writers' careers but in their lives overall. The specificity of her letters served as proof. "I've been meaning to tell you how much I loved your review of the Cheever stories," Judith wrote after sympathizing with Anne's frustration at her children's encroachment on her writing time. "Much as I love your reviews, I hope you're not giving too much of yourself to others and that a new novel is just about spinning off the typewriter. Yes? All your hungry readers (myself included) keep asking how long." Judith's gentle encouragement and atten-tive check-ins had the intended effect; just shy of a year after those summer letters went back and forth, Anne Tyler delivered the manuscript of her next book.

· · · · · · ·

A few times a year, Judith had lunch with Betty Prashker (née Arnoff), her former Doubleday office mate from the 1940s. After taking a ten-year hiatus to raise three kids, Prashker had returned to publishing. She was at Doubleday again, as a full editor this time. Ken McCormick, still editor in chief, had been instructed by the house's executives to bring more women into upper-level roles; by the late 1960s, American businesses were under pressure to attend to the shifting political sands. "Feminism, which one might have supposed as dead as the Polish Question," wrote Martha Lear in the *New York Times* in March 1968, "is again an issue. Propo-nents call it the Second Feminist Wave." The headline asked the question, "What do these women *want?*" The movement's answer: "full equality for all women in America . . . *now.*" Betty Prashker was one of McCormick's affirmative action hires.

Prashker was an ardent advocate of women's voices and rights and considered herself a feminist. She'd go on to publish several of the movement's most import-ant titles, including Kate Millet's 1970 *Sexual Politics*, a book Prashker felt had life-changing possibilities for women. Two years after that, she published Phyllis

Chesler's *Women and Madness*. Both books helped build the zeitgeist of the second feminist wave and sold well. They helped build Prashker's clout at work. Judith, though, was not keen to join the political cause. She felt misaligned with its messaging, which she saw as encouraging women to adopt stereotypically masculine traits in "a strident or angry way." "I think sometimes they emphasize the wrong goal in the feminist movement," Judith told me. "What I really feel deep down is that we're individuals rather than men and women. I am a certain kind of woman. I used my femininity, it was just natural to me. It's hard to define how, but you do." She added, "I *cannot* claim to have very strong feminist genes."

"Judith was not a marcher," her longtime Knopf colleague Ann Close told me. "But she was paying attention. We all were." Judith may have preferred to remain outside the fray, but it wasn't because she saw no need for change or had no frustrations of her own.

One might assume that, by the early 1970s, Judith's worth was obvious to all those she worked with. Jane Becker (née Lippman and who, at the time, was going by her first married name and is best known by her later married name, Friedman, would become a revolutionary force in publishing; she founded and became president of the first audiobooks division of a trade publisher, was CEO of HarperCollins, and cofounder of Open Road Media), then a young colleague of Judith's who'd come to Knopf about the same time Gottlieb became editor in chief, recognized Judith's authors as among Knopf's most important. John Updike and Anne Tyler, Friedman told me unequivocally, "needed [Judith] desperately." But Gottlieb didn't see things quite the same way. With regard to Anne Tyler, he told me, "There wasn't anything you could do with her except give her nice jackets and publish her books. I don't think most of [Judith's literary] writers needed, wanted, or appreciated editorial input." He discredited Judith's critical role in her books' success and devalued her, in house, in kind.

Over lunch, Prashker and Judith swapped stories about their families, talked shop about the books they each were working on, and discussed the state of publishing at large. Then the subject of salaries came up. "Judith began telling me a little bit about Bob Gottlieb and what she was making at Knopf," Prashker told me. "I said to Judith, 'You've got to tell him that he has to pay you more money because that's ridiculous!'"

For years, Dick had been urging Judith to ask for more money. Her compensation, he felt, was far lower than it should be, especially given the profits her writers earned for Knopf. And Judith, Dick surmised, was making a fraction of what the male editors made. "Dick would just go through the roof!" Chris Vandercook told me. "But Judith would say, 'No, no, no.' She was sort of the opposite of a strident feminist. And Dick wasn't going to fight it for her. It was hers to fight.

And, after all, he would just sort of say, 'Okay, have it your way.' But he would have loved to see her be more insistent." Julia Child had long been beating a similar drum. Judith told me Julia "felt that women were not listened to" and encouraged her editor to "get up and speak your mind and fight."

Betty Prashker's outrage over what she saw as Judith's unfair pay left Judith equal parts embarrassed and emboldened. The idea of advocating on her own behalf, though, was deeply uncomfortable for her. Still, Judith decided it was time. She screwed up her courage and approached Bob Gottlieb about a raise. He turned down her request.

When I asked him about the incident decades later, Gottlieb told me he didn't recall the details. "Everybody was always asking me for a raise," he said. "Judith didn't say, 'I'm worth this, and if you don't give it to me, I'm leaving.' That's what a person would say who was assertive. Not everyone can go around wasting their time intuiting your feelings which you're afraid to express. Judith was at a certain level that other editors were at, and she was paid in relation to that. She made as much as the colleagues who produced as much as she did." Gottlieb told me: "I have always been a feminist. I hired women. I admired them. I worked with them. I paid them." Plus, Gottlieb added when we spoke, Judith "had a rich husband." His assumption was beside the point. It was also untrue. Though the couple lived comfortably, they weren't wealthy; with only a brief exception early on in their relationship, Judith had been her household's primary earner. She would remain so until its end. They relied on Judith's salary to live.

Judith's situation wasn't one to which Gottlieb himself could relate. "In my entire career, only once did I ever ask for a raise, because money was thrust at me," he told me. His was an experience utterly foreign to most women in the paid workforce at the time, including his women colleagues at Knopf. "Even I, who came along with the women's movement," Knopf's longtime managing editor, Kathy Hourigan, told me, "would never, ever say, 'I need more, I deserve more money than this.' I would never have asked Bob for more money. I don't know why, it was just not done. I was not raised to. It was crass, or something like that. I came into publishing because it was idealistic." It had been Judith's stance, too, up until that point, and in her humiliation at Gottlieb's rejection of her request, she internalized it doubly. Judith never asked for a raise at Knopf again.

Instead, she returned to thinking about social change primarily through others' authorial voices. She was looking not so much for stories that reflected the priorities of the women's movement, but with her own experience and tastes. If she was going to contribute to shifts in the cultural conversation, it wouldn't be from out in front. Rather, she preferred to remain off to the side and out of view, exerting influence in her own quiet way.

CHAPTER 12

I t was morning, almost time to leave for work. Judith had woken early, as always, and did her yoga stretches while the coffee brewed. Dick was still in bed. In the fridge was a bowl with a kitchen towel over the top. She pulled the bowl out, releasing the sweet smell of fermenting yeast into the room. She'd begun the bread dough the previous evening; it had become a nearly daily routine. Overnight, the dough had risen slowly, more than doubling in size. A living thing.

Judith rolled up her pajama sleeves and sprinkled flour onto the countertop. Then she turned the dough out of the bowl and began to knead, rising on her tiptoes for leverage. With the heels of her hands, she pushed the dough away, then folded it over itself and pulled it back toward her body over and over and over again. Judith's arm muscles began to burn as she lost herself in the rhythm. She loved the physicality of bread making: the outlet for frustration that kneading provided and the quotidian alchemy of dough. When, at last, the mass became smooth and resilient, Judith tucked it back into its bowl and covered it once again. After work, she'd punch the dough down and shape it into loaves before baking them to have with dinner that night and for breakfast the following day.

· · · · · · ·

By the fall of 1968, the "Food Establishment" had grown to be something of a taste-making, if insular, little world. In a piece for *New York* magazine, Nora Ephron wrote about the increasingly influential crew, citing its leaders as James Beard, Craig Claiborne, and Julia Child. Judith wasn't named, but the piece pointed directly at her centrality to the scene. Ephron described the group's typical member as one who aspires to write cookbooks (that is, if they hadn't already). "His publisher, if he is lucky, is Alfred Knopf," she wrote.

Cookbooks were increasingly seen as shapers of culture, and Judith was behind the best of them. In April 1968, Knopf had celebrated the launch of Julia Child's *The French Chef Cookbook*. Judith had planned to print forty thousand copies to start, but Gottlieb insisted the house aim much higher than that. By then, more than a million people were regularly watching Julia Child on TV. Gottlieb upped the first run to a hundred thousand, then arranged a deal with Bantam to print a paperback edition (it came with a $340,000 guarantee). The multifront strategy sent sales through the roof; *The French Chef Cookbook* sold more than two hundred thousand copies in its first three years.

Child's first solo cookbook launched just a month after John Updike's *Couples*. The novel had served as an important litmus test and bellwether not only for Americans' shifting attitudes toward sex but toward the pursuit of pleasure overall. And what John Updike's novel did for sex, Julia Child was doing for food. By the late 1960s, "Liberated men and women, who used to brag that sex was their greatest pleasure," Ephron wrote, "began to suspect somewhat guiltily that food might be pulling ahead." "It's as though you suddenly released something that had been suppressed since the Puritan age," Judith told me. And while Judith resisted joining the feminist movement, she was delighted to be at the vanguard of the American revolution in food.

On October 22, 1970, Knopf published *Mastering the Art of French Cooking*, Volume Two, authored by Julia Child and Simone Beck. (Louisette Bertholle, with whom there had been some creative discord, wasn't in on the book's second act.) Convincing Knopf to do a follow-up to *Mastering* had been a cinch, requiring none of the strategic maneuvering or convincing on Judith's part that the first book had. It was proof of how far both Judith and Julia had come in their careers.

There were so many good recipes that had been cut from the first volume for length that the content of Volume Two was already halfway written by the time the contract was signed. And although it didn't take as many years of work as the initial *Mastering*, Judith, Julia, and Simca treated the second book with the same intense rigor and focus as they had the first book. And no symbol spoke more powerfully of the seriousness of Judith and Julia's quest to make over American attitudes toward cooking and food than Volume Two's approach to bread.

Mastering the Art of French Cooking hadn't included a recipe for a classic French baguette, and Judith felt it was essential that Volume Two fill in the gap. Without a foolproof bread recipe, she argued, the book would be incomplete. At first, Julia was reluctant. Most French home cooks, she pointed out, never baked loaves of their own. Instead, they bought their *pain quotidien* at their local *boulangeries*. That was all well and good in France, Judith said, but the French bread on offer in the United States left much to be desired. Judith and Julia went back and forth, but ultimately Judith won out.

For a full year, Julia worked obsessively to perfect a bread recipe that could help her replicate the loaves she'd eaten in France—namely the baguettes—one that American cooks could successfully execute at home. Paul Child—who by then for all intents and purposes had become his wife's assistant—sent Julia's trials for Judith to taste via overnight mail. Round after round failed to impress. Judith rolled up her sleeves in her home kitchen and joined the elusive pursuit, testing and commenting on many iterations of Julia's recipe. Judith brought those of her colleagues who were eager to learn into the mix, too. "The revolt against plasticized bread is in such full swing chez Knopf these days," Judith declared. "*Vive la révolution!*" When, at last, the *Mastering* team was satisfied with their recipe, it was thirty-two manuscript pages long. Judith helped Julia pare it back to nineteen pages before the book went to the printer.

Mastering, Volume Two was a success even before it hit shelves. There were so many preorders on the initial run of one hundred thousand copies that a second printing of half as many went to press before the book's publication date. Unanimously, critics raved. *Newsweek* declared the book "without rival, the finest gourmet cookbook for the non-chef in the history of American stomachs." In *Life*, Gael Greene, a reporter who'd quickly grown influential in the world of food, called Volume Two, "ambitious, inventive, slightly permissive, and rigidly authentic." Greene dubbed the book an essential text. No serious scholar of the kitchen will want to function without it," she wrote. PBS seized on the opportunity for promotion, too, debuting a new season of *The French Chef*—in color for the first time—concurrent with the book's launch. Public television affiliates from across the country had contacted Knopf, asking if the house would arrange for Child to help promote the new season of her television show. It was Jane Friedman, then twenty-five years old and hungrily ambitious, who came up with a solution equally beneficial to the TV network, Knopf, and Julia Child herself.

Friedman had begun at Random House in 1967, when, she told me, she walked into the house fresh out of college and said, "I want to be a publisher." She went on to say, "I was given a temporary job as a Dictaphone typist. That was terrific. Then, right around the time Bob, Tony, and Nina came in, I was offered this job working in publicity at Knopf." Trouble was, Friedman recalled, "no one knew what publicity was!" At the time, she said, the house relied entirely upon reviews. That, Friedman knew, was but one component of what could be a grander scheme to promote books *and* the personalities behind them. "What I was interested in was how we could bring authors to the public," she said. So she made a proposal, building on the scrappy self-promotional trips Julia Child and Simone Beck had taken back in 1961 and 1962. Why not put a little extra effort behind publicizing *Mastering*, Volume Two, and have the house send Julia Child out on tour?

Friedman put together a list of cities with both public television stations that aired *The French Chef* and also thriving retail stores. Julia would do a cooking demo at each store and sign copies of her book, and advertisements in local media paid for by the hosting shop would make her appearances known. Someone in each locale would host a little party on the author's behalf, and Julia would do spots on local radio stations and TV channels while in town. When Friedman had finished arranging the cross-country schedule, she had orchestrated what would come to be known in publishing history as the first modern book tour. Together, Jane Friedman and Julia Child hit the road, stopping first in Minneapolis in November 1970. On the morning of the tour's inaugural event, Friedman woke early to find hundreds of women already lined up down the block. In city after city, the results were the same: fans by the thousands clamored to see the French Chef in the flesh. Most important to Knopf, the vast majority bought her book. Via Julia Child, Judith had won over the nation's middle-aged bourgeoisie with regard to food. But to remain ahead of the curve and prove herself hip to the times, Judith, who'd turned forty-six earlier that year, needed to capture the attention and trust of American youth.

· · · · · · ·

Judith was at her desk, trying to wrap things up so she could leave. It was the Tuesday before Thanksgiving 1970, and the Knopf office was already half-empty. Dick had called midmorning, asking when she'd be ready to hit the road. He wanted to try to make an early start, beating the traffic out of the city to get a jump on the long drive to Greensboro, Vermont. Since Monty, her father's, death in January 1968, Judith's mother, Phyllis, had been spending more and more time up north. Slowly, she was leaving the apartment at 139 East 66th Street behind, moving toward making her full-time home in Vermont.

Things were changing in rural places across the country like the Green Mountain State. Following the 1967 Summer of Love, thousands of young people—most of them privileged and white—left American cities and universities and headed for the hills. Judith watched with curiosity as the phenomenon swept Vermont. VW vans and Beetles "sped up I-89 and I-91, veered off at various exits and headed into the hinterland," wrote lifelong Vermonter Joe Sherman, "indiscriminately carrying radical militants against the war in Vietnam, acid-tripping God seekers, college dropouts, runaway kids, body odor, marijuana, and LSD." Vermont was an easy drive from cities like Boston and New York, and land there could still be gotten cheap. Between 1967 and 1973, an estimated hundred thousand new arrivals poured into Vermont, increasing its population by nearly a fifth. "There were these little pockets of young people rebelling," Judith told me, "families living together—they all had lots of children—producing everything and weaving their own clothes." The young idealists gave their communal operations names like Total Loss Farm, Earth People's Park, Tree Frog, and Hamburger Hill. It was being called a movement "Back to the Land."

Ever since Rachel Carson exposed the far-reaching deadly effects of DDT in her 1962 book *Silent Spring*, the environmental movement had been gaining speed. That same year, Cesar Chavez, Dolores Huerta, and Larry Itliong founded the National Farm Workers Association, that later became the United Farmworkers (UFW), to collectively combat the exploitation of laborers in American agriculture. Racial inequity and poor working conditions in the U.S. food system were issues as old as the nation itself. But since World War I, the demographic subject to such mistreatments had shifted markedly. In 1917, the U.S. and Mexican governments had struck a deal to provide American landowners with cheap labor from Mexico to work their orchards, ranches, and fields. The policy, which admitted "otherwise inadmissible aliens" from Mexico into the United States, was reinstated during World War II. Braceros, as Mexican migrant workers were called, weren't protected by American labor laws, so U.S. landowners could pay them a great deal less than their American-born counterparts. The program increased profits for landowners and lowered prices of domestically produced food. In 1951, the Bracero Program was codified into law. That year, 192,000 Braceros entered the United States; by 1956, that number had risen to 445,000. By the early 1960s, people of Mexican origin played an outsize role in producing and harvesting America's food.

In their call to reform unjust labor practices, the UFW connected the dots of immigration, race, labor, the environment, and food. And though it would be years before the political establishment addressed such concerns in earnest, the counterculture responded right away. If "the man" controlled your food, their thinking went, "the man" controlled you, too. They'd take matters into their own hands, DIY their way to cleaner food, and resist injustice along the way. To the British food writer Jane Grigson, whose books Judith was publishing the American editions of, Judith wrote, "There is a tremendous surge of interest in natural things among the young in this country," including "organic gardening" and "stalking the wilds for natural foods."

Judith wanted to do a book channeling that collective spirit into accessible, beginner-friendly terms. But first she'd need an author with the right viewpoint and expertise. When, in the fall of 1970, she read an article on organic gardening in *Quadrille*, Bennington College's alumni magazine, it sparked an idea. The piece was written by Catharine "Kit" Osgood Foster, a recently retired longtime professor of literature at Bennington. Kit kept a large, chemical-free garden and wrote about it regularly in a column for the Bennington village newspaper. Alongside her husband, Thomas Henry Foster—a poultry farmer turned Vermont congressman with a conservationist bent—Kit Foster had become a leading voice in the northeast's sustainable agriculture crusade. After months of racking her brain to land on someone to write an organic gardening book for Knopf, Judith finally knew who to ask.

Before packing it in for the Thanksgiving holiday, Judith wrote to Foster. "Dear Kit, I was just browsing through the most recent issue of Bennington's *Quadrille* last night and I was caught by your piece on organic gardening," she began. "For some time I've been trying to get someone to do a really good little book on the subject, which is so obviously increasing in interest, particularly to young people today. I notice that you have retired from teaching and are doing a column for *The Bennington Banner*, which leads me to believe that you might have the time to tackle such a project." Would Kit be interested? Judith asked. The week after the holiday, Judith received a response. "How good to hear from you after all these years," Kit wrote. She enthusiastically agreed to take the project on; she'd start in right away.

In her letter, Kit noted the "drastic change" in Bennington's culture. "I miss all the old-timers," she wrote, "but do enjoy this new generation of wacky, do-good, warm-and-insolent young kids nowadays." The same demographic enthused by the idea of planting lettuce, potatoes, and beets had proven themselves open to broadening their palates as well. And though she was a generation their senior and not as outwardly politically engaged, Judith shared the counterculture's openness to culinary diversity and change. For a full decade by then, she'd been helped along by Craig Claiborne's multicultural approach to covering food for the *New York Times*.

"When it is a question of restaurants, New York could be called an international festival," Claiborne had written in 1961. In May of the following year, the *Times* began running a weekly restaurant review, making it the first bona fide restaurant section in a major American newspaper. To rate his picks, Claiborne adapted the star system developed by the *Guide Michelin* in France. And though

Claiborne never lost his love of French gastronomy and technique, his coverage stretched far beyond *la belle cuisine française*.

In August 1961, Claiborne reviewed Viet Nam, a "small, poorly air-conditioned, unpretentious place with an interesting cuisine modestly priced" that was, purportedly, the only Vietnamese restaurant in the United States at the time. When he premiered his weekly review column for the *Times* on May 18, 1962, of the five Manhattan eateries he covered, only one of them was French. Claiborne wrote up "one of New York's most unusual Northern Italian" places, a seafood house, an American restaurant that served "Near Eastern bread," and a Chinese spot on West 125th Street in Harlem called Tien Tsin.

Judith and Claiborne had, by then, become close colleagues and friends. He often invited her to accompany him when he was working on an article. "He'd always call up and make the reservation in my name," Judith told me. She was impressed by Claiborne's curious and conscientious approach. "He wanted to make the food page intelligent, and widen people's horizons," Judith said. When he stepped down as the *Times*'s food editor in 1971, Claiborne devoted himself full-time to chronicling the dynamic, shifting culinary landscape of New York. Judith wanted to use that same energy and open curiosity to continue growing Knopf's cookbook line. She had helped the nation fall in love with French cooking via Julia Child, but she wanted to keep pushing, exposing Americans to more cultures and cuisines and expanding their sense of taste. She began with *A Book of Middle Eastern Food* by Claudia Roden.

Roden was born into a Syrian Jewish family in Cairo in 1936. She'd grown up in an elite cosmopolitan milieu. As a teen in 1951, she'd been sent to boarding school in Paris, and in 1954, she enrolled at St. Martin's College in London to study painting. During those same years, her family was pushed out of Egypt under political pressure and her parents relocated to London. In Egypt, Roden's mother, Nelly Sassoon, hadn't regularly prepared the family's meals. The family had been wealthy and paid household help for that. But in London, where there were no restaurants serving Middle Eastern fare, Nelly grew into a passionate and talented home cook. For Roden, eating dishes from the Middle East at her mother's table in exile became proxy for returning home.

Roden began collecting stories and recipes from the Egyptian friends who gathered at her parents' house on Friday nights. And though she'd hardly set foot in a kitchen before then, Roden became committed to learning to cook. "The dishes that Claudia associated with the past, with family, with memory were what [she] wanted to re-create to make that tie again," Judith later said. Roden decided to put all the history, lore, and kitchen know-how she'd picked up into a book. *A Book of Middle Eastern Food* was published in the UK in 1968.

Dick's brother Russ, a political journalist, was posted in Israel at the time. He and his wife encountered *A Book of Middle Eastern Food* there. Russ was no cook, but he knew good writing when he saw it. His wife, though, was able and enthusiastic in the kitchen. She was struck by the cookbook's clarity and her success with its recipes. Russ sent a copy of *Middle Eastern Food* to the Joneses in New York. "This little book is the talk of the town," Russ wrote his sister-in-law. He wondered if Judith might be interested in purchasing the cookbook's American rights.

Judith was captivated by Roden's vividly wrought details and *Middle Eastern Food*'s yearning, almost elegiac, tone. She also recognized the book's thoroughness of instruction and the ambition of its scope. Roden had attempted to translate and transmit an entire culinary culture for readers who might know little, if anything at all, of the Middle East. Later, Roden would say she'd been writing "not for myself and all the Egyptian Jews" but for Brits who'd most likely never even seen or tasted olive oil before. Like *Mastering the Art of French Cooking*, *A Book of Middle Eastern Food* was intended as a teaching tool for cultural outsiders. But unlike Julia Child, Claudia Roden wrote as an insider, parsing and narrating foodways to which she herself belonged.

Judith knew that she and her authors "had to take people by the hand and teach them . . . Ever more so if you're talking about an 'exotic' cuisine where you're flying blind, maybe making a dish you've never even tasted." Judith would later credit the clarity of cookbook authors like Roden to their having learned to cook themselves later in life. "They didn't cook at grandma's knee—all was done in the kitchen 'out there' . . . so they understood all the things they needed to explain." Judith felt fortunate that Roden, in her accomplishment of that difficult task, had happened across her path. "We didn't know what Middle Eastern food was in this country," Judith recalled. She thought Claudia Roden's book had the potential to do for Middle Eastern food what Julia's had done for the cuisine of France, and she was eager to bring it to the States.

Judith worked her connections, trying to track down Roden so she could personally express her interest in publishing her book. But before Judith was able to find a contact for the author, Bob Gottlieb took a business trip to London. While there, he met with Jill Norman, Roden's British editor at Penguin Books. Norman was the preeminent publisher of cookbooks in the UK, the British counterpart to Judith Jones. She gave Gottlieb a copy of Roden's book, and when Knopf's editor in chief returned to New York in December 1970, it was with the British edition of *A Book of Middle Eastern Food* tucked under his arm.

Knowing nothing about cookbooks himself, Gottlieb handed Roden's book off to Judith to get her take, unaware that she already had her own copy, and had, by then, been cooking from it for months, and was determined to pursue the book for Knopf. Telling me the story years later, Judith said, "When I said I wanted to publish the book, [Gottlieb] said, 'Well, *I've* decided that we should publish this book.'" She laughed a little cynically at the memory. "It was in some ways kind of handy because it became partly his discovery, too." Judith didn't bother arguing with Gottlieb about who'd discovered Roden's book. She knew such nitpicking would likely backfire and get in the way of the work she was itching to do. With Gottlieb behind the project and Roden's agent's contact information finally in hand, Judith made her move.

"Dear Miss Roden," she wrote on December 18, "I can't tell you how pleased I am to be sending you this contract for your *Book of Middle Eastern Food*. It is a book that I have quite fallen in love with and I am sure we are going to have great fun publishing it here. Already I have a hard time hanging on to the Penguin copy," the one Gottlieb had brought back from the UK. "It keeps being stolen from my desk by the curious who have heard such good things about the book around the office and then they turn quite greedy and don't want to give it up." Judith said, "I had to take home my own Nelson edition which was sent to me recently by a sister-in-law temporarily posted to Israel, whose bible—or rather survival kit—your book has become to her." Judith told Roden her book would need quite a lot of work before it could be published in the United States. The measurements needed translating from metric to American usage, the index, to be completely reorganized, and American readers would need guidance on how to source ingredients not carried by most supermarkets.

Roden was elated by Judith's interest. Even overseas it was, by then, clear that if you were going to publish a cookbook in the United States, you wanted to do it with Knopf. And by the time Judith boarded a plane for France for the Christmas and New Year's holiday stretch that December of 1971 ("Mostly a pleasure trip," Judith wrote Kit Foster, "but with a little work thrown in to ease the old New England conscience"), Roden had accepted Judith's offer, and the Knopf edition of *A Book of Middle Eastern Food* was underway.

· · · · · · ·

The following spring, while Judith awaited chapters from Kit Foster and revisions from Claudia Roden, she received a call from Roberta Pryor, a powerful agent with the International Famous Agency (which would later be known as International Creative Management, or ICM, Partners). A client of Pryor's, a film professor at UCLA, had sent along a packet of vegetarian recipes by a student of his named Anna Thomas, who'd taught herself to cook in a student kitchen on a shoestring budget. It was a phenomenon Judith had observed growing in strength and speed. To Jane Grigson in the UK, she reported, "An adherence to vegetarian diets [is] beginning to revolutionize eating habits here." Thomas often invited her fellow film students over to eat. They thought her food was something special and suggested Thomas write her recipes down and try making them into a book.

In April 1970, when the United States invaded Cambodia, student protests on the UCLA campus shut classes down for most of spring term. Thomas, with nothing much to do besides attend protests and march (which she did plenty of), decided to take her friends' advice. She started keeping a careful record of what she cooked, but hadn't a clue about the publishing industry or how it worked. That spring, she mentioned what she was doing to a professor of hers. Intrigued, he made some suggestions for putting together a coherent manuscript, and said he'd ask his agent, Roberta Pryor, if she'd be willing to shop Thomas's book around. Thomas organized and compiled her recipes and put them into her professor's hands. He passed them on to Pryor who, despite her track record landing deals, was inexperienced with cookbooks. She knew who Judith Jones was, though, and sent Thomas's work to her.

Steeped in the roiling times, Thomas had been politically radicalized down to the way she cooked and ate. And her location on a college campus in Los Angeles, where student housing bumped up against immigrant enclaves, put her right at the nexus of expanding offerings and changing tastes in food. In the days before food coops, farmers markets, and natural grocers became commonplace, small mom-and-pop ethnic groceries were the readiest source of all things free of sulfates, dried, bulk binned, and whole. Such novel ingredients livened up drab American fare. In Thomas's inventive, playful recipes, Judith saw an American everywoman, low on cash but big on spunk and ideals.

Judith was impressed by Thomas's clarity, purpose, and "a certain joy" that came through in her words. She wrote Thomas directly saying she had "the makings of an excellent book," but that the prose could use some "toning down." Judith reported that one of her colleagues at Knopf with whom she'd shared Thomas's pages felt the writer was "so preachy" in her vegetarian zeal "that it turned her off." Despite plant-based diets' increasing popularity, many cookbooks extolling the lifestyle prized piousness over taste. A flavorless politics of the table was not one sensual Judith could get behind. Thankfully, Anna Thomas was no ascetic. "The recipes themselves are so very good," Judith wrote; she'd tried a few herself at home. Judith saw a ready market for Thomas's book, and told the young writer she'd like to take it on. "Let me know," she wrote. "Even call me collect if you would like."

Thomas responded, excited. She hadn't expected anything to come of her amateur recipes, let alone a book deal. She agreed to make the cuts Judith suggested "with no regret at all," and to "tighten her wording," too. But she was adamant that the book position vegetarianism as a lifestyle of abundance rather than focusing on what the diet lacked. Thomas said the book was intended as "a delight and a celebration of life." "I hope we can make it happen," Thomas wrote Judith in June 1971, "and that the book does well for us all."

Next thing Thomas knew, Roberta Pryor was on the phone. "We have an offer, and I think we should take it," Thomas remembers the agent saying. The advance Judith was offering was small—only a couple thousand dollars to put toward a no-name author and a niche cookbook. It wasn't enough to cover both Thomas's rent and fund her student film, but it was still a meaningful sum; it meant she wouldn't have to take time off from school to work a side job as she had in previous terms. Thomas told Pryor she'd do the book; "I said, 'Yeah, okay, fine,'" Thomas told me, "and I went back to working on all my schoolwork and stuff I was doing at the time. I was really immersed in it." She had no idea what lay ahead.

In late June, Judith wrote to Thomas, "I'm eager to get it out for both our sakes because so much is being done in this area of cooking now that we want to get ahead of the other books that are bound to be coming out." She wanted Thomas to start in right away. "If you feel I'm setting an impossible deadline, please let me know." Thomas said she'd do her best to adhere to Judith's ambitious timeline and got right down to work.

Over four months in the spring and summer of 1971, Thomas completely reworked her book. She and Judith agreed they'd call it *The Vegetarian Epicure*, a "very fetching" title, Judith thought. When Thomas began to submit her revised chapters, Judith was pleased. She felt Thomas's slightly adjusted tone was "just right," "personal and relaxed and wonderfully enthusiastic—and yet no feeling of over-selling." The editor had only one bone to pick. "I made a vow to myself that I would never publish a cookbook that used powdered garlic," she wrote. "Particularly in a book like this that is so full of fresh and glorious things it should not have to appear." Judith asked that Thomas, "please," not make her go back on her word.

· · · · · · ·

By mid-June that summer, Judith had half of Kit Foster's *The Organic Gardener* in hand. She was concerned. The book wasn't shaping up as she had hoped it would. Just as a cookbook's recipes had to be crystal clear and its tone encouraging to those learning in their kitchens at home, Judith knew Foster's instructions had to be equally workable and succinct. Otherwise, Judith feared, novice gardeners would lose heart and give up. She sat with the pages of *The Organic Gardener* for a couple of weeks, gnawing on her pencil in her office. Before leaving for Greensboro for a few days for the Fourth of July, Judith wrote to Foster. "Now that I have more distance on these four chapters, I am frankly worried that you are not doing more of that sifting and assimilating process for the reader and giving us the essence of all you have learned in language that is totally comprehensible." Judith had tested the waters with a colleague of hers at Knopf, an eager but inexperienced gardener who worked in advertising and publicity; she'd hoped, Judith reported in her letter to Foster, that *The Organic Gardener* would be for her. But skimming through a few pages, Judith's coworker found the book "beyond her." Foster may have been respected as a scholar and practiced in the garden, but when it came to writing for a popular audience, Judith had picked an amateur. "I'm afraid that you continue to give us too many options, documenting more thoroughly than we want or can absorb how other people do things. I feel I should stress again that we the readers all want you to make the decisions for us," Judith wrote. "That is why we're buying the book."

She took it upon herself to comb through Foster's overwrought instructions herself. Over the holiday weekend at her mother's place in Vermont, Judith claimed a small plot of land for herself off to the side of the house, and spent all weekend working outdoors in a worn chambray shirt and old blue jeans. Judith had come full circle since her days on the Bennington farm. While as a young student she'd resented having to put in time on the farm, in middle age, she found the same tasks invigorating and fun. Dick snapped a photograph of his wife standing beside a mound of soil she'd worked hard to dig and turn. In the photo, a bandana keeps her hair out of her face. She stares into the lens, radiant in the country air, a picture of vigor and youth. Back in New York the following weekend, her skin bronzed from the sun, Judith wrote Foster, "We had a gorgeous weekend up in northern Vermont (Greensboro) and I started a compost heap which a woodchuck feasted happily on. We also planted a tidy lettuce and herb patch over an old garden site and I drove everyone quite out of their minds saying constantly Kit says to do it this way or that. (I didn't realize how much I'd learned!)" Foster's prose may have left much to be desired in terms of style, but her methods worked.

While Judith waited, anxious and impatient, for Foster to send in new and reworked chapters of *The Organic Gardener*, the revisions of Anna Thomas's *Vegetarian Epicure* arrived at Knopf right on schedule. Judith marked up the pages and mailed them back. She was delighted with Thomas's work; the writer had taken the editor's notes without resistance, while still maintaining the original spirit of the book and authenticity of her voice. Under Judith's clear guidance and steady pressure, Thomas moved through her work quickly and efficiently. "I was a completely unwashed newbie," she told me. "Judith was very straightforward and clear in terms of what needed to be done, but also always very encouraging. She would send these wonderful letters that, in retrospect, I realize were very diplomatic." Though she was a first-time author, Thomas recognized her editor's acuity. "You have the ability," she wrote Judith in late July 1971, "to put your literary and informational finger on all my weaknesses and at the same time make me feel that I'm doing everything well. I see the manuscript improving with your editing and am so pleased."

In mid-August, Thomas sent Judith forty-four new recipes and a fully revised manuscript of *The Vegetarian Epicure*. She enclosed a note asking her editor to let her know as soon as possible if she needed anything more from her; classes were starting back up soon, and Thomas needed to return her focus to her studies and film. Judith was impressed. "You must be feeling very pleased with yourself for having gotten so much done, so well and so quickly. Thank you for being so very dependable and working so very well despite the pressure I'm afraid I inflicted." Judith had what she needed from Thomas, and said she'd take things from there. In early October, the editor sent the pages of *The Vegetarian Epicure* off to the printer, and set a publication date for the following spring.

• • • • • • •

In January 1972, Judith squeezed into an eight- by seven-foot galley kitchen in a Greenwich Village apartment, notebook and pencil in hand. She watched as the fingers of the cook, Madhur Jaffrey, danced about, pinching spices from tins and sprinkling them into oil that had been heating on the stove; the rich, earthy scent of toasting cumin, coriander, and mustard seeds filling the air. As Jaffrey shimmied the skillet around on the burner, careful not to singe the fragrant contents of the pan, Judith scribbled down a note: stir constantly, do not let spices burn. She couldn't believe this magnificent cook's book had nearly been lost.

In November 1971 Elaine Markson, a literary agent then working at Knox Burger & Associates, had written to Judith. She had a cookbook, titled *Curry: Myth and Reality*, whose path to publication had run aground, Markson said, and she wondered if Knopf might want to take it on. Its author, Madhur Jaffrey, had been born in Delhi, India, and had studied theater at the Royal Academy of Dramatic Art in London, headed for a career as an actress. And it was in London, at age nineteen, that Jaffrey began to cook. Like Claudia Roden, Jaffrey hadn't spent time in her kitchen as a girl. But living abroad she'd missed the flavors of home. So Jaffrey had asked her mother to send her her handwritten recipes, and began to learn how to prepare Indian dishes.

Madhur Jaffrey, née Bahadur, came to the States with Saeed Jaffrey in 1957;

the pair married the following year. By the early 1960s, she was cooking for large gatherings of friends, many of whom, like the Jaffreys, had immigrated to New York from India. She continued to act professionally as she became a mother, bearing three daughters in the four years from 1959 to 1963. Madhur and Saeed's marriage ended in 1965; Madhur sent their daughters to India to stay with her mother and sister while she went to Mexico to secure a divorce. That same year, the film *Shakespeare Wallah* premiered. Madhur Jaffrey played the starring role. To build publicity around the film in the United States, its producer, Ismail Merchant, talked Craig Claiborne into profiling Jaffrey. She was, after all, not only a talented and beautiful actress but also an outstanding cook. "Indian Actress Is a Star in the Kitchen, Too" was the headline of Claiborne's July 1966 profile of Jaffrey in the *New York Times*.

Not long after, Jaffrey had a deal with Harcourt, Brace & World for an Indian cookbook titled *Curry: Myth and Reality*. But, Markson told Judith when she reached out to her, the editors involved had since left the house, and the book had been abandoned partway through. Harcourt was primarily a textbook publisher, and no one on its editorial staff had stepped in to complete work on Jaffrey's book. Under pressure from Markson, Harcourt agreed to cancel their contract with Jaffrey. She was now free to resell her book. Judith's interest was piqued. Though she'd tasted a few Indian dishes while dining out with Craig Claiborne, Judith knew virtually nothing of Indian food.

Indian chefs had been cooking food in New York for seven decades by then; J. Ranji Smile, who arrived in 1899, is said to have been the first. But that food was heavily Americanized, made more familiar for an audience to whom Indian flavors and cooking techniques were utterly foreign and strange. As Jaffrey later wrote in the 2011 reissue of the book, at the time of her arrival in the States, "There was no place in . . . America where top-quality Indian food can be found, except, of course, in private Indian homes." Well into the 1960s, Indian food remained all but unknown to white Americans, even those who lived in the most diverse cities like San Francisco and New York. This was in large part due to the low numbers of immigrants who had been allowed into the United States from India; they'd been barred since the Immigration Act of 1917 and the national origins quota system instituted in 1921. With the passage of the Hart-Cellar Act in 1965, that finally began to change.

Hart-Cellar abolished the quotas that had flung open the doors of the United States to immigrants from Northern and Western Europeans while keeping them barely cracked to those from the rest of the world. (In 1960, 84 percent of immigrants to the United States had been born in Europe or Canada, while 6 percent hailed from Mexico, less than 4 percent from elsewhere in Latin America and

South and East Asia, and fewer than 3 percent from everywhere else.) Proponents of immigration reform positioned Hart-Cellar as part of a larger move toward expanding civil rights. As Massachusetts senator Edward Kennedy said, "Our streets may not be paved with gold, but they are paved with the promise that men and women who live here—even strangers and new newcomers—can rise as fast, as far as their skills will allow, no matter what their color is, no matter what the place of their birth." Hart-Cellar led to marked demographic shifts in the U.S. and changed how identity was expressed in American culture at large. Judith saw an opportunity to capture the rise of identity politics through cookbooks. She asked Markson to send her a copy of Jaffrey's work to date.

Madhur Jaffrey's pages enveloped Judith into a world of parathas, chutneys, koftas, and pullao. She hadn't seen or tasted foods like those before, and she knew immediately that she wanted the book. On Friday, January 21, 1972, Judith met with Jaffrey at Knopf. The editor told Jaffrey she thought some changes to the introduction, the title, and a few details about styling would strengthen the book. "She seems so cooperative and enthusiastic," Judith wrote to Markson after the meeting. "I am sure we are going to be very happy working together." The following Monday, the editor put Jaffrey's book contract through in the mail.

Judith had no budget to hire recipe testers; indeed, Bob Gottlieb was still giving her only scant support with which to make cookbooks. But it was just as well: "I don't believe in testers!" Judith told me. "I think that you have to test your own recipes." But cooks, Judith knew, were often too close to their own work to be objective. She'd learned that a second person in the kitchen could be useful, someone to pose questions and take detailed notes on measurements; techniques; and, when necessary, to lend an extra hand with the cooking itself. Judith loved to jump in and act the part.

In her own tiny kitchen, Jaffrey took the lead while Judith wrote down details about textures, colors, methods and measurements, ingredient sourcing, and serving style. Like the book's potential readers, Judith was new to this cuisine, and her eagerness to learn at Jaffrey's elbow was genuine. Jaffrey, for her part, was impressed by the level of Judith's commitment and involvement in her book. Judith "was there all the time," she later said, and grew to "know the book intimately, just as intimately as I know the book. How rare is that?" Judith didn't think of her methods as extraordinary but rather as the essential work necessary to build both a book and an author. Her role, as Judith saw it, was to "let that voice come out," and "to learn to gauge what that writer really wants out of the collaboration. And it *is* a collaboration," Judith emphasized to me. Together, author and editor reworked Jaffrey's pages into a Knopf cookbook: precise, well organized, and heavily detailed, yet still clear enough for a novice to use.

. . . .

By that point, Judith had worked on enough cookbooks to establish her own style for the form. It was "a new way of doing cookbooks, a better way, a more serious way," former *Times* food critic Ray Sokolov later said. But the high standard Judith had set for cookbooks at Knopf required a huge amount of careful attention and time. She had arrived at the point where she could no longer do it alone. She needed help with some of the fussier, most time-consuming editorial tasks. In summer 1971, Judith was in up to her neck preparing books by Anna Thomas, Kit Foster, and Claudia Roden for publication. Judith's colleague Ann Close reached out to Mildred ("Millie") Owens, a former in-house Knopf copy editor, to help Judith with the finicky finish work needed on the *Book of Middle Eastern Food.* Owens had recently gone freelance and moved from New York to Vermont, a connection Close knew Judith would appreciate. She was also, apropos to the subject at hand, a serious home cook. Right away, Owens proved herself quick and fastidious, someone Judith could rely on and trust. The timing proved not a moment too soon, as by the fall of 1971, Judith was in way over her head.

In the same month she signed Madhur Jaffrey, Judith took on yet another ambitiously complex cookbook, this one on Chinese cuisine. Its author was the Shanghai-born Manhattan restaurateur Irene Kuo. Though Chinese restaurants had grown popular in the United States, Judith had yet to see a cookbook that she felt clearly taught, explained, and celebrated China's rich and diverse culinary culture. When she read Kuo's manuscript, she knew she had to have the book. Kuo was not only talented at the stove but also with her pen. "She had a gift with language," Judith later said. "She talked about 'velveting' little pieces of chicken, 'slippery coating' them. You could practically eat the words, they were so seductive."

Millie Owens gave Judith the reliable support she needed. In February 1972, as Judith sent off the latest manuscript in need of Owens's careful touch, she wrote, "Thank heavens I am able to turn this over to your capable hands because I have an uneasy feeling that it still needs a very sharp eye and a good deal of common sense applied to it." Owens's foremost job was to ensure the consistency and clarity of every recipe in a book. But Judith also asked her to weigh in on bigger-picture aspects, including overall structure, organization, terminology, and flow, and the style, content, and tone of the headnotes to each recipe. When Judith sent Owens Madhur Jaffrey's manuscript, she enclosed a note detailing "what needs to be done on Jaffrey's book," and asked Owens for suggestions for the book's title as well. "You really feel she has translated these dishes to America just as she herself has been transplanted." For that reason, "the title must be personal," Judith said.

Food had become a haven for Judith, a space in which she felt safe. "My little cocoon," she said. It also became a crucible through which she grew and transformed. It didn't happen in isolation but rather together with her cookbook authors, the vast majority of whom were women, extraordinary ones at that. "They weren't little housewives," Judith explained. "It took courage to be who they were." Judith wanted her cookbooks to invite intimate engagement, to become a part of reader-cooks' worldviews and lives. "How we finally broke through," Judith told me, "was doing, *creating* cookbooks that empowered you, that stimulated you. That you're really learning. And once you've learned that technique you don't have to read the five pages. It's up here," she said, pointing to her head.

CHAPTER 13

The gifts poured in to room 905. Dick brought Judith tulips. Alfred Knopf had sent a mixed spring bouquet. His second wife, Helen (they'd married in Rio in April 1967, less than a year after Blanche's death), had sent yellow tulips; and Judith's cousin Jane Gunther an azalea plant. There were roses from world-renowned pianist Arthur Rubinstein and his wife, Nela; Judith had acquired his two-part memoir for Knopf. Bob Gottlieb and his wife, Maria, had sent Judith a mustard pot. Aunt Helen, slippers. And, together, the Childs and James Beard had sent a dozen splits of champagne, a preemptive toast to Judith's recovery and return to good health. It was Saturday, February 26, 1972, and Judith was in bed at Lenox Hill hospital, groggily waking up from an anesthetic sleep.

Two weeks earlier, the editor had been at work on a run-of-the-mill day when she began to bleed while standing in the cubicle of her assistant, Nancy Nicholas. It came on suddenly and heavily, that rush of red between her legs; "she poured blood," Nicholas recalled. But rather than go to the hospital, Judith "went to the bathroom," Nicholas said, then "came back to her desk." "It seemed impossible" to Nicholas, given the amount of blood she'd seen moments before. But Judith finished out the day as though nothing were amiss.

Judith's periods had never stopped giving her problems. Long after she'd abandoned the possibility of bearing children, she'd learned that the cyclical agony she experienced and her inability to conceive had a cause and a name: endometriosis. In the bodies of those afflicted, the endometrium—the lining of blood and tissue that thickens inside the uterus each month in preparation to receive a fertilized egg—grows elsewhere in the body. Endometriosis causes inflammation, excessive bleeding, nausea, and fatigue during menstrual periods, and often gives rise to chronic pain and infertility. Its cause remains unclear. And while treatment options have improved for the roughly 10 percent of women and girls of reproductive age afflicted by the condition, at the time of this writing, there is still no cure.

The night of the incident, Judith went to the hospital seeking help. They told her to see her doctor. The following day, her gynecologist told Judith that a radical hysterectomy—the removal of the uterus, cervix, ovaries, and fallopian tubes—would be the only fix. Judith kept quiet about it at work. Endometriosis had long been understudied and ignored by the medical community at large. The symptoms women suffering from the condition reported were often considered psychosomatic and far less severe than those experiencing them said they were. As more and more women entered the paid workforce in the mid–twentieth century, doctors began calling endometriosis the "career women's disease." Medical practitioners believed that by delaying marriage and pregnancy to pursue careers, women brought that affliction upon themselves. Doctors' skepticism rendered many women silent about the malady, muzzled by stigma and shame.

In the two weeks between her initial appointment and her operation, Judith carried on as usual, her schedule fully packed. Two days after seeing the doctor, she flew to Boston to meet with the crew of *The French Chef* at WBGH. She spent most of the weekend in Cambridge with the Childs, then, on Sunday, went to Ipswich to have lunch with John Updike before catching the train back to New York. The following workweek proceeded as usual, though Judith did cancel her evening plans. Saturday, February 19, Judith and Dick went to Connecticut for lunch with Dick's daughter Bronwyn, then hosted Judith's mother, Phyllis, and aunt Hilda for dinner that evening at home. Pamela, Dick's other daughter, and her family came to visit on Tuesday after Judith got home from work.

Judith had kept her assistant in the dark about what was afoot. The editor said only that she'd be out of the office for a while, and asked Nicholas to forward any mail that arrived at Knopf in her absence to her home address. On the night of February 24, Judith checked into the hospital. She had surgery the following morning.

Over the next few days, visitors spilled into Judith's room. In the evenings, Dick brought dinner he'd prepared so the two could eat together. He stayed until Judith was worn out from talking and ready to sleep. On Sunday, March 5, Judith was discharged and returned home. Enforced rest wasn't easy for the editor, especially not with the crop of books she had that year. John Hersey's, *The Conspiracy*, had launched on January 1; Judith hated being laid up during its initial publicity buzz. Anna Thomas's *The Vegetarian Epicure* was due out in spring, and Kit Foster's gardening book in summer. Judith had muscled her way through fraught work on a solo cookbook with Simone Beck; *Simca's Cuisine* would come out later that year. And Claudia Roden's *A Book of Middle Eastern Food* was on the list for fall. In April, Knopf would put out the American edition of *The Least and Vilest Things*, a debut novel with a feminist hue by Elizabeth North, a British mother of four. Judith had purchased its American rights the year before; Knopf would publish North's book under the title *Summer Solstice*. There was Anne Tyler's latest, *The Clock Winder*, forthcoming in May, and a short story collection from John Updike called *Museums and Women* in early fall. Nineteen seventy-two was shaping up to be a tremendous year for Judith at Knopf. And though she may have been bedridden, she refused to be derailed.

To lessen the menopausal symptoms the hysterectomy would induce, Judith began hormone replacement therapy (HRT). It was the same pharmaceutical regimen Julia Child had been put on after her own hysterectomy almost exactly a decade before. When Judith confided in Julia about her surgery, Julia urged her not to follow in her post-op path. In 1968, Julia had been diagnosed with breast cancer and her surgeons removed her breast. Julia was certain the synthetic hormones—the same ones Judith's doctors were recommending she take—had caused the malignancy. "Well," Judith told me, "I had a very forceful doctor who said, 'You *must* take these hormones; you won't be yourself.'" So Judith put her trust in modern medicine and began taking the pills. She was told that the surgery combined with HRT would make "a new woman" of her with "at least three more hours of energy a day."

Just two weeks after surgery, Judith was working full tilt again. To her trusty copy editor, Millie Owens, Judith wrote in early March: "I am at home recuperating from an operation (nothing serious—a hysterectomy—but it takes time to mend). Right, on to business then." She waited but a few days more before she began socializing again; on March 10, Judith hosted family for dinner at home with Dick. The following Monday, she went into the office for the first time to check in. And on Thursday, the 16th—just three weeks out from her surgery—Judith and Dick boarded a plane to Puerto Rico for a quick vacation. They were back in Manhattan Sunday night. On Monday morning, March 20, Judith returned to the office full-time. The week before, she had turned forty-eight years old; she was firmly middle-aged. She was firing on all cylinders, and her list was beyond full. After so many years of tireless work and mounting crescendo, her career was reaching its dynamic peak.

. . . .

Early on a bright summer morning, Judith dug through a moving box of clothes, looking for something suitable to wear to work. She and Dick had just moved back to 139 East 66th Street, not to the small, quirky penthouse this time—they felt they'd outgrown it—but to Phyllis's more spacious apartment, 9N. Since Judith's mother had moved full-time to Vermont, the unit had been sitting empty, collecting dust. To provide a down payment, Dick and Judith sold their apartment upstairs, which they had been subletting since Chris and Audrey's arrival a decade earlier. They financed the rest at a hefty interest rate (in 1972, there was no other kind). Apartment 9N would be the Joneses' final address in New York. On top of the move, Judith had been monstrously busy since she'd returned to the office that spring. She'd had no time yet to unpack. She dug out a skirt and blouse that she thought would do for the day, and ironed them on a towel flung over a taped-up box marked "books." Dressed, she hurried out the door and set off at a brisk pace to walk to work. Kit Foster's *The Organic Gardener* was set to arrive at Knopf that day.

In the year and a half since Judith had signed Kit to do her gardening book, food as a means of social activism had burst onto the scene. In their monthly supply letter in June 1971, the United Fresh Fruit and Vegetable Association issued a response to the "Organic Food Kick," which was gaining followers by the day. The Big Ag-controlled group wanted to dispel what they called myths of harm caused by chemical pesticides and fertilizers to the natural environment and humans, both. In September of that year, timed almost as if in direct response, Frances Moore Lappé released her book, *Diet for a Small Planet*. Based in Berkeley, California, Lappé had grown up, she wrote, "believing my government represented me—my basic ideals." But she'd learned, "'my' government was not mine at all. Something had to be done, *now*." *Diet* channeled the younger generation's growing disillusionment with government policy into actionable steps on an individual scale. Lappé urged readers to think globally while acting locally, treading more lightly on Earth by eating organic and vegetarian while simultaneously working for political change.

Diet hit the bestseller list; it became an instant classic among the progressive left. But Lappé's recipes, which focused on self-sacrifice as an act of political martyrdom, were flavorless and drab. Judith was irked that *Diet* had beaten the books she'd done with Kit Foster and Anna Thomas to shelves. But she took heart knowing that both her authors' books had a strength Lappé's lacked: they had pleasure at the fore. Everyone, Judith knew, regardless of their politics, preferred delicious food over dull. She believed it would be enough of a leg up to help Thomas's and Foster's books break through. And though Judith would have preferred her books to have been the first out of the gate, she couldn't deny that *Diet* primed the pump for both *The Vegetarian Epicure*'s and *The Organic Gardener*'s success.

In April 1972, when the first copies of *The Vegetarian Epicure* had come in, Judith mailed a copy to Anna Thomas in L.A. "Here is the masterpiece! I find it irresistible," the editor wrote. The *Times* called the book "lovely" and "comprehensive. . . . There is nothing cranky about the food; it just tastes very good and is easy to cook," critic Nika Hazelton said. Judith wrote Thomas to report that "a man, name of Battersby, I believe, who is starting a new magazine, to be called FOOD AND WINE, came to see me about some Knopf good backlist books he wanted to have reviewed. He said if the magazine got off the ground, he would like to have a regular feature on vegetarian cooking and I recommended you. So I hope maybe something will come of it." She continued, "I also had lunch recently with William Maxwell," the *New Yorker* editor and writer whose own writing Judith edited at Knopf (she'd published his memoir, *Ancestors*, the year before). "He said that your book had literally saved his life. They have two teenage daughters who have both turned vegetarian and the whole family had been eating dreary basement vegetarian fare until you came along."

At first, all Judith's praise had little impact on Thomas; she was consumed with classes and making her film. But one day, when she was walking down Hollywood Boulevard with friends, one of them exclaimed, "Look at that!" Thomas looked up to see copies of her book taking up an entire bookshop window's display. "It was around that time," Thomas told me, laughing, "I began to realize it was a thing." Receiving royalty checks and notices about the sale of foreign rights made the book's success even more real. "Your book seems to be doing so steadily well," Judith wrote Thomas. "I'm sure [it] has lots of life in it for some time to come and should buy you a good deal of film." *The Vegetarian Epicure* was a hit.

Kit Foster's *The Organic Gardener*, which came out soon after *The Vegetarian Epicure*, quickly found an audience, too. Its emphasis on ecological smallholder gardens and farms provided a timely retort to the 1971 appointment of Earl Butz as secretary of agriculture. Butz urged American farmers to plant commodity crops like feed corn and soy "fencerow to fencerow"; his mantra was "get big or get out." The *Times Book Review* celebrated the utility of Foster's book, calling it "gently forceful" and "wholesome as the fresh Vermont mountain air." The paper gave the book more play still in their year-end book review. The coverage paid off. Before the 1972 holiday shopping blitz was over, *The Organic Gardener* had gone into its third printing. Judith wrote Kit: "I am happy to see I find the paperback copy in a lot of the special health food stores and such around here. And I suspect it is going to be around for a long time."

Over that spring and summer, Judith prepared for the launch of Roden's *Book of Middle Eastern Food*; it would come out in September 1972. The editor helped craft flap copy intended to give the book the broadest possible appeal. Since Richard Nixon had taken office as president in January 1969, the cost of eating in America had been on the rise. Meat, in particular, had skyrocketed in price. "At a time when food costs are soaring," Judith wrote, "here is a cuisine that is particularly appealing because it offers new and delicious ways of using less expensive cuts of meat and nutritious grains and legumes." While Judith knew Roden's book would be attractive to already adventurous cooks and eaters, she hoped to use the framing of affordability to seduce many more. The editor sent personalized letters to specialty food shops and bookstores across the country, urging them to both stock the products needed to makes Roden's dishes and to prominently display her cookbook alongside. Judith thought placing essential ingredients and the cookbook next to one another would incline customers to buy both.

Roden footed the bill to fly to New York from London for her book's release. She could stay only a few days, as she had three children under twelve back home. Judith wanted to help Roden make the best of her short time in the States. To give the book and its unknown author the strongest possible start, Judith had asked James Beard for help. Since she'd met him when preparing to launch *Mastering* in 1961, the two had become acquaintances, saying hello at food events and such. But in the early 1970s Judith had gotten it into her head that somebody needed to do a book on bread. "All these sixties counterculture people were making their own bread," she told me, "and there were no bread books!" Judith thought Beard, with his name recognition, his cooking school, and his huge nationwide readership, was the perfect person for the job.

At lunch, "We just had fun and hit it off," Judith recalled. At the time, Beard was putting together *American Cookery*, which Little, Brown would publish in 1972. He couldn't yet see beyond the project with which he was still in the midst, but Beard said he'd give some thought to doing a bread book for Knopf down the line. "We had a second lunch and maybe a third," Judith told me, before, at last, Beard said to her, "Look, I'd like to do that bread book." Judith, Beard, and his cowriting team began work right away on what became the 1973 bestseller, *Beard on Bread*. Judith grew to know Beard—Jim, to those he knew personally—closely, as both an author and friend. She particularly appreciated his generosity when it came to helping others; Judith saw it as a characteristic that "kind of went with food." When the prepublication galleys of Roden's *Book of Middle Eastern Food* came in, Judith gave a copy to Jim. He was impressed and offered to put the weight of his name behind the book. "A landmark in the field of cookery," he called *A Book of Middle Eastern Food.*

He also offered to host a fete to celebrate the launch of Roden's book, with an invite list four pages long. It was a veritable who's who of the American food scene, a world that had continued to grow in size and influence. Ray Sokolov, food critic of the *Times*, came, as did Paul and Julia Child. So did Joseph Baum of the Four Seasons restaurant; Gael Greene; the Canadian food writer Helen McCully; and Mimi Sheraton, who'd just written a remarkable piece on tasting everything in the Bloomingdale's food department—1,196 items over 11 months—for *New York* magazine. Judith made sure to invite everyone in her Rolodex who was at all connected to food, as well as editors and reporters from all the glossies and the *New Yorker*, the *Washington Post*, *Newsweek*, and *Time*. Generally speaking, Judith spent as little time with "the foodies," as she called them, reflecting on that era, as she could. She wished she could entirely avoid their "very catty" scene. But she understood that showing her face and making contacts in the food establishment was a crucial part of promoting cookbooks. Judith wrote to Roden, preparing her for the fractious milieu. "All this sounds terribly crass," Judith conceded, "but that's how one sells books."

Roden didn't find the overt marketing of herself and her cookbook distasteful at all. In fact, she loved being in the limelight on tour. Soon after she returned home to London after the initial publicity blitz, the author wrote Judith saying she wanted to return again to the States to do more events. Judith connected Roden with Jane Friedman, who'd piloted Julia Child's 1968 book tour to such success. Together, Judith, Friedman, and Roden made a schedule for Roden to give talks and cooking demonstrations across the United States for several weeks in 1973. And while *A Book of Middle Eastern Food*'s sales may have been modest in comparison to *The French Chef*'s, Judith was nonetheless pleased at how Roden's book caught on. In May 1973, Judith wrote, "Your lovely Middle Eastern Food, while it did not exactly take the whole country by storm immediately, continues to delight us because people keep on discovering it and the orders are coming in steadily week by week, which means it is being bought."

While Claudia Roden was out on tour in the spring of 1973, Knopf published Madhur Jaffrey's *An Invitation to Indian Cooking*. Just as she'd done for *Middle Eastern Food*, Judith rolled up her sleeves and got to work spreading word about the book. She wrote to bookstores across the country, asking that they put Jaffrey's book on prominent display. She also reached out to specialty grocers in New York and DC, requesting that they stock some of the harder-to-find ingre-

dients in the book like whole spices, fresh cilantro, and ginger root. Jane Fried-
man arranged for Jaffrey to give cooking demonstrations at New Jersey's busiest
Bloomingdale's branches in Hackensack and Short Hills. And Judith got Jim
Beard to let Jaffrey use his teaching kitchen to hold classes in Manhattan. Judith
put the book in the hands of Ray Sokolov at the *Times*; he wrote it up the month
it launched, calling *Invitation* "the most useful and interesting introduction to
Indian food that I have ever seen." (In the same review, he covered *The Classic
Italian Cookbook* by Marcella Hazan. Soon thereafter, Judith would bring Hazan
to Knopf.) To Leo Lerman, an editor at Condé Nast, Judith wrote. "I understand
you were hoping to have Jaffrey do something for *Vogue* for a midsummer issue.
I know other magazines are interested and we want to get her as much exposure
as possible, but you are there first so could you let me know as soon as possible,
particularly if you want to use something from the book." It was only later that
Jaffrey realized the impact of Judith's multipronged approach. "She was really
making an author," she said.

It wasn't only Indian food Judith felt she must make legible to an American
audience; it was also the cultural context of Jaffrey herself. In *Invitation*'s introduction, Judith had insisted Jaffrey address potential barriers of understanding
and any tentativeness on readers' parts. "I have tried to begin each chapter with
the simpler recipes, those which are easier to make and not too surprising to
the palate," the editor coached Jaffrey to write. Judith saw it as incumbent upon
her authors to explain their identities to their readers, rather than putting the
onus on a book's audience to do the work of understanding themselves. While
the ease-in method may have increased the popular appeal of non-European
cuisines, it further exoticized authors of color and their food. Judith's approach
revealed the assumed whiteness of cookbooks' readership, as well as of her own
gaze.

The subjects of food writing in America were becoming increasingly diverse,
but the gatekeepers of the culinary media were not. The world of cookbooks was
a privileged one; only those with ties and access to white culture-making institu-
tions and people in power got in. Julia Child, Kit Foster, and Anna Thomas were
all prime examples. Julia Child had worked her own personal ties to the publishing
world to push *Mastering* through to publication, while Judith had hand-picked
Foster from the faculty of one of the priciest private colleges in the United States.
And Thomas had hardly had to leave her student flat to get an agent to sell her
book to Knopf. With the exception of her cookbook authors who'd been born
abroad, the circles in which Judith moved remained almost entirely white. (Two
decades into the twenty-first century, the racial gap in publishing still yawns appallingly wide; in 2018, it was estimated that between 76 and 84 percent of those

working at all levels of the publishing industry self-identified as white.) It wasn't a disconnect Judith paid much attention to, or a tension she seemed to perceive at all. Indeed, she'd never given much thought to how racial and class dynamics were reflected in America's food. It wasn't until Judith encountered a remarkable American cook that her thinking began to change.

CHAPTER 14

Judith sat at her desk beside a stack of copies of *The Taste of Country Cooking*. She picked one up and flipped through its pages, glancing at the menu for "Breakfast Before Leaving for Race Day" with sour-milk griddle cakes and pear preserves; "Hunting Season Dinner" with purée of black-eyed peas, lamb's quarters, and green tomato preserves. It was the spring of 1976. For that time of year, the book's author, Edna Lewis, suggested a breakfast of pan-fried shad with its roe, wild strawberry preserves, those most fleeting seasonal delights, as well as steamed whole hominy, honey from woodland bees, and dandelion blossom wine. Turning back to the book's introduction, Judith found herself moved, all over again, by *Taste*'s opening lines. "I grew up in Freetown, Virginia, a community of farming people. It wasn't really a town," Lewis had written. "The name was adopted because the first residents had all been freed from chattel slavery and they wanted to be known as a town of Free People. My grandfather had been one of the first." It had taken four years, but the book was finally done, and it was gorgeous. Knopf would publish *Taste* just weeks before the nation's bicentennial anniversary, July 4, 1976. The whole country was abuzz with discussion of what, two hundred years into its existence, it meant to be American and how to commemorate the nation's history. Judith aimed to position Edna Lewis's *The Taste of Country Cooking* as a powerful and provocative response, one packaged in the unlikely form of a cookbook.

It had started back in September of 1971 when Evangeline Peterson, a philanthropist involved in arts and education, who was then a recently divorced mother of two teenage children and completing her social work degree, wrote to her friend Bob Bernstein, head of Random House, asking for his help. Peterson had been writing a cookbook together with Edna Lewis, a cook who'd long been renowned among New York's elite. In late 1948, Lewis became chef and part owner of Café Nicholson on East 58th Street near the Queensboro Bridge. The restaurant was the brainchild of antiques dealer Johnny Nicholson and photographer Karl Bissinger; they were partners in business and in life. Like Judith, the two men had been in Paris the heady summer of that year. They'd palled around with Tennessee Williams and Gore Vidal, part of the gay bohemian scene. Both writers became regulars of Café Nicholson and brought with them a star-studded clientele. Paul Robeson dined there. Eleanor Roosevelt did, too. A photo taken in the restaurant's garden features Tanaquil Le Clercq, who danced for Balanchine at New York City Ballet, standing beside a table at which Tennessee Williams, Gore Vidal, the novelist Donald Windham, and the abstract painter Buffie Johnson were seated.

Café Nicholson quickly earned a reputation for its salon-like atmosphere and its superb, French-inflected fare. When William Faulkner dined at the café, he popped into the kitchen to ask Lewis if she had trained in Paris. "I was flattered of course," Lewis later said, "but more flattered that I hadn't." Lewis had learned everything she knew about food from her late mother, and she honed her craft at a woodstove in the Virginia countryside. Lewis's cooking drew together a range of culinary influences, but its roots were in the American South. Fellow southerners living in New York, including Truman Capote and Tennessee Williams, begged Lewis to prepare fried chicken and biscuits, foods that worked on them like Proust's madeleines, conjuring memories of home.

Café Nicholson was heralded for its food, but its chef remained largely hidden from view. When Clementine Paddleford reviewed Nicholson in the *New York Herald Tribune* in 1951, she homed in on the restaurant's—by which she meant, though did not say, Edna Lewis's—flawless chocolate soufflé. While Lewis cooked in the kitchen alongside her younger sister, Ruth, Johnny Nicholson worked the dining room. The restaurant's food might have been Black, but its public face was white.

· · · · · · ·

Lewis left Café Nicholson in 1954. She and her husband, Steve Kingston, moved to New Jersey, where they tried pheasant farming for a while. But when a disease decimated their flock, the venture flopped. Broke and deflated, they moved back into the city—Harlem this time—to try to get back on their feet and remap a plan for their lives. The move put Lewis at the heart of the Black Arts Movement that explored the question, per the poet and publisher Haki Madhubuti: "How do we become a whole people, and how do we begin to essentially tell our narrative?" The movement—whose most influential figures included Amiri Baraka, Audre Lorde, Ntozake Shange, Larry Neal, Nikki Giovanni, Sonia Sanchez, and June Jordan—made an indelible imprint on Lewis's political and artistic sense of self. In an act of self-determination, she opened a restaurant of her own in Harlem. But, as the vast majority of restaurants do, it closed not long after its debut. With no high school diploma and few job options available to her, Lewis reluctantly turned to domestic work.

At a time when more and more white women were entering the paid workforce outside the home, opportunities for women of color lagged far behind. In 1960, more than 33 percent of all Black women were employed as domestic servants ("private household workers," the census called them), while only 3.2 percent of white women held such jobs. The divide illuminated the friction and dissonance between the largely white second wave feminist movement, whose leaders included Betty Friedan and Gloria Steinem, and the activism of Black women. While white feminists largely emphasized the fight for gender equality with their white male counterparts, Black women organized not only around their own and their families' needs but on behalf of liberation more broadly. The lawyer and priest Pauli Murray used her legal expertise to advocate for civil and human rights protections for women of color, queer women, and femmes, while welfare activist Johnnie Tillmon crusaded for governmental support to ensure poor women's and mothers' access to food, stable housing, and affordable health care and childcare.

Throughout the 1950s and 1960s, Lewis worked, cooking and doing household chores, in white women's homes, as she had, intermittently throughout her youth in Virginia. Among New York's elite, word of Lewis's exceptional cooking quickly spread. By the mid-sixties, her employers and their friends had begun to ask her to cater tony dinner parties and private events. That's how Lewis met Evangeline Peterson, and it was Peterson who proposed Lewis write a cookbook. Lewis insisted that she was a cook, not a writer. Peterson volunteered to help.

Together, they'd compiled some of Lewis's most inventive recipes into *The Edna Lewis Cookbook*. The book spoke to Lewis's experience, skill, and range, as well as the globalization of the American palate of the times: There were coquilles St.-Jacques; gazpacho; shrimp curry; pork ribs smothered in ground peanuts;

and ketjap benteng asin, a sweet Indonesian soy sauce. The *Edna Lewis Cookbook* marked Lewis's unwillingness to be defined by or adhere to "the knee-slapping, cornpone image of Southern food" or those who cooked it. Peterson hoped she might be able to work her connections to get somebody with pull with the food media to help spread the word about the book. Bob Bernstein pointed Peterson toward Judith, who he thought might have some ideas.

Peterson promptly wrote to Judith, asking if the editor would take a look at her and Lewis's work. Lewis's cooking, Peterson said, was the best she'd ever tasted, including in Paris. She also mentioned the seed of an idea she had for a next book. During their time working together on the cookbook, Peterson wrote, Lewis spoke often of the foods she'd helped to grow, cook, and eat as a child in Freetown, Virginia. It was there that Edna Lewis was born in 1916.

Lewis's kin had cleared the land themselves. Education was a top priority— Lewis's grandfather helped establish a one-room schoolhouse and hired Isabella Lightfoot, a Black graduate of Oberlin, to teach. But subsistence living was at Freetown's core. Lewis's family and their neighbors hunted, raised livestock, planted fruit trees, and lived by the season's rhythms and demands. They gathered mushrooms from the woods and wild asparagus along the fence rows; and they knew where in the creek the lushest clusters of watercress grew. The community was anchored by intergenerational collectivity and an ethic of care for the land. Their communal way of life served as a retort to the white supremacist system of capitalism its residents sought to escape.

By economic measures, Freetown and its residents were poor; what money they had came mostly from wages they earned working piecemeal jobs for nearby white families. It was work Lewis, her sisters, and mother all did at times. In those white households, Black folks learned French cooking. It was a legacy imprinted on Virginia's Piedmont region by Thomas Jefferson, a notorious Francophile and slaveholder. Over the generations, the women of Freetown integrated the techniques of *la cuisine bourgeoise* with traditions of their own. As Lewis later wrote, "What began as hard work became creative work. . . . It has nothing to do with reading or writing. Many of those cooks could not read or write." With experimentation and ingenuity, the people of Freetown developed a vernacular cuisine reflective of their place, race, and time. It was a culinary riff as Black and American as jazz. That distinct regionality, ethos, resourcefulness, and skill made Lewis's cooking stand out.

Peterson had heard Lewis speak eloquently about the flavor of wild greens and homemade preserves, the taste of fruits that were never sprayed, and eggs from hens who were free to roam and peck. "It's not our intention to write a 'natural foods' cookbook," Lewis's collaborator wrote to Judith. "Rather, what we have in mind is a book which will describe the natural or commonsense approach to food gathering and preparation which has been typical of many generations in the particular area of the country in which Edna grew up."

Judith asked to see a copy of the pair's current cookbook. But by the time Peterson had reached out to Judith, *The Edna Lewis Cookbook* was already on its way to press. Judith, however, was intrigued by what Peterson had written about Lewis's past. She asked to see a fleshed-out proposal of the next book's concept and a few sample recipes whenever the duo had something to show.

Two months later, Peterson wrote Judith somewhat at a loss. "Attached are some of Edna's reminiscences about special holidays in Orange County," she said. "The way of life and special customs of Freetown are especially fascinating, although we're not certain they belong in the book." When Lewis spoke of Freetown, Peterson wrote, she sometimes made mention of "the shackles of slavery" in the same breath that she exalted the honey of ripe peaches. Lewis wanted to include mention of her enslaved grandmother, how she'd been forced to leave her babies alone in their cribs all day while she laid bricks. Such stories, Peterson feared, would interfere with the "lightness and easy flow I so wanted to achieve." Before pushing the project any farther along, she wanted Judith to weigh in.

Before encountering Edna Lewis, Judith had never taken a sustained look at the deep pain contained in the stories of American food. But she didn't share Peterson's concerns about Lewis's desire to mention the more political or difficult contours of her past at all. Rather, she felt such details lent Lewis's story historical context illustrative of the essential contribution the book stood to make. Just before Christmas 1971, Judith responded to Peterson: "The material is so interesting and remembered with such genuineness of heart. If you can keep this sort of thing up, it seems to me you might very well have a book that I feel we could publish successfully. And I know the recipes are going to be good." Judith encouraged Peterson to continue following Lewis's lead. In February 1972, Peterson sent Judith a more detailed outline with a note saying she and Lewis could adjust the proposed length "according to what aspect of the book we decide to emphasize—the reminiscences or recipes." Judith invited the pair in to the office to meet.

Edna Lewis cut a figure in her full-length, brightly colored batik skirt with a matching scarf draped around her long, elegant neck. In the decades she'd lived in New York, she'd become more outward in her articulation of her Black identity as she learned more about the history and politics of the African diaspora. By then, Lewis was working part-time in the African Hall of the American Museum of Natural History. She spoke to visitors about the myriad influences of African cultures on the United States while donning African-inspired garb she sewed herself. She wore her graying hair pulled back into a tidy bun and long earrings that swung as she moved her head. "I was immediately struck by Edna's regal presence," Judith later wrote.

The three women sat and talked in Judith's office. Judith asked Lewis a few questions prompted by the anecdotes on the pages Peterson had sent in. Lewis spoke lyrically of her upbringing in Freetown and the worldview it had nurtured in her. Judith was moved by Lewis's story, and her detailed remembrance of it all. It was obvious to Judith that Lewis had another book in her, one even more personal and poetic than what the outline Peterson had put together proposed. On April 4, the pair signed a contract with Knopf for a cookbook to be delivered by end of July 1973.

The manuscript was slow in coming. But in April 1973, when Judith read the pages that had finally arrived, she sounded the alarm. The book as it was written wasn't working at all. Peterson's translation, Judith determined, was muffling Lewis's singular voice. Peterson, to her credit, agreed. In February 1974, more than six months after the book's due date, all three parties signed off on a severance agreement, terminating Peterson's role in the book. It was then that Judith began working closely with Lewis herself. "We decided that we would try to talk out the book and that after each session she would go home and immediately put down what she had told me. It worked miraculously. The first sample Edna brought me . . . was written on legal-size lined yellow paper, and the words flowed," Judith later wrote. Working in tandem, they were underway.

By the time Judith met Edna Lewis, Black American women had been resourcefully blending Indigenous, European, and African ingredients and culinary techniques for more than two centuries, resulting in what is considered the first truly American cuisine. For just as long, Black women's artistry had been appropriated by white women; Black women's food was often featured in cookbooks, but their recipes were rarely credited as their own. Of the estimated one hundred thousand collections of recipes printed in the first two centuries of the United States's existence, only about two hundred were attributed to Black cooks. Black women's "poignant absence" from southern cookbooks belied their centrality in the construction and keeping of southern food traditions and American culture at large.

It wasn't until the Great Migration that southern Black culture gained visibility and influence outside the region; from 1917 to 1970, more than six million Black southerners left for the cities of the North and Midwest. In 1918, Black folks started a renaissance in Harlem, an upswell of music, poetry, and artistic styles described as both "fine" and "folk." They brought their cooking, too.

Black food traditions with roots in the South were lumped together under the banner of Soul. "Soul food" was narrowly linked to poverty, racist imagery, and "backwards" ways, rather than recognized as a product of the diverse traditions and creative inventiveness from which it was born. In the wake of the civil rights movement, Black food writers began to push back against such reductive stereotypes. In 1970, poet, radio broadcaster, and self-described "Gullah-Geechee girl" Vertamae Smart-Grosvenor put out *Vibration Cooking*. The next year, chef, social worker, and scholar Helen Mendes published *The African Heritage Cookbook*. Both books combined African American culinary history and innovation with a feminism oriented toward Black women's self-love. They were infused with "culture, emotional flexibility, and strength," what the writer Alice Walker later dubbed "womanism," and anticipated the notion of intersectionality, "a lens through which you can see where power comes and collides, where it interlocks and intersects," a theory coined by law professor Kimberlé Crenshaw in 1989. But Judith hadn't registered the publication or impact of such critical corrective works. She knew nothing about the nuances of Black American foodways, nor of their immense influence on the nation's food overall. Other than Edie, her family's maid when she was a child—who was not African American but Caribbean by birth—Judith hardly knew any Black people at all.

In the summer of 1974, Lewis went home to Virginia for several weeks, as she did each year. She was there to help her sister pick and put up the summer harvest and to celebrate Homecoming. Lewis wrote to Judith about her days. She was picking wild blackberries, making German sweet pickles, and picking crab apples for jellies, she said. She'd also gone to several local archives, searching for records that named Freetown's first settlers and detailed their purchase of the community's land. Though autonomous Black communities like Freetown proliferated in the South after the Civil War, their existence had been omitted from dominant historical narratives of the nation's past.

Reading Lewis's missives from Orange County, Judith could tell the writer was getting closer to the essence of the book. Judith urged Lewis to keep digging for as much historical detail as she could find. "The book is rooted in tradition. The more you know about the past, the more graphically you can describe it. Gather as much information as you can. I am glad you are having a rewarding time again [with] all the good things of the earth. I envy you. All the right feelings are here, and it shouldn't be hard to put together. It is going to be a wonderful book, I'm convinced."

Judith was as eager as Lewis to dive into the world of Freetown and learn more about its past. Since returning from France, Judith had trained her culinary interest outward, focusing on foreign cuisines. Before meeting Lewis, Judith hadn't given much credence to America's foodways at all. But Lewis's distinct way with food and the particularities of place and culture from which she had sprung began to reshape Judith's perspective on U.S. regional cuisines. Judith wanted to ensure that Lewis's book positioned her not only as an adept and resourceful cook but as a bearer of critically important American history as well.

. . . .

That autumn, when Lewis returned to New York, she and Judith worked with sustained focus to finalize the manuscript. Lewis tested the recipes in the South Bronx apartment she shared with her husband and her niece, Nina, the daughter of Edna's younger sister Naomi. Naomi had previously lived with them, too, but, suffering from a flare-up of tuberculosis brought on by the incineration of trash in her building, she'd left her daughter in Edna's care, and had gone to seek treatment at the Hospital of the University of Pennsylvania in Philadelphia. Ruth, another Lewis sister—the same one who'd formerly been in the kitchen with Edna at Café Nicholson—worked at UPenn as a data processor, which enabled her to keep a close eye on Naomi, who stayed with Ruth for several months to recuperate after her hospital release.

Nina watched as her aunt Edna worked diligently to adapt the dishes, which she'd learned to cook on a woodstove, to a modern kitchen range. Lewis threw out attempt after failed attempt; her aunt wasn't satisfied, Nina told me, until she felt she'd successfully replicated the taste of home. At one point, Lewis even had her sister Jenny mail her a box of ash from her woodstove in Virginia to help evoke the flavor she was reaching toward. Once each recipe had been finalized and her aunt Edna's notes were all written out, Nina typed them up and sent them to Judith. Judith added each new recipe to the book's file as she received them, and began organizing the book into sections by season, working on Lewis's detailed observations from her recent trip home and smoothing out her prose.

In the spring of 1976, when the advance reader copies of *Taste of Country Cooking* came in, Judith couldn't wait to show off the book. She sent out copy after copy, each with a personalized letter, telling everyone she knew in the food world about Edna Lewis and her remarkable book. Judith began with her own authors; she was intent that they know one another's work. To Anna Thomas, whose second volume of *The Vegetarian Epicure* was nearly complete, Judith wrote, "I'm sending you a lovely book which we're just about to publish the end of this month on country cooking written by a remarkable black woman who grew up on a farm in Jefferson country. It's really as much a memoir as a cookbook and I think you'll find it very special. Do write me something about it if you love it as I suspect you will." Judith sent a copy to Mary Frances Kennedy (M. F. K.) Fisher, the California-based writer with whom Judith had struck up a relationship by post in the late 1960s; Judith subsequently become the writer's editor when she published Fisher's *Among Friends* in 1971. Fisher frequently wrote reviews for the *New Yorker*; Judith hoped she'd review Lewis's book there. Fisher "galloped through" *The Taste of Country Cooking*, and told Judith she found Lewis's writing "dignified" and "reticent" in a most uncommonly lovely way. To Craig Claiborne, who was still writing for the food section at the *New York Times*, Judith wrote, "It is such a beautiful expression of a time when eating was both a time for gathering and celebrating and a reward for hard work. I think you will lose your heart to it." Judith sent a copy to David Willis McCullough of the Book-of-the-Month Club, too. He responded with a note calling *Taste* beautiful, and said it was among the "most readable" cookbooks he'd ever seen.

When *The Taste of Country Cooking* launched in June 1976, Mimi Sheraton reviewed the book in the *Times*. In December 1975, she'd replaced Craig Claiborne as the paper's restaurant critic, becoming the first woman to hold the job. Sheraton called *Taste* "a rare combination of simplicity and sophistication," and highlighted Lewis's "style and precision." She swooned over the menus and recipes, a mix, she noted, of dishes commonly thought of as part of the southern food canon, like fried chicken, peach cobbler, griddle cakes, and "more elegant choices" involving wild mushrooms, pheasant, and quail. But the critic made no mention of the memoir-like essays threaded throughout the book or the hard-to-stomach historical anecdotes that punctuated the text. Perhaps Sheraton thought the *Times*'s readership had no appetite for those sorts of heavy matters in the food pages, or that such subjects didn't belong in cookbooks at all. *Taste* was full of stark truths many Americans had long suppressed or had resisted looking directly at. But the book had been ingeniously designed as something of a Trojan horse; in the guise of a cookbook, *Taste* was a work of revisionist history served up slant.

Taste hit shelves just a month before the bicentennial. The anniversary arrived in the midst of an era, as writer and Random House's first Black editor, Toni Morrison, put it, of "contested, fought over, fought for, and fought against public (and publicly expressed) life . . . where issues of conscience, morality, law, and ethics were liberationist rather than oppressive." It was a moment of reflection on the nation's identity, and reckoning with the events that had shaped it over time, including the Civil War. That fall, when Georgian Jimmy Carter won the Democratic bid for the presidency, Americans were reminded of the animosity still smoldering between North and South; it was the first time that a candidate from the Deep South had been the national face of a major political party in 128 years.

Time's September 20, 1976, special issue was titled "The South Today: Carter Country and Beyond." On the cover was an audacious image meant to provoke: the Stars and Stripes enjoined with the Stars and Bars of the Confederate flag. Contributor Paul Gray wrote, "Blacks in increasing numbers are examining their American experience, and for most that story takes shape in the South." The issue pointed to the groundswell of recently published and forthcoming titles that examined the Transatlantic slave trade and the legacy of the peculiar institution itself. On the list was Alex Haley's landmark *Roots*, due out from Doubleday shortly after the *Time* issue hit the newsstands. Lewis's *Taste* was named, though not in the literary roundup. It was siloed in "Modern Living: A Home-Grown Elegance" instead. *Time* called *Taste* one of the most "beguiling—and authoritative—books on the subject" of southern food published to date. (The only other southern cookbook that received mention was *American Cooking: Southern Style*, part of the Time-Life series; it was written by Lewis's dear friend Eugene Walter, an Alabama-born bohemian and gourmand who'd helped George Plimpton start the *Paris Review* in 1953.)

Judith was miffed. She believed *Taste* transcended the food genre and deserved attention as a work of literature and cultural history. "It seems to me, too, that Edna Lewis says some good things about our heritage that I hate to see just buried in a cookbook," she'd said to Bob Manning, an editor at the *Atlantic*, when she'd written encouraging him to excerpt *Taste* in the magazine. "I really feel this book is something special and that Edna Lewis as a black woman writes in a way that no one has quite done—since M. F. K. Fisher perhaps did with her much more privileged past." But critics continued to miss the larger significance of Lewis's book. Knopf seemed to be missing it, too. The house put little effort into publicizing *Taste* when it launched, and for most of the summer of 1976, the book was hard to find in stores. In mid-August, while on her annual pilgrimage home, Lewis wrote to Judith, frustrated and confused. "Everyone I meet talks about the book and everyone seems to have trouble finding it," she remarked.

Try as she did, Judith couldn't convince Knopf to put more muscle behind marketing and distributing *Taste*. Exasperated, in November she wrote to her colleague Dick Liebermann in the sales department, saying Mimi Sheraton was planning to include *Taste* on her list of the year's best books on food in the *Times*. "Now that the hardcover edition of Edna Lewis's *The Taste of Country Cooking* is back in stock I hope we can make a big effort to get it in the stores for Christmas. It has been very hard to find recently in most bookstores—even the paperback—and a lot of people have been asking for it, particularly after the TIME cover story on the South singled it out." Judith ended her memo on a terse note: "Let's try to have it in the stores by the time that [*Times*] article comes out."

On December 5, 1976, Sheraton's roundup ran in the *Times*. In it, she lambasted the explosion in the number of cookbooks published each year as causing a dip in the genre's overall quality. She laid blame at the feet of people of "inordinate wealth" and their endless quest for "new sensations" on their tongues. "But blasé palates," Sheraton wrote, "will get little help from publishers this year for the pickings are among the leanest in a long time." Among the hundreds of culinary books published in 1976, Sheraton wrote that only a handful "seem worthy of shelf space." One of them, she said, was Edna Lewis's *The Taste of Country Cooking*, Sheraton called it "the single most beguiling cookbook of the year." The review gave *Taste* a bump, as did its selection as a book club read by *Better Homes & Gardens* and *Country Journal* in early 1977. Still, sales of Lewis's book remained disappointingly slow.

Personally, though, the impact of working on *Taste* was enormous on author and editor, both. Lewis began hearing from local historical societies about *Taste*'s importance, saying the book illuminated contours of the region's past they hadn't known (or, more likely, had chosen not to see) before. They believed Lewis's work could help broaden the historical narrative of the South that had long focused on "the big houses" and the mythology of enslaved Black people's lives. "Many people think Blacks were only field and house workers," Edna wrote Judith, but "I know of persons that were blacksmiths, carpenters, masons, midwives." Another historian wrote Lewis that her book helped correct the notion that, after Emancipation, all Black people "left for the cities" and abandoned country life. Yet another remarked that *Taste* made clear to him how little was understood about the organization of Freetown and how important it was to study those people and better understand their way of life. "I had never thought of the people of Freetown in those terms. Although I did think they were special," Edna wrote Judith. "We shall see what will come of this idea. It becomes more and more exciting." Lewis's gratitude to her editor was immortalized in print: Lewis's dedication for *Taste* reads: "To the memory of the people of Freetown and to Judith B. Jones, with many thanks for her deep understanding."

Judith, too, found herself profoundly changed by working with Edna Lewis. She had been moved by Lewis's gentleness, quiet confidence, and her unshakable sense of self. "My whole experience with Edna taught me a lot about what I care about, I mean, human nature and that you're responsible for other people," Judith told me. Working so closely on *Taste* helped Judith recognize the depth of her ignorance about her own country and the privilege of her editorial lens. She began to change the way she approached working across lines of identity, especially race and class. "[People] are different, they have different backgrounds, but nobody's better than the other person," Judith told me. "You try to take people for what they are and isolate that quality and encourage it."

If *Taste* couldn't hit big in the culture at large, Judith aimed to at least get Lewis duly recognized within the intimate, quietly powerful culinary circle she'd helped build. In October 1977, Judith invited Edna to New York for a luncheon to celebrate the launch of Irene Kuo's *The Key to Chinese Cooking*. After six years of grueling work, the five-hundred-page book was finally done. (To date, it is still widely considered the best English language Chinese cookbook of all time.) As

Judith's cookbook roster grew, she insisted her authors become familiar with one another's work in order to understand their place within food culture at large. She also wanted them to get to know one another personally. It had been a profound realization for Judith to discover that she wasn't alone in using food to buck tradition in both her work and her larger life. She wanted to ensure her authors had a chance to experience that sense of shared purpose and identity, too. Over the meals Judith and her cookbook authors shared at restaurants, in Judith's apartment, and in their respective homes, the women offered one another mutual uplift and support, traded contacts and publicity strategies, introduced one another to television producers and magazine editors, and hosted events on one another's behalf. It became an informal alliance, a culinary coalition of sorts.

That day at her Manhattan restaurant, Kuo laid out a dazzling spread of dishes, recipes for which she'd included in her book. Among those at the table was Marion Cunningham, a talented cook from California whom Judith had met through Jim Beard, whose assistant Cunningham had become. Judith had since tapped Cunningham to update the nearly two thousand recipes in the 1896 classic *The Boston Cooking-School Cook Book* by Fannie Merritt Farmer—which had come to be known simply as *The Fannie Farmer Cookbook* in later editions—for a new Knopf version. Lewis was awed by Kuo's cooking, but it was the effect of gathering like-minded women that impressed her most. Cunningham, who was fifty-five years old at the time, and Lewis, sixty-one, hit it off right away. Not only would they remain close friends for the rest of their lives but together they'd come to be known as the grande dames of American home cookery. There was such intimacy in swapping stories of past, place, labor, and kin with others who were leading unorthodox lives and who shared an understanding of the language of food, Edna noted in a letter she wrote to Judith afterward. "Everything gave one the feeling of complete familiarity. I felt I gained something—a fresh point of view."

When they were together, Judith and her authors reflected their individual worth at one another. As a group, they were better able to recognize the meaning and importance of their work in food, translating what had long been relegated to the realm of unpaid, domestic labor into careers in the public sphere. Their collective, alternative approach to womanhood and care work permeated American culture. Together, they wrote new rules, charted new paths, and forged new identities in and through food that others would build on for years to come.

CHAPTER 15

Judith had been driving for hours; the trip from Manhattan to the Northeast Kingdom is more than three hundred miles long. As she turned off the interstate and onto Vermont's winding two-lane roads, she cranked her window down to let in the clean country air. Dick, in the passenger seat beside her, followed suit. Judith felt her shoulders fall away from her ears. Being in Vermont always put her into a state of ease and calm. But that summer of 1980 was different. She and Dick weren't going to Phyllis's house in Greensboro to vacation and rest. They were going there to work.

After decades of helping shape others' voices, Judith had decided she was ready to give writing a try. In the late 1970s, she and Angus Cameron, her now retired former mentor at Knopf, began work on a fish and game cookbook for L.L.Bean. About the same time, Judith and Dick joined forces to do a book on bread. Judith had caught the bug during the baguette trials for *Mastering*, Volume Two. Her interest in bread making had been growing since. Judith and Dick experimented with baking everything from the chewy wheat berry loaf in Anna Thomas's *Vegetarian Epicure* to the more than one hundred recipes in *Beard on Bread*. Judith found particular satisfaction in the convergence of good flavor, thrift, and the vigorous physical activity that came from making one's own loaves. But when Dick first posited the idea of their doing a bread book of their own, Judith hadn't been so sure. "With all those cookbooks being published year after year," Judith said, "it's very hard to find something fresh." All the noise made Judith more choosy than ever about which cookbooks she took on. Before she committed to doing one of her own, she would need to be certain that there was a "significant contribution" they could make, and determine "whether we could honestly say something new."

After reviewing all the books on bread they could find, the Joneses decided there was plenty on the subject that had yet to be explored in text. They'd had a great deal of fun getting young people, including their grandchildren, nieces, and nephews, into the kitchen by way of bread, and they thought a book on baking with children would provide a fresh angle, and thus stood to break through. Dick and Judith sold *Knead It, Punch It, Bake It!* to Thomas Y. Crowell, rolled up their sleeves, and got to work. But soon, they'd gathered so much rich material that, before their children's baking book was anywhere near complete, they'd put together a second proposal for a more globally comprehensive look at bread. Harper & Row, which had acquired Crowell in 1977, bought Dick and Judith's *The Book of Bread*.

It was the first time Judith and Dick had officially collaborated on a book since doing *How to Live in Paris on Practically Nothing* three decades before. But they'd long been deeply enmeshed in each other's work. Judith often used Dick as a sounding board, calling him from the office several times a day to run ideas past him or to read something aloud so that he could weigh in. And Dick, who in the 1970s began to write almost exclusively about food, bounced every one of his story leads off his wife.

When Judith first began working with Edna Lewis, she'd realized what a dearth of writing there was on the history and culture of American food. Dick took up the call. He successfully pitched the idea of a regular column exploring U.S. regional food to *Gourmet* magazine, and began traveling all over the country to report. As much as Judith could, she tagged along. "We went to some fabulous places," she told me. The people of a given town "would come out and do a big barbecue, some kind of a church supper" or the like. "We did a lot of interviewing of families and people around the country about their attitudes toward food. Dick was very good at getting people to talk," Judith said. While Dick asked his questions and listened attentively to what his subjects said in response, Judith stood by quietly observing and taking notes. As Dick gathered what he needed to write each piece, Judith picked up ideas for cookbooks to do at Knopf. "It was very handy," she said. The more they learned, the more the Joneses realized how many stories there were to tell about American regional cuisines. Judith encouraged

Dick to run with the theme and turn it into a book. His years of research went into *American Food: The Gastronomic Story*, which Dutton published in 1975.

After the challenging and often strained years of raising Audrey and Chris, being on the road, alone together with a collective aim, helped restrengthen the couple's bond. "We had a great time," Judith told me. "I could have done it for years." The appeal of cowriting a bread book was as much about Dick and Judith's genuine interest in baking as it was an excuse to work closely side by side.

Judith meticulously outlined the project from beginning to end while Dick took on the lion's share of research, sourcing different types of grains and flours, collating baking tips and tricks, gathering details to add color to the book, and drafting recipes as he went. Sometimes, Dick would mix a sourdough starter or begin a trial for a new kind of loaf on his own. But the couple did most of the recipe testing in tandem, mixing, kneading, baking, and tasting together as a team. At day's end, they were often dusted in flour, their fingers and forearms tired and sore.

Dick and Judith worked steadily, and were on track to deliver both bread manuscripts to their editors on time. But then in early 1980 Judith discovered a lump in her breast. A biopsy revealed it was cancer. Surgery was scheduled to remove the breast. And for a time, Judith and Dick's work on their books ground to a halt.

As she lay recovering in her hospital bed, Judith was furious at herself for ignoring Julia Child's advice not to go on hormone replacement therapy after her hysterectomy in 1972. Instead of trusting her friend's firsthand experience, Judith had believed her doctor when he'd assured her the drugs were not only effective but safe. As it turned out, synthetic hormones had been linked to endometrial and breast cancer in labs as early as the 1930s, but physicians optimistically chose to see that as correlation as opposed to cause. Doctors withheld the cautionary findings from their patients; selling prolonged youth and sex appeal with hormone replacement therapy was too profitable to undermine. As such, women were denied the ability to weigh the possible risks HRT presented to their long-term health with the benefits they wrought. Thus, when patients agreed to take the hormones, they weren't consenting in full.

For weeks after her mastectomy, Judith was in agony. For relief, she relied on the pranayama techniques she'd learned from her longtime yoga instructor, Al Bingham, and tried to breathe through the pain. To help cope with her fear and uncertainty about her prognosis, Judith leaned on faith and prayer. She was relieved when, late in the spring of 1980, her first round of follow-up scans came back clean. She began to recoup her peace of mind after that.

On top of Judith's cancer diagnosis and surgery, Dick, then sixty-four, had been confronted with severe health issues of his own. Decades of drinking too much, bouts of depression, and a recent, nearly fatal, stroke had all taken a toll on the health of his body and mind. (In fact, Judith hadn't told anyone about her cancer until Dick had been released from the hospital.) Neither Judith nor Dick wanted to retire or give up the work they so loved, but they understood they had to reduce their level of stress; it had been a trying, exhausting stretch. For both of them, their bodies had made it painfully clear: they needed a break to reset and get back on track at a more sustainable pace. So Judith requested extended leave from the office for July and August of 1980. She gathered up her authors' manuscripts; she'd take them with her to Vermont. Then she and Dick packed up their car with flour and yeast and drove north. The couple planned to use the summer to recuperate, recalibrate, and complete their books in Phyllis's Greensboro house.

After unpacking and settling in, Judith and Dick set up for their first bake. But when Judith went to preheat the oven, she discovered it didn't work. Phyllis said the appliance had short-circuited, and as she didn't cook, she hadn't bothered to get it fixed. Judith was beside herself. How, without an oven, would she and Dick finish testing the recipes for their books? They would need to find somewhere else to complete the task at hand, and they'd need to do it fast.

Judith and Dick weighed their options. They had other family in Greensboro they could call upon. There was Jane and John Gunther's place; but the house at "Jane's Rock" was always full of guests, as the Gunthers often hosted members of the literati there. "It wasn't so much *had* you published a book, but how many? And have you written one that won a Nobel Prize?" Jon Morey, Judith's nephew, her sister Susan's son, told me, laughing at the competitive snobbery of the Gunthers' summer scene. What's more, Jane was mystified at the amount of attention Judith gave to cookbooks. "I think she fell into it and it took more time than she would have liked," she said to me. Judith felt Jane's judgment palpably. There were Phyllis's sisters, Hilda and Helen, who each had their own homes on Caspian Lake, both with room to spare. But like Judith's mother, they had a tendency to hover, raising their eyebrows at the nature of Dick and Judith's work and dispensing a steady stream of disapproving comments. Judith could do without more of her aunts' condescension. And besides, she and Dick were too proud to plead for a summer's worth of hospitality on such short notice. For years, the Joneses had toyed with the idea of finding a country place of their own, but it was Phyllis's broken oven that finally gave them the push.

It was Jane who spotted the advertisement for a little house in Stannard, Vermont, that summer of 1980. The place was only half-finished, the Realtor told Jane when she called. Its owner, Carlos Montoya—son of the famous flamenco guitarist of the same name—was in the boom-and-bust restaurant business. He'd run out of funds before he'd completed building his new home and was in a financial bind. Montoya wanted to sell the house, but in the meantime, he was looking for someone to rent. It was a quirky place, the Realtor explained to Jane, but it was fully furnished and available right away. Jane roped in Audrey, who was in town visiting, and the two drove across the valley to take a look at the property.

The dwelling was rough-hewn, but it was cheap and boasted a spectacular view. Jane had a quick look around, then headed back to Greensboro and told Judith and Dick she thought she'd found a suitable spot for them. The Joneses drove out the next day to see the house for themselves. Stepping out of their car, with the sweeping vista before them, Judith was sold on the spot. Inside the house, the walls were unpainted, and most of the rooms lacked doors. But that didn't deter Judith and Dick. Once they laid eyes on the large industrial-style range in the kitchen, they were sure it was meant to be. The Joneses drove right back to Greensboro and handed over a month's rent. Then they went to Phyllis's, packed up their things, drove back to Stannard, and settled in.

In the house on the hill, there was no one nagging Dick and Judith to have a cocktail or take a break to swim. Away from Judith's clucking mother and aunts, the couple could work in peace. "We really came to have our own place, and just to be quiet," Judith told me. For the remainder of that summer, they tested, refined, and revised the recipes and headnotes for their books. They lovingly nicknamed the little house Bryn Teg, Welsh for "fair hill." Over dinner in the evenings, Dick and Judith began to scheme. "We realized this was it," Judith told me. "We could have Vermont and have our own life and do the creative things we wanted to do." She and Dick decided they'd try to buy Bryn Teg.

"As you know, we are much taken with the Carlos Montoya house," the Joneses wrote to the Realtor who'd handled the lease, "and are enjoying the privilege of living in it this month. It is unique in the sense it was designed for very specific tastes, and at the same time seems to have been built to give a rare kind of reward to people like ourselves. We'd like very much to take advantage of the fact it is for sale." Dick and Judith were poker-faced in their offer letter, masking their excitement and enthusiasm in hopes of bargaining down the price. They exhaustively detailed the house's faults: It lacked permanent electrical fixtures, baseboards, and ventilation in the downstairs bathroom. There was exposed wiring, the screens in the house's exterior doors were torn, and the shower upstairs didn't work. The chimney needed flashing, the back steps would have to be rebuilt, and the exterior planking needed to be sealed or it would rot away. "We are interested in taking on these problems, and to purchase for a fair price the house as it is furnished and the land," they wrote. They were able and willing to pay $70,000. It was a bid of hope.

A few rounds of back-and-forth ensued. For a couple of extra thousand dollars, Montoya said he'd include all forty-two acres surrounding the house. Over Labor Day weekend, Montoya's calico cat, whom he had abandoned and who had been at the house with Dick and Judith since they'd moved in, gave birth to a litter of kittens. The couple took it as a good omen; a christening of sorts. By the end of the holiday weekend, they'd reached a deal. Bryn Teg would be theirs.

All through that fall, and the winter and spring of 1981, Judith and Dick prepared for the coming summer at Bryn Teg. They bought boxes of nails and new screens for the exterior doors; knobs, hinges, and handrail brackets; lamps and a knife rack; a dining table and chairs; mattresses, box springs, down pillows, and a braided rug; silverware, a wine decanter, and terra-cotta tiles for the kitchen floor. They scraped together another thousand dollars to purchase two more acres of land along Town Highway 11, giving them a contiguous tract that ran all the way down to the road at the rocky pastures' edge. On Memorial Day weekend 1981, when the last threat of frost in the Northeast Kingdom had finally passed, Dick and Judith moved their things in to Bryn Teg. That summer, dressed in old jeans and worn flannel button-down shirts, Judith and Dick planted a row of raspberry canes along the edge of the yard. They picked stones from a plot of level ground just downhill from the house where they planned to grow vegetables. "Turned out it was very swampy," Judith said to me. "I knew nothing, just learned by trial and error." Judith laughed as she recalled their early, amateur gardening days.

Bryn Teg changed the way Dick and Judith thought about food, and the way they cooked and ate. There on the mountain, meals took shape around what was at hand, whatever they could gather or manage to grow. Together, the couple explored the corners and contours of their land. Guided by books and knowledge-able locals alike, they came to know the many edible things that thrived there. They learned to fry milkweed pods and forage for mushrooms, chokeberries, and wild greens. "We didn't know how rich this fifty-odd acres was with food when we bought it, did we?" Dick later said in an interview. "No," Judith agreed, "it's like a gift. We're learning so much. At our age, it's like starting over."

The couple delighted in the slower pace and physicality of rural life and of country cooking, too. "I can remember the feeling of going out just before supper—the light is so beautiful at that hour," Judith said to me. "And thinking, 'Oh I wonder what's in the garden,' or picking a handful of raspberries to go into dessert and running across the lawn there, just feeling that you wanted to cry with pleasure." Bryn Teg marked a new chapter in the couple's marriage and a turning point in Judith's career.

Judith had been at Knopf for more than two decades when she and Dick bought their place in Vermont. Her relationships with the authors on whom she had built her career—namely John Hersey, John Updike, Anne Tyler, and Julia

Child—were well established by then. Judith still attended carefully to her writers, but once she'd learned what each needed from her, working with them became less of a heavy lift. Finally confident in her job security, her editorial style, and her list at Knopf, Judith felt she could at last put some space between herself and Manhattan, and the publishing world as a whole.

After that unbroken stretch of time in Vermont, it was jarring to go back to the Knopf office after Labor Day. Judith wrote to Anne Tyler, with whom she was putting the finishing touches on Tyler's forthcoming novel, *Dinner at the Homesick Restaurant*, "I'm back—in flesh, if not yet entirely in spirit." But there was much that required Judith's attention that fall. She needed to be present in New York. That October, John Updike's third book chronicling Harry Angstrom, *Rabbit Is Rich*, hit shelves. The book's main character remained somewhat unlikable; it was part of his appeal. "He is suspicious of intelligent women and complications rub him the wrong way. He tries to like everybody, and can't. He wants to be innocent, and isn't. But he dreams for the rest of us. He is our Canada goose," wrote John Leonard in the *Times*. The novel sold like hotcakes right away and won both a Pulitzer and a National Book Award, a triumph for John Updike, Judith, and Knopf.

In contrast, when Judith and Dick's *Knead It, Punch It, Bake It!* launched that same season, critics barely registered its arrival. Judith couldn't help her disappointment, but she held out hope for *The Book of Bread*, which was due out in the next summer. As Mimi Sheraton noted in her year-end roundup of books on food, the tide in cookbooks was beginning to turn. "To judge by the current outpouring of new cookbooks, huge and hefty encyclopedic volumes seem to be on the wane. . . . [T]here are now many slim books that seem to be focusing on narrower aspects of particular cuisines. . . . [M]any of these new books offer a bonus by leavening the mix with fascinating insights into the customs, traditions and lore that surround the foods. The results make good reading as well as good cooking." To Judith, the piece signaled that, though *Knead It, Punch It, Bake It!* may have been before its time, the pump had been primed for single-subject cookbooks like *The Book of Bread*. She would begin sending advance copies of it out late in spring 1982 in anticipation of the book's release. But first, Judith had Anne Tyler's latest novel to launch.

In March, when Knopf published *Dinner at the Homesick Restaurant*, critics showered Tyler with praise. "[I]n recent years her narratives have grown bolder and her characters more striking," the *Times* said. They called the book "Funny, heart-hammering, wise, it edges deep into truth," pushing "deeper than Miss Tyler herself has gone before." The novel was "a border crossing," the author's "probable ultimate achievement," the *Times* said. *Homesick* became a finalist for the National

Book Award, the PEN/Faulkner Award, and the Pulitzer Prize for Fiction, and thrust Anne Tyler into fame. The book enjoyed "new spurts of selling with all the excellent short notices" and mentions as one of the "year's best." It was "a most unusual thing to have happen to a novel these days," Judith proudly wrote to Tyler.

· · · · · · · ·

Judith had her green pencil in hand and the latest pages from Angus Cameron spread before her on her desk. It was autumn 1982. Their *L.L.Bean Game and Fish Cookbook* had been under contract since December 1979, and their manuscript submission date had long since come and gone. All week, she had been trying to get through Angus's latest batch of recipes—there were to be nearly five hundred in the book in all. She wanted to finish making her comments and send the pages back to Angus so he could take one final pass. But Judith hadn't been able to sustain her focus. The phone had been ringing off the hook. Reporters had been calling incessantly, wanting to talk to her about *The Book of Bread*. She'd just started in on the recipe for stuffed hearts of venison when her assistant popped her head in the doorway. The poor young woman looked almost sheepish as she asked Judith if she had a few minutes to spare. There was another reporter on the line, she said, who wanted to know if Judith could give a quick comment about *Bread*.

Coverage of *The Book of Bread* had been thin the season when it was published, but in the fall, it began to mount. The reviews were good. Barbara Kafka called *The Book of Bread* "a classic, ludic and comprehensive" in the December issue of *Vogue*. In the *Times*, Mimi Sheraton said she especially liked the "interesting history of bread baking" and "an excellent chapter on the use of yeast." But the press seemed more interested in *Bread*'s authors—Judith specifically—than the book itself. "Judith Jones is known as the country's best cookbook editor," Sheraton said. A long piece in the *Arizona Republic* and *Washington Post* about the book and Dick and Judith ran under the headline "Authors Work Bread Making into Busy Lifestyle." "She would be known as Julia Child's editor if she weren't also James Beard's editor. And Marcella Hazan's. Simone Beck's. Madhur Jaffrey's. Irene Kuo's," reporter Phyllis Richman wrote. "There are, after all, far more great cooks than great editors. The gentle handling that a soufflé requires is nothing compared to the handling of an author." "You need that sense of person and of presence," Judith said in the interview with Richman before Dick had cut in. "Darling, you try to make the book say something. That's what makes you a good editor," he said. "Sometimes, I almost feel in the relationship of a therapist," Judith explained in response. After working all her adult life on behalf of her authors and largely out of view, Judith herself had become a subject of interest and was on display.

The buzz around Judith continued well into 1983, when *The L.L.Bean Game and Fish Cookbook* finally came out in the fall of that year. Marian Burros, who took over for Mimi Sheraton as food critic of the *New York Times* in January 1983, covered the book in her Christmas roundup that year. She noted its writers' biographical details—"This book is the result of a collaboration between Angus Cameron, an avid hunter and former book editor, and Judith Jones, who is a cookbook author and editor"—and said the book stood out, especially "in a lean year for memorable cookbooks." No one, Burros noted, had "written such a compendium in the previous 50 years," nor, she said, echoing James Beard's enthusiastic blurb on the book's jacket, need anyone else "write another game book for at least half a century." She called *Game and Fish* "a definitive work." (Indeed, at the time of this book's writing, Judith and Angus Cameron's book remains the best-selling fish and game cookbook of all time.)

By the following summer, Dick and Judith had contracted L.L.Bean to do a second book, this one on New England food. It gave the Joneses an excuse to delve deep into the culture and history of Vermont and to spend even more time at Bryn Teg. As was his wont, Dick took the lead on research, putting his small-town newspaper reporting skills to use. "We subscribed to lots of New England papers and read the food pages," Judith told me, "and all during the week he would make little dishes that he had gotten there." On weekends, when Judith joined her husband in Vermont, the couple would "go down to town and talk. It was such fun! I didn't want to miss any of that," she said.

That summer of 1984, a young reporter named Rux Martin drove up to interview Dick and Judith about their work and regional approach to food. Martin observed Judith as she worked "unhurriedly" making lunch, "using ingredients gathered from her garden and the fields around the house," and peered over the lip of the bowl as Judith stirred the batter of a blackberry buckle for dessert. It was a test of one of the more than 800 recipes Dick and Judith would include in their L.L.Bean New England book. In the profile based on her visit that day, Martin wrote that the Joneses' "relaxed, pluralistic vision . . . is refreshing in food writing, which often creates an unrealistically 'pure' view." "When people say, 'Oh, you're a gourmet cook,'" Judith had said to Martin, "I get cross, I really hate that." Judith told Martin she corrected such people by saying, "I'm interested in good food."

Judith, who'd turned sixty in March 1984, was growing more comfortable having a public platform and license to speak on her own behalf. In the spotlight, she dropped the mask of reserve and openly asserted her own strong opinions and tastes; the irreverent ethos and exacting standards that had long guided her came clearly to the fore. The power of others' approval had almost completely lost its hold on her. In her late middle age, Judith had grown less faithful to the establishment and more disillusioned with it as well.

CHAPTER 16

I t was late September 1986, and the leaves in northern Vermont had already started to turn. Judith and Dick had gone up to Bryn Teg for a long weekend to prepare to close the house up for winter. They'd spent the day trimming back the perennial flowers and berry bushes which, by then, had begun to thrive. They picked the last green tomatoes from their withering vines. The first hard frost could come any night.

Still dressed in her gardening clothes, the knees of her jeans encrusted with dirt, Judith gathered up an armful of papers and went to the pond. The year before, Dick had had it made as a gift for her; all her life, Judith had loved to swim. Judith had watched with delight as big yellow excavators had crawled up the hill, come to dig out a marshy dip in the land at Bryn Teg. In a matter of days, as if by magic, the hole had filled with cold, clear water from the mountain springs that coursed underneath the land.

Dick had a small dock built, and a bench placed down by the cattail-lined shore. There, he and Judith often read or worked together in easy silence. Sometimes Dick would sit by the pond alone to watch his wife as, lithely and without hesitation, she entered the water. Before breakfast each morning and again in late afternoon, Judith always did her laps. Except when there were visitors who followed her down to the pond, she swam in the nude.

That evening, before Judith could go for her swim, there was a manuscript she needed to revisit. At summer's end, a British agent named Alan Davidson had sent her a book by Patience Gray. Gray was a writer, translator, and textile designer. Through the war years, she'd supported two children as a single mother, cobbling together odd jobs. In 1958, she'd become the first "woman's editor" at the *Observer* in the UK. In 1961, Gray was let go from her post at the paper. After that, she and her lover, the sculptor Norman Mommens, left England first for Greece, then moved on to Italy. In 1970, the couple settled on a once-working sheep farm without running water or electricity in the remote region of Apulia.

Gray began to gather the regional history and lore of her new surroundings, as well as recipes, personal vignettes, and instructions for foraging wild foods. She learned all she knew "from people who have never read a book." Gray feared that if the region's deep traditions weren't written down, they would soon be lost. "Things only become history once they have disappeared," she wrote. Eventually, she compiled everything into a genre-defying book she titled *Honey from a Weed*. Alan Davidson had been trying, as yet unsuccessfully, to sell it since 1982.

Judith settled onto the bench by the pond, and flipped open the manuscript. Gray's prose was enchanting, unflinching, and vividly wrought: "We plucked the birds, emptied their crops, removed their entrails and severed their necks and coral feet," she'd written. *Honey from a Weed* was fascinating, and Gray's voice was resonant and clear. But Judith knew the book's potential for commercial success was limited at best.

By the mid-1980s, bookselling and the publishing industry were undergoing rapid and dramatic change. Independent bookshops were falling like dominoes to multi-outlet bookselling chains. Companies like B. Dalton Bookseller, Waldenbooks, and Borders, which often anchored shopping malls and suburban strips, were able to buy books in bulk and sell them at lower prices than the indies could. In 1987, when Barnes & Noble purchased all 797 of Dalton's retail locations, it was well on its way to becoming the biggest American bookseller of all. A similar pattern of conglomeration was changing the nature of publishing as well. Powerful houses backed by immense wealth, like Knopf's parent company, Random House, were increasingly buying up smaller presses. "Salability" had become the industry's mantra. Judith had seen the change coming for some time by then.

"I feel frustrated," she'd written Claudia Roden in 1978. "It is a rough business, trying to do good books, to get them the audience they deserve, to keep them in stores, keep them in print. More and more it's the good, solid, marginal book that is getting hurt in these days of bigness." For more than three decades, Judith had put her energy and faith into as-yet unknown authors and "small treasures" like *Honey from a Weed*. It's how she'd built her unique, multigenre list, especially when it came to food. But with new financial pressures at play, Judith was forced to adjust her approach. Gray's book, Judith knew, was likely to have limited reach; many of its recipes weren't replicable in the modern world, at least not outside Puglia. Gray's vantage point and subject were unique—therein lay *Honey from a Weed*'s specialness—but that level of specificity would almost certainly limit the book's commercial appeal and sales. "Before, you could bring out a book and it sold under twenty thousand copies, maybe fifteen thousand when you were introducing a new author. And you, *we*, were satisfied with that! *You*, the *publisher*, built the platform. But now, it seems to have to come from the outside in. It's a different ball game, and harder to take chances," Judith told me. "It's partly because of the money. Publishing has changed."

Judith finally responded to Alan Davidson in November 1986. "I have been neurotic about not answering you on Patience Gray," she began. "Twenty years ago I wouldn't have hesitated. But the sad fact is that it is getting harder and harder for a conglomerate such as we are when it comes to the sales force to publish the odd and unusual. By the time any word of mouth gets going, the books can't be found because they are swept out of the stores (that is, if they are even in the chain stores, which this book wouldn't be)." Judith continued, resigned, "The truth is that I can't bear to say no and yet I know I must. I can't take it on at this point in the life of Knopf."

Knopf's stability had been unsettled by Alfred Knopf's death at the age of ninety-one in August 1984. For the first time in the seven decades since Alfred and Blanche founded the house, Knopf had a chance to chart a new course and to redefine itself. In 1987, after nearly twenty years as editor in chief, Bob Gottlieb left Knopf for the *New Yorker*; he'd hold the same title at the magazine as he had at the publishing house. Before leaving, Gottlieb had recommended to Si Newhouse and Bob Bernstein that Sonny Mehta become his successor at Knopf.

Mehta, the son of an Indian diplomat, had made a name for himself in paperback publishing in London, at Paladin and then at Pan Books's Picador imprint. One of his first major successes had been Germaine Greer's 1970 *The Female Eunuch*, one of the definitive works of feminism's second wave. Later, Mehta had put such novelists as Ian McEwan and Salman Rushdie on the map. He had a keen nose for talent, and a bullish energy for marketing as well. Gottlieb thought Mehta was the right man to shepherd Knopf into the publishing industry's new era of high competition and faster pace. When word of who Knopf's new editor in chief would be was announced, the press went mad. Mehta was enigmatic and, though he was a well-known player in British publishing, he was relatively obscure in the United States. He struck many as an odd pick to lead the most illustrious publishing house in the United States.

For his first three months on the job, Mehta flew back and forth across the Atlantic, slowly acclimating to Knopf while tying up loose ends at Picador, the paperback imprint he had launched at Pan Books. To find his feet, he'd need to "learn how things functioned over here," he told me; his mandate had been to "change as little as possible at first, to keep things going as it had gone." He also needed to meet the principals among his new staff. Mehta told me, "I knew very few people here when I came to Knopf." Bob Gottlieb suggested he start with Judith and Nina Bourne.

"I was totally intimidated by these women," Mehta told me years after the fact. "They were both so impeccably polite. But I think it was their certainty more than anything else. I seem to remember Judith carrying most of that lunch." Mehta quickly saw that Judith "had an innate curiosity and cosmopolitanism. She was a reader and a thinker. I liked her sophistication," Mehta said. He would come to know it all as "so much a part of her character" as a person and editor, both. "Judith," Mehta told me, "was the most civilized person in publishing."

Before meeting her that day, Mehta had known Judith by reputation; according to him, everyone in publishing did. "People associate Judith with cooking almost exclusively. But I didn't. I associated her with John Updike and Anne Tyler," he said. And while Mehta had no particular interest in or experience with cookbooks, he knew that Judith's stood apart. Her food writers "were experts, they were people who knew what they were doing. They were the best in their areas. Judith had an eye and an understanding of the culture, their particular cuisines," he told me. Beyond Judith's cookbooks' distinction, the new editor in chief also knew how central they'd become to the house. "Judith's cookbook line was the backbone of Knopf at that stage," he told me. For nearly twenty years, Bob Gottlieb had remained blasé about the importance of cookbooks at Knopf and, by extension, about Judith's value not only to the publishing house but to food culture as a whole. But Mehta saw Judith in a completely different light. "I just knew that she was a kind of a legend," he said.

Mehta felt like an outsider in New York's publishing scene, and in his early days at Knopf, he was convinced he'd made a mistake accepting the job. Judith went out of her way to make him feel welcome. "She was extremely kind to me,"

Mehta said. In addition to being in awe of her exceptional list, he admired her "eye for small touches" and her firm but "gentle" way as an editor. "Judith never took an axe to a manuscript," Mehta said. He began to see Judith as a friend and ally, and to lean on her for perspective and professional advice.

Not long after his start, Mehta received a new memoir by the British businessman turned writer Peter Mayle; Mehta had published him in the UK. Mehta asked Judith, who he knew had lived in France, if she would weigh in. Judith took the manuscript home and returned it the next day. She said she found Mayle's book delightful and believed it stood to do well. Mehta bought the book, and Judith became the writer's editor. In 1989, Knopf published Mayle's *A Year in Provence*. It went on to sell more than six million copies and to be translated into more than forty languages.

Mehta made his reverence for Judith clear; he promoted her to vice president and gave her a significant raise. It was a show of Mehta's respect and his acknowledgment of her importance to the house. Still, the increase in pay was far from commensurate with Judith's output or that of her authors' value to Knopf (by 1994, Anne Tyler's book advances were up to $1,750,000). In 2002, the median income for men across all roles in publishing, regardless of their longevity in the field, was $90,000, compared to $70,000 for women. For those who'd been in editorial more than eleven years, the average pay was $87,000, and $168,000 for those who'd been in management roles for the same amount of time. In 2002, Judith had been working with Mehta for fifteen years, and at Knopf for forty-five. She was senior editor and vice president. Her tax return for that year shows her salary was $115,020.54.

Judith did not achieve pay parity while working for Mehta. Still, under his leadership, she experienced a kind of editorial freedom previously unknown to her. He gave Judith license to take risks as she saw fit. "Basically she reported to me and I let her do what she wanted," Mehta told me.

Ever since *The Taste of Country Cooking* came out in 1976, Judith had wanted Edna Lewis to do a second book. No one had made more of an impact on Judith's thinking about America's food and its history, or on regional food writing as a whole, than Lewis. Judith knew Edna had more to say. For years, Edna had been writing to her editor about her radicalizing politics and her commitment to celebrating and documenting the past and present of Black southern food. "After looking over my grandfather's life and the times he lived in and the time I knew him and his neighbors, I see them as a people that had a unique spirit of strength and unity," Edna had written to Judith back in 1977. "They were denied human identity. They were classed as farm livestock and sold as such. It was their great spiritual strength and unity that helped them to combat the humiliation of slavery and . . . to cope. They did retain an identity of their own—a hidden Africanism. They did not seem to have expressed a physical means of reacting, but react they did—with dignity. I haven't figured out just how it should be put," Edna wrote to Judith. "I'll wait for your thinking on it."

In 1981, Edna sent Judith a one-page proposal, written longhand, for her next book. In March 1982, they signed a contract for the project with a $20,000 advance. But as eager as Lewis was to write another book, her priority was paying her bills. *Taste* had brought Lewis increased name recognition and clout, but it hadn't provided much in the way of actual financial gain. And, as for so many who work in food service, especially people of color, Lewis's income had remained unpredictable and unstable. Knopf's payment for her second book wasn't enough to support Lewis in full. So, though she was in her mid-sixties by then, Lewis continued to do the grueling work of cooking professionally.

Meanwhile, the food world helped themselves to Lewis's talent and recipes without compensating her properly—or sometimes at all—for her contributions and skill. When, in the autumn of 1979, *Bon Appétit* magazine talked Lewis into developing and printing an original recipe for them without pay, Judith flew into a rage. She wrote to Marilou Vaughan, the magazine's managing editor, "When you and I last talked in late September . . . I tried very hard to make you realize how important it was that professional writers/cooks be paid a fair fee for original work. It not only takes time, shopping, testing, and typing up recipes (in Mrs. Lewis's case she has to hire a typist), but, in addition, one is paying for expertise—the years of experience that go into developing the creativity and taste and judgment that make a recipe genuinely distinctive. You said that you paid only the superstars like Julia Child and James Beard for their time and effort, but I fail to understand the rationale behind that policy. Certainly Edna Lewis's time is just as valuable." Judith went on, detailing Lewis's distress over the situation and naming an amount she thought the magazine should offer Lewis as compensation in order to make amends. She added that she was sending a copy of her letter to both Julia Child and James Beard, "because I think they should know the policies of a magazine that they seem to respect and have worked with so very amicably." Vaughan responded flatly: "When Mr. Beard and Mrs. Child give us stories, they could be selling those stories elsewhere; therefore, they are compensated. If you believe that Mrs. Lewis can command that kind of market for an article, then of course you are free to seek it."

It was not an isolated incident, and the more the overt exploitation of Lewis persisted, the more protective Judith became. In 1983, Fearrington House, an upscale inn and restaurant in Pittsboro, North Carolina, hired Lewis as a consulting chef for their opening. But after she'd designed Fearrington's menu and trained their kitchen staff to be able to replicate her dishes, Lewis was let go without due notice or severance pay. As has happened to Black women throughout American history, Edna Lewis's talents had been appropriated to promote and uphold white enterprise. When Edna sought legal counsel for lost wages, R. B. Fitch, Fearrington's proprietor, grew defensive and angry. Edna wrote Judith, seeking advice. Judith, irate on Edna's behalf, took up the cause.

"I could only guess at the embarrassment that would be felt as a result of your decision not to ask her back," Judith wrote Fitch in April 1984. "Obviously it is hard for anyone to negotiate with an employer, and if you had sensitivity you would know it is particularly hard for Edna," she said. Judith had learned firsthand how challenging it was to advocate for oneself as a woman in the workplace. She knew Lewis's Blackness made it that much harder still. "The unmistakable conclusion on the part of it all," Judith put it pointedly in her letter to Fitch, "is that you simply exploited her for the publicity and have been unfair about not wanting her to share in the rewards."

Lewis was out of cash and emotionally bruised when she started her next post in the kitchen in Charleston, South Carolina, in 1985. She'd been hired at Middleton Place, a plantation that had once relied on slave labor to produce rice, a cash crop that had been particularly valuable in the eighteenth and nineteenth centuries. Lewis was well aware of Middleton's complicated history, but she needed the job. What's more, she craved more knowledge about the foodways of the American South and the influence of enslaved African people on their present and past. Working as the chef at Middleton gave Lewis a chance to become familiar with a part of the South whose culinary traditions were largely unknown to her. The Carolina Low Country was nothing like Virginia's Piedmont, where she'd grown up. Culturally and climatically, the two regions were worlds apart.

Edna wrote Judith about the new ingredients and dishes she was learning about. She learned to use okra, benne seeds, and rice far more often than wheat. Lewis had grown up inland; in Freetown, oysters had been a once-a-year holiday treat. But in her kitchen in Charleston, Lewis had an abundance of mollusks, shrimp, crabs, and fish to work with. At Middleton, Lewis began to research historical preparations and amplify the ingredients that enslaved Africans and Black Americans had ingeniously learned to prepare. She wanted to prevent her ancestors' traditional cooking techniques from falling into disuse. But her enthusiasm for the culinary riches of South Carolina was overwhelmed by homesickness; Lewis had no people in the Low Country, and she missed the cultural vitality of New York. So at the start of 1987, she returned north.

Judith hoped that, with Edna nearby again, they could hurry her book along.

Judith found a cowriter, Mary Goodbody, to help Edna complete the book. Good-body drove down to Manhattan from her home in Connecticut a couple of days a week to spend early mornings with Lewis in the kitchen of Uncle Sam's, a steakhouse where she'd been hired as the chef. Goodbody taped their conversa-tions and took notes as Lewis cooked, then she worked it all together into recipes and prose. By midyear, 1987, Judith had a full manuscript of Lewis's next book in hand. Knopf published *In Pursuit of Flavor* in the autumn of the following year.

Judith hoped Mehta's Knopf would get behind *Pursuit* in a way the house, under Gottlieb, hadn't with *Taste*. After all, Judith pointed out, interest in Amer-ican food was at an all-time high. "People aren't just looking for more regional recipes," she wrote in a memo to her colleagues, "they're looking for cookbooks that feed their hunger to know more about their own heritage." No author was better positioned, Judith believed, than Edna Lewis to capitalize on the trend. So Judith was not only exasperated but stung when Knopf threw only meager support behind printing and distributing Lewis's latest book.

"I am not able to understand the reason for the reduction of printing from 25,000 to 17,500 on this book," Judith wrote Mehta in July 1988. The Book-of-the-Month Club, she pointed out, "is using it as the MAIN selection for their cooking and crafts club, is running with us and has ordered a printing of 29,000, and I cannot remember in my many years at Knopf a time when a book club has printed more of a cookbook than we have (usually their sales on a successful book are about 1/3 of ours)." Mehta justified his choice by saying that cookbooks were losing their appeal, and, as such, Knopf had to exercise caution when it came to the size of their first runs. But Judith didn't buy her boss's excuse. "It's interesting that I don't hear about the dire slump in the cookbook market from Peter Workman or people I know at S&S and Morrow and Crown," she retorted testily.

Judith was not going to let the issue rest. Edna Lewis had recently been fea-tured in both *Connoisseur* and *National Geographic* magazines, Judith pointed out. Alice Waters, who'd made a name for herself at her Berkeley restaurant, Chez Pa-nisse, had publicly credited Lewis both as an inspiration to her personally and as a pioneer of America's growing farm-to-table trend. Indeed, Lewis had "become something of a cult figure," Judith said. And while she conceded that Lewis, who'd turned seventy-two in April 1988, was "reluctant to go on a nationwide promotion tour . . . she has a special magic. And there isn't a publisher who does cookbooks who wouldn't give anything to have her on their list (and they've tried)." Judith concluded her letter to Mehta on a damning note: "It's not much of a reward for sticking with Knopf to launch her with so little confidence."

Mehta's assessment of the marketplace wasn't entirely off base. Cookbooks were no longer the powerful shapers of culture they'd been from the time Julia

Child launched in the early sixties through the late seventies. As glitzy cook-books written by well-known restaurant chefs began to emerge on the scene in the mid-eighties, more modest books on home cooking had begun to lose their commercial edge. Even if Mehta had a point, Judith felt it was no justification for abandoning Edna Lewis in-house. Not only did Judith have great faith in the appeal of Lewis's food and instruction style, she felt that Lewis, as an established Knopf author and leading expert on her subject, deserved far more resources and support than she was getting. But Mehta dug in his heels and stuck to *Pursuit*'s reduced print run.

Judith could have capitulated then, taking Mehta's diminished support of Lewis as a sign that it was time to give up on the kinds of cookbooks on which she'd built her line at Knopf. It would have been a reasonable thing to do; she was sixty-four years old, nearing the age at which most working Americans retire. But resignation had never suited Judith. Instead of dropping the cause, she took Mehta's treatment of Lewis as a challenge to think bigger and more strategically, and to try to build upon her decades of experience publishing in the culinary space to redirect the winds of change.

As food became more and more a subject of interest in American popular culture, Judith noticed the pendulum was beginning to swing back from whence it came. "The kind of miraculous thing with this opening up of real interest in food—one's own roots and the connections and memories, and the books that were being done and magazines and all that—is that people were ready to say, 'Hey, there's some-thing in America, too!'" "Re-creating the past and feeling pride in it" had become central to the nation's way with food. Judith believed the time was right to explore in depth the question: What is American cuisine?

Traversing the country with Dick over the years, Judith had observed that the impulse among recent arrivals was often to assimilate their ways of cooking and eating to the United States rather than to maintain the food cultures they'd brought with them. "What makes American food so different," Judith wrote in her proposal for an ambitious cookbook series on the myriad food cultures of the United States she'd decided to call Knopf Cooks American (KCA), "is that it's a melting pot or more accurately a flavorful stew of the different waves of immi-grants and what they brought with them, what they encountered when they got here, and how they adapted to new circumstances."

Given Mehta's feelings about how the cookbook market had changed, Judith knew she'd have to justify such a pursuit. She had to prove she was not naive to what was happening in publishing. "One of the discouraging aspects of the cook-book market is that a good cookbook does not have the shelf life that it did in the past," Judith said. "By establishing this series as something unique and enduring we hope to reverse that pattern." It was grandiose, but she believed she had enough experience and influence in food by then to pull it off. "Over the years, Knopf has been recognized as the preeminent publisher of great teaching cookbooks that set a new standard in cookbook writing," she wrote in a rare moment of laying claim to her own success. Judith felt confident that "a library of cookbooks that tell different aspects of the American story is bound to have immediate and continuing appeal." If Mehta had doubts, he kept them to himself. He gave Judith and her series the go-ahead.

A book by Bill Neal, a North Carolina–based chef, kicked things off. Neal had trained in classical French technique. He'd been deeply influenced by that country's precise and elemental approach to cooking. But he'd come to believe that his place—the American South—had a culinary language as rich and worthy of honor as that of France. Like Edna Lewis, Neal had grown committed to documenting and articulating the region's varied traditions, and of being part of their contemporary revival as well. At Crook's Corner, the idiosyncratic Chapel Hill restaurant he opened in 1982, Neal prepared canonical southern dishes like Brunswick stew, she-crab soup, and hush puppies using the best regional products he could find. He was tireless in his search for farmers producing heritage grains for the freshest, most flavorful cornmeal. He got to know the fisherfolk who plied the waters of North Carolina's Outer Banks, and the orchardists who still tended the Piedmont's heritage varietals. He cooked dishes familiar across the South, but inflected them with accents of his own. Most restaurants in the early 1980s either fell back on tradition or leaped wildly into a modernist future. Neal's middle ground—tinkering with the old ways while exalting heritage products and honoring history—was, at the time, seen as revelatory and bold.

Knopf published Bill Neal's *Biscuits, Spoonbread, and Sweet Potato Pie* in 1990. It was a deep dive into baking traditions from Alabama to Mississippi, Virginia's Tidewater to the Appalachian hills. By detailing and parsing so many iterations of dishes universal throughout the South, Neal beckoned readers to more carefully consider a region too often mistaken, by northerners especially, as a monolith. *Biscuits* was not a nostalgic book, but rather one that pointed toward an ever-changing notion of America's identity through its food.

Judith selected other authors for KCA who were equally authoritative and highly specific in their approach. There were *Hot Links and Country Flavors: Sausages in American Regional Cooking*, by health researcher-turned-chef-turned-sausage-entrepreneur Bruce Aidells and Denis Kelly, and the cheekily titled *Barbecued Ribs, Smoked Butts and Other Great Feeds* by native Alabamian Jeanne Voltz. Like Judith and Julia Child, Voltz had been part of the early wave of women who brought intellectual seriousness to the subject of food. She was among the first newspaper editors in the United States to bring rigor to culinary journalism, first as the food editor at the *Los Angeles Times* before moving over to the same role at *Woman's Day* magazine.

Most of those who wrote KCA's books, though, were little, if at all, known. Judith had met some of her authors during her travels with Dick. Others she'd encountered in the food pages of small-town and regional newspapers and magazines. "I got some very good cookbooks" that way, Judith told me, "and some very good writers, too!" She commissioned Nancy Verde Barr to chronicle the Italian American community of Providence, Rhode Island, and Joan Nathan—now considered food writing royalty—to write a definitive volume on Jewish American cuisine. There were books on fruit preserves, the shellfish of the Florida Gulf Coast, and another on the borough of Brooklyn's rich and crazy culinary quilt. "We did the Northern Heartlands," Judith told me, alluding to the KCA title that explored the foodways of the upper Midwest—including Dick's home state of Minnesota—a region whose culinary traditions "hadn't really been explored," Judith said. "I kind of got to know that part of the country through my marriage, and the newspaper out there." *Blue Corn and Chocolate* mapped the culinary evolution of ingredients native to the Americas (though Judith stopped short of finding an Indigenous author to write the book). As part of the KCA series, the editor even reissued *Helen Brown's West Coast Cook Book*, which had anticipated in 1952 what would come to be known as California cuisine.

Judith put out the first four books in the series in 1990. Between 1991 and 1997, she added in excess of a dozen more. It was a feat of ambition, organization, and attention to detail, working on so many cookbooks at once. Judith's assistant, Kathy Zuckerman, who'd started at Knopf a year after Mehta became editor in chief, played a vital role in keeping everything straight. "In the early ones, like *We Called It Macaroni*, I went to the Met[ropolitan Museum of Art] to try to find art for the pages," Zuckerman, now vice president and executive publicist at Knopf, told me. For Joan Nathan's book *Jewish Cooking in America*, Judith sent Zuckerman downtown to research and eat. "There were places in the city that I'd never even heard of, like Russ and Daughters and so forth. So I went down there for knishes, and then again to help get art. That was really fun," Zuckerman said.

The final titles in the KCA series were its most boundary pushing. Judith tapped Ken Hom, a first generation Cantonese-American chef who'd learned to cook in his uncle's restaurant in Chicago, to write *Easy Family Recipes from a Chinese-American Childhood*. Hom's book was a guide to preparing the dishes that had been passed on to him by his family, as well as a deeply personal comment on hyphenated ethnic identity. Anne Mendelson, who was then reviewing cookbooks for the *Los Angeles Times*, carefully tracked the evolution of KCA. She called Hom's book "an astonishing testimony to Judith's instinctive sense that nothing was more deeply, truly American than the cooking of immigrant families, families who were sustained by food traditions linking them to a former homeland while they made a new life for themselves here." For *Latin American Cooking Across the U.S.A.*, Judith paired Cuban-born historian and activist Himilce Novas with Rosemary Silva as a cowriting team. "The mere fact that she was eager to champion stateside Latin American food as quintessential American food is extraordinary," Mendelson later said. So, she noted, was the fact that Judith insisted on publishing a Spanish-language edition of that book. At the time, few publishers in the United States were actively confronting the question of linguistic access in print. Putting out two editions of *Latin American Cooking* was not only a progressive political statement on Judith's part but an unprecedented move in both the realm of cookbooks and in commercial book publishing overall.

Mendelson called KCA "Judith's finest and bravest project" of her entire cookbook career. The series, she said, "defied the expectations of snobs," and was a retort to all things "gourmet" and "the very cheffy phenomenon of New American cuisine" which had been moving steadily to the fore. Judith had little interest in perpetuating that trend. "We began to get more and more that every restaurant chef felt he had to have a book," Judith told me. "And I felt that they *didn't* have to have books, because it wasn't the kind of cooking you did at home. They're two different worlds." She was speaking from firsthand experience.

In the late sixties, Judith had signed the renowned Swiss-born chef Albert Stockli to do a cookbook. Even though Stockli hired someone to help him write and test recipes for *Splendid Fare*, which Knopf published in 1970, "I spent quite a lot of time with him to get it on track," Judith recalled. "I had notes all over the recipes he'd done, and I said to him, 'You know, you say put this in a six-hundred-degree oven. Who's got a six-hundred-degree oven?'" Stockli saw the editor's point. "He went out and bought that terrible kind of stove you got in those days with four little burners that took half an hour for the water to boil. He almost fainted! He couldn't believe that it was so difficult to cook with this dinky little stove. But he acknowledged it, and at least *said* he tested all his recipes in that country kitchen. Now that's pretty good! And unless chefs could do that translating, you didn't learn anything from them!" Ever since, Judith had avoided pursuing books with celebrity chefs. But she wasn't ignorant to the larger shifts afoot in publishing, and was open-minded enough to give it another go.

Partway through her work on KCA, Judith signed a deal with Oprah Winfrey's personal chef, Rosie Daley, to do a cookbook. Though Judith knew it was

Oprah's enormous celebrity that would sell the book, she justified the project to herself by framing Rosie's food, at its core, as home cooking. Judith found, though, that the problems that cropped up working with Rosie were the same sort she'd encountered with Stockli; in their draft form, the recipes Daley sent Judith were unusable for home cooks. They often lacked a complete ingredient list, and the instructions were disorganized, vague, and unclear. Chris Vandercook, Judith's adopted son, remembered being with Judith in Vermont the summer that Daley's recipes, sent by fax, came in. "Each would require days of work," he told me. Judith rose to the challenge, meticulously working through all the material and going back to Daley again and again until they got each recipe right. And when *In the Kitchen with Rosie* came out in 1994, it took off right away. It sold more than six million copies in hardcover, making it one of the best-selling cookbooks of all time and a cash cow for Knopf. But even the book's enormous success didn't alter Judith's convictions; she was no more interested in celebrity chefs, or publishing their cookbooks, after *Rosie* than she'd been before. Increasingly, though, she stood alone in resisting the wave: The year before *Rosie* came out, the American food media at large underwent a radical shift, one that made publishing celebrity chefs virtually obligatory for any cookbook editor who wanted to keep their job.

In November of 1993, the Food Network launched and practically overnight changed the entire landscape of American food media. The channel featured programs starring chefs like Emeril Lagasse, David Rosengarten, and Debbi Fields, the founder of Mrs. Fields baked goods. The Food Network's programs amplified professional chefs' visibility by moving them out of restaurant kitchens and into viewers' living rooms. It was all performance; the way food preparation appeared on screen had little relevance to home cooking. Prep work was done ahead and cook times were collapsed to meet network standards, compressing hours', if not days', worth of planning and labor into thirty-minute slots. Not only were such cooking shows inaccurate portrayals of the realities of home cooking, they didn't inspire its viewers to cook more. On the contrary. As cooking shows proliferated in the United States, Americans spent less and less time cooking. Still, viewers gobbled up the Food Network's programming: By the end of 1993, the channel was beaming into more than 6.8 million American homes.

Held up against the Food Network, Judith's Knopf Cooks American series appeared modest, almost quaint. Despite KCA's groundbreaking contributions and Americans' seemingly bottomless appetite for food media, most of the books in the series didn't sell well. It wouldn't be until the early twenty-first century, when regionality and authenticity became the guiding ethos in American food, that KCA would finally be celebrated for its prescience and import. Judith would

continue to work on select cookbooks until the end of her time at Knopf. But between the lackluster consumer reception of KCA and the advent of cable food TV,
the editor felt strongly that America's golden age of cookbooks—those written by
and for those who actually cooked at home, the sort she'd championed since her
earliest days at Knopf—was over and done.

CHAPTER 17

The editor and the poet sat together at the dining room table in Judith's apartment in New York. It was fall 1991. Judith had cooked and served a simple but elegant lunch: an omelet, a green salad, and a tartlet for dessert. They'd each had a glass of wine. Judith had cleared the dishes and made a pot of coffee before spreading the poet's pages across the table. They were all marked up in green. It was time to get down to work on fine-tuning the forthcoming collection by Sharon Olds. It had been a long and winding path, but after more than three decades at Knopf, Judith, at sixty-seven years old, had come full circle back to her first great love, poetry.

Judith had been tentative about publishing poetry since her disappointment with the reception of Sylvia Plath's *The Colossus* in 1962. She had taken a chance on a collection called *Heaved from the Earth* by Besmilr Brigham that Knopf published in 1971. It hardly sold at all. That same year, Judith advised Bob Gottlieb not to take on *The Collected Poems of Frank O'Hara*. In her reader's report, she'd written, "Except for two or three general pieces, they are <u>much</u> too fugitive, and too tied to specific shows and fleeting references to survive collecting in a book.

A good university press item, perhaps, if O'Hara were Ruskin—or ever Roger Fry or Clive Bell. But, as he was not, hopeless." Gottlieb didn't agree and went ahead anyway. O'Hara's collection won the National Book Award for Poetry in 1972. Judith had been wrong. She had remained somewhat skittish about publishing poetry since.

"I am very much out of step with what's going on today in poetry," Judith wrote to Brigham, who wanted to do a second collection with Judith at Knopf. "I have very little patience with the lack of form, the lack of sustained imagery, the lack of vision. The whole trend today is to spill it all out, freely with seemingly little concern as to whether one is honestly communicating. And audiences seem to lap it up. But I am very old-fashioned and I do ask for more." She went on, "I've become increasingly disenchanted with our ability to publish poetry at all successfully. I'm afraid it takes someone with more conviction than I have."

That someone was Alice Quinn, who began at Knopf in 1972 when she was twenty-three years old. Quinn started out in advertising with Nina Bourne, then moved over to an editorial role. One of the first ideas she put forth to Bob Gottlieb was that Knopf do more with poetry. He gave her permission to start a series of four books a year with the usual modest print runs of poetry books of the time. Quinn turned to Judith for help. She knew Judith had published Sylvia Plath. "The fact that she had fostered a relationship with her" impressed Quinn, she told me. "Judith was very important to me, because she was the person most obviously interested in poetry at Knopf."

Just as the series was getting off the ground, Quinn received a debut collection called *Satan Says* from a then-unknown poet named Sharon Olds. At the time, Olds was in her mid-thirties, married with two kids. Though her life may have appeared outwardly conventional, her poetry was anything but. *I have done what you wanted to do, Walt Whitman, / Allen Ginsberg, I have done this thing, / I and the other women with this exceptional / act* Olds wrote in "The Language of the Brag." Quinn asked Judith if she'd give Olds's poems a look.

"Judith responded to *Satan Says* right away," Quinn told me.

The themes of Olds's poetry were redolent of those of Sylvia Plath: sex and rage, marriage, and family life all featured prominently. The intoxication of love. The ache of passing time. Olds's verse trod similar territory as the prose of Anne Tyler, too. As Quinn put it, Olds set herself apart with her "willingness to take on the dramatic aspects of what are for most of us big subjects—love, physical love, marriage, parenthood, vulnerability, estrangement, loss, and more." But Judith and Quinn decided they should pass. Although the series was relatively new, the list was already backed up. Quinn wrote to Olds apologetically. She and Judith had decided they would try to get Olds's second collection.

Olds found a home for *Satan Says* at the University of Pittsburgh Press. It published the poet's debut collection in 1980. Olds's linguistic range, which drew from both sophisticated literary tradition and workaday expletives, along with her twinned descriptions of sexuality and violence, caught critics' attention right away. Many heralded her work as daring and exceptional in form and control, while others lambasted it as vulgar. Helen Vendler, one of America's most prominent poetry critics, referred to Olds's work as pornographic. The controversy only added to the book's allure; *Satan Says* sold and sold.

When Quinn and Judith received the manuscript for Olds's second collection, they were floored. "Sharon's compass for the kind of poem she would write was set with her first book," Quinn said of Olds's career in 2017, more than twenty years after she first edited the poet at Knopf, "so we were prepared for the territory, the angle of vision." But they hadn't quite expected the shuddering impact of Olds's second book of poems. "The book was extraordinary," Quinn said of *The Dead and the Living*, which Knopf published in 1984, "and the reviews and response of poets [were] predictably intense." The collection won a National Book Critics Circle Award. To date, *The Dead and the Living* has sold more than fifty thousand copies, making it one of contemporary poetry's best-selling books. Olds struck again in 1987 with her "shockingly intimate" *The Gold Cell*. Poems seemed to tumble out of her; it was Olds's third collection in seven years.

When *The Gold Cell* was off at the printer, Quinn announced that she was leaving Knopf to join the fiction department at *The New Yorker*; the magazine's editor, William Shawn, had tapped her himself. Nine months after Quinn's arrival, the magazine's longtime poetry editor, Howard Moss, died suddenly. With Bob Gottlieb now at the publication's helm, Quinn succeeded Moss in his position while continuing on in the fiction department. "I knew when I left that nobody but Judith should work with Sharon," Quinn said to me. Initially, when Quinn told Olds that Judith would be editing her at Knopf, Olds was both "a little intimidated," the poet told me, and also surprised. Judith did, after all, still give off "an aura of restraint," Quinn explained, and Olds's poetry was "so sensual and visceral." But, as Quinn had come to understand, that first impression of Judith was incorrect. Olds soon saw it, too.

Olds's fourth collection, *The Father*, was a painfully honest excavation of her shifting feelings toward the man who'd raised her through his battle with cancer and in the wake of his death. In "Beyond Harm," Olds wrote, *A week after my father died, / suddenly I understood / his fondness for me was safe—nothing / could touch it.* When the manuscript came in, Judith asked Bobbie Bristol—an editor who, in 1974 at the age of twenty-five, had come to Knopf to assist Angus Cameron—to read it and give her opinion. Bristol, like Olds, had at first seen Judith as "reserved, formal, and proper," but in time, that impression washed away. "I mean, it wasn't as if she was relaxed about everything," Bristol told me. "Obviously, no. She had very high standards, and there were things she didn't like." But Bristol had come to recognize Judith's earthiness and generosity, her openness and her deep spirituality, which, Bristol said, "was really surprising and very real."

Bristol knew poetry. She had, by then, brought Galway Kinnell—who'd won both a Pulitzer Prize and the National Book Award for his 1982 *Selected Poems*—to Knopf from Houghton Mifflin; Bristol published his 1990 collection, *When One Has Lived a Long Time Alone*. Bristol knew Sharon Olds, too. The two had met through the Community of Writers, an annual writer's conference held near Lake Tahoe in California, and had become friendly with each other by the time Judith replaced Quinn as Olds's editor. Bristol read Olds's manuscript as Judith had asked. The subject of the collection could have been "unbearable," Bristol told Judith. But instead, Olds had rendered it both magnetic and accessible with "unmistakable power and her great bravery." "Her probing of the wound," Bristol wrote, "is painful but precise." It was exactly what Judith needed to hear. She acquired Sharon Olds's *The Father* for Knopf in July 1991.

When it was time to finalize the collection for publication, Judith invited the poet to her apartment for a working lunch. "I hadn't expected to ever be there," Olds told me. "I was glad she offered wine so the edge was taken off my nerves." Olds noted the editor's "elegance and beauty" as she prepared their meal; Judith, Olds said, was "powerfully attractive, unselfconscious and economical. She moved gracefully, as if in a kitchen dance." When they ate, Olds was struck by Judith's "enjoyment of the food, and that sparkle in her eye." That's when, Olds told me, she realized her new editor was "a fellow sensualist."

It was high pleasure for Judith to attend so carefully to verse. Poems were all breath and feel. The way desire burns. The tender pain of sorrow kept. Even more than in writing about cooking and food, poetry was an attempt to capture embodied experience in language distilled. Judith offered Sharon clear feedback and advice on the terrain the poet traversed in her work, as well as on her style. "Her sympathetic nature," Olds said, was "held well this side of any kind of sentimentality. She was very articulate, very smart." She was grateful for Judith's astute "judgments, which were never unkind. She could put them into words that were clear." The editor was prone to reticence, the poet saw. "I mean she didn't say all she saw. She had a lot of self-possession," Olds said to me.

The Father was published in 1992 to wide acclaim. "Praise *The Father*. Praise Sharon Olds," wrote Adam Mars-Jones in the *London Review of Books*. "Celebrate the autobiographical mode in American poetry, its risks and rewards. Praise directness cut with understatement, starkness with an obliquity that can still take the reader off guard." Olds credited the collection's success in no small part to Judith's practiced skill as an editor, but also to her innate perceptiveness and sensitivity. "She knew a lot about feelings," Olds said. "I loved her editing." On a broadside of her poem "The Protestor," which she gave Judith as a gift, Olds articulated her admiration and gratitude: "For Judith—Wise guide, elegant guardian, generous & game, whose loving heart loves & sees. With love, Sharon."

In the years that followed, as Olds and Judith continued to work together, their relationship deepened. They began to socialize outside of work, in a small group connected by Knopf, poetry, and Vermont. In the late 1990s, Galway Kinnell and Bobbie Bristol married. Like Dick and Judith, Galway and Bobbie split their time between New York and the Northeast Kingdom. Since the early 1960s, Galway had been restoring an old farmhouse in Sheffield, just a short drive northeast of Bryn Teg. Sharon would sometimes visit Galway and Bobbie in Vermont to work; Galway and Sharon had long been dear friends and colleagues, and together founded New York University's Creative Writing Program in 1981. When Sharon visited Sheffield in the summers, Bobbie and Galway, Sharon, Judith, and Dick would have dinner together, talking for hours over several bottles of wine. Judith and Galway played cutthroat games of croquet on the lawn while the others looked on, bemused.

It was Judith's ongoing attention to her work, though, that moved Olds most of all. Judith helped pace the poet, who sent her editor poem after poem, mostly scrawled in longhand with margins full of notes. The poet admired the editor's courage and conviction, too. Though critics sometimes spewed venom at Olds and readers sent hate mail, Judith never wavered in her support, remaining true to the work and the transcendent power of language. "Judith was not intimidatable," Olds said.

Late in 1995, Judith sent Olds's fifth collection, *The Wellspring*, off to the printer. Knopf set the book's publication date for May of the following year. Judith and Dick booked tickets to visit the Roths, the couple's dearest friends from their time living in France, in Paris in early spring of 1996; they'd be back in New York for the book's launch. Judith sent an advance reader copy of *The Wellspring* to the Sri Lankan–Canadian poet and novelist Michael Ondaatje. He wrote that Sharon Olds's latest poems were "pure fire in the hands—risky, on the verge of falling, and in the end leaping up. I love the roughness and humor and brag and tenderness and completion in her work as she carries the reader through rooms of passion and loss."

• • • • • • •

In late January 1996, while up to use the bathroom during the night, Dick fell in the apartment at 139 East 66th Street, hitting his head on the sink. He'd had a series of mini strokes by then. The next morning, Judith took her husband to see his doctor, where Dick was diagnosed with a broken neck. He was sent to Lenox Hill Hospital, where they determined the best way to proceed would be to operate on the break and then attach to his head a "halo," a device meant to keep his neck in place while it healed. But during surgery, Dick fell into a coma, one from which he never emerged. He died on February 4, a week after entering the hospital. The official cause was pneumonia. He was eighty years old.

Family and the couple's closest friends gathered for a memorial at Bryn Teg. Judith scattered her husband's ashes across the spring-greening hill. Galway Kinnell captured the ache-filled day in verse: *Judith moves like a dancer / on sea swells, in a cloud / of the dust and ashes of this ardent man / who, as he grew older, more and more / gave himself to his love of poetry.* He continued, *Each of us / scoops up a handful of this intimate / grit and follows in her wake. / Some fling the ashes, others / sift them slowly through their fingers / as if feeling for something lost.*

For the first time in nearly forty-eight years, Judith found herself alone.

· · · · · · ·

It was early July 1996, and Judith was in Vermont. It had been five months since Dick's death. Late one evening, she left Greensboro, where she'd had dinner with family, and set off back to Bryn Teg. Madoc, Judith's little Welsh corgi, sat beside her in the car. It had been raining on and off all day, and hard. A mile and a half from home, Judith saw water coming over Messier Road; a culvert had flooded. She squinted through the dark, trying to gauge how deep the swollen creek had become. She felt sure she could make it through. But as she drove on, her tires sank into the mud. Judith began to feel a rushing current pressing against the sides of her car. Realizing she was in trouble, she honked for help several times, but no one came. Judith opened her door; she would deal with the car later and walk the rest of the way home. But she'd underestimated the water's depth. In an instant, Judith was swept off her feet.

She clutched her dog, Madoc, tightly as she was carried downstream. Judith was bumped into fallen trees, then pinned against a log. To avoid drowning, she had no choice but to let Madoc go. She was sure he was gone for good. Judith let the water pull her under a log, then came up gasping on the other side. Reaching out in the dark, she grabbed a young tree and hauled herself up onto the bank. Then she started to scream. Madoc, who'd managed to make his own way to shore, heard Judith and began swimming toward her in the relative calm along the brook's edge. Only once her dog was back in her arms did Judith begin to cry. Police and firefighters found her the next morning. Judith's ribs were bruised. Her abdomen was, too. She had cuts and scratches all over her arms. She was hypothermic. Still, she told officials she was "doing okay."

The story made all the regional papers: Against the odds, Judith Jones, a seventy-two-year-old vice president of Alfred A. Knopf, had survived a flash flood. For a piece about the incident, the *Vermont Times* spoke to Rux Martin, the journalist who'd interviewed Judith and Dick during their early years at Bryn Teg. Martin had never lost sight of the will, self-possession, and hardiness she had seen in Judith during their first encounter. "Unforgettable," Martin said. "Only Judith would come through like that."

Some tenacious power had taken hold of Judith in the water and dark. "I felt a lot of fight in me," Judith told a reporter for the *Vermont Times*. "I felt angry at nature. I wasn't going to let it get me." After her brush with death in the water that night, Judith grew determined not to succumb to fear. She would not relinquish the life she'd built or her place in the world just because she'd lost Dick.

• • • • • • •

In 1997, Judith signed Nina Simonds, an American food writer who studied Asian cultures and cuisines, to do a book for Knopf; it would later be titled *A Spoonful of Ginger*. Though Judith had worked on cookbooks about the food traditions of the Far East—there was Irene Kuo's *The Key to Chinese Cooking*, then *At Home with Japanese Cooking* by Elizabeth Andoh, which Knopf published in 1980—she'd never visited that region of the world herself. What if, Judith proposed to Simonds, she tagged along on the author's next trip to gather research for the book? Judith needed a way to get back on the horse again without Dick. Simonds thought it a splendid idea. She got right to planning. "Hello You Guys! Here's where we want to go," Simonds wrote in December 1997 in a note she faxed to Judith and her assistant, Kenneth Schneider, who had started with her in 1995 when he was twenty-eight years old. Ken quickly grew devoted to Judith; he would remain with her until the end of her career. Judith adored Schneider, too, and relied heavily on him, especially for help in keeping up with new communications technology and the quickening pace it was fostering in publishing. Judith struggled to adjust; "She didn't necessarily want to live in the modern world," her friend and former colleague Bobbie Bristol told me.

Simonds, like most of Judith's authors by then, ran all her communications with her editor through Schneider. "If you want to come," Simonds wrote, "you must visit Hong Kong (I have great connections at the Mandarin Hotel). I would probably take you then to Laos and then fly back to Bali. I know you want to be back to plant your garden in Vermont. Think about it and we'll talk." Judith saw it as a rare opportunity not to be missed: exploring new places and with an eye toward learning, led by a knowledgeable guide. By Christmas, she'd committed to accompanying Simonds and her partner, Don, on their trip.

But before going anywhere else, Judith knew she had to face Paris—and with it, the permanence of Dick's absence—alone.

In March 1998, Judith traveled to France solo for the first time in her life. Jacques Roth picked her up at the airport, just as he'd always done for her and Dick. In a spiral-bound notebook, Judith wrote, "We had a lovely talk driving into Paris and then there was Bettina waiting, her eyes dancing with delight—yes, we will all grow old together—and joy. Table laid as always with breakfast—croissants and brioches—and the usual nap—almost 2 hrs." Then it was off to Claudia Roden's little flat at 34 Rue Saint-Dominique; the author was in London, and she'd lent Judith her apartment for the week. "What a nice place to make a nest in the heart of this beautiful city that's just bursting into spring and heart-breakingly lovely," Judith wrote. She went for a long walk past the apartment where she and Dick stayed the last time they were together there, "and onto the street market still bustling in the late afternoon and bursting with fresh things—morels, strawberries, *asperges*, little artichokes." She got a Langres cheese, some *charcuterie*, a croissant for the following morning, "and some lovely baby batons about 8" long just warm from the oven, so irresistible I eat one on the street." That night, Judith fell into bed early and slept long and hard.

The next day, though, Judith's spirits fell from their heights. She'd dreamed about Dick. In Judith's sleep, Dick had come across a puppy, "a small messy ball of fur," and, on the spot, convinced her they must take it home. Since Dick's death, it was the first conjuring of him "in which he is really alive and present and so touchingly himself and our relationship so exactly the way it was," Judith wrote. "A miracle," she called it. It shook her nonetheless. "Broke for lunch, then tried the sculpture gardens. But somehow I needed guidance and someone to share with— a disheartening experience, going it alone."

Judith "walked all the way back home," hoping it would help her find some equanimity. But soon after she got back to the apartment to put her feet up, the phone in Roden's apartment rang. It was Judith's assistant, Ken, announcing "that we have been sold to Bertelsmann. Most disturbing," Judith wrote. "Why? Isn't Si making enough [off] of us?" "Si" was S. I. Newhouse, heir to Advance Publications, a magazine and media empire that included Condé Nast. Since 1980, he'd owned Random House. "Why a foreign publisher? Why does the government allow this kind of monopoly? What happened to the antitrust laws?" Judith asked into the void. The news left Judith agitated. "About 7:30 I venture forth to dine alone, determined not to be deterred and to enjoy it. Made me feel quite the adventurer on this trip alone," she wrote. Paris seemed at once so familiar, and yet, without Dick, was cast entirely anew.

It had been fifty years since Judith first arrived in Paris. That time, in so many ways, set her on her path. She'd grown accustomed to the place of that experience in her narrative, how those years had shaped her thinking, her family, her ambition, and career. But it was different now, Judith saw. All of it. Dick was gone. Knopf had been sold; commodified, again. The foundation of her life had shifted indelibly. That part of the story, *her* story, had drawn to a close. A person could get stuck in the past, Judith knew, trying to retrieve it, to re-create it, mired in nostalgia. Or she could throw open the doors of her life, as she'd done half a century before, in pursuit of newness and adventure, and thus find a way forward into her final, as yet uncharted, chapter. For Judith, it was an obvious choice.

· · · · · · ·

In early 1998, before leaving for Paris, Judith had contracted for a book with Julia Child and the French-born chef and author Jacques Pépin, with whom Judith had first worked in 1984. Julia and Jacques had known each other since the 1980s. Together, they'd cofounded the gastronomy program at Boston University in 1991, and had both been teaching there since. Their joint cookbook was to be a companion piece for PBS's forthcoming series *Julia and Jacques Cooking at Home.* Early in the process, Geoffrey Drummond, the series's producer, had reached out to Judith to float the idea of doing a book of recipes to accompany the show. *Julia and Jacques* was set to premiere in 1999, and, with the program's star power, PBS was expecting it to be a hit. The book would follow the formula Judith and Julia had developed for their 1968 collaboration, *The French Chef Cookbook*, making it possible for home cooks to replicate the dishes they saw Julia and Jacques preparing on screen. With Sonny Mehta backing her, Judith began negotiating terms with Drummond.

It wasn't an easy deal to land; Drummond drove a hard bargain. Julia remained quiet in the background, relying on the producer and her agent to do the talking on her behalf. Julia's cool distance during the process of setting terms irked Judith, especially after all the two women had been through and built together. Still, Judith stood firm. She believed Knopf was the right house, and she the right editor, for the book; "I was very sure of my ground on that," she told me. In the end, the advance Knopf agreed to was huge: $1,000,000 for world rights, including electronic versions in all languages. It seemed to Judith an almost obscene sum. "To me, that's pretty scary, to have a million dollars in my pocket," she told me. But by then Julia Child had global reach, and Mehta believed Knopf's investment was likely to pay off. Once matters of money had been settled, Judith seized the reins, making her priorities for the book plain: she would not allow lust for celebrity to supplant the book's essential pragmatism and quality. To Drummond, she wrote, "Above all, the book should be directed at the home cook, who today is more uncertain than ever about how to take the first steps." Drummond may have had jurisdiction over the series's production, but Judith planned to keep the cookbook firmly under her control.

She quickly got to work securing a cowriter for the project. The television series was set to begin taping that spring, and Judith needed someone to be on set with Julia and Jacques in Cambridge at Julia's house (Paul Child had died in May 1994) more consistently than she could herself, someone to watch the two cooks in action and get those finicky recipe details down for the book. Julia, who'd turned eighty-five years old in August 1997, was exceptionally sharp and able-bodied for a person her age, but she'd lost some of her capacity for granular specificity and patience for revision of her younger years. And, crucially, Judith needed someone to keep the project on schedule; in order to optimize its sales potential, the cookbook needed to be published concurrent with the debut of the TV series in September 1999. In mid-February 1998, Judith hired David Nussbaum, a food writer she'd been referred to by Rux Martin, who had, by then, become an esteemed cookbook editor herself, first at Chapters Publishing and, after Chapters was acquired by Houghton Mifflin (later Houghton Mifflin Harcourt) in 1997, as a senior editor. (Martin remained at HMH for the rest of her career, rising through the ranks first to executive editor, then to vice president and director. She was best known for her eponymous cookbook imprint.) In late April 1998, Judith traveled to Cambridge to observe the team in action and offer a guiding hand. "Your presence," Nussbaum observed, "was really helpful. Together with you, Julia is more focused and assertive about what she wants to say—and just how—which is incredibly valuable. The vitality of your creative partnership is evident." After ensuring the team was moving in the right direction, Judith returned to New York and prepared for her trip to Asia.

On May 13, Judith flew with Simonds and her partner from New York to Tokyo. They began their whirlwind tour in Singapore, then carried on to Malaysia, Kuala Lumpur, and Penang. She and Nina went to Bangkok, then Laos's Vientiane. They ended in China—Beijing, and then, to cap off the trip, Hong Kong.

When Judith got back to New York at the end of May, she was exhausted but exhilarated; before her plane even touched down, she'd found herself scheming more trips with other authors. Her appetite for travel had come roaring back. But in the immediate future, she had the Julia and Jacques book to attend to. She'd hated, with such a high-stakes project in process, to be away and unavailable to advise and troubleshoot. So despite her jet lag, Judith headed into the office first thing the morning after landing, and got right back to work on the book.

For much of her time at Knopf, Judith's cookbooks had been illustrated with drawings, but in the 1980s, photographs started to take their place. And by the late 1990s, visual culture had so firmly taken hold that photographs had become a requisite component of any cookbook hoping to achieve commercial success. The Jacques and Julia book needed a photographer. Judith had worked with several in the past, but she had yet to find someone whose style she felt accurately represented the pleasing but unfussy aesthetic of most home cooks. She had an idea, though, of where she might find a photographer who could.

Since its debut issue in 1994, Judith had been watching *Saveur* magazine evolve with great interest. The magazine's founding editors veered away from fine dining and celebrity chefs, aiming instead to "tell the life story of food" within a larger cultural context, for readers who "see the world food first." *Saveur*'s editors' approach reflected and resonated with Judith's own.

In the fall 1997 issue, Judith had been struck in particular by the magazine's images. On the cover was a photograph of a cone of skin-on French fries wrapped in waxed paper. The food, Judith remarked, looked appealing but unadulterated, like itself. It was nothing at all like the highly styled food photos that had become so popular in food media. She checked the issue's table of contents, then flipped to the cover story on page 122. Alongside the headline "Hot Potato" was a full-page photograph of three different cuts of golden fries, each in a dinged-up, run-of-the-mill metal mixing bowl, all held in the hands of a chef whose face the viewer could not see. She checked the photo credit: Christopher Hirsheimer, it read. Judith filed the name away.

When, in late May 1998, Judith was back in the office after her Asian sojourn, she asked Ken Schneider to get her the number for *Saveur*'s SoHo offices. On the line, she asked the receptionist for (Ms.) Christopher Hirsheimer, the executive editor of the magazine, and was put through. Judith introduced herself. "I saw your photographs in *Saveur* and I love what you do." Judith, Hirsheimer recalled, asked if she would be interested in shooting a book project for her at Knopf. Hirsheimer was unfamiliar with the book publishing landscape and with Judith personally, and demurred, saying she'd think it over. Afterward, she mentioned the call to

Dorothy Kalins, another founding editor, who, Hirsheimer recalled, exclaimed, "Judith Jones? You're kidding! That's great! Do it, whatever it is!" Hirsheimer called Judith back, and they set a date to meet at Knopf.

"I didn't give it any thought," Hirsheimer told me. "I had such a busy job, you can imagine, we were starting up, doing everything." The morning of her meeting with Judith, Hirsheimer got to the *Saveur* offices early, "because I thought, oh god, I should probably take some photographs or something with me," she said, laughing. "I was going through the photos for the magazine, and I just grabbed a folder out. It was a story about potatoes. I just thought, oh, I'll take those. It was just kind of nothing for me. Most people would have had a book and a whole thing. I just had these transparencies in a manila folder. Whatever professional is, this was the opposite of that."

At Knopf, Ken Schneider brought Hirsheimer back to Judith's office. Hirsheimer was bowled over. "It looked like a movie set, and Judith was central casting," she said. Judith offered Hirsheimer a seat and the two got to talking. "It was so natural between us," Hirsheimer told me. Eventually, she handed Judith the photos she'd brought. "Judith just opened them up and held them up toward the window and said, 'Oh! These are the exact photographs that drew me to you! This potato story!'" Hirsheimer recalled. "So it was sort of kismet." By the end of the meeting, Hirsheimer had agreed to take on Jacques and Julia's book.

In late 1998, Hirsheimer traveled with Judith to Cambridge to begin shooting. Julia and Jacques cooked, and the PBS staff used the dishes to style their own stills under artificial light. But "that wasn't me," Hirsheimer said. "It was all men photographers doing all that lighting, and I didn't know how to do any of that." Her approach was different. After the television staff were done shooting, Hirsheimer would take the dishes to a place with natural light—near a window, on the floor, or outside—to compose her shots for the book.

"Judith wasn't a visual person," she told me, "but I could see what she was trying to do with the images, what they represent." Judith allowed the photographer to execute her task in whatever way she saw fit; "She wasn't put off by my idiosyncratic way of shooting," Hirsheimer told me. At *Saveur*, Hirsheimer was "writing recipes, editing other people's recipes, finding recipes, and assigning stories. So we had these overlapping jobs," Hirsheimer told me. "I understood what she was doing, and really respected it, because I was trying to do that myself in my other job. We worked very well together in complex situations. [We] just had that kind of trust."

Hirsheimer was amazed at the level of seventy-four-year-old Judith's engagement with the whole process; "She was so meticulous, she was *in* the recipes," she recalled. "As the author was preparing the food—which Judith always wanted them to do, she didn't want it to be a stylist—she would sit, always, on a little stool right there with that green pencil." Judith would note aloud any discrepancy between what she observed the cooks doing as they prepared a given dish before her and the working version of its written recipe. "She was always doing that, and always to make it better," Hirsheimer said. "She was so involved, but in a way that you really trusted her. She made so many people look good."

Julia and Jacques Cooking at Home came out in September 1999, right on schedule. Judith and Julia's work together was nearing its end; *Julia and Jacques* would turn out to be Julia's penultimate cookbook. In 2000, she would publish one last book with Knopf, *Julia's Kitchen Wisdom*, again cowritten with David Nussbaum. In 2001, Julia moved to Santa Barbara, California, where she had summered as a child and where, late in their life together, she and Paul had wintered to escape the cold of the Northeast. Julia donated her house in Cambridge to her alma mater, Smith College, and her kitchen to the Smithsonian Institution's National Museum of American History in Washington, DC. In her final years, Julia began working with her great-nephew, Alex Prud'homme, on a memoir about her formative years in France. She died on August 13, 2004, two days shy of her ninety-second birthday, before the book was complete. Knopf published *My Life in France* in 2006; its final lines read: "[I]t now reminds me that the pleasures of the table, and of life, are infinite—*toujours bon appétit!*" Julia was both mourned and celebrated around the world; she had, across the decades, become a true icon. For Judith, Julia's death was more personal: the loss of a lifelong collaborator and a bookend to an era in American food culture that they, together, had begun.

Judith, though, wasn't done making her mark. She continued to work in the food space, both nurturing and learning from younger talents as they came up in a rapidly changing media landscape. Her relationship with Christopher Hirsheimer turned out to be among the closest and most generative creative relationships of Judith's late career. After *Julia and Jacques*, Hirsheimer shot many more of Judith's books in the following years. "We spent so much time together," Hirsheimer told me. Traveling in tandem and working on shoots, and they swapped stories constantly. "She told me the story of being in Paris when she was young and living in this fabulous apartment and starting a dinner club when 'the grown-ups' were away,'" Hirsheimer recalled. "I came back to Colman [Andrews] and said, 'we have to get Judith to write that.'"

Judith published her essay, "Le Cercle du Cirque," in the April 2001 issue of *Saveur*. It featured a photograph of her in Paris in 1951, her hair pinned up in a twist, her face lit by candlelight. She gazed steadily into the camera, her eyebrows raised audaciously. "I believe that some of us are genetically predisposed to love food," Judith's essay began. "But even though one may possess a fair share of these genes, it takes a moment of awakening to fully realize their potential, particularly if one was brought up, as I was, to look upon a passion for food as an embarrassing weakness to be curbed—like being oversexed." She went on to tell the story of setting sail for Paris in 1948, of meeting Pierre Ceria and learning to cook from him as they conducted their love affair. She recounted how she, Paul Chapin, and Ceria started the supper club in the princess's apartment, and of how that time had set her life on its course. "The experience opened up a new world to me. Although I returned to editing in New York . . . in time, I managed to sneak back into the kitchen, in my own way, and have been shamelessly loving it ever since, learning and helping others to discover the joys—the art—of cooking," she wrote.

Judith sent a copy of the article to her friend, cowriter, and former mentor, Angus Cameron. "I was simply delighted to read your piece," he replied. He saw the moment as an opportunity to offer some unsolicited advice. It was high time, he said, that Judith do a book of her own. Angus wrote her repeatedly in the fall and early winter of 2001 with ideas for directions she might take. "You should write a big general book about cooking, called in principle maybe 'publishing books on cooking,'" he said. A few weeks later he wrote, "You must do a book and the first and easiest should be a collection of familiar essays about the Julias, etc. Its working title might be *Great Cooks—An Editor's Memoir of Writer-Cooks*. Of course, someday you must do *The Memoirs of a Cook Book Editor*. I will get two and possibly three books out of you." And in one of the last letters he ever wrote to Judith, Angus was adamant: "<u>I am now more than ever convinced that you yourself should do a book</u>," he said. "It should be a book about learning from experts how to improve one's cooking by editing and publishing them. <u>You must write. You have a talent for it</u>. Love, Angus."

Cameron died in November 2002, at the age of ninety-three. Mourning his loss, alone in her apartment, Judith flipped through years' worth of their correspondence. She reread the letters he'd written her urging her to write over and over again. Judith hadn't ever really considered telling her story in print. She had to admit, though, that she'd enjoyed doing the piece for *Saveur*; it had exercised a different part of her mind than editing. And writing alone was entirely different from doing so collaboratively: more introspective, and pleasingly challenging. And if there was anyone whose editorial vision Judith trusted, it was Angus Cameron. His words felt, to her, at once like a challenge and a final benediction of sorts. Perhaps, Judith thought as she tucked his letters back into their envelopes, it was time she try to find her own voice on the page.

CHAPTER 18

It was late in the evening. Judith sat on the back deck at Bryn Teg. Her hair was still damp from her evening swim. A clean plate and an empty wineglass sat on the table beside her; she'd cooked herself dinner and eaten by candlelight, as she'd continued to do each evening since Dick's death. Away to the northwest, the Green Mountains were cast in silhouette, a rugged underline of the dimming sky. The sinking sun dragged its embers down, setting the shelved clouds above the ridge aflame. The birds had grown quiet. Bats darted and swooped. From below in the pasture came the soft snap of cattle tearing at meadow fodder with their teeth and the slow, heavy thud of their footfall as they grazed. With the help of her cousin and neighbor John Reynolds, Judith had brought a small herd of Black Angus to Bryn Teg earlier that year; they were raising them for beef. Judith shivered, the chill of dusk setting in. It was June 2006, nearly the summer solstice. Soon, the days would begin to grow shorter in a long, slow denouement. Judith could feel the turn coming like a charge; she was brimming with it. She stilled herself, her gaze fixed in reverie as the horizon smoldered.

After the sky had deepened to nighttime blue, Judith gathered her dishes and went inside. She was weary; it had been a long, full day. She'd been up early, done her yoga, and then had gone down to the pond for her morning swim. She dove in, and then paused to pull a few cattails from the muddy bank; the reedy marsh plants were forever encroaching on the open water, threatening to turn the pond back into the wetland it had once been. After tossing the long stalks ashore, Judith finished her laps among the bullfrogs' throaty calls and the dragonflies flitting about in the morning mist. After breakfast, she'd holed up in her office to work on manuscripts. Updike had a book—a collection of essays and criticism titled *Due Considerations*—coming out the following year. So did Lidia Bastianich, an Italian chef and entrepreneur who Judith had begun working with in 2001. Their first cookbook collaboration had been *Lidia's Italian-American Kitchen*; in 2004, they'd done another, *Lidia's Family Table*. By the summer of 2006, Bastianich and Judith were putting the finishing touches on their third book together, *Lidia's Italy*. The book was set for publication in April 2007.

Judith had been startled out of her concentration by the sound of gravel crunching under tires coming up the driveway; it was her friends, the skilled collectors of wild foods, Nova Kim and Les Hook. They were stopping by to drop off a basket of mushrooms and to make a plan to go foraging with Judith later that week. It was almost lunchtime when they arrived, and Judith asked if they'd like to stay. But they were on the go; they had a circuit of restaurant chefs to whom they needed to deliver their wares that afternoon. When they'd gone, Judith fixed herself something to eat, then took her dog for a walk down to the end of the long, steep driveway to get the mail. It was late in the afternoon by the time she settled down to tend to her own writing.

After *Saveur* published Judith's essay about Paris, Christopher Hirsheimer had talked Judith into writing more pieces for the magazine; Judith wrote an essay on sorrel and gooseberries, "The Lemons of the North," that ran in the July 2001 issue. In the summer of 2000, Hirsheimer had come to Bryn Teg to shoot Judith's gooseberry bush in full fruit. While there, she photographed Judith walking down to the pond for her swim, her dog, Madoc, at her heels. When Judith emerged from the water, she told Hirsheimer about the beaver that had settled in the pond in 1999, felling trees near the waterline, building a dam and a lodge, and slapping its tail in warning every time Judith came near. Judith had realized it wouldn't take long before the dam clogged the pond's drainage system and it flooded the low-lying parts of the property and likely the dirt road below, too. She had agonized over what to do. Finally, she'd asked David, her stepdaughter Bronwyn's husband, to try to kill the creature so that she might have some peace again. Early one morning, in the first gray light, Judith woke to gunshots. She ran down the stairs and outside to see David standing beside the beaver—all fifty pounds of him—lying limp in the grass.

Judith was at once relieved and at a loss: to merely scrap the carcass, she felt, would be a waste and an act of disrespect. Judith thought of Angus Cameron and how he'd taught her about the long history of hunting beavers not only for their fur but for their meat as well. She thought, too, of Dick, who had fried up a beaver tail given him by a local hunter and contributed the resulting recipe to Judith and Angus's *L.L.Bean Game and Fish* book. While the beaver's body was still warm, Judith instructed David to cut open the animal and remove its liver. In the kitchen, she coated the organ in flour, fried it in plenty of butter, and ate it for breakfast in tribute. Later, she skinned and fried the animal's fatty tail, and braised its legs for supper.

Hirsheimer told Judith the story was too good not to publish. Judith accepted the assignment, and "Beaver Tale" ran in the June/July 2003 issue of *Saveur*. Judith wrote the piece with good humor, but also reverence, nodding at the interdependence between humans and that which sustains us. She was taken aback when she received a wave of hate mail in response to the piece, condemning her cruel behavior and ignorance of beavers' crucial role in maintaining ecological health.

The outrage affirmed Judith's suspicion that Americans knew next to nothing about the true sources of their food. It was something she'd been thinking about more and more over time as she worked with Kit Foster, Edna Lewis, Angus Cameron, and, later, the painter, winemaker, gardener, and avid home cook Edward Giobbi (in 1991 Judith had published his *Pleasures of the Good Earth* as part of the Knopf Cooks American series). And though *Saveur*'s readers' blowback surprised Judith, it did not silence her. On the contrary, Judith found herself more motivated than ever to speak up, and not just on her views about food.

In March 2004, Judith turned eighty years old. And while no one asked or pressured her directly, she knew the question of her retirement hung in the air. More and more, publishing was becoming a young person's game; everything kept moving faster and faster, pegged to the pace of new media and changing trends. Judith had struggled to adapt to some of the changes. Still, she had no desire to leave her job, and she saw no good reason why she should. She remained curious and committed to her work, publishing a slew of books each year. And she was lithe and vigorous despite her age; she practiced yoga each morning at home and the weekly yoga class she'd organized at the office many years before. She walked to work, took the subway, rode the bus. She went with friends to the theater and to hear music. She was active in her church. She did all her own shopping and cooking. She spent more and more time at Bryn Teg; between FedEx, fax machines, and the internet, she could be away from the office for longer stretches while remaining in the loop. Judith had been traveling, too. She continued in the tradition of her and Dick's annual pilgrimage to Paris, and took trips with her authors: to Israel with Joan Nathan and Bronwyn to shoot the photos for Nathan's 2001 book, *The Foods of Israel Today*, and to Naples and Rome with Lidia Bastianich.

Judith and Bastianich had quickly grown close. At first, Bastianich's writing was stiff and stilted. "I was afraid it wasn't good enough and that I wasn't a writer," she told me. But Judith pushed Bastianich to deepen her authorial voice. "I really began to expand myself in those books with her," Bastianich told me. Judith guided her author patiently through her fear and insecurity, instructing Bastianich to put everything down as it came into her mind. Judith, Bastianich recalled, said, "'I'll take care of cleaning it up.' That liberated me. Whenever I needed guidance, whenever I didn't know, Judith was there." Their relationship became an intimate one. "Judith permeated your life," Bastianich told me. "All the time she spent with me, nurtured me, she helped me be who I am." She did not take Judith's attention for granted; she understood that to be nurtured by such talent was a privilege and a gift. "I mean, she was this great literary mind. And she knew exactly what she wanted. She was right, you know. History has proven her right all the way."

It may have been clear to Bastianich that Judith still had plenty of capacity and verve, but she saw that Judith was facing a pervasive cultural disregard for women of advanced age. "Here in America, the respect may not be for the older people as much. Judith felt that," Bastianich told me. Judith was well aware of the outside world's perception of her as a fragile granny figure, an old lady ready to be put out to pasture. Old women, it seemed, had no worth in American culture; there was no room for them in public life. Judith decided to address the elephant in the room directly, and in print, no less.

In August 2005, Judith published an essay she called "A Recipe for Life: A Ripe Old Age" in *Vogue*. "We live in a society that disparages age, and it is easy to feel that you should be stepping aside to let someone more youthful take over," she wrote. She knew people around her whispered, wondering why she wasn't packing it in. "Why do I continue to work? To me, it is more a question of 'Why retire?' I find that the very word has unappealing connotations—to retreat, withdraw." As she'd continued to accrue years of wisdom and experience, she felt she had more, not less, to offer and pass on. Aging, Judith had come to feel, wasn't something to be resisted, but rather a badge of honor one should wear with pride. "Every office," she wrote cheekily, "needs to have a little ripe fruit and aged cheese around."

A photo of Judith in her office at Knopf accompanied the piece. She wore a purple wool pencil skirt and a fetching lavender blouse. Around her neck was a bright silk scarf. Manuscripts in process covered the surface of her desk. On the bulletin board on her wall were snapshots of her authors, many of whom, by then, had become the editor's dear friends. It was a reflection of Judith's life as she herself perceived it still to be: engaged, busy, colorful, and full. Unless someone forced Judith out, she planned to stay in the game as long as she could.

Jonathan Segal, a longtime editorial colleague of Judith's and a fellow gastronome, seized on the moment of chutzpah. The two editors had been working alongside each other for decades; Segal came to Knopf in 1989, lured there by Sonny Mehta from his position at the *New York Times Book Review*. Segal and Judith had bonded over their love of France and *la belle cuisine*, and had shared many meals. Judith hadn't shown off the pieces she'd done for *Saveur*, nor her most recent one in *Vogue*, but Segal was aware of them nonetheless. So were others at Knopf. In casual conversation, someone in the office had mentioned to Segal that they thought Judith should write her story. And one day, he approached Judith and proposed the idea. She could chronicle her life through her adventures in food and her work with cookbooks, Segal said. As he spoke, Judith couldn't help but hear the echo of Angus Cameron's encouragement at the end of his life. Segal told Judith that Knopf would do the book—he'd edit it himself—and gave her time to think.

Judith was ambivalent. Writing an article here and there was one thing, but a book, entirely another. She knew, from decades of experience supporting authors, how long and arduous the work was, how much energy and focus it required. Besides, she was still working full-time. She wondered if she should divide her attention like that, or if she really had the time she'd need to write. More than that, though, Judith wasn't sure she wanted to reveal so much about herself, and to step into the publicity spotlight as she knew she would have to if the book was to find an audience. "I mean, I've worked with some wonderful books, I've worked with some wonderful people," Judith told me. "It goes back to what I said before. A certain amount of luck, that certain things came my way. I think I'm naturally modest. I'm not that impressed with myself." But she had never shied away from a challenge, and she wasn't keen to appear uncertain or afraid before a colleague. "Maybe that made me work harder to try," Judith told me. She told Segal she would do it. She would write a book of her own.

Judith approached her memoir with characteristic diligence, energy, and pluck. She went back through old marked-up manuscripts, photographs, editorial files, and notebooks and letters from her youth, all kept in boxes and rusting filing cabinets at 139 East 66th. As she began attempting to put the events of her life down on paper, though, Judith found the writing surprisingly hard. She tried to channel the advice she'd long given her authors: to begin by writing just "as though I were talking to you as I'm talking now," Judith told me. She tried to keep her worry about the book's structure and finessing the language at bay until after she'd gotten the bones of the stories down, which, she discovered, she could not do on the computer but only by writing longhand. "I had to leave that damn little machine in the other room," Judith told me, "and just have that yellow pad. I can't do it on that machine. It freezes me somehow." Still, she found it difficult to assess the quality of her own work. "It's hard to judge objectively. And I do think I'm hard on myself," Judith said. She persisted nonetheless.

By spring 2006, Judith had most of her manuscript in working shape. It had been more challenging than she'd imagined, carving out time for her own writing while going into the office daily and remaining available to her authors and their needs. She'd spent the fall of 2005 and first months of 2006 finalizing the latest novels from both Anne Tyler and John Updike, due out within weeks of each other (Tyler's *Digging to America* came out in May 2006, and Updike's *Terrorist* in mid-June). She'd also been working closely with a first-time cookbook author, Hiroko Shimbo, on *The Sushi Experience*, and with Madhur Jaffrey on *Climbing the Mango Trees: A Memoir of a Childhood in India*, the author's first book of prose. By March 2006, both culinary titles were at the printer and set to launch in October of that year. Judith was looking forward to spending most of the summer at Bryn Teg, where she could write the final two chapters of her book in quiet and begin revisions on the rest. The retreat away from New York felt more necessary than ever. Before she left, though, she had a public appearance to make in New York. Earlier that year, the James Beard Foundation had contacted Judith, saying they were honoring her with a Lifetime Achievement Award. They hoped she would accept in person at their annual awards dinner.

James Beard had died in January 1985, and soon thereafter, Julia Child had called Peter Kump, a former student of Beard's and founder of the Institute of Culinary Education, urging him to do something with Beard's Greenwich Village town house, where he'd lived and out of which he'd run his cooking school. In November 1986, Kump, Jacques Pépin, the writer Calvin Trillin, and other major players in the food world had presided over the opening ceremony of the James Beard Foundation. Its mission was "to provide a center for the culinary arts and to continue to foster the interest James Beard inspired in all aspects of food, its preparation presentation, and of course, enjoyment." Over the years, the foundation had evolved into the self-appointed arbiter of the world of restaurants and culinary media; to win a James Beard Award was an anointment, a mark of acceptance into the food scene 'in' crowd. Judith didn't put much stock in the foundation's awards, and didn't care for all that competition and glitz. Still, Judith felt a swell of pride. For forty-five years, she'd been editing cookbooks that shaped

American culture, but the impact of her work had been little recognized. On May 6, 2006, donning a brocade jacket and flowing full-length black skirt, Judith stood at a glass podium in front of a packed house and graciously accepted her award. Publishing at large had yet to celebrate Judith's living legacy, but the food world recognized her as royalty.

In Vermont, a couple weeks later, Judith tackled the final section of her memoir with renewed vigor and purpose. She opened the chapter she was calling "Treasures of the Good Earth" in 1980, the summer she and Dick found Bryn Teg. There on the mountain, steeped in the magic of that place, the words came easily to Judith. She found the final chapter, "The Pleasure That Lasts the Longest," more difficult to write. It began with Dick's death in the winter of 1996. The memories of the initial shock and disorientation that followed were painful to revisit. But as Judith constructed sentence after sentence, she began to recognize how much she'd grown in the decade since. "I doubted that I would ever find pleasure in making a nice meal for myself and sitting down to eat it all alone," Judith wrote. "I was wrong." She saw more clearly than ever how, in the kitchen and at the table, life goes on. Judith felt it was an important message to share with readers. Until getting it down on the page, she'd been unaware of how much she'd needed to articulate it for herself, too.

Knopf published *The Tenth Muse: My Life in Food*, in October 2007. With her star-studded list of authors all lined up in the book, for the first time, Judith's outsize role in American food culture was made undeniably clear. In teasing the book for the dining section of the *New York Times*, Julia Moskin wrote, "Ms. Jones may not be the mother of the revolution in American taste that began in the 1960s and transformed the food Americans cook at home. But she remains its most productive midwife." She went on: "[S]he has exposed millions of Americans to new ways of thinking and tasting during her 50-year career."

Dorothy Kalins wrote *The Tenth Muse*'s review for the *Times*. "If we had in our libraries only the food books Jones has edited, what an impeccable culinary education that would be: a curriculum of foods of the world, rigorous, responsible and delightfully authentic." But the one-note sunny tone of *The Tenth Muse* did give Kalins pause. She wrote that she wished Judith had been more candid and revealing of her life's complexity and depth. "[W]e know that accomplishments like hers never come without struggle, profound disappointment, angst, even a touch of self-doubt. Jones is perhaps too much a lady, or too much a Vermonter, for such revelation . . . saving perhaps the messy bits (and the juicy bits) that have inevitably been a part of that life for the next volume. We're still hungry for more."

Judith relished the attention and was unfazed by the critique; she believed deeply in privacy and discretion, and had deliberately kept much about her authors and her own life off the page. "I've had people saying, 'Oh, I wish you'd done more,' And I say, 'Oh, who cares,'" she told me, laughing. "I do think that Americans love to create heroes for themselves." She had no qualms about reserving certain parts of her life and story only for herself. "Sorry, but you'll just have to decide whether I slept with the chef!" she said.

At eighty-three years old, Judith went out on tour. "It was the first time, except for sales conferences, where I had a big audience," she told me. Speaking before rooms full of admirers, Judith felt as young and vital as she had in years. "I loved connecting, I loved getting laughs. All anxiety just left me. There's always some person you want to keep the smile on their face. But it's more than that. It's giving, *sharing* something that meant a lot to you," she said, her eyes alight.

Judith used the public platform to freely speak her mind. She told stories of learning to grow her own produce at Bryn Teg, hunting for mushrooms in the Vermont woods with Nova and Les, and raising grass-fed cattle for beef. Those experiences "added to that whole sense of where your food comes from," Judith told her audience, and "enriched her cooking," too. Such involvement with her food and its production, Judith explained, helped her feel she was responding constructively to Big Food and its ill effects on ecological and human health as well. She had been deeply influenced by journalistic exposés like Eric Schlosser's 2001 *Fast Food Nation*, and Michael Pollan's *Omnivore's Dilemma*, which came out 2006. "It's so horrifying what we've allowed the food industry and Big Ag to do," Judith said in December of 2007 at Politics and Prose, a bookstore in the nation's capital.

While on tour, Judith also spoke out about what she saw as the misuse of celebrity. Julie Powell's book, *Julie and Julia: 365 Days, 524 Recipes, 1 Tiny Apartment Kitchen: How One Girl Risked Her Marriage, Her Job, and Her Sanity to Master the Art of Living*, was published in 2005. In it, Powell chronicled her experience cooking her way through *Mastering the Art of French Cooking* while navigating life and love as a young adult in New York City. She punctuated her book with fictionalized biographical sketches of Julia Child's life. *Julie and Julia*, which had begun as a blog, became a bestseller. At Politics and Prose, an audience member asked Judith if she'd read Powell's book and, if so, to share her feelings about it.

Judith didn't hold back in her response. "I first heard about it when [Powell] had her blog," she began. "In fact, she called me and asked if I would come out to watch her cook. I didn't know anything about the blog, and I agreed at a certain date." In the meantime, Judith said, "I watched the blog, and I thought, this girl could not care one bit about cooking. It's all an exploitation of Julia, she's just using her. She only has a vocabulary of four-letter words! So I called up and said I would not be coming." She and Julia had talked about Powell's project as well, Judith said, and Julia had some choice words about the whole thing. "Then she went on to do a book about this, got a huge advance from some publisher," Judith said, the energy rising in her voice. "And now, they're making a movie!" Judith delighted in pulling back the curtain. She went on to tell her audience that Nora Ephron had written the screenplay and would be directing the film, and that Meryl Streep had been cast as Julia Child. "I'm a character in it who, at the last minute, turned down the dinner," Judith said, incredulous. "Here she'd made this beautiful dinner for me and I didn't come. So"—she paused for a moment, collecting herself—"I don't know. Maybe it gets people to Julia and, if so, that's just fine. But I can't really respect it. Maybe it's my age."

Julie & Julia, the film, debuted in theaters in August 2009. *The Tenth Muse* had increased Judith's visibility, but only among a niche readership. The movie, though, brought Judith widespread public exposure. At Nora Ephron's request, Judith attended the premiere; she watched uneasily as Erin Dilly played her on-screen. Judith left the theater annoyed. (She wasn't alone in being irked by the film's portrayal of her. In 2012, Anne Tyler, who rarely gave interviews, told the Associated Press that she thought the movie was "stupid" because of its gross mis-representation of Judith as someone who, at the last minute, would no-show to dinner on account of rain. "Judith Jones would go through a blizzard," Tyler said. "She's the most indomitable person.")

In September 2009, a month after *Julie & Julia*'s premiere, Knopf published Judith's second book, a collection of essays and recipes titled *The Pleasures of Cooking for One*. Judith had written it quickly; she'd signed the contract in March 2008. The book was done on a shoestring budget: Judith's advance from her employer of nearly fifty years was $25,000. Christopher Hirsheimer took the photographs for free.

In early 2009, Judith had taken the bus to Lambertville, New Jersey, to the Canal House studio Hirsheimer shared with her business partner, Melissa Hamilton. She brought with her several bags of food for the shoot and John Updike's final manuscript; he'd died in January of that year at the age of seventy-six. While Hirsheimer and Hamilton styled and shot, Judith sat at a little table by the window, her green pen in hand, marking up Updike's pages. The editor was wearing, Hirsheimer recalled, a lovely green sweater. "I looked up and the light was kind of falling softly across her. I just took my camera and I said, 'Judith, just stay there. Don't move. You just look so beautiful. I'm going to take a pho-tograph for your author's page.'" "All right," Judith responded. "And as a present, I'm going to read you this passage from John Updike's book that has never been heard."

"It was," Hirsheimer told me, "*such* a special moment . . . and that, that was the payment." She went on: "I *loved* working with her. She was funny, and she had a wicked sense of humor. We had so much fun together. I think I can say we loved each other. We were a little bit kindred spirits; we recognized each other somehow. You never know where you're going to get the good stuff from. It comes, you just have to be aware."

Judith's *The Pleasures of Cooking for One* may not have contained the sorts of "messy" and "juicy" details some had found lacking in *The Tenth Muse*, but nonetheless, it was a more personal book than her memoir had been. In *Pleasures*, Judith expounded upon her notions of pragmatism and thrift. She encouraged home cooks to make their kitchens their own. "I like to walk into a kitchen and feel that the space expresses the personality of the cook who inhabits it. Too many kitchens today seem like sterile laboratories—there's no one home." She used luscious, evocative language in her headnotes and recipes, an approach to food writing she'd long encouraged her authors to practice; you want the reader, Judith said, to be "just *panting* by the time you get to taste [the recipe]. You can't stand it!" She encouraged reader/cooks to loosen up in the kitchen; "This is apt to be a messy-looking pancake," she wrote in the headnote for Wild Rice Pancake, "But who cares? It's just for you, and it's delicious." Above all, *Pleasures* was an articulation of an ethic that Judith had spent a lifetime building. "Cooking is a sensual experience, and you really should allow all your senses full play," she wrote in her introduction. "Enjoy the feel of ingredients, observe what is happening, taste as you go along, and drink in the heady smells that arouse your anticipation . . . even if it's just for you—or especially if it's just for you." The book was a manual for living as much as for cooking, positioning pleasure as a means of resisting homogenization, convention, commodification, and alienation from one's own body. A worthy purpose in and of itself.

By the time the *Pleasures* book tour was over in early 2010, Judith had to concede that she was beginning to tire. She was eighty-five years old. "She was slowing down," her longtime assistant, Ken Schneider, told me. "Definitely in terms of acquisitions. She wanted to spend more time at Bryn Teg. I think she was, you know, ready to relax a bit." Schneider's hesitation mirrored Judith's own; paring back was anathema to how she had lived her entire life. She'd always been full steam ahead. It took Judith some time to wrap her head around the change, but in the fall of 2011, she retired as senior editor and vice president of Knopf.

Judith did not stop working, though. She was still very much in demand. She reviewed manuscripts for colleagues and friends; they were piled on her coffee table, dining table, and in the little dining nook where she ate most of her meals. And she started a third, and final, book of her own, *Love Me, Feed Me*, about living alongside, and cooking for, the dogs she'd cared for throughout her long life, and the joy they brought her in return. Judith worked on the book at her apartment at 139 East 66th Street and at Bryn Teg, where she was finally free to spend the entire summer; she left New York in late May, and didn't return until autumn. In Vermont, Judith hired a local woman to transcribe her handwritten pages into typed text. Judith's eyes had gotten bad; to read, she held a magnifying glass in hand. When Knopf published *Love Me, Feed Me* in October 2014, Judith was ninety years old.

On the morning of January 1, 2015, Judith met Meri Zeinklishvili-Dubrova at 139 East 66th Street. It was a first date of sorts; Meri had been asked to the apartment by Bronwyn to interview for the position of live-in caregiver for Judith. For some time, Judith had been slipping in and out of lucidity; she'd be perfectly sharp one moment and disoriented the next, conflating the past with the present and forgetting where she was. By the time she wrapped up the short regional publicity tour for *Love Me, Feed Me*, the episodes were increasing in frequency. Judith knew something was wrong, though she was loath to admit it. But Bronwyn and Chris, the family members closest to her, were worried. At last, they insisted Judith see a doctor. The diagnosis was Alzheimer's. The illness had taken hold slowly—Judith's strong social ties and intellectual engagement had likely helped to stave off cognitive decline. Bronwyn visited more and more often, staying longer than she had in the past. When Judith fell while out walking Mabon one day and fractured her hip, Bronwyn knew the time had come. It wasn't safe for Judith to live on her own anymore. Bronwyn began exploring avenues for in-home support.

It was clear to all involved that Judith was going to resist that kind of help. It would require of her an unprecedented admission of vulnerability and dependence. If Judith was going to allow someone into her home, it would have to be someone extraordinary. Bill Needelman, a close friend of Jane Gunther, connected Bronwyn with Meri; Meri had cared for his mother, a member of the Manhattan Project, for five years. Needelman thought Meri was just the sort of person Judith might not only concede to accept into her life but actually enjoy spending time with.

Meri Zeinklishvili-Dubrova had been born in the city of Kutaisi, in the Republic of Georgia. The city was cosmopolitan, and her household was, too. She read widely, was exposed to multiple languages, and played the piano from an early age. At university, she studied sociology and psychology. She'd become a schoolteacher and then, at twenty-eight years old, a principal. She stayed at the school for fifteen years, time during which she completed a master's degree, married, and had two children. In 1999, when her son was nineteen and her daughter nine, Meri immigrated to the United States; political and economic conditions in Georgia were strained. Her husband and daughter came with her. Her son stayed.

The family settled in Orlando, where Meri enrolled in school again; she studied to become a medical assistant, and worked at Florida Hospital Celebration Health as a patient care technician in the intensive care and progressive units and the emergency room. She excelled at the work; she was thrice honored with a model of excellence award. After several years, in search of educational opportunities for her daughter, Meri relocated to Brooklyn and began working as a caregiver.

Judith was skeptical at first. Meri was undeniably warm, kind, and capable. She was easy to talk to and was intelligent, attentive. Still, Judith tried to hold out, unprepared to relinquish her independence. But Bronwyn was clear about Judith's needs, and offered Meri the job. Meri would live with Judith for ten days at a stretch, and then Bronwyn would rotate in for two or three. It came together quickly; the day after Meri's interview, she began working with Judith.

Meri admired Judith from the start; "She had a very big wish to live. Not all people have that," she told me. But she understood that Judith was uneasy about her presence. If the two had any chance of building a comfortable rapport, Meri knew she would have to find a way to engage with Judith on genuine terms. Meri paid close attention to Judith's home, using the objects therein as clues to her new charge's personality and proclivities. Books, a good portion of which Judith had edited herself, filled every room of the apartment. "She loved literature, that was clear," Meri told me. While Judith rested, Meri perused the shelves. In Judith's library, "I found her thoughts on Dostoyevsky," she said. "I have a master's degree in Russian literature, this is my subject, my 'bread,' so to speak. So we started to talk about that." They connected over a shared love of classical music, too; Meri had studied music for many years and played, still. "This is what helped me to know her," Meri told me. But it was in their time cooking and eating together that the two forged their deepest bond.

Judith wasn't as steady on her feet as she'd once been, so they struck a deal: Judith would do the chopping, and Meri helm the range. On occasion, they went out to eat; Judith introduced Meri to Indian food, which she'd never tasted before. When Meri went home to Brooklyn on her days off, she'd prepare Georgian dishes and bring them back for Judith to try. Together, they made Jane Gunther's hundredth birthday cake in August 2016, a lavish, multitiered thing with icing piped on top.

In the evenings, Judith would put on music while they prepared dinner. When everything was ready, Meri set the table and lit the candles and they'd eat together, "sitting and talking about life," for two or three hours. Judith told Meri about her parents; her father's warmth and her mother's rigid expectations. She talked about Bennington, where she fell in love with poetry and Roethke. She talked about Doubleday, and going to Paris; about falling for Pierre Ceria and discovering Anne Frank. She talked about meeting Dick, and how she knew, so quickly, that they would be together. Meri saw that Judith's deep longing for, but inability to have, children of her own had made an indelible mark; "She filled up her life a different way," Meri said. Judith talked a great deal about her relationship with Dick. Meri was struck by the unusualness of the couple's marriage, how Dick had done so much of the cooking and household chores, working piecemeal while Judith pursued an absorbing full-time career. Judith was transparent that their marriage hadn't always been easy. But Meri saw what the longevity and steadfastness of Judith's partnership with Dick had given her; "She was able to do it"—everything she accomplished in her life, Meri said, "because she had such big protection from Dick. She wanted very much to be married, and she did *everything* to save this marriage."

The two women went together to Bryn Teg. The first summer they spent there, in 2015, Judith offered the guest bedroom on the second floor next to her own, but Meri insisted it should remain available for family and friends. "Okay," Judith said, "then would you like to sleep in Julia's bed?" "Who's Julia?" Meri asked. "Julia Child!" Judith said, as though it were obvious. "Julia Child was sleeping in this house?" Meri asked, gobsmacked. "Yes," Judith said, every time she visited, sometimes "all month long!"

Meri accepted, and settled into, the small room just off the kitchen on the ground floor. There was a twin bed set against the windowed wall. The other long wall was lined with records and cassettes, and a small piano. Meri offered to play; Judith enthusiastically agreed. Every day, "we had music hour," Meri told me. "She was lying on my bed, and I was sitting there, playing piano for her." They walked Mabon, Judith's latest dog, together several miles a day. Judith swam. They went into town for Reubens and homemade potato chips. They went to church on Sundays. They cooked and cooked and cooked. They hosted visitors; Kathy Hourigan came early in the season, and Chris came all the way from Hawaii. Bronwyn came often from her home in Burlington and stayed for several days at a time. John Reynolds was a daily presence, coming by to feed the cows and often staying to talk for a long, long time. There were frequent dinners with Judith's nephew Jon Morey and his second wife, Durrell; they married that summer and had bought a house just down the lane from Bryn Teg upon retiring from their respective medical careers. Les and Nova brought mushrooms. Bobbie Bristol dropped by from time to time. Judith, it was clear to Bristol, had not only gotten over her initial suspicion of her caregiver, but had connected with her deeply. "I think," Bristol told me, "Meri was the last great love of Judith's life."

In October 2016, after returning from Vermont and getting Judith settled back into her apartment in New York, Meri left for a few days in Brooklyn with her family while Bronwyn stayed with Judith. When Meri got home and opened her bag, she found a copy of *Love Me, Feed Me* tucked among her things. She opened to the title page. "For Meri—From whom I've learned so much. A wonderful cook who is such fun to cook with because she loves the art of cooking. I have loved working with you so much. Keep up the good work. Love, Judith."

CODA

By early 2017, it was clear that Judith was failing. In tandem, Meri and Bronwyn began to orchestrate visits from loved ones. Christopher Hirsheimer visited that spring. Meri opened the apartment door, then went to get Judith. "Judith, it's Christopher Hirsheimer. Do you remember me?" Hirsheimer recalled asking gently. "She looked much littler," she said, "and I put my hand out like to shake her hand. And Judith pointed her finger at me and said, 'You're not going to get off that easily!' And she hugged me." Hirsheimer laughed. "She remembered *everything*. I was talking about things we had done together, having dinner with Julia, being with Marion Cunningham, all of these people, and the funny times we'd had and when we'd find ourselves in fixes and catch each other's eye. It was a lovely visit. That was the last time I saw her."

I went to see Judith that spring, too. I was almost scared to touch her at first; she looked shrunken and frail. Meri walked Judith gently by the arm and brought her through to the dining room. In all our meals together, Judith and I had never eaten there.

Meri had laid the table with crystal and china. She'd prepared lunch, too; chicken salad and cold white wine. She helped Judith into her chair and gestured for me to sit beside her. Meri left us alone to talk.

Judith took small bites of her lunch. I took nervous sips of wine.

I had plenty to report, so I filled the silence, telling Judith about the house my husband and I had bought and my twin babies, who'd been born the September before. She asked to see photos, and I pulled out my phone and showed her a picture of my children perched atop the kitchen counter, one gleefully clutching tin measuring cups, the other raising a wooden spoon into the air. Judith pointed at the child with the spoon held in salute and then looked at me, grinning wryly. "They're going to be tough," she said. I beamed.

A while later, Meri came back in with dessert; a specialty cake her family had sent from Georgia. She spoke a bit about the confection's history and context as Judith tucked into a slice with gusto.

Dabbing chocolate from her lips with her napkin, Judith piped up: "I'm trying to get Meri to do a book! You know, the food and stories of her youth, from home!"

I looked up at Meri. "It's true," she said.

We all laughed. Judith may have been fading, but she was still very much herself.

I didn't linger long after lunch. I hugged Judith, and kissed her soft cheek. She asked me to come back again soon and bring my kids. I told her I'd love that. Then we said goodbye.

· · · · · · · ·

In late May, Judith and Meri made the long drive to Bryn Teg. Judith was weaker than she'd ever been and took long naps in the afternoon. Still, she held on to her vigor. The two women cooked together and walked every day. Visitors cycled through the house. After her recent hip surgery, Judith wasn't steady enough to navigate getting in and out of the pond, but she insisted on swimming nonetheless. Meri drove her to an indoor pool in nearby St. Johnsbury, where Judith swam laps as spring turned to summer in Vermont.

On August 2, 2017, a clear day with high clouds billowing on the breeze, Judith died peacefully at Bryn Teg. Meri had just stepped out of the room for a moment. Bronwyn was resting; they'd been taking turns through the nights at Judith's bedside, knowing any moment could be her last. Chris was by Judith's side when she took her last breath.

· · · · · · · ·

National newspapers marked Judith's passing in reverent prose. "Authors and publishing colleagues called Ms. Jones an extraordinary editor—imaginative, versatile, fascinated with stories, curious about people and places, a deft wordsmith and above all insatiable for the pleasures of French cooking," wrote Robert D. McFadden in the *New York Times*. "She talked about it, wrote about it and practiced its arts in her kitchens in Manhattan and rural Vermont." The *Times*'s obituary highlighted Judith's more literary accomplishments as well. "A Knopf vice president, Ms. Jones edited some of America's best novelists and nonfiction writers. She shepherded all but one of Mr. Updike's scores of books of fiction, short stories, poetry and essays to publication, and edited Ms. Tyler's novels on the American family and works by Mr. Hersey, Elizabeth Bowen, Peter Taylor and William Maxwell." The *Washington Post*'s food editor, Joe Yonan, referred to Judith as "the legendary editor who rescued Anne Frank's 'The Diary of a Young Girl' from a publisher's reject pile" and wrote, "Mrs. Jones helped open a world of cuisines to a public previously bound by convenience foods, and her impact on cookbook publishing, home cooking and the American palate was monumental." The *Los Angeles Times* said Judith was beloved "both as a person and as an editor." "Few better embodied and lived out the ideal of a life in New York publishing" than she, wrote Hillel Italie. For the first time, the full range of Judith's career and the magnitude of her cultural impact were being celebrated publicly.

On October 4, 2017, hundreds upon hundreds packed into the Church of the Holy Trinity on East 88th Street in Manhattan. We had convened to celebrate Judith's life. It seemed as though the entire worlds of food and books had come to pay their respects. I found a place at the far end of one of the long, burnished pews and slipped in.

Judith's adopted son, Chris Vandercook, spoke, and then Lidia Bastianich stepped up. The Attacca Quartet played Mozart's "Andante Cantabile" from the String Quartet No. 14 in G Major, K. 387, offering time for reflection. Kathy Hourigan, Knopf's longtime managing editor and one of Judith's dearest friends, read a few words on Anne Tyler's behalf. Then the whole sanctuary sat rapt listening to Matthew Ernst, Judith's stepdaughter Bronwyn's son, read "The Wild Swans at Coole" by W. B. Yeats, one of Judith's favorite poems.

Jonathan Segal, Judith's colleague and editor at Knopf, spoke about the many lunches he'd shared with Judith, and how she nearly always began their meals together by smiling mischievously and saying, "I think I'll have a glass of red." Knopf's director of publicity, Kathy Zuckerman, who'd once been Judith's assistant, spoke of Judith's mentorship of her over the years, and how they'd bonded over a belief in the supernatural and a shared dislike for smoking pot. That got everyone laughing through their reverence and tears. Then Sharon Olds rose to speak. Her white-gray hair fell all the way to her waist. She'd pulled it back off her face with tiny, twinkling butterfly clips. Olds adjusted her glasses, then touched both her hands to the adornments in her hair. "Judith loved the pagan sparkles," she said. A few words from Sonny Mehta and a deeply felt remembrance by Judith's stepdaughter Bronwyn closed out the proceedings that afternoon.

I was overcome by how much a true reflection of Judith's spirit and multiplicity the service was, and by the great numbers who showed up to celebrate her remarkable life. But as I rode the train north later that afternoon, I felt frustrated and angry, too. The deep love and admiration so many had for Judith had been palpable that day. But that sort of public recognition hadn't been shown to her when she was alive. Not in the way Judith deserved.

In the fall of 2019, Sharon Olds said to me, "I think a lot about how extraordinary it is for her as a woman to have been in the work she was into, to have been so important, so valued, and so high up. I'm sure there were people who used that to, you know, look down on women and the whole cooking editor persona. But I think of her as having been amazing to do what she did." Olds continued, "It was because of her gifts."

And because she carried with her, always, that most vital lesson: first, listen. Judith understood that this is how you free yourself. That this is how we free one another. She understood that it was never, really, about her at all.

"She had a human use for art as the thing it is for all of us: an opening," Olds said. "We all need that, more room in which to feel."

ACKNOWLEDGMENTS

I wrote this book in solitude, but it—and I—were and are upheld by a collective of brilliant minds and tender hearts.

First, and always, to Judith Jones. For going deep from the jump. For always beginning with lunch. For walks in New York and swims in Vermont. For asking, on our very first meeting, "And you? What do *you* want to do with your life?" and for reminding me to always snatch the phone. You demonstrated how to boldly and fearlessly bring love—*real* love—into one's work and thus revealed to me so many possibilities for building a rich, full life. I loved you so much; I love you still. It's been a great honor to spend these many years with you.

To Bronwyn Dunne, for telling me to keep calling Judith after our work together was done. For inviting me into the family fold. For asking, that day in Hardwick, if I'd like to come to the apartment at 139 E. 66th Street to have a look. For entrusting me with the stories and extraordinary lives of your father and Judith, your *belle-sœur.*

To everyone who shared memories of Judith—both on and off the record—over the years. Your touch is upon these pages. This book wouldn't exist without you.

To the Julia Child Foundation (JCF), for recognizing the importance of Judith's life and the urgency of recording her stories, for reaching out to the Columbia Center for Oral History (CCOH) Research for guidance, and to Mary Marshall Clark at CCOH, on the receiving end, for looking up at me from your laptop during our class break that fateful October morning in 2012 and saying, "You might be interested in this query—you're a food person." To Todd Schulkin and Alex Prud'homme at JCF: Todd, thanks for answering my eager email and giving me a chance, and Alex, for coffee in Lefferts that snowy day and for handing me Judith's phone number. You two opened the door; walking through it changed my life. Thank you to JCF for the funds that supported my research of, and time with, Judith in 2013. You watered the seed and made this work possible.

To Natalie Conn, who captured my oral history interviews with Judith in photographs and video, for your careful, beautiful work and easy presence. The Salt Institute DNA runs deep. You're a joy to work with.

To the faculty of the New York University Food Studies doctoral program—especially Drs. Amy Bentley, Krishnendu Ray, and Jennifer Berg—who allowed me to continue to pursue this deep study on the program's dime, even though it (and I) seemed, at times, odd fits. To the women who saw to it that I didn't abandon this project despite the academic slog: Drs. Megan Elias, Marcie Cohen Ferris, and Dana Edell. And to Carol Gilligan, who focused my attention on listening, who asked, "What happens if you replace judgment with curiosity?" and who said to me, "You know, this is a book."

For the many students I've taught over the years at NYU Gallatin School of Individualized Study and at the Wallkill Correctional Facility via the NYU Prison Education Program (especially Sophia Hampton, Robert Clinton, Mychal Pagan, Sarika Tatineni—for notes, too!—and my late, beloved friend, Marvin Mayfield), thank you for keeping me humble, for reminding me how much I don't know, for asking unwieldy questions, for being receptive to wonder, and for remaining open to changing your minds.

To Emma Tsui, beside whom I wrote most of this book's very first draft as a doctoral dissertation over so much tea and cookies during those difficult years; for being with me as I began to make a book to help with the pain of being unable to make a baby. For showing up so reliably and helping me put my head down and get on with it day after day after day. And for all the struggle and laughter shared since.

To Kathy Zuckerman and Kathy Hourigan, for giving me entry to Knopf, both its people and its vast collection of invaluable archival materials. Your generosity is testament to the importance of amplifying Judith's remarkable life and story.

To the fastidious archivists at the Harry Ransom Center at the University of Texas at Austin and the devoted librarians at Kingston Public Library, for supporting all my research needs. To my local indie bookstore, Rough Draft, in my hometown of Kingston, New York: thank you for getting me the mountains of books I need to own so that I may write in them, supporting sales of all three of my books, and for opening your doors to all of us.

To the National Endowment for the Humanities, for the lifeline of a year-long Public Scholars grant that arrived in the summer of 2020 when it was unclear to me how, or whether, I would complete this book. And to Rux Martin and Francis Lam, for helping the committee see me amid a sea of worthy and deserving applicants. Public funding for the arts and humanities makes so much vital research and creative work possible, but access to it remains frightfully narrow and its gates are too tightly kept. Here, a wish for expansive growth of that use of public funds.

To the people and publications who helped me think through this work in its early stages and gave me a platform via which to share: Julia Turshen, Francis Lam, and the rest of the team at *The Splendid Table*; Joe Yonan and the *Washington Post*; Emily Firetog and Jonny Diamond at *Literary Hub*; and Kerry Diamond and the rest of the Cherry Bombe team.

To my agent, Kari Stuart: I guess the third time's the charm. From that spring day in April 2018 that we were introduced (Thank you, thank you, Samin Nosrat, my gratitude to you is bottomless!), I knew you were the one I'd been looking for. Thank you for believing in me, and in this story, from the very start. Thank you for reading—I mean really, *really* reading. Thank you for keeping your cool every time I lost mine. Thank you for having a moral compass—and following it—in an industry that often doesn't. Thank you for pushing me to really think about what I want and need, going after it on my behalf, and for allowing me to say no, too. Thank you for understanding what it is to be a breadwinner while in the trenches of twin motherhood; never having to explain the conditions of my life to you is a gift. I feel inexplicably lucky to be in your able hands.

To Julia Cheiffetz: for believing Judith's story deserved to be told, for the original acquisition of this book, and for coming up with its bold and brilliant title.

To Kate Napolitano: for accepting the arranged marriage between us with openness and for adopting and nurturing this stepchild of a book as your own. For your time, your responsiveness, your whip-smart mind, your irreverence, and your good taste. For your love of the analog. For listening closely and reading with curiosity. For being on top of your shit and for being accountable and clear. For being part of the sisterhood of industry exes, and thus getting it—all of it, I mean. For telling me a book lives in the body and that it was high time to get this one out of mine. You are a *brilliant* editor. The whole package, the real deal. I'm so glad the twisting, potholed path that has been this project led me to you. Would that I be so lucky that we may work together again.

To the entire team at Atria Books: Libby McGuire, for putting Kate and me together. Sean deLone, for your patience with the tedium and staying with me on some steep learning curves. Debbie Norflus, for your excitement and organization. Jolena Podolsky, for your energy and knowledge of arenas that make my brain short-circuit. Mark LaFlaur, my goodness, you run a tight ship! What a boon you are to all authors whose work comes under your watchful read. Martha Schwartz, copy editor and fact-checker extraordinaire: So few writers have the benefit of your level of rigor and integrity these days. Thank you for your hawk's eye, and specifically for saving me from errors of sloppiness, inaccuracy, and incorrect grammar and syntax. You are a treasure! To all those working behind the scenes in art and design, proofreading, marketing, and beyond, this book would still be but a ream of paper without your tireless work. Thank you!

To Michelle Blankenship of Michelle Blankenship PR, thank you for saying yes to taking on this campaign, for your enthusiasm, your patience, and your incredible wealth of experience.

The community of women writers, storytellers, and editors who nourished me through this process and who know precisely both what this kind of work takes and how much it can give: Ruth Franklin, for working with me on my first attempt at profiling Judith, for your wrenching honesty that snowy day at Le Pain Quotidien, for being the first to show me that motherhood and a writing life can coexist, for your unflinching clarity about the cost, and for everything since. Ariana Gonzales Stokás, for immediate intimacy and depth, for seeing mangroves and rhizomes everywhere, and for your intuition about Steve and me. Ashley Cleek, for your big, wandering brain and your bigger, boundless heart. To Angela Garbes, who helps me feel like a writer always, but did especially during that hardest year, when I wasn't putting a single word on the page. Thank you for sticking with me, and flying east. I can't wait to see what you do next and to sauna with you again. Molly Wizenberg, for understanding what it means to claw oneself out of an industry marriage as a mother-writer, for reading hundreds of pages of half-baked mess, and helping me start to weed out a path forward. Thank you to writer-mother-thinker-feeler sisters-in-arms: Pia Padukone and Emily Van Duyne, for writing me letters out of the blue—and to Amy Reading, for accepting mine—and your friendship and solidarity ever since. Jenn Sit, first my editor, now one so dear to my heart: thank you for being so damn good at what you do, for showing me how good the editor-author thing can be, and for allowing the professional boundary between us to metamorphose into such cherished friendship. To Bobbie Bristol and Rux Martin, for talking and feeling ad nauseam about Judith with me. For inviting me into your homes, giving me places to be still in Vermont, and for the invaluable perspective and richness of intergenerational friendship. May we continue to run the dogs, tromp through the woods and fields, pass the books and articles back and forth, tend the gardens, and cook and eat and wash up after the meals side by side for many years to come. In *The Cancer Journals,* Audre Lorde said the thing truer than I'm able to myself: "The novel is finished at last. It has been a lifeline. . . . My work kept me alive . . . my work and the love of women. They are inseparable from each other."

To Ross Gay, Ada Limón, and Robin Wall Kimmerer, for indelibly rearranging the furniture of my mind and spirit. Your words became ballast and lifeblood during the serest times, and reading and thinking with you remains a great joy of my life. Thank you for the work you've done and all that you continue to do.

For Caitlin Welles and Suse Volk: I think it's unlikely I'd be standing where I am—certainly not so steadily—without your insight, intelligence, kindness, and guidance. Thank you.

To my chosen family and Hudson Valley community, who hold and feed me (and often my children, too!) emotionally, intellectually, physically, and spiritually: To Molly McHenry, for helping me see how to do the work, and for showing me boundaryless, unconditional love. For all those walks in the cold. For Ross, Aracelis, and Naomi. For Dionysian revelry. For bringing Olivia Hamilton, God O, with her matchless intellect and spirit, into my life. And for always, always being on the other end of the line. I thank my lucky stars (and Martín!) every single day for giving me you. For Emily Echevarria, for being a true sister across all these thirty-plus years. I can't wait to see what the next thirty bring. Ali Gruber, Chris and Jake Baker, KayCee Wimbish, Katrín Björk, Jenny Bowskill, Sydney Maresca, Abigail Baim-Lance, Konstantine Barsky, Alia O'Connor, Igor Bernstein, and Maija Niemisto.

To Steve Leibovitch, for having the foresight to say no until you finally said yes. Thank you for letting me find you. You are, as Ariana says, a deep well; thank you for drawing from it to share with me your attention, your affection, and your tenderness. I love you.

To my dog, Zadie, for helping this big old house never be a lonely one, for every moment spent in the woods and the water, and for getting me outdoors and moving every day.

To my sister-in-law, Marissa Cinquanti Franklin, for not blinking when you found out I was a writer, for committing to the work yourself, and for being one of only two humans on the planet whose taste in books I take as gospel.

To my brother, Peter Franklin: I still can't say anything about us without crying. For singing with me when we were too angry and sad to speak words of our own during those years of fracture and loss. For starting again with me over and over. For being my family when it became just us two and as we've picked up and made more humans along the way. And for being the first person I ever told aloud that, if I was being really honest about what I wanted to do when I grew up, it was write about food. I love you.

To Chris Bradley, for seeing and naming the light in my face after my very first meeting with Judith in January 2013. For cooking and sharing countless meals. For understanding appetite. For taking so many risks and adventures with me. For providing our children with the yin to my yang in parenting. And for staying close and sticking with this changed, and changing, family we made.

To the teachers and administrators at George Washington Elementary School, and to everyone who has ever helped care for our children for a minute or years on end: I don't have enough gratitude (or cash) to compensate you for the support you've given our family. To the wild-spirited staff at Hillside Nursery and Livingston Street Early Childhood Community (I'm looking especially at you, Cheryl Demuth, Matthew Wetzler, and Katelyn Semon!). To Danila Monteiro: I would never have become a working mother-writer without your steadiness, reliability, care, and friendship. You are family in every true sense of the word. Thank you for bringing Nina Langley into the fold and, to both of you, for the raucous joy of your growing families: Danilo, Sammy & Olivia, Gary and Thomas. *Muito amor, muito obrigada!*

And to my children, C and E: in making you and in becoming your mother, I was remade. Every day, you show and teach me purpose, laughter, boldness, joy, mettle, faith, and endurance. This family that we are continually expands the bounds of what I imagined as possible in belonging, love, and care. Thank you for your patience with me all those early, early mornings when you woke to find me reluctant to peel myself away from the quiet world of books, and all the times my attention was spread too thin. Thank you for being curious about my work and for being my foremost reason to set it aside. I love you. I love you. I love you.

AUTHORS FOR WHOM JUDITH JONES SERVED AS EDITOR

Bruce Aidells
Donald Allen
Elizabeth Andoh
Lucy Ash
John Ashbery
W. H. Auden
Ilsa Barea
Nancy Verde Barr
Lidia Matticchio Bastianich
James Beard
Simone Beck
Emily Bernard
Louisette Bertholle
Elizabeth Bjornskov
Elizabeth Bowen
Kay Boyle
Jean Anthelme Brillat-Savarin

Seymour Britchky
George Brockway
Lucile Brockway
Helen Brown
Albert Camus
Penelope Casas
Gerda Charles
Julia Child
Craig Claiborne
Isabel Colegate
Richard Collin
Rima Collin
Marion Cunningham
Rosie Daley
Pierre Daninos
Elizabeth David
Annabel Davis-Goff

Edith de Born
Roy Adries de Groot
Luís de Sttau Monteiro
Jane Doerfer
Beth Dooley
Century Downing
Nathalie Dupree
Merle Ellis
Susan Engberg
Jason Epstein
Nan Fairbrother
Michael Field
Robert Finigan
M. F. K. Fisher
Catharine O. Foster
Eugene R. Gaddis
André Gide
Edward Giobbi
Victoria Glendinning
Jon Godden
Rumer Godden
Sherry Golden
Shirley Ann Grau
Francine du Plessix Gray
Jane Grigson
Dag Hammarskjöld
David Hapgood
Marcella Hazan
Victor Hazan
Shirley Hazzard
Shelby Hearon
Mary Roblee Henry
John Hersey
Janie Hibler
Ken Hom
Barbara Howes
Langston Hughes
Madhur Jaffrey
Evan Jones

Edmund Keeley
Denis Kelly
Rod Kennedy, Jr.
Thomas Kinsella
Alfred A. Knopf
Edwin H. Knopf
Mildred O. Knopf
Robert Kotlowitz
Irene Kuo
Margaret Lane
George Lang
Margaret Laurence
Herbert Leibowitz
Jeanne Lemlin
Jeanne Lesem
Edna Lewis
David Littlejohn
Tanya Bastianich Manuali
Lydie Marshall
William Maxwell
Gretchen McHugh
Anne Mendelson
William Meredith
Marian Morash
Joan Nathan
Bill Neal
Himilce Novas
Justin O'Brien
Frank O'Connor
Ned O'Gorman
Frank O'Hara
Sharon Olds
Elisabeth Lambert Ortiz
Millie Owen
Scott Peacock
Angelo M. Pellegrini
Jacques Pépin
Ursula Perrin
Brenda Peterson

Donn Pierce
Sylvia Plath
J. F. Powers
Alex Prud'homme
Arnold Rampersad
Julia Randall
John Crowe Ransom
Claudia Roden
David Roessel
Waverly Root
Elisabeth Rozin
Arthur Rubinstein
Nela Rubinstein
Jean-Paul Sartre
Leonardo Sciascia
Florida Scott-Maxwell
Jeannette Seaver
Arthur S. Seiderman
Hiroko Shimbo
Rosemary Silva
Nina Simonds
Desmond Smith
Lacey Baldwin Smith
Mason Smith
W. D. Snodgrass
Raymond Sokolov
André Soltner
Muriel Spark
Katy Sparks
Ann Spencer

Matthew Spender
Lyn Stallworth
Jeffrey Steingarten
Michael Steinman
Holly Stevens
Wallace Stevens
Albert Stockli
Andrea Strong
Caroline Stuart
Dabney Stuart
Peter Taylor
Janet Teissier du Cros
Anna Thomas
Olivier Todd
Andrew Todhunter
Virginia Tranel
Charlotte Turgeon
Anne Tyler
Art Ulene
John Updike
Alexander A. Ushakov
Vassilis Vassilikos
Jeanne Voltz
Philip M. Wagner
Mary Ward
Andrew Weil
Roger Weingarten
Richard Wolff
Kenneth Wollitz
Susan Yankowitz

PERMISSIONS AND CREDITS

The author wishes to acknowledge the generosity of the following for their assistance in accessing archival materials, and their permission to reprint extracts from their respective holdings in this work:

The estate of Judith B. Jones, with deep gratitude to Bronwyn Dunne.

The families of: Galway Kinnell, with thanks to Bobbie Bristol; Edna Lewis, with thanks to Afeworki Paulos and Nina Williams-Mbengue, as well as Mattie Scott and the late Ruth Lewis Smith; Evangeline Peterson, with thanks to Ralph and Ed Rugoff; Angus Cameron, with thanks to Kevin Cameron; and Theodore Roethke, with thanks to Beatrice Lushington and Pat Turner.

Anne Tyler, Sharon Olds, Anna Thomas, and Bobbie Bristol for permission to quote from their own correspondence with Judith Jones.

The Alfred A. Knopf, Inc., Archive at The Harry Ransom Center at the University of Texas at Austin.

Faber and Faber Ltd for permission to quote from the literary estate of Sylvia Plath, and The Harry Ransom Center © Sylvia Path. Reproduced by permission of the Sylvia Plath Estate.

NOTES

Unless otherwise noted, all direct quotes and anecdotes from Judith Jones come from interviews conducted by the author between April and June 2013 that were originally commissioned by the Julia Child Foundation. Recordings of these interviews are held by Arthur and Elizabeth Schlesinger Library on the History of Women in America, Radcliffe Institute for Advanced Study, Harvard University, Cambridge, MA, and can be accessed online at https:// id.lib.harvard.edu/alma/990144277390203941/catalog.

Many of the materials cited in this book are privately held by the estate of Judith Jones and are not, at the time of writing, accessible to the public. These holdings are referred to throughout as Judith Jones Private Collection. Precise dates of events in Judith Jones's life, unless otherwise noted, come from her datebooks, held in said collection.

All notes credited to Knopf private files refer to materials held in a nonpublic records storage facility and are the property of Alfred A. Knopf, Inc. The author was granted access to said files for research purposes for this book.

All notes credited to Harry Ransom Center come from Alfred A. Knopf, Inc.,

Records (Manuscript Collection MS-00062), Harry Ransom Center, University of Texas at Austin.

Throughout the following references, Judith is identified by her married name, Judith Jones, for consistency over time.

INTRODUCTION

xi   *"Dear Miss Plath: Sylvia":* Judith Jones to Sylvia Plath, August 22, 1961, Harry Ransom Center, University of Texas at Austin.

xii   *Theodore Roethke had written her:* Theodore Roethke to Judith Jones, February 23, 1960, Theodore Roethke Collection, held in the University of Washington Libraries, Special Collections.

xii   *"one of the few remaining editors who":* John Hersey, interview by Jonathan Dee, "The Art of Fiction, No. 92," *Paris Review*, no. 100 (Summer-Fall 1986), https://www.theparisreview.org/interviews/2756/the-art-of-fiction -no-92-john-hersey.

xiii *"body of work as an editor":* Sonny Mehta in a speech delivered by video on Judith Jones for the James Beard Lifetime Achievement Award in 2006.

xiii *"very delicate and graceful":* Anne Tyler, quoted in Hillel Italie, "Judith Jones Dies at 93; Changed American Cuisine by Publishing Julia Child," *Los Angeles Times*, August 2, 2017, https://www.latimes.com/local/obituaries/la -me-judith-jones-20170802-story.html.

xiv   *"the invisible hand":* Laura Shapiro, "Remembering Judith Jones, a Culinary Luminary," panel discussion with Joan Nathan, Ray Sokolov, Laura Shapiro, Anne Mendelson, Madhur Jaffrey, and Bronwyn Dunne; moderated by Andrew F. Smith, The New School, October 24, 2017. A video recording and transcript of the event is available on YouTube at https://www.youtube.com /watch?v=shHZywNaISU.

xiv   *"For a long time, the women":* Charlotte Druckman, "Judith Jones, In Her Own Words," Eater, September 23, 2015, https://www.eater.com/2015 /9/23/9355183/judith-jones.

xiv   *"imaginative, versatile, fascinated with stories":* Kim Severson, "Remembering Judith Jones and Her Recipe for Food Writing," *New York Times*, August 2, 2017, https://www.nytimes.com/2017/08/02/dining/judith-jones-food-edit or.html.

xv   *"Food started getting serious respect"; "When you talk about the cookbook revolution":* Ruth Reichl, quoted in Severson, "Remembering Judith Jones and Her Recipe for Food Writing."

CHAPTER 1

1   *The publishing house's offices:* "The History of Doubleday," Doubleday, https://www.randomhouse.com/doubleday/history/; Al Silverman, "The Curious Family Establishment: Doubleday," in *The Time of Their Lives: The Golden Age of Great American Book Publishers, Their Editors, and Authors* (New York: Truman Talley Books/St. Martin's Press, 2008), 180–213.

1   King Kong *premiered there:* "History in the Making," Rockefeller Center, https://www.rockefellercenter.com/history/.

4   *the family was feeling the strain:* Jonathan Morey, interview with author, August 5, 2019.

5   *"deliciously mischievous":* Profile, season 9, episode 911, "Judith Jones," Fran Stoddard in conversation with Judith Jones, aired January 11, 2010, on Vermont Public Television, https://www.pbs.org/video/judith-jones-ipj8vz/.

5   *Most days, after school:* Judith Jones to Phyllis Hedley Bailey, February 22, 1936, Judith Jones Private Collection; Judith Jones, *Love Me, Feed Me: Sharing with Your Dog the Everyday Good Food You Cook and Enjoy* (New York: Alfred A. Knopf, 2014), 14.

5   *But every Monday:* Jones, *Love Me, Feed Me,* 14.

5   *She sent Judith horseback riding:* Judith Jones to Phyllis Hedley Bailey, February 22, 1936, Judith Jones Private Collection.

5   *"thick layers of jam and cream":* Judith Jones to Phyllis Hedley Bailey, November 18, 1935, Judith Jones Private Collection.

5   *"lovable"; "magnetic":* Brearley Yearbook, class of 1941, Judith Jones Private Collection.

6   *"education as a sensual and ethical":* traditional Bennington commencement statement, *Bennington College Handbook,* https://www.bennington.edu/current-students/student-handbook.

6   *Phyllis kept a copy:* Jonathan Morey, interview with author, August 5, 2019.

6   *The college prized the literary and performing arts:* Thomas P. Brockway, *Bennington College: In the Beginning* (Bennington, VT: Bennington College Press, 1981), 49.

7   *"the educational advantages of metropolitan life":* Brockway, *Bennington College,* 49.

7   *In 1927, Doubleday merged with George H. Doran Company:* Silverman, *The Time of Their Lives,* 190.

8   *"I sell books, I don't read them":* Silverman, *The Time of Their Lives,* 190.

8   *"things were quite simple":* Alfred A. Knopf, quoted in introduction to Silverman, *The Time of Their Lives,* 7.

8 *"working together with their authors"*: Keith Jennison, quoted in introduction to Silverman, *The Time of Their Lives*, 6.

8 *"to the fullest extent"*: John Hersey, interview by Jonathan Dee, "The Art of Fiction, No. 92," *Paris Review*, no. 100 (Summer-Fall 1986), https://www.theparisreview.org/interviews/2756/the-art-of-fiction-no-92-john-hersey.

8 *Doubleday was short on staff:* David Paul Nord, Joan Shelley Rubin, and Michael Schudson, eds., *A History of the Book in America*, vol. 5, *The Enduring Book: Print Culture in Postwar America* (Durham: University of North Carolina Press, 2009); Silverman, *The Time of Their Lives*, 181.

8 *Baum, born in 1988:* Marina Sassenberg, "Vicki Baum, January 24, 1888–August 29, 1960," The Shalvi/Hyman Encyclopedia of Jewish Women, Jewish Women's Archive, December 31, 1999, https://jwa.org/encyclopedia/article/baum-vicki.

9 *the work ethic she learned in the ring:* Baum, quoted in Irene Gammel, "Lacing Up the Gloves: Women, Boxing and Modernity," *Cultural and Social History* 9, no. 3 (2012): 369–90, https://mlc.ryerson.ca/assets/blog/Lacing%20Up%20the%20Gloves.pdf.

9 *"I don't know how the feminine element"*: Gammel, "Lacing Up the Gloves."

9 *"waded through thousands of words"; "I do want to compliment you"; "You blended"; "We regret you had to"*: Ken McCormick to Judith Jones, March 31, 1942, Judith Jones Private Collection.

9 *"absolute pride and joy"*: Judith Jones to Phyllis Hedley Bailey, undated, Judith Jones Private Collection.

9 *bedspread; starched white curtains:* Judith Jones to Phyllis Hedley Bailey, May 7, 1943, Judith Jones Private Collection.

10 *"We wanted a college where"*: Lee Lescaze, "At Bennington the Toughest Lesson Is Coping with Freedom," *Washington Post*, December 26, 1979, https://www.washingtonpost.com/archive/politics/1979/12/26/at-bennington-the-toughest-lesson-is-coping-with-freedom/42c29454-aec9-4892-b52a-f3f0899beffb/.

10 *"the little red whorehouse on the hill"*: Kathleen Norris, *The Virgin of Bennington* (New York: Riverhead, 2001), 10.

10 *The young women planned:* Judith Jones to Phyllis Hedley Bailey and Charles Bailey, May 21, 1943, Judith Jones Private Collection.

10 *"a scrupulous craftsman"*: Cyril Clemens, "The Poems of Theodore Roethke," *New York Times*, October 5, 1941, https://timesmachine.nytimes.com/timesmachine/1941/10/05/105899444.html?pageNumber=63.

10 *"completely successful"*: R. Victoria Arana, *W. H. Auden's Poetry: Mythos, Theory, and Practice* (Amherst, NY: Cambria Press, 2009), 44.

10 *"his poems have a controlled grace"*: Elizabeth Drew, "Open House," *The Atlantic*, August 1941, https://www.theatlantic.com/magazine/archive/1941/08/open-house/653476/.

10 *Roethke had a reputation as:* Stanley Kunitz, "Theodore Roethke," *New York Review of Books*, October 17, 1963, https://www.nybooks.com/articles/1963/10/17/theodore-roethke/.

10 *"Motion is equal to emotion"*: David Wagoner, quoted in "Theodore Roethke," Poetry Foundation, https://www.poetryfoundation.org/poets/theodore-roethke.

10 *"Don't be so guarded—let your mind buzz around!"*: unnamed student, quoted in "Theodore Roethke," Poetry Foundation, https://www.poetryfoundation.org/poets/theodore-roethke.

10 *"perfectly tremendous"*: Kunitz, "Theodore Roethke."

10 *"we all decided"*: Judith Jones to Phyllis Hedley Bailey and Charles Bailey, May 21, 1943, Judith Jones Private Collection.

11 *"We have a new teacher up here"*: Judith Jones to Charles Bailey, September 3, 1943, Judith Jones Private Collection.

11 *For Burke, the scope of literature's impact:* Kenneth Burke, *A Rhetoric of Motives* (Berkeley: University of California Press, 1969).

11 *"form attitudes or induce actions"*: Burke, *A Rhetoric of Motives*, 41.

11 *The shift toward producing:* Sofie Sherman-Burton, "Food for Thought: The History of Agriculture at Bennington College," December 14, 2017, https://silo.tips/download/food-for-thought-the-history-of-agriculture-at-bennington-college.

11 *"community spirit"*: Judith Jones to Charles Bailey, July 7, 1943, Judith Jones Private Collection.

11 *"I can't . . . manage to summon"*: Judith Jones to Charles Bailey and Phyllis Hedley Bailey, May 21, 1943, Judith Jones Private Collection.

12 *"Dearest Mums, . . . With the coming"*: Judith Jones to Phyllis Hedley Bailey, September 20, 1943, Judith Jones Private Collection.

12 *"the belief that everything in the finite world"*: Judith Jones, "The Nature of the Transcendence in the Poetry of Gerard Manley Hopkins," June 1945, 1.

12 *"Listen how / Circling other skies"*: Judith Jones, "Poem," Theodore Roethke Collection, held in the University of Washington Libraries, Special Collections.

12 *"To Judy, a good writer"*: Theodore Roethke, inscription in the first edition copy of *Open House*, Judith Jones Private Collection.

13 *She'd been made head editor of Silo:* Judith Jones, letter to her parents, 1945, exact date unknown, postmark ripped, Judith Jones Private Collection.

13   *"You can tell our worthless friend":* Judith Jones to Phyllis Hedley Bailey, un-
      dated, Judith Jones Private Collection.

13   *"One thing that distinguishes":* Jones, "The Nature of the Transcendence in the
      Poetry of Gerard Manley Hopkins," 1.

13   *"popp[ed] off one by one":* Judith Jones to Phyllis Hedley Bailey, May 7, 1943,
      Judith Jones Private Collection.

14   *announcing both the couple's engagement and wedding:* "Miss Susan Bailey En-
      gaged to Marry," *New York Times,* October 2, 1942, https://timesmachine
      .nytimes.com/timesmachine/1942/10/02/85053748.html?pageNumber=22;
      "Miss Susan Bailey Is Wed in Capital," *New York Times,* November 30, 1942,
      https://timesmachine.nytimes.com/timesmachine/1942/11/30/85614075
      .html?pageNumber=20.

14   *"I should think you'd be":* Judith Jones to Phyllis Hedley Bailey, May 7, 1943,
      Judith Jones Private Collection.

14   *"to live an audacious life":* "Remembering Judith Jones: An Audacious Life,"
      Bennington College, August 3, 2017, https://www.bennington.edu/news
      -and-features/remembering-judith-jones-audacious-life.

CHAPTER 2

15   *He looked dapper, if a bit offbeat:* McCormick's physical appearance details are
      in Al Silverman, "The Curious Family Establishment: Doubleday," in *The
      Time of Their Lives: The Golden Age of Great American Book Publishers, Their
      Editors, and Authors* (New York: Truman Talley Books/St. Martin's Press,
      2008), 185.

15   *"baby" and "sweetie":* Lisa Drew on McCormick, quoted in Silverman, *The
      Time of Their Lives,* 205.

16   *The median income:* U.S. Census, https://www.census.gov/library/publica
      tions/1953/demo/p60-014.html.

16   *By 1947, women's employment:* "A Return to an Ideal of Civilized Happi-
      ness," Roundabout Theater Blog, https://blog-archive.roundabouttheatre
      .org/2016/11/30/a-return-to-an-ideal-of-civilized-happiness/.

16   *Many who wanted to work were regularly refused jobs:* The era of women en-
      tering the public sphere during the war and then being told to return to
      the domestic sphere is well documented. A good summary can be found in
      "Women and Work After World War II," part of the PBS *American Experi-
      ence* series, https://www.pbs.org/wgbh/americanexperience/features/tupper
      ware-work/.

16   *Early in that spring term:* Dana Goodyear, "The Gardener," *New Yorker,* Au-

gust 24, 2003, https://www.newyorker.com/magazine/2003/09/01/the-gar
dener-2.

16 *"Dear Ted, . . . All winter I have been":* Judith Jones to Theodore Roethke,
April 14, 1946, Theodore Roethke Collection, held in the University of
Washington Libraries, Special Collections.

16 *"Tried to sell"; "much too nice"; "But perhaps it is out of kindness":* Judith Jones
to Theodore Roethke, April 14, 1946, Theodore Roethke Collection, held in
the University of Washington Libraries, Special Collections.

17 *$35 a week:* Jay Parini, *Empire of Self: A Life of Gore Vidal* (New York: Dou-
bleday, 2015), 50.

17 *national average of $3,000 per year:* "Income of Families and Persons in the
United States: 1947," February 7, 1949, https://www.census.gov/library
/publications/1949/demo/p60-005.html.

17 *"It kept me in cocktails":* Gore Vidal quoted in Parini, *Empire of Self,* 50.

17 *tawny hair; gold-flecked eyes:* Stephen Spender, quoted in Parini, *Empire of
Self,* 76.

17 *Vidal's promiscuity . . . slept with both women and men:* Charles McGrath,
"Gore Vidal Dies at 86; Prolific, Elegant, Acerbic Writer," *New York
Times,* August 1, 2012, https://www.nytimes.com/2012/08/01/books/gore
-vidal-elegant-writer-dies-at-86.html.

18 *the house had nearly five thousand employees:* Silverman, *The Time of Their Lives,*
193.

18 *there were only two Black employees:* Silverman, *The Time of Their Lives,* 194.

18 *In Judith's memory:* According to Judith Jones in our first interview, there
were three women in an editorial capacity at Doubleday at the time; she did
not recall the name of the third woman. According to Al Silverman's *The
Time of Their Lives,* Judith Jones and Betty Arnoff (later Prashker) were the
only women editors at Doubleday in the immediate postwar years.

18 *"It was a leisurely process":* Betty Prashker, interview with author, April 4,
2019.

19 *"It wasn't a lot of work":* Betty Prashker, interview with author, April 4, 2019.

19 *Betty's parents were away for the summer:* Betty Prashker, interview with author, April 4, 2019.

19 *Betty, Judith, and their friends were:* Betty Prashker, interview with author,
April 4, 2019.

19 *Many of the GIs filtering home had developed:* Nina Renata Aron, "This Brilliant 22-Year-Old Is the Reason You Can Get Great Literature in 'Quality
Paperback,'" Medium, October 4, 2017, https://medium.com/timeline/jason
-epstein-paperback-books-1110113fea0c.

19   *In 1943, the CBW began printing:* "The Council on Books in Wartime, 1941–46," Books for Victory, March 3, 2013, http://www.booksforvictory .com/2013/03/the-council-on-books-in-wartime-194146.html.

19   *By the end of the war, when its operations ceased:* Aron, "This Brilliant 22-Year-Old Is the Reason."

19   *The CBW kept publishers and magazine presses:* In 1942, a group of booksellers, publishers, librarians, and authors had joined forces to come up with a way to use books as "weapons in the war of ideas," spurring an initiative they called the Council on Books in Wartime which set to work manufacturing reprints of popular books and shipping them abroad to the troops. Men who'd left school to join up could continue their learning and entertain themselves. It may have been patriotic, but it wasn't selfless; the CBW created an opportunity for publishers to boost sales despite the economic crunch of wartime.

19   *the most ambitious educational experiment:* "Education: Beginning of the End," *Time,* July 30, 1951, 58, https://content.time.com/time/subscriber /article/0,33009,815174,00.html.

19   *sent American vets to college:* Keith W. Olson, "The G. I. Bill and Higher Education: Success and Surprise," *American Quarterly* 25, no. 5 (December 1973): 596–610, https://doi.org/10.2307/2711698.

19   *With literacy and leisure time on the rise:* David Paul Nord, Joan Shelley Rubin, and Michael Schudson, eds., *A History of the Book in America,* vol. 5, *The Enduring Book: Print Culture in Postwar America* (Durham: University of North Carolina Press, 2009).

19   *golden age of publishing:* According to Silverman, the golden age of publishing began in 1946, after the end of World War II, and had ended by the early 1980s.

19   *"Print was king":* Silverman, introduction to *The Time of Their Lives,* 5.

20   *"There were so many authors":* Betty Prashker, interview with author, April 4, 2019.

20   *"She'd have a drink or two":* Betty Prashker, interview with author, April 4, 2019.

20   *"Well I'm here":* Theodore Roethke to Judith Jones, February 5, 1947, Judith Jones Private Collection.

21   *"Please forgive me":* Judith Jones to Theodore Roethke, June 17, 1947, Theodore Roethke Collection, held in the University of Washington Libraries, Special Collections.

21   *"Dearest Ted, . . . I imagine your silence":* Judith Jones to Theodore Roethke, July 1947, Theodore Roethke Collection, held in the University of Washington Libraries, Special Collections.

21 *He wrote, begging Judith:* Theodore Roethke to Judith Jones, July 19, 1947, Judith Jones Private Collection.

21 *"Dear Puss, I waited around":* Theodore Roethke to Judith Jones, August 11, 1947, Judith Jones Private Collection.

21 *"I'm in a strange state":* Theodore Roethke to Judith Jones, August 11, 1947, Judith Jones Private Collection.

21 *"I do miss you very much":* Theodore Roethke to Judith Jones, August 11, 1947, Judith Jones Private Collection.

21 *"Darling: This is just a last shot":* Theodore Roethke to Judith Jones, August 13, 1947, Judith Jones Private Collection.

21 *Jane's little flat:* Jane's apartment, in which Judith temporarily lived, was at 19 Washington Square North, according to the return address on some of Judith's letters to Roethke in the months after Jane left Jack Vandercook.

22 *how to file for a divorce:* While, in 1940, only two out of every thousand marriages in the United States ended in divorce; by 1946, that rate had nearly doubled. World War II brought couples together. It also drove them apart. Frank Olito, "How the Divorce Rate has Changed over the Last 150 Years," Insider, January 30, 2019, https://www.insider.com/divorce-rate-changes -over-time-2019-1#in-the-40s-the-annual-divorce-rate-reached-34 -divorces-for-every-1000-americans-7; Corinne Purtil, "The Unromantic, Untold Story of the Great US Divorce Spree of 1946," Quartz, June 26, 2018, https://qz.com/1314011/the-unromantic-untold-story-of-the-great -us-divorce-spree-of-1946/.

22 *"Dreadful as it seems":* Jane Vandercook to Judith Jones, September 22, 1947, Judith Jones Private Collection.

22 *Roethke had left Knopf:* Theodore Roethke to Judith Jones, March 30, 1947, Judith Jones Private Collection.

22 *Roethke wrote brusquely:* Theodore Roethke to Judith Jones, November 3, 1947, Judith Jones Private Collection.

22 *"I am going to devote":* Judith Jones to Theodore Roethke, fall 1947, Theodore Roethke Collection, held in the University of Washington Libraries, Special Collections.

22 *"Forgive me dear":* Judith Jones to Theodore Roethke, fall 1947, Theodore Roethke Collection, held in the University of Washington Libraries, Special Collections.

22 *"Love me please":* Judith Jones to Theodore Roethke, fall 1947, Theodore Roethke Collection, held in the University of Washington Libraries, Special Collections.

23 *"the world of thoughts"*: Judith Jones to Theodore Roethke, undated, early 1948; *"really unliterary"*: Judith Jones to Theodore Roethke, July 1947, Theodore Roethke Collection, held in the University of Washington Libraries, Special Collections.

23 *"viciousness"*; *"contempt for the ones"*: Judith Jones to Theodore Roethke, July 1947, Theodore Roethke Collection, held in the University of Washington Libraries, Special Collections.

23 *"It was a very nice feeling"*: Judith Jones to Theodore Roethke, fall 1947, Theodore Roethke Collection, held in the University of Washington Libraries, Special Collections.

23 *"I know I am lazy"*: Judith Jones to Theodore Roethke, fall 1947, Theodore Roethke Collection, held in the University of Washington Libraries, Special Collections.

23 *"I have been trying to think of all possible alternatives"*: Judith Jones to Theodore Roethke, fall 1947, Theodore Roethke Collection, held in the University of Washington Libraries, Special Collections.

23 *"or use it for a chance to get more money"*: Theodore Roethke to Judith Jones, October 6, 1947, Judith Jones Private Collection.

23 *"Thank you for your thoughts"*: Judith Jones to Theodore Roethke, undated, Theodore Roethke Collection, held in the University of Washington Libraries, Special Collections.

23 *He was attentive, acting supportive:* Theodore Roethke to Judith Jones, October 21, 1947, Judith Jones Private Collection.

23 *"Darling, I got the raise"*: Judith Jones to Theodore Roethke, fall 1947, Theodore Roethke Collection, held in the University of Washington Libraries, Special Collections.

23 *"I'm delighted about the raise"*: Theodore Roethke to Judith Jones, November 9, 1947, Judith Jones Private Collection.

24 *"I have been in a completely frenzied state"*: Judith Jones to Theodore Roethke, late 1947/early 1948, Theodore Roethke Collection, held in the University of Washington Libraries, Special Collections.

24 *"though not for long"*: Theodore Roethke to Judith Jones, late 1947, Judith Jones Private Collection.

24 *"Darling . . . this is the second night"*: Judith Jones to Theodore Roethke, February 1948, Theodore Roethke Collection, held in the University of Washington Libraries, Special Collections.

24 *"Look, it just might be"*: Theodore Roethke to Judith Jones, February 25, 1948, Judith Jones Private Collection.

24 *"Really, Ted . . . get off your own letter"*: Judith Jones to Theodore Roethke,

undated, early 1948, Theodore Roethke Collection, held in the University of Washington Libraries, Special Collections.

24 *"It's been dismal here":* Judith Jones to Theodore Roethke, undated, early 1948, Theodore Roethke Collection, held in the University of Washington Libraries, Special Collections.

25 *"It is getting warmer":* Judith Jones to Theodore Roethke, undated, early 1948, Theodore Roethke Collection, held in the University of Washington Libraries, Special Collections.

25 *She was jubilant:* To Roethke, in an undated letter from the spring of 1948, Judith wrote, "I sail two weeks from this Tuesday and actually I cannot sleep I am so excited. I am not sure that two and a half weeks is really going to be long enough to give me a good breather, but at least it will be something," Theodore Roethke Collection, held in the University of Washington Libraries, Special Collections.

25 *"I am very tired of being mournful":* Judith Jones to Theodore Roethke, undated, late 1947/early 1948, Theodore Roethke Collection, held in the University of Washington Libraries, Special Collections.

25 *By the time Judith's cousin Jane's divorce:* Judith wrote to Theodore Roethke in the summer and fall of 1947, telling him of Jane and John Gunther appearing together in public. In a letter whose postmark is ripped, Judith wrote that Jane was "stepping around at a great rate at fancy parties and fancy people with Mr. Gunther, celebrating (I guess I told you!) Jack's hasty marriage to the NBC copy-girl, age 22."

25 *"The new couple made plans to elope":* Daily *Illini,* "Gunther to Marry," March 6, 1948.

25 *"It will be very good for me":* Judith Jones to Theodore Roethke, spring 1948, Theodore Roethke Collection, held in the University of Washington Libraries, Special Collections.

26 *(Koestler took a shine to many women):* "The Koestler Question," *Irish Times,* March 6, 1999, https://www.irishtimes.com/news/the-koestler-question -1.160241; Theodore Dalrymple, "A Drinker of Infinity: Arthur Koestler's Life and Work Embodied in the Existential Dilemmas of Our Day," City Journal, Spring 2007, https://www.city-journal.org/html/drinker-infinity -13022.html.

CHAPTER 3

28 *liberation brought an end to the city's Nazi occupation, but:* "Paris is still, physically, living largely on vegetables and mostly without heat," wrote Janet
Flanner in *Paris Journal, 1944–1965* (New York: Atheneum, 1965), 4.

28 *"Parisians, who expected to fill up":* Flanner, *Paris Journal*, 5.

28 *"Generously uncovered pink thighs":* Jean Galtier-Boissière, quoted in Antony
Beevor and Artemis Cooper, *Paris After the Liberation, 1944–1949* (New
York: Doubleday, 1994), 60.

28 *"Fashion is a veneer":* statement made by the fashionable Louise de Vilmorin,
as quoted in Alistair Horne, *Seven Ages of Paris* (New York: Alfred A. Knopf,
2002), 386.

28 *That summer, when Judith and Sarah arrived, saw more American tourists:*
Flanner, *Paris Journal*, 88–91; Beevor and Cooper, *Paris After the Liberation*,
59–60.

28 *new ideas flowed freely:* Horne, *Seven Ages of Paris*, 384.

28 *Judith and Sarah moved to the more modest:* Judith's datebook notes that on
June 17, she and Sarah moved to the Hôtel Montalembert.

28 *A young Simone de Beauvoir:* Deirdre Bair, *Simone de Beauvoir: A Biography*
(New York: Touchstone, 1990), 273.

29 *He'd gone to Europe to escape: The Pillar and the City* was published in the
spring of 1948, and Gore Vidal couldn't bear its scrutiny and mixed reviews;
Jay Parini, *Empire of Self: A Life of Gore Vidal* (New York: Doubleday, 2015),
72–74.

29 *Vidal went first to Rome:* Parini, *Empire of Self*, 74–79.

29 *Judith bumped into Vidal on the street:* Judith's 1948 datebook marks July 5 as
her first time socializing in Paris with Vidal. She continued to see a good
deal of him that summer; her datebook notes meals and outings together on
July 5, 9, 14, 15, and 21.

29 *Williams was a social magnet:* Fred Kaplan, *Gore Vidal: A Biography* (New
York: Doubleday, 1999), 277.

29 *Truman Capote blew in, flaunting:* Capote's amethyst ring, which he alleged
was given to him by the French Nobel Prize winner Gide, shows up in many
writings about Capote's time in Paris after the war. It is described in most
detail on pages 89–90 of George Plimpton's oral history, *Truman Capote:
In Which Various Friends, Enemies, Acquaintances, and Detractors Recall His
Turbulent Career* (New York: Nan A. Talese, 1997).

29 *Capote and Williams lunched:* Parini, *Empire of Self*, 79.

29 *the French novelist, freedom fighter:* Malraux's *Les Voix du Silence* was pub-

lished in 1951. The English translation of Malraux's book, *The Voices of Silence*, was published in 1953.

30 *One fellow in particular caught:* Jones, *The Tenth Muse*, 20, and Judith Jones's unpublished manuscript about her time in France, held in Judith Jones Private Collection.

30 *On their first date:* From Judith Jones unpublished essay on Restaurant 4 Rue du Cirque, Judith Jones Private Collection.

30 *The Left Bank's clubs drew:* Beevor and Cooper, *Paris After the Liberation*, 59–60.

30 *"the young, rootless, and vaguely politicized":* Colin Jones, *Paris: Biography of a City* (New York: Viking Penguin, 2005), 432.

30 *He took her to lunch in a little auberge:* Jones, *The Tenth Muse*, 21.

31 *"Paris is such a wonderful city":* Judith Jones to Charles Bailey and Phyllis Bailey, quoted in Jones, *The Tenth Muse*, 19–20.

31 *One warm August afternoon, Judith wandered:* Judith didn't know the date of the mishap, but the entry in her datebook from August 23, 1948, reads: "lunch-1, Tuileries, Chris & John Krisch, bank, embassy, etc." The combination of the Tuileries, where Judith told the story of having her purse stolen, and the bank and embassy flurry that follows, makes this timing a best guess.

31 *"Dearest ones . . . The question is one":* September 14, 1948, Judith Jones to Charles Bailey and Phyllis Bailey, Judith Jones Private Collection.

32 *Born Marguerite Chapin:* "Marguerite Caetani Dead at 83; Literary Editor Was a Duchess," *New York Times*, December 19, 1963, https://times machine.nytimes.com/timesmachine/1963/12/19/89993986.html?page Number=33; Judith Jones unpublished manuscript about time in France, Judith Jones Private Collection.

32 *Judith wrote home about the "Bard boy":* Judith Jones to Charles Bailey and Phyllis Hedley Bailey, September 14, 1948, Judith Jones Private Collection.

33 *"I have so many irons in the fire":* Judith Jones to Charles Bailey and Phyllis Hedley Bailey, September 20, 1948, Judith Jones Private collection.

33 *Since August, she'd done odd jobs:* Judith Jones to Charles Bailey and Phyllis Hedley Bailey, October 5, 1948, Judith Jones Private Collection.

33 *The idea for the Cercle Rue du Cirque:* The details about the pop-up restaurant at 4 Rue du Cirque come from an unpublished essay Judith wrote about the restaurant years later. In her private collection are two versions, both that she hoped to sell to magazines. The piece, in those iterations, was never published.

35 *"1,000 francs for dinner":* Jones, unpublished essay.

35 *"An hors d'oeuvre of lobster":* Jones, unpublished essay.

35 *"I know you didn't send me to an expensive college":* Judith Jones to Charles Bailey and Phyllis Hedley Bailey, October 13, 1948, Judith Jones Private Collection.

35 *"Hello? Is this* Weekend *magazine?":* Judith's 1948 datebook says she moved back into the Lenox on Tuesday, December 7, and had an appointment with Dick at *Weekend* on Thursday, December 9. The story of "snatching the phone" comes from Judith Jones interviews with author, April–June 2013; and Jones, *The Tenth Muse,* 33.

35 *The magazine, Lord conceded:* Sterling Lord, interview with author, May 12, 2020.

CHAPTER 4

37 *Weekend, a glossy offshoot:* Many of the details about *Weekend* come from Sterling Lord's memoir, *Lord of Publishing* (New York: Open Road, 2013).

37 *the office was still only half unpacked:* Details from photos of *Weekend*'s offices in Judith Jones Private Collection.

38 *He told her to come in at nine the next morning:* Judith's 1948 datebook says she met *Weekend*'s staff and Dick at 5 p.m. on December 9, and started work at the magazine's offices at 9 the next morning.

38 *She was distracted by thoughts of him that Friday:* Details from Judith Jones's 1948 datebook, Judith Jones Private Collection.

38 *That day, Dick invited Judith to lunch:* Judith's datebook for 1948 says Judith and Dick first had lunch on Monday, December 13.

39 *Over lunch, he told Judith:* Details about the Jones family are drawn from the author's interviews with Judith Jones, as well as Dick's mother, Elizabeth Jones's, letters to her son and the unpublished memoir she wrote about her life and work in newspapers, all of which are held in Judith Jones Private Collection.

39 *"A curious person":* Judith Jones to Sarah Moore, April 27, 1951, Judith Jones Private Collection.

40 *In mid-February 1949, Judith typed an official-looking letter:* Letter subject "Release from Duty," February 15, 1949, Judith Jones Private Collection; Lord, *Lord of Publishing,* 32–35.

40 *In February 1949, Judith moved in with Dick and Sterling:* Judith sent home a packet of letters in early 1949 with the return address 80 Rue Lauriston, Paris 16.

40 *"I know it is hard for you":* Judith Jones to Charles Bailey and Phyllis Hedley Bailey, 1949, quoted in Judith Jones, *The Tenth Muse: My Life in Food* (New York: Alfred A. Knopf, 2007), 35–36.

41 *In March 1949, Ken McCormick had written to Judith:* Kenneth McCormick to Judith Jones, March 1949, Judith Jones Private Collection.

41 *"My job is an easy, undemanding one":* Judith Jones to Sarah Moore, April 27, 1951, Judith Jones Private Collection. The first evidence of Judith's independent literary-agenting business venture comes from the return address on the letter Judith wrote on behalf of Theodore Roethke to Phoebe Pierce at *Flair* magazine in New York, dated January 28, 1950, Judith Jones Private Collection.

42 *It was an advance copy of a book:* Carol Ann Lee, *The Hidden Life of Otto Frank* (London: Viking, 2002), 244–45.

42 *"History cannot be written solely":* Translation and quotation from Ruth Franklin's "Ghost Stories" Substack, July 4, 2022; "Nach Appell von Minister: Anne will ihr Tagebuch veröffentlichen," March 28, 1944, Anne Frank House, https://www.annefrank.org/de/timeline/74/nach-appell-von-minister -anne-will-ihr-tagebuch-veroffentlichen/?utm_source=substack&utm _medium=email.

42 *The girl began to revise her diary:* My knowledge of Anne Frank editing her own diary before her father, Otto Frank, edited it for publication is largely a credit to the writer Ruth Franklin and Dr. Carol Gilligan, both of whom have made deep studies of Anne Frank's life and writing. Other accounts include Erin Bartnett's May 18, 2018, article in Electric Literature, "Researchers Have Found Two New Pages in Anne Frank's Diary. Should We Read Them?" https://electricliterature.com/researchers-have-found-two -new-pages-in-anne-franks-diary-should-we-read-them/.

43 *"we Jews were to tell how we lived":* The Diary of Anne Frank (London: Macmillan Children's Books, 1995), 167.

43 *"The Anne that appeared before me":* "The publication of the diary," Anne Frank House, https://www.annefrank.org/en/anne-frank/diary/publication -diary/.

44 *In response, Meyer wrote an article:* "How Did Anne's Diary Become So Famous?," Anne Frank House, https://www.annefrank.org/en/anne-frank /diary/how-did-annes-diary-become-so-famous/.

44 *the diary was handed off to Barbara Zimmerman:* Matt Schudel, "N.Y. Review of Books Founder Barbara Epstein," *Washington Post,* June 19, 2006, https:// www.washingtonpost.com/archive/local/2006/06/19/ny-review-of-books -founder-barbara-epstein/10abf4cd-a088-48a2-acfa-a0cfce41f7df/.

44 *many believe that it was actually Barbara Zimmerman who ghostwrote:* Cynthia Ozick, "Who Owns Anne Frank?," *New Yorker,* September 28, 1997, https://www.newyorker.com/magazine/1997/10/06/who-owns-anne-frank.

44 *"a born writer":* Meyer Levin, "Life in the Secret Annex," *New York Times,*
June 15, 1952, https://www.nytimes.com/1996/10/06/books/life-in-the-se
cret-annex.html?searchResultPosition=1.

44 *the review catapulted the Doubleday edition:* The story of Anne Frank and
her diary has been widely documented (see, for example, "Who Is Anne
Frank?," Anne Frank Center USA, https://annefrank.com/about-anne
-frank/). Among the works consulted here are *Anne Frank: The Book, the Life,
the Aftermath* by Francine Prose (New York: Harper, 2009); *An Obsession
with Anne Frank: Meyer Levin and the Diary* by Lawrence Graver (Berkeley:
University of California Press, 1995); and *The Stolen Legacy of Anne Frank:
Meyer Levin, Lillian Hellman, and the Staging of the "Diary,"* by Ralph Mel-
nick (New Haven: Yale University Press, 1997).

44 *"the most popular secular book":* Brenda Goodman, "Puppet Show with Dark
Tale to Tell: Anne Frank's," *New York Times,* January 25, 2006, https://www
.nytimes.com/2006/01/25/theater/newsandfeatures/puppet-show-with
-dark-tale-to-tell-anne-franks.html.

45 *It was her own endeavors, not Doubleday's:* Judith Jones to Phyllis Hedley
Bailey and Charles Bailey, early 1950, Judith Jones Private Collection.

45 *They called the book* How to Live in Paris*:* Edwin Boone to Judith Jones, April
30, 1951, Judith Jones Private Collection.

45 *"I tell you it's really just because":* Judith Jones to Charles Bailey and Phyllis
Hedley Bailey, 1950, Judith Jones Private Collection.

45 *"away a good deal":* Judith Jones to Sarah Moore, April 27, 1951, Judith Jones
Private Collection.

45 *"I am playing politics":* Judith Jones to Charles Bailey and Phyllis Hedley
Bailey, March 19, 1951, Judith Jones Private Collection.

45 *"I must confess":* Judith Jones to Sarah Moore, April 27, 1951, Judith Jones
Private Collection.

46 *They'd found a cheap room:* Jones, *The Tenth Muse,* 42.

46 *the* charcuterie, *the* boucherie*:* Jones, *The Tenth Muse,* 36–37.

46 *The wheat harvest, in 1948:* Flanner, *Paris Journal,* 93.

46 *They learned to be humbly curious:* Jones, *The Tenth Muse,* 27–47.

47 *"You're allowed to have deck chairs":* Judith Jones to Phyllis Hedley Bailey and
Charles Bailey, spring 1950, Judith Jones Private Collection.

47 *"rather fabulous American":* Judith Jones to Phyllis Hedley Bailey and Charles
Bailey, December 21, 1950, Judith Jones Private Collection.

47 *For their Christmas meal:* Jones, *The Tenth Muse,* 41.

48 *"I would be willing to consider this":* Judith Jones to Charles Bailey and Phyllis
Hedley Bailey, spring 1951, Judith Jones Private Collection.

49   *Judith worried that if:* Judith Jones to Charles Bailey and Phyllis Hedley
      Bailey, Spring spring 1951, Judith Jones Private Collection.
49   *"Dearest ones. Am writing":* Judith Jones to Phyllis Hedley Bailey and Charles
      Bailey, postcard, date ripped, Judith Jones Private Collection.

CHAPTER 5

Dates in chapter 5 come from Judith's 1951 datebook, Judith Jones Private Collection.

52   *he'd just moved into a tiny basement office:* David Margolick, "Sterling Lord,
      Premier Literary Agent, Is Dead at 102," *New York Times,* September 4, 2022,
      https://www.nytimes.com/2022/09/04/books/sterling-lord-dead.html.
52   *At the time, most American mothers:* U.S. Department of Health, Education,
      and Welfare, "Vital Statistics of the United States, 1951," vol. 1, https://
      www.cdc.gov/nchs/data/vsus/vsus_1951_1.pdf.
53   *"I fell in love with her in an instant":* Bronwyn Dunne, interview with author,
      May 13 and 14, 2019; Bronwyn Dunne, email correspondence to author,
      November 12, 2020.
53   *an idea for an historical book:* Dick Jones published *The Minnesota: Forgotten
      River* as part of the Rivers of America series, edited by Carl Carmer, pub-
      lished by Holt, Rinehart & Winston in 1962.
53   *"I miss you horribly":* Judith Jones to Richard Evan Jones, January 26, 1952,
      Judith Jones Private Collection.
54   *"I'd be able to close up my desk":* Judith Jones to Richard Evan Jones, January
      26, 1952, Judith Jones Private Collection.
54   *"I am after all free":* Judith Jones to Richard Evan Jones, February 9, 1951,
      Judith Jones Private Collection.
54   *"I'm really quite expert now":* Judith Jones to Richard Evan Jones, February
      1951, exact date unknown, ripped, Judith Jones Private Collection.
54   *"let [them] know that I was entirely responsible":* Judith Jones to Richard Evan
      Jones, 1952, exact date unknown, postmark ripped, Judith Jones Private Col-
      lection.
54   *Still, the house didn't offer Judith a job:* Judith Jones to Richard Evan Jones,
      1952, Judith Jones Private Collection.
55   *"I must confess that I find":* Judith Jones to Theodore Roethke, November 14,
      1952, Theodore Roethke Collection, held in the University of Washington
      Libraries, Special Collections.
55   *"The thought of the Radio City rat race":* Judith Jones to Charles Bailey and
      Phyllis Hedley Bailey, February 1, 1951, Judith Jones Private Collection.

56　*Though medical intervention had failed:* Judith had been seeking treatment for her painful, heavy periods for years by then. In the fall of 1947, she wrote to Roethke describing the scene and alluding to the mysterious contents of the shots: "They assure me that twill cure all," Theodore Roethke Collection, held in the University of Washington Libraries, Special Collections.

56　*Judith, too, wrote a couple of pieces for* Yankee*:* Judith's pieces in *Yankee* were published in 1955. One, in May, was entitled, "They Want to Grow Up"; another, "La Mode Sportif"; and in August, she had two features in the magazine, "Future Fashions" and "Becoming Models: How One 'Daughter's Debut' Led to a New England Wide School for 'Natural Femininity.'"

56　*She signed up to be a substitute teacher:* Judith Jones, *The Tenth Muse: My Life in Food* (New York: Alfred A. Knopf, 2007), 52–53.

56　*"Any man who has been named":* "McCarthyism and the Red Scare," University of Virginia, Miller Center, https://millercenter.org/the-presidency/educational-resources/age-of-eisenhower/mcarthyism-red-scare.

CHAPTER 6

59　*Blanche Knopf was often displeased:* "Mrs. Blanche Wolf Knopf of Publishing Firm Dies: Helped Husband to Found Company in 1915," *New York Times,* June 5, 1966, https://timesmachine.nytimes.com/timesmachine/1966/06/05/93844557.html?pageNumber=86.

59　*Knopf was then considered:* There are many references to Knopf's elite reputation in mid–2000 century publishing, especially *The Art of Prestige: The Formative Years of Knopf, 1915–1929* by Amy Root Clements (Amherst: University of Massachusetts Press, 2014); "Living in a Dream World: Alfred A. Knopf, Inc.," in Art Silverman's *The Time of Their Lives: The Golden Age of Great American Book Publishers, Their Editors, and Authors* (New York: Truman Talley Books/St. Martin's Press, 2008); Laura Claridge's *The Lady with the Borzoi: Blanche Knopf, Literary Tastemaker Extraordinaire* (New York: Farrar, Straus and Giroux, 2016); Robert Gottlieb's memoir, *Avid Reader: A Life* (New York: Farrar, Straus and Giroux, 2016); and notes, journals, and memoirs that accompany the voluminous archives of Alfred A. Knopf (both the person and the publishing house) at the Harry Ransom Center, University of Texas at Austin.

60　*Knopf published their first hit:* Chip McGrath, "The Life and Times of Alfred A. Knopf," *Literary Hub,* October 1, 2015, https://lithub.com/the-life-and-times-of-alfred-a-knopf/, excerpted from Charles McGrath, introduction to *Alfred A. Knopf, 1915–2015: A Century of Publishing* (New York: Alfred A. Knopf, 2015).

60   *"Madison Avenue ballyhoo"*: "The Borzoi Credo," explicitly stating Knopf's priorities as a publisher, ran as an advertisement in the *Atlantic Monthly* in 1957, https://www.randomhouse.com/knopf/about/credo.html.

60   *Blanche Knopf hadn't set out to hire a lady editor:* Judith often refers to herself as a "lady editor" in her correspondence from her early days at Knopf.

61   *"I don't think a lady publisher"*: "Mrs. Blanche Wolf Knopf of Publishing Firm Dies."

61   *In her heyday, Blanche Knopf:* Claridge, *The Lady with the Borzoi.*

61   *"courage went a kind of stubbornness"*: John Hersey to Alfred A. Knopf, June 22, 1966, Harry Ransom Center, University of Texas at Austin.

61   *Elizabeth Bowen noted the "effrontery"*: Claridge, *The Lady with the Borzoi*, 37.

61   *"the soul of the firm"*: Claridge, *The Lady with the Borzoi*, 3.

61   *her outsize impact didn't earn her:* This is major theme of Claridge's *The Lady with the Borzoi*, but is best articulated on pages 1 to 6 and 24.

61   *From a young age, Blanche had suffered:* Claridge, *The Lady with the Borzoi*, 161; Megan Tatum, "DNP: The Dangerous Diet Pill Pharmacists Should Know About," *Pharmaceutical Journal* 302, no. 7926 (June 13, 2019), https://pharmaceutical-journal.com/article/feature/dnp-the-dangerous-diet-pill-pharmacists-should-know-about.

62   *"one of the most brilliant and disturbing memoirs"*: Charles Poore, "Memories of a Catholic Girlhood by Mary McCarthy," Books of the Times, *New York Times*, May 18, 1959, https://archive.nytimes.com/www.nytimes.com/books/97/11/23/home/mccarthy-catholic.html.

62   *Jack Kerouac's* On the Road*:* David Margolick, "Sterling Lord, Premier 62 Agent, Is Dead at 102," *New York Times*, September 4, 2022, https://www.nytimes.com/2022/09/04/books/sterling-lord-dead.html.

62   *"Dearest Ted . . . I have been meaning"*: Judith Jones to Theodore Roethke, June 24, 1957, Theodore Roethke Collection, held in the University of Washington Libraries, Special Collections.

64   *"American everyman"*: Christopher Lehmann-Haupt, "John Updike, a Lyrical Writer of the Middle-Class Man, Dies at 76," *New York Times*, January 28, 2009, https://www.nytimes.com/2009/01/28/books/28updike.html.

64   *"what happens when a young American family man"*: Adam Begley, *Updike* (New York: Harper, 2014), 166–67.

64   *"moving and brilliant"*: David Boroff, "You Cannot Really Flee," *New York Times*, November 6, 1960, https://www.nytimes.com/1960/11/06/archives/you-cannot-really-flee-rabbit-run-by-john-updike-307-pp-new-york.html. *Rabbit, Run* sold only moderately well, about twenty-six thousand copies. It was *Couples*, in 1968, that shot him to commercial fame, selling

more than two hundred thousand copies within three years of its publication; Henry Raymont, "John Updike Completes a Sequel to 'Rabbit, Run,'" *New York Times*, July 27, 1971, https://archive.nytimes.com/www.nytimes.com/books/97/04/06/lifetimes/updike-r-rabbit.html.

64 *His 1946* Hiroshima: Will Hersey, "John Hersey's *Hiroshima* Is Still Essential Reading, 75 Years Later," *Esquire*, April 23, 2021, https://www.esquire.com/uk/culture/books/a36196920/john-hersey-hiroshima/.

65 *"When I get fired from Knopf":* Judith Jones to Richard Evan Jones, 1957, Judith Jones Private Collection.

66 *In an office often rife with tension:* Descriptions of Alfred and Blanche Knopf's contentious dynamic come from the author's interviews with Judith, as well as various Knopf correspondence held at the Harry Ransom Center, Claridge's *The Lady with the Borzoi*, and Silverman's *The Time of Their Lives*, and the author's interview with Robert Gottlieb on June 20, 2019.

66 *It was a cookbook, he said, that had just come in:* Knopf published Elizabeth David's *Italian Food* in 1958, the year after Judith started at the house. The original edition was published in London by Macdonald in 1954.

66 *"Everybody knew that I had spent that time in Paris":* Judith Jones, interview by Linda Kulman, "Judith Jones Toasts a Culinary Life in 'Tenth Muse,'" Book Tour, NPR, January 8, 2008, https://www.npr.org/2008/01/08/17809903/judith-jones-toasts-a-culinary-life-in-tenth-muse.

66 *At the time, most cookbooks:* See Megan J. Elias's *Food on the Page: Cookbooks in American Culture* (Philadelphia: University of Pennsylvania Press, 2017).

66 *Not one of the French cookbooks Judith tried:* The Joneses had "half a hundred" cookbooks, wrote Craig Claiborne in "The Joneses Delight in Keeping up With Cuisine," *New York Times*, August 3, 1961, https://timesmachine.nytimes.com/timesmachine/1961/08/03/118046282.html?pageNumber=10.

66 *"Thanks for letting us take our time":* William Koshland to Avis DeVoto, November 30, 1959, Harry Ransom Center, University of Texas at Austin.

68 *"You really have got something here":* Avis DeVoto to Julia Child, December 25, 1952, quoted in Bob Spitz, *Dearie: The Remarkable Life of Julia Child* (New York: Alfred A. Knopf, 2012), 241.

68 *"more complex and difficult to handle":* Dorothy de Santillana to Julia Child, Louise Bertholle, and Simone Beck, March 21, 1958, quoted in Spitz, *Dearie*, 285.

68 *"Believe me, I know how much":* Paul Brooks to Julia Child, Louise Bertholle, and Simone Beck, November 10, 1959, quoted in Spitz, *Dearie*, 296.

68 *"Do not despair":* Avis DeVoto to Julia Child, November 10, 1959, quoted in Spitz, *Dearie*, 296.

CHAPTER 7

69 *that morning in April 1960:* Bob Spitz's *Dearie: The Remarkable Life of Julia Child* (New York: Alfred A. Knopf, 2012, 302) says the meeting took place on May 5, 1960, but this does not align with when Avis called Julia with the good news of Knopf's acceptance of the book on April 9, 1960, or when Julia sent in new title suggestions for the book on May 3, 1960. The meeting had to occur in April.

69 *"I don't know of another book that succeeds":* Judith Jones, internal Knopf Memo, 1959, Harry Ransom Center, University of Texas at Austin.

70 *Alfred Knopf was a bon vivant:* David Strauss, *Setting the Table for Julia Child: Gourmet Dining in America, 1934–1961* (Baltimore: Johns Hopkins University Press, 2011), 31.

70 *He'd been at Bobbs-Merrill:* John J. Simon, "Angus Cameron: Leading US Publisher Who Survived Community Witchhunt Smears," *Guardian,* November 29, 2002, https://www.theguardian.com/news/2002/nov/30/guardianobituaries.booksobituaries.

71 *"the foremost United States book editor":* Simon, "Angus Cameron."

71 *he caught and sold whitefish:* Douglas Martin, "Angus Cameron, 93, Editor Forced Out in McCarthy Era," *New York Times,* November 23, 2022, https://www.nytimes.com/2002/11/23/arts/angus-cameron-93-editor-forced-out-in-mccarthy-era.html.

71 *"Both as aspirant cook and editor":* Quotes from Cameron's report are courtesy of Jonathan Coleman, held in their original at the Harry Ransom Center, University of Texas at Austin.

71 *The book was an astonishing achievement:* Avis DeVoto to Julia Child, March 25, 1958, Arthur and Elizabeth Schlesinger Library on the History of Women in America, Radcliffe Institute for Advanced Study, Harvard University, Cambridge, MA.

72 *Blanche Knopf fidgeted grumpily:* Story retold by Judith in interviews with the author, and also in Jonathan Coleman's unpublished biography, "What He Stood For: The Courage and Many Worlds of Angus Cameron."

72 *"Our publication proposal":* Judith Jones to Julia Child, April 9, 1960, Arthur and Elizabeth Schlesinger Library, Radcliffe Institute.

72 *Knopf offered $1,500 for the book:* Houghton's advance was $250, while Knopf's was $1,500, Spitz, *Dearie,* 242, 303.

72 *Judith reiterated the book's brilliance:* Judith Jones to Julia Child, April 9, 1960. Arthur and Elizabeth Schlesinger Library, Radcliffe Institute.

72 *"It means that we can have truly meaningful":* Julia Child to Judith Jones, May 14, 1960, Harry Ransom Center, University of Texas at Austin.

72 *"The final manuscript can be ready":* Julia Child to Judith Jones, June 10, 1960, Harry Ransom Center, University of Texas at Austin.

72 *In 1950, McGraw-Hill and General Mills jointly published:* "25 Best-Selling Cookbooks of All Time," Daily Meal, https://www.thedailymeal.com /cook/25-best-selling-cookbooks-all-time-slideshow. The closest competition *Betty Crocker* had is *My Better Homes and Gardens Cook Book*, published in 1930, which has sold approximately thirty million copies.

73 *"the latest short cuts":* Betty Crocker's Picture Cook Book (McGraw-Hill and General Mills, 1950), 5.

73 *American wives did the lion's share:* "Post-War Consumerism," Women & the American Story, New-York Historical Society, https://wams.nyhistory.org /growth-and-turmoil/cold-war-beginnings/post-war-consumerism/.

73 *"dream come true":* Betty Crocker's Picture Cook Book, 5.

73 *"Dear Mrs. Child . . . I'd like to suggest":* Judith Jones to Julia Child, May 27, 1960, Harry Ransom Center, University of Texas at Austin.

74 *"Perhaps Americans think":* Julia Child to Judith Jones, June 25, 1960, Harry Ransom Center, University of Texas at Austin.

74 *"you are the final authorities":* Judith Jones to Julia Child, June 20, 1960, Harry Ransom Center, University of Texas at Austin.

74 *"A good cassoulet":* Julia Child to Judith Jones, June 25, 1960, Harry Ransom Center, University of Texas at Austin.

75 *"Mastering the Art of French Cuisine/Cooking/Cookery":* Julia Child to Judith Jones, October 30, 1960, Harry Ransom Center, University of Texas at Austin.

75 *"We have all liked the idea of playing":* Judith Jones to Julia Child, November 18, 1960, Harry Ransom Center, University of Texas at Austin.

75 *"I have made all the corrections":* Julia Child to Judith Jones, September 14, 1960, Ransom Center, University of Texas at Austin.

75 *"I think you are a wonder":* Judith Jones to Julia Child, April 5, 1961, Harry Ransom Center, University of Texas at Austin.

76 *"I hope you're not getting too discouraged":* Judith Jones to Julia Child, April 19, Harry Ransom Center, University of Texas at Austin.

76 *"The book . . . is more important":* Julia Child to Judith Jones, April 24, 1961, Harry Ransom Center, University of Texas at Austin.

76 *Perhaps you consider yourself:* From "The Colossus," in *The Colossus and Other Poems* (London: Heinemann, 1960).

76 *Plath, who'd been placing:* Sylvia Plath, Poetry Foundation, https://www.po etryfoundation.org/poets/sylvia-plath.

77 *He'd written to Plath:* Harold Strauss to Sylvia Plath, June 26, 1952, Harry Ransom Center, University of Texas at Austin.

77 *"not in the position to concentrate":* Sylvia Plath to Harold Strauss, July 8, 1952, Harry Ransom Center, University of Texas at Austin.

77 Mademoiselle's *annual college issue:* Plath's one-month stint is thoroughly detailed in Elizabeth Winder's *Pain, Parties, Work: Sylvia Plath in New York, Summer 1953* (New York: Harper, 2013). For photographs of Plath and Bowen, see Michelle Legro, "Pain, Parties, Work: Sylvia Plath in New York, Summer 1953," Marginalian, https://www.themarginalian.org/2013/06/12 /pain-parties-work-sylvia-plath-in-new-york-summer-1953/.

77 *"pain, parties, and work":* Plath quoted in Andrew Wilson, "Sylvia Plath in New York: 'pain, parties and work,'" *Guardian,* February 2, 2013, https:// www.theguardian.com/books/2013/feb/02/sylvia-plath-young-new-york -andrew-wilson.

77 *In August, she attempted:* Elizabeth Winder, *Pain, Parties, Work: Sylvia Plath in New York, Summer 1953* (New York: Harper, 2013), 225.

77 *"I blissfully succumbed":* Paul Alexander, "What Sylvia Plath's Letters Reveal About the Poet We Thought We Knew," *Washington Post,* October 18, 2017, https://www.washingtonpost.com/entertainment/books/what-sylvia -plaths-letters-reveal-about-the-poet-we-thought-we-knew/2017/10/18 /fffbc4c8-b34d-11e7-be94-fabb0f1e9ffb_story.html.

77 *After her attempted suicide:* "Sylvia Plath," Poetry Foundation, https://www .poetryfoundation.org/poets/sylvia-plath.

77 *There, at a launch party:* Plath's letter recounting the events of that first meeting, written on February 26, 1956, can be seen at https://www.bl.uk/collec tion-items/sylvia-plaths-journal-26-february-1956.

77 *"chicken & squash ready":* Quoted in Lynda K. Bundtzen, "Lucent Figs and Suave Veal Chops: Sylvia Plath and Food" *Gastronomica* 10, no. 1 (Winter 2010): 79–90. JSTOR, https://doi.org/10.1525/gfc.2010.10.1.79.

77 *"Whoa, I said to myself":* Bundtzen, "Lucent Figs," originally quoted in Sylvia Plath, *The Unabridged Journals of Sylvia Plath,* ed. Karen V. Kukil (New York: Anchor Books, 2000), 269.

77 *"Disease of doldrums":* The Unabridged Journals of Sylvia Plath, 423.

78 *"A much more difficult job for a poetrywriter":* Sylvia Plath to Mary Stetson Clarke, April 10, 1959, *The Letters of Sylvia Plath,* vol. 2, *1956–1963,* eds. Peter K. Steinberg and Karen V. Kukil (New York: Harper, 2018), 310.

78 *That June, she submitted it to Knopf:* Plath submitted it to Knopf on June 8, 1959. The manuscript was then titled *Devil of the Stairs.* After Knopf passed, Plath sent the book to Viking and Farrar Straus and Cudahy, both in October 1959.

78 *"impressed enough":* Judith Jones, *The Colossus* reader's report, December 7, 1960, Harry Ransom Center, University of Texas at Austin.

78   *Poetry, like food, was a shared passion:* Chris Vandercook, interview with author, May 22, 2019.

78   *"This girl is a poet":* Judith Jones, interoffice memo, December 7, 1960, Harry Ransom Center, University of Texas at Austin.

78   *"so deliberately stolen":* Judith Jones, interoffice memo, December 7, 1960.

78   *"'Poem for a Birthday' at the end of the book":* Judith Jones to Stanley Kunitz, January 25, 1961, Harry Ransom Center, University of Texas at Austin.

79   *"I feel I have lied [sic] with these poems":* Judith Jones to Sylvia Plath, March 29, 1961, Harry Ransom Center, University of Texas at Austin.

79   *"GOOD NEWS GOOD NEWS GOOD NEWS":* Sylvia Plath to Aurelia Schober Plath, May 1, 1961, *The Letters of Sylvia Plath*, vol. 2, 615–16.

79   *Plath conceded, without a whiff of defensiveness:* Meanwhile, Plath had written to Roethke directly—the two had met at a party in London in February of that year. Plath wrote "I find he is my influence"—enclosing a copy of her book, saying she was negotiating with Knopf, and pointing to the sequence of poems in question "which show me so far under your influence as to be flat out"; Sylvia Plath to Theodore Roethke, April 13, 1961, *The Letters of Sylvia Plath*, vol. 2, 602.

79   *"a good and reasonable number":* Sylvia Plath to Judith Jones, April 5, 1961, Harry Ransom Center, University of Texas at Austin.

79   *Judith wrote that she liked:* Judith Jones to Sylvia Plath, April 28, 1961, Harry Ransom Center, University of Texas at Austin.

79   *"I am pleased that our opinions seem":* Sylvia Plath to Judith Jones, May 2, 1961, Harry Ransom Center, University of Texas at Austin.

79   *"and will result, I think":* Sylvia Plath to Judith Jones, May 2, 1961, Harry Ransom Center, University of Texas at Austin.

79   *"lady editor":* Sylvia Plath to Aurelia Schober Plath and Warren Plath, *The Letters of Sylvia Plath*, vol. 2, 641. Bernard Bergonzi reviewed the UK edition of *The Colossus* in the *Guardian* on November 25, 1960, praising Plath's "highly personal tone and way of looking at the world," and noted that she wrote with "a degree of assurance that would be rare in her contemporaries of either sex on this side of the Atlantic." Despite the whiff of pat sexism in the commentary, Bergonzi concluded that Plath's collection offered an answer in the affirmative to "those inquiring spirits who demand if there are any new poets worth reading." (Bergonzi quotes can be seen at Lauren Niland, "Sylvia Plath—Reviews from the Archive," *Guardian*, October 27, 2012, https://www.theguardian.com/theguardian/from-the-archive-blog/2012/oct/27/sylvia-plath-reviews-archive. It was no small thing for Plath to revise her collection in light of such a glowing review.

80   *"a trial run"*: Sylvia Plath to Judith Jones, May 2, 1961, Harry Ransom Center, University of Texas at Austin.

80   *"hastening . . . to let you know"*: Judith Jones to Sylvia Plath, August 22, 1961, Harry Ransom Center, University of Texas at Austin.

CHAPTER 8

81   *Claiborne had been made food editor:* Thomas McNamee wrote *The Man Who Changed the Way We Eat: Craig Claiborne and the American Food Renaissance* (New York: Free Press, 2012), the only biography on Claiborne as of 2021. A list of all the *New York Times* food critics is available at Amanda Kludt, "A Timeline of All New York Times Restaurant Critics," Eater, September 16, 2011, https://ny.eater.com/2011/9/16/6650353/a-timeline-of-all-new-york-times-restaurant-critics.

82   Gourmet *editor, Ann Seranne assigned Claiborne:* Craig Claiborne's first column, "Steeped in History," devoted to the history of tea, ran in the January 1955 issue of *Gourmet*; see http://www.gourmet.com.s3-website-us-east-1.amazonaws.com/magazine/1950s/1955/01/a-history-of-tea-craig-claibornes-gourmet-debut.html.

82   *"a really remarkable book"*: Judith Jones, interview by Bob Spitz, March 18, 2009, quoted in Bob Spitz, *Dearie: The Remarkable Life of Julia Child* (New York: Alfred A. Knopf, 2012), 312.

82   *On a sweltering 93-degree day:* Judith wrote to Julia Child that she'd cooked "in 93 degree heat at noon," Judith Jones to Julia Child, August 11, 1961, Harry Ransom Center, University of Texas at Austin.

83   *"They live by the dictum"*: Craig Claiborne, "The Joneses Delight in Keeping Up With Cuisine," *New York Times*, August 3, 1961, https://www.nytimes.com/1961/08/03/archives/the-joneses-delight-in-keeping-up-with-cuisine-couples-cooking-zeal.html.

83   *"probably the most comprehensive"*: Craig Claiborne, "Cookbook Review: Glorious Recipes; Art of French Cooking Does Not Concede to U.S. Tastes," *New York Times*, October 18, 1961, https://www.nytimes.com/1961/10/18/archives/cookbook-review-glorious-recipes-art-of-french-cooking-does-not.html.

84   *the Kennedys hired René Verdon:* Craig Claiborne, "White House Hires French Chef," *New York Times*, April 7, 1961, https://www.nytimes.com/1961/04/07/archives/white-house-hires-french-chef-macmillan-treated-to-trout-in-wine.html.

84   *just days after* Mastering's *launch:* The date of this spot is unclear; both Bob

Spitz's *Dearie* and Alex Prud'hommes *The French Chef in America: Julia Child's Second Act* (New York: Alfred A. Knopf, 2016) allude to the spot—Prud'homme, on page 40, says it happened in October 1961—but do not give its exact date.

84 *close to ten thousand television sets:* "1945: 'Television,'" in *World Book Encyclopedia* (Chicago: World Book, 2003), 119.

84 *nearly a hundred commercial stations:* Claudia Reinhardt and Bill Ganzel, "Farming in the 1940s: TV Turns On," Wessels Living History Farm, https://livinghistoryfarm.org/farming-in-the-1940s/tv-turns-on/.

84 *fifty-two million TV sets:* Winthrop D. Jordan, *The Americans: A History* (Boston: McDougal Littell, 1996), 798.

84 *four million households:* Spitz, *Dearie*, 313.

84 *Julia and Simca practiced doggedly:* Spitz, *Dearie*, 314; Prud'homme, *The French Chef in America*, 40–42.

85 *"Our publishers are beginning to think":* Julia Child to Dorothy Child, October 22, 1961, Arthur and Elizabeth Schlesinger Library on the History of Women in America, Radcliffe Institute for Advanced Study, Harvard University, Cambridge, MA.

85 *"I hope by now you have received":* Judith Jones to William Hogan, October 30, 1961, Harry Ransom Center, University of Texas at Austin.

85 *"The girls are going good":* Paul Child to Judith Jones, November 24, 1961, Harry Ransom Center, University of Texas at Austin.

86 *Known as "the Dean of American Cooking":* There are several biographies of James Beard, the most recent—and most thorough—being John Birdsall's *The Man Who Ate Too Much: The Life of James Beard* (New York: W. W. Norton, 2020).

87 *"I've been up to my ears":* Sylvia Plath to Judith Jones, October 7, 1961, Harry Ransom Center, University of Texas at Austin.

87 *in February 1961, Hughes assaulted her:* James Tozer, "How Pregnant Sylvia Plath Was Beaten by Ted Hughes Two Days Before She Miscarried Their Second Child, Her Lost Letters Reveal," *Daily Mail*, April 11, 2017, https://www.dailymail.co.uk/news/article-4403400/Sylvia-Plath-letters-revealing-Ted-Hughes-abuse-sale.html; see also Emily Van Duyne, *Loving Sylvia Plath: A Reclamation* (New York: W. W. Norton, 2024).

87 *"Having seen some short stories of yours":* Judith Jones to Sylvia Plath, November 22, 1961, Harry Ransom Center, University of Texas at Austin.

87 *"It enables me to go on writing":* Sylvia Plath to Judith Jones, December 12, 1961, Harry Ransom Center, University of Texas at Austin.

88 *"I suspect that by now":* Judith Jones to Sylvia Plath, January 11, 1962, Harry Ransom Center, University of Texas at Austin.

88 *"Thanks very much for your letter"*: On February 2, 1962, Sylvia Plath wrote Judith Jones that she'd received the proofs of *Colossus* and had only minor corrections to make. Almost as an afterthought, she added that the family had welcomed a new addition two weeks earlier: a son, Nicholas. "Now all is peaceful again, I am back at my novel," she said (Harry Ransom Center, University of Texas at Austin).

88 *"Opinion makers"; "I feel certain I am going to get"*: Judith Jones to Sylvia Plath, April 3, 1962, Harry Ransom Center, University of Texas at Austin.

89 *"He just sort of gave up"*: Chris Vandercook, interview with author, May 22, 2019.

89 *"Judy; one of the things"*: Chris Vandercook, interview with author, May 22, 2019.

CHAPTER 9

92 *the couple continued in their routines:* Bronwyn Dunne, interview with author, May 13, 2019.

92 *Dick settled in at his office:* Alexis Bierman, email correspondence with author, July 18, 2019.

92 *"Judith didn't take part":* Chris Vandercook, interview with author, May 22, 2019.

92 *After they'd hung up the phone:* Chris Vandercook, interview with author, May 22, 2019; Alexis Bierman, interview with author, June 6, 2019.

92 *"It was like a folie à deux":* Alexis Bierman, interview with author, June 6, 2019.

92 *In fact, after Chris and Audrey moved in:* Meri Zeinklishvili-Dubrova, interview with author, October 3, 2019.

93 *"Sometimes, they had a couple glasses":* Chris Vandercook, interview with author, May 22, 2019.

94 *"almost flattened"; "perfectly delighted":* Sylvia Plath to Judith Jones, May 5, 1962, Harry Ransom Center, University of Texas at Austin.

94 *"I'm sure you must be feeling terribly neglected":* Judith Jones to Sylvia Plath, August 30, 1962, Harry Ransom Center, University of Texas at Austin.

94 *It was a shame, Moore wrote Judith:* Marianne Moore to Judith Jones, April 7, 1962, Harry Ransom Center, University of Texas at Austin.

94 *"hoped I would have more letters":* Judith Jones to Sylvia Plath, August 30, 1962, Harry Ransom Center, University of Texas at Austin.

94 *"I am sorry Miss Moore eschews":* Sylvia Plath to Judith Jones, September 5, 1962, *The Letters of Sylvia Plath*, vol. 2, *1956–1963*, eds. Peter K. Steinberg and Karen V. Kukil (New York: Harper, 2018), 818–19.

95 *The couple briefly tried:* Details of the Ireland trip from Emily Hourican, "The Irish Sojourn of Sylvia Plath," *Irish Independent,* September 23, 2006, https://www.independent.ie/lifestyle/the-irish-sojourn-of-sylvia-plath-26416786.html.

95 *"I have managed a poem a day":* Sylvia Plath, October 12, 1962, in *Letters Home: Correspondence 1950–1963,* ed. Aurelia Schober Plath (New York: Harper & Row, 1975), 466.

95 *Koshland gave the novel a quick read:* On November 7, 1962, William Koshland wrote "We have had sent to us *The Bell Jar* by Victoria Lucas and somehow or other can locate no correspondence as to how it came to us. It's all the more embarrassing that we're going to have to say that we are not going to make you an offer for it." Harry Ransom Center, University of Texas at Austin.

95 *Heinemann's letter explaining that* The Bell Jar *was:* Elizabeth Anderson to William Koshland, September 11, 1963, Harry Ransom Center, University of Texas at Austin.

95 *"knocked galley west"; "But we still cannot warm up":* William Koshland to Elizabeth Anderson, November 30, 1962, Harry Ransom Center, University of Texas at Austin.

96 *"entitled to a first look":* William Koshland to Elizabeth Anderson, November 30, 1962, Harry Ransom Center, University of Texas at Austin.

96 *Heinemann responded quickly and curtly:* Elizabeth Anderson to William Koshland, December 10, 1962, Harry Ransom Center, University of Texas at Austin.

96 *"Dear Sylvia Plath: I know that you have heard":* Judith Jones to Sylvia Plath, December 28, 1962, Harry Ransom Center, University of Texas at Austin.

97 *"it was only recently that the peculiar intensity":* Al Alvarez, "A Poet's Epitaph," *Observer Weekend Review,* February 17, 1963, https://www.newspapers.com/clip/28202446/a-poets-epitaph-sylvia-plath/.

97 *It was Blanche Knopf who circled back:* Correspondence between Blanche Knopf and Charles Pick at Heinemann from March 15 to April 3, 1963, Harry Ransom Center, University of Texas at Austin.

97 *"It is a tragedy that Sylvia Plath died":* Blanche Knopf to Charles Pick, April 3, 1963, Harry Ransom Center, University of Texas at Austin.

98 *"Have no idea how much it pulled":* Julia Child to Judith Jones, March 14, 1962, Harry Ransom Center, University of Texas at Austin.

98 *"Get that tall, loud woman back":* Alex Prud'homme, *The French Chef in America: Julia Child's Second Act* (New York: Alfred A. Knopf, 2016), 39.

98 *"They have no mazuma":* Julia Child to Judith Jones, March 14, 1962, Harry Ransom Center, University of Texas at Austin.

98 *"I would have been the complete mother":* Julia Child quoted in R. W. Coffey, "Their Recipe for Love," *McCall's*, 1988, 98.

98 *its author was, privately, recovering at home:* Judith Jones told me about Julia's hysterectomy in our interviews, and, in an email response to my query on March 9, 2020, Bob Spitz confirmed that this was the operation. There is no mention made of the hysterectomy in any of Julia Child's biographies, and so the exact cause of the surgery is unknown.

98 *She scheduled the procedure for early January 1962:* Avis DeVoto alluded to it in a letter she wrote to William Koshland, dated January 13, 1962: "She returned from the hospital Thursday. Operation very successful, and she will have to take things quietly for several months, but goes up and downstairs, and moves around. A great relief," Harry Ransom Center, University of Texas at Austin. Julia's friend Pat Pratt said, "Julia refused to let health matters faze her. She treated herself like a car; if you had a flat tire you went ahead and fixed it," Spitz, *Dearie: The Remarkable Life of Julia Child* (New York: Alfred A. Knopf, 2012), 389–90; Grant Mack, "Julia Child Didn't Like Talking About Her Experience with Cancer," Showbiz CheatSheet, October 19, 2020, https://www.cheatsheet.com/entertainment/julia-child-didnt-like-talking-about-her-experience-with-cancer.html/. Bob Spitz made no mention of the surgery in his exhaustive biography of Julia Child. When I wrote to him on March 9, 2020, asking why, he responded the same day saying, "I chose not to include it in the book because I felt it was too personal to Julia and did not add to the narrative."

98 *"The unpalatable truth must be faced":* Wilson quoted in Nancy Krieger, Ilana Löwy, Robert Arnowitz, et al., "Hormone Replacement Therapy, Cancer, Controversies, and Women's Health: Historical, Epidemiological, Biological, Clinical, and Advocacy Perspectives," *Journal of Epidemiology & Community Health* 59 (August 2005): 740–48, http://dx.doi.org/10.1136/jech.2005.033316.

98 *"fully-sexed"; "nature's defeminization":* Robert A. Wilson and Thelma A. Wilson, "The Fate of the Nontreated Postmenopausal Woman: A Plea for the Maintenance of Adequate Estrogen from Puberty to the Grave," *Journal of American Geriatric Society* 11 (April 1963): 347–62, https://doi.org/10.1111/j.1532-5415.1963.tb00068.x; see also Judith A. Houck, "'What Do These Women Want?': Feminist Responses to Feminine Forever, 1963–1980," *Bulletin of the History of Medicine* 77, no. 1 (Spring 2003): 103–32, https://doi.org/10.1353/bhm.2003.0023.

99 *"An interesting, adult series":* Julia Child to WGBH, April 26, 1962, Arthur and Elizabeth Schlesinger Library on the History of Women in America, Radcliffe Institute for Advanced Study, Harvard University, Cambridge, MA, quoted in Prud'homme, *The French Chef in America*, 40.

99 *Child would tape four half-hour shows:* Julia Child to William Koshland, May 28, 1962, Harry Ransom Center, University of Texas at Austin.

99 *"TV is certainly a much more difficult medium":* Julia Child to William Koshland, August 6, 1962, Harry Ransom Center, University of Texas at Austin.

99 *"The sales may not be spectacular":* William Koshland to Julia Child, June 12, 1962, Harry Ransom Center, University of Texas at Austin; William Koshland to Julia Child, August 23, 1962, Harry Ransom Center, University of Texas at Austin.

99 *Book-of-the-Month promptly distributed twelve thousand copies:* https://julia childfoundation.org/timeline/#.

99 Mastering *was the first cookbook Book-of-the-Month:* William Koshland to Julia Child, August 23, 1962, Harry Ransom Center, University of Texas at Austin.

99 *In October, James Beard asked Child to come teach:* Julia Child to William Koshland, October 6, 1962; Julia Child to Judith Jones, December 18, 1962, Harry Ransom Center, University of Texas at Austin.

99 *"most lucid volume":* Craig Claiborne, "How to Cook by the Book," *Saturday Evening Post*, December 22–29, 1962, 74, https://www.saturdayeveningpost .com/reprints/how-to-cook-by-the-book/.

99 *"Don't look now":* William Koshland to Julia Child, January 11, 1963, Harry Ransom Center, University of Texas at Austin.

100 *"26 programs in all":* Julia Child to Judith Jones, December 18, 1962, Harry Ransom Center, University of Texas at Austin.

100 *It would be called* The French Chef: Julia Child to William Koshland, October 6, 1962, Harry Ransom Center, University of Texas at Austin.

100 *Within weeks, Julia Child was drawing a viewership unprecedented for WGBH:* Spitz, *Dearie*, 346.

100 *"I am flabbergasted":* Judith Jones to Julia Child, May 3, 1963, Harry Ransom Center, University of Texas at Austin.

100 *Friedan—once a boots-on-the ground reporter:* Debra Michals, ed., "Betty Friedan," National Women's History Museum, 2017, https://www.womens history.org/education-resources/biographies/betty-friedan.

100 The Feminine Mystique *touched a nerve:* "Betty Friedan and 'The Feminine Mystique,'" *The First Measured Century: The Other Way of Looking at American History*, PBS, https://www.pbs.org/fmc/segments/progseg11.htm.

100 *"It was work in the guise of leisure":* Betty Fussell, *My Kitchen Wars* (New York: North Point Press, 1999), 153–54.

101 *Within months, Americans were watching Child:* Spitz, *Dearie*, 346.

101 *When Knopf moved their offices:* Judith Jones, interviewed by Bob Spitz, March 18, 2009, quoted in Spitz, *Dearie*, 300.

102 *He represented writers including:* "Diarmuid Russell Dies at 71, Founded Literary Agency," *New York Times*, December 18, 1973, https://timesmachine.nytimes.com/timesmachine/1973/12/18/issue.html.

102 *Judith knew immediately:* Judith Jones to Bob Croft, July 28, 1993, Knopf private files.

102 *"turned out to be the only person":* Anne Tyler, "Still Just Writing," in *The Writer on Her Work*, ed. Janet Sternburg (New York: W. W. Norton, 1980), 14.

102 *"one knew immediately":* Judith Jones to Bob Croft, July 28, 1993, Knopf private files.

CHAPTER 10

104 *He was prone to dark moods:* Chris Vandercook, interview with author, May 22, 2019.

104 *Joneses rarely went to bed at the same time:* Chris Vandercook, interview with author, May 22, 2019.

104 *Within months of her death:* It was Al Alvarez, the critic who'd kick-started Plath's posthumous ascent to fame, who connected Ted Hughes with the *New York Review of Books*; Alvarez wrote regularly for the magazine right from the start. On November 13, 1964, Ted Hughes wrote to Judith: "What I suggest is that you arrange with the *New York Review of Books* (which has printed several of her poems) to reprint that article by Alvarez (he's one of their regular reviewers) when the book comes out: it will reach a big audience that way, and you could reprint on the jacket of the book all the more pertinent remarks he makes, together with any others you think necessary." Harry Ransom Center, University of Texas at Austin.

105 *The NYRB was intended to be:* Christopher Lehmann-Haupt, "Jason Epstein, Editor and Publishing Innovator, Is Dead at 93," *New York Times*, February 4, 2022, https://www.nytimes.com/2022/02/04/books/jason-epstein-dead.html.

105 *the Review needed "literary-intellectual":* *Esquire* called the *NYRB* "the premier literary-intellectual magazine in the English language," Matt Schudel, "N.Y

Review of Books Founder Barbara Epstein," *Washington Post,* June 19, 2006, https://www.washingtonpost.com/wp-dyn/content/article/2006/06/18 /AR2006061800775.html.

105 *"As you probably know":* Judith Jones to Ted Hughes, March 11, 1964, Harry Ransom Center, University of Texas at Austin.

105 *"We understand from Faber and Faber":* Judith Jones to Ted Hughes, August 11, 1964, Harry Ransom Center, University of Texas at Austin.

105 *"Dear Mr. Hughes, I was reasonably certain":* Judith Jones to Ted Hughes, November 9, 1964, Harry Ransom Center, University of Texas at Austin.

106 *Hughes wanted a larger advance:* Ted Hughes to Judith Jones, November 13, 1964, Harry Ransom Center, University of Texas at Austin.

106 *"everybody hated" Plath:* A widely quoted statement by Ted Hughes after Plath's death; see, for example, Daphne Merkin, "A Matched Pair," *New York Times,* December 21, 2003, https://www.nytimes.com/2003/12/21/books/a -matched-pair.html.

106 *"extraordinary talent"; "last and major work":* Ted Hughes to Judith Jones, November 13, 1964, Harry Ransom Center, University of Texas at Austin.

106 *"without a hitch":* William Koshland to Peter du Sautoy, Esq., at Faber and Faber, November 12, 1964, Harry Ransom Center, University of Texas at Austin.

106 *"Something amazing":* Robert Lowell quoted in Dan Chiasson, "Sylvia Plath's Joy," *New Yorker,* February 12, 2013, https://www.newyorker.com /books/page-turner/sylvia-plaths-joy; see also Stephen Tabor, *Sylvia Plath: An Analytical Bibliography* (Westport, CT: Meckler, 1987). After *Ariel*'s initial publication in March 1965, reprints were issued on January 14, 1966 (3,180 copies), July 6, 1967 (2,500), and March 20, 1972 (2,000).

106 *"The publishing of poetry":* Judith Jones to Ted Hughes, October 12, 1965, Harry Ransom Center, University of Texas at Austin.

106 *"a brilliant first novel":* Orville Prescott, "Return to the Hawkes Family," *New York Times,* November 11, 1964, https://archive.nytimes.com/www.nytimes .com/books/98/04/19/specials/tyler-morning.html.

107 *"His reviews had a lot of influence":* Judith Jones to Bob Croft, July 28, 1993, Knopf private files.

107 *"Dear Anne, I am terribly sorry":* Judith Jones to Anne Tyler, August 1, 1973, Harry Ransom Center, University of Texas at Austin.

108 *"good writer-editor relationship":* Judith Jones to Bob Croft, July 28, 1993, Knopf private files.

108 *"Writers are rare who can":* Christopher Lehmann-Haupt, "A Small Pebble with a Big Splash," *New York Times,* December 23, 1965, https://archive .nytimes.com/www.nytimes.com/books/98/04/19/specials/tyler-tin.html.

108 *"not merely good, but wickedly good"*: Viv Groskop, "The Beginner's Good-bye, by Anne Tyler," *Independent*, April 28, 2012, https://www.independent.co.uk/arts-entertainment/books/reviews/the-beginner-s-goodbye-by-anne-tyler-7687286.html.

108 *Judith took a deep breath and dashed:* "The rains came hard all day Wednesday, but Life still made it to the stands," Judith Jones to John Updike, November 8, 1966, Harry Ransom Center, University of Texas at Austin.

108 *"John Updike has vast talent, charm":* Jane Howard, "John Updike Has Talent, Charm, and a New Book—but Can a Nice Guy Finish First," *Life*, November 4, 1966, 74.

109 *"beautifully written, an exquisitely artful book":* Howard, "John Updike Has Talent, Charm, and a New Book."

109 *"unquiet adulthood":* Christopher Lehmann-Haupt, "John Updike, a Lyrical Writer of the Middle-Class Man, Dies at 76," *New York Times*, January 28, 2009, https://www.nytimes.com/2009/01/28/books/28updike.html.

109 *mundane beauty:* In his foreword to *The Early Stories: 1953–1975* (New York: Alfred A. Knopf, 2003), xv, Updike noted that as a writer his "only duty [has been] to describe reality as it had come to me—to give the mundane its beautiful due."

109 *Wasn't a fashion glossy such as Vogue:* John Updike to Judith Jones, November 25, 1970, Judith Jones Private Collection.

109 *Updike was aware his endless requests might test:* John Updike to Judith Jones, August 20, 1965, Harry Ransom Center, University of Texas at Austin.

110 *Updike often wrote or called his editor daily:* John Updike to Judith Jones, February 12, 1970, Harry Ransom Center, University of Texas at Austin.

110 *"tried to tell him what to do":* Charlotte Druckman, "Judith Jones, In Her Own Words," Eater, September 23, 2015, https://www.eater.com/2015/9/23/9355183/judith-jones.

110 *"As for the jacket":* Judith Jones to John Updike, February 24, 1970, Harry Ransom Center, University of Texas at Austin.

110 *"Dear John, I think it would be grand":* Judith Jones to John Updike, January 6, 1968, Harry Ransom Center, University of Texas at Austin.

111 *recalled a day when Updike came into the office:* Kathy Zuckerman, interview with author, July 15, 2019.

111 *Updike wrote Judith recounting Davison's grumblings:* John Updike postcard, to Judith Jones, May 5 (year of postmark ripped), Judith Jones Private Collection.

111 *John wrote his editor to tell her he'd just drawn up:* John Updike to Judith Jones, January 16, 1973, Harry Ransom Center, University of Texas at Austin.

111 *"I think you came out rather nobly":* Judith Jones to John Updike, November 8, 1966, Harry Ransom Center, University of Texas at Austin.

111 *"On May 22, 1966, Julia Child became the first":* "1966," Julia Child Foundation, https://juliachildfoundation.org/timeline/#.

111 *"catapulted her into a whole other stratosphere":* Russ Morash, quoted in Spitz, *Dearie: The Remarkable Life of Julia Child* (New York: Alfred A. Knopf, 2012), 364.

111 *"Our Lady of the Ladle"; "the most influential cooking teacher"; "a cult from coast to coast"; the "year everyone seems to be cooking in the kitchen with Julia":* "Everyone's in the Kitchen," *Time,* November 25, 1966, https://time.com/4230699 /food-everyones-in-the-kitchen/.

111 *after two years of quietly battling cancer:* Laura Claridge, *The Lady with the Borzoi: Blanche Knopf, Literary Tastemaker Extraordinaire* (New York: Farrar, Straus and Giroux, 2016), 323, 327.

111 *wife of "the publisher"; "a figure in the publishing field in her own right"; "[Alfred] and Blanche are like Jupiter and Juno":* "Mrs. Blanche Wolf Knopf of Publishing Firm Dies: Helped Husband to Found Company in 1915," *New York Times,* June 5, 1966, https://timesmachine.nytimes.com/timesmachine /1966/06/05/93844557.html?pageNumber=86.

112 *Judith had been unable to outgrow:* Nancy Nicholas, interview with author, July 2, 2019.

112 *"most important prerequisite for an editor":* Judith Jones to Margaret Laurence, October 2, 1971, Harry Ransom Center, University of Texas at Austin.

CHAPTER 11

113 *"rumor has it":* Wilfred Sheed, "Play in Tarbox," *New York Times Book Review,* April 7, 1968, https://archive.nytimes.com/www.nytimes.com/books /97/04/06/lifetimes/updike-r-couples.html.

114 *She finally had a secretary:* A letter dated February 15, 1966, is the first archival mention Judith makes of having a secretary of her own, Harry Ransom Center, University of Texas at Austin. Kathy Hourigan, who was the longtime managing editor at Knopf until her retirement in December 2023, began at Knopf in 1963. She told me it was "some time" after she began at the house that she began working as Judith's assistant.

114 Sex and the Single Girl *hit big:* Jennifer Scanlon, "Sensationalist Literature or Expert Advice?," *Feminist Media Studies* 9, no. 1 (2009): 1–15, https://doi .org/10.1080/14680770802619433.

114 *"make you see":* Charles Poore, "The Group," *New York Times,* August 29, 1963,

https://archive.nytimes.com/www.nytimes.com/books/97/11/23/home
/mccarthy-group.html.

115 *"nice girls"*: Normal Mailer, "The Mary McCarthy Case," *New York Review of Books*, October 17, 1963, https://www.nybooks.com/articles/1963/10/17/the-mary-mccarthy-case/.

115 *Regardless whether they liked it or not:* Apoorva Tadepalli, "What Elites Got Wrong About Mary McCarthy's *The Group*," *Literary Hub*, December 20, 2020, https://lithub.com/what-elites-got-wrong-about-mary-mccarthys-the-group/; Elizabeth Day, "The Group by Mary McCarthy," *Observer*, November 28, 2009, https://www.theguardian.com/books/2009/nov/29/the-group-mary-mccarthy.

115 *"Welcome to the post-pill paradise":* John Updike, *Couples* (New York: Alfred A. Knopf, 1968), 52.

115 *Since the early sixties, he and his wife:* Adam Begley, *Updike* (New York: Harper, 2014), 208–9, 211.

115 *"His tongue searched":* John Updike, *Couples*, 194–95.

115 *The house's founder agreed it was too risky:* Alfred Knopf to John Updike, August 10, 1967, Harry Ransom Center, University of Texas at Austin.

115 *Once both Judith and Alfred signed off on a final draft:* Judith Jones, Knopf interoffice memo, August 7, 1967, Harry Ransom Center, University of Texas at Austin.

116 *"Knopf was the publishing house of my dreams":* Robert Gottlieb, interview with author, June 19, 2019.

116 *"To have gotten even one"; "almost a publishing business in themselves":* Bennett Cerf, *At Random: The Reminiscences of Bennett Cerf* (New York: Random House, 1977), 288.

116 *"It was ridiculous":* Kathy Hourigan, interview with author, June 20, 2019.

116 *"When I got there, everybody had been":* Robert Gottlieb, interview with author, June 20, 2019.

117 *"She was a lady":* Robert Gottlieb, interview with author, June 20, 2019.

117 *"You never know what other editors do":* Robert Gottlieb, interview with author, June 20, 2019.

117 *"a commentary on America":* Kirkus Reviews, "Couples," April 1, 1968, https://www.kirkusreviews.com/book-reviews/john-updike/couples-3/.

117 *"fancied-up pornography":* Diana Trilling, "Updike's Yankee Traders," *Atlantic*, April 1968, https://www.theatlantic.com/magazine/archive/1968/04/updikes-yankee-traders/659541/.

117 *"America's Most Explicitly Sexual Novel Ever":* Los Angeles Times, quoted at Christopher Carduff, "John Updike: Novels 1968–1975," Library of America,

https://www.loa.org/books/627-novels-1968-1975/#:~:text=(The%20 Los%20Angeles%20Times%20called,of%20promiscuity%20among%20 a%20tight.

117 *"He describes the sexual experiences":* Ludwig B. Lefebre, "Couples: A Novel by John Updike," *Psychology Today*, December 1966, 6, 8.

117 *"The Adulterous Society":* Time, April 26, 1968, https://content.time.com /time/magazine/0,9263,7601680426,00.html.

117 *sixth printing:* Judith Jones to John Updike, September 5, 1968, Harry Ransom Center, University of Texas at Austin; "We're in the 7th now—192,000 copies!," Judith Jones to John Updike, July 18, 1969, Harry Ransom Center, University of Texas at Austin.

117 *more than two hundred thousand copies:* Henry Raymont, "John Updike Completes a Sequel to 'Rabbit, Run,'" *New York Times*, July 27, 1971, https:// archive.nytimes.com/www.nytimes.com/books/97/04/06/lifetimes/up dike-r-rabbit.html.

117 *Over dessert, Russell told Judith:* Judith Jones to Anne Tyler, October 16, 1969, Harry Ransom Center, University of Texas at Austin.

118 *"Everything I wanted to write"; "living in a very small commune"; "I was trying to convince myself":* Anne Tyler quoted in Patricia Rowe Willrich, "Watching Through Windows: A Perspective on Anne Tyler," *Virginia Quarterly Review* 68, no. 3 (Summer 1992), https://www.vqronline.org/essay/watching -through-windows-perspective-anne-tyler.

118 *She also wrote and published:* The short stories Tyler published between 1965 and 1970 appeared in *Harper's, Southern Review, New Yorker, Mademoiselle, Ladies' Home Journal,* and *McCall's.*

118 *"special kind of detachment":* Judith Jones to Peter Taylor, April 10, 1970, Harry Ransom Center, University of Texas at Austin.

118 *"very much continuing to go her own way":* Judith Jones to Albert Goldman, April 10, 1970, Harry Ransom Center, University of Texas at Austin.

118 *"It seems to me that since I've had children":* Anne Tyler, "Still Just Writing," in *The Writer on Her Work*, ed. Janet Sternburg (New York: W. W. Norton, 1980), 9.

118 *"This is a more mature book":* Judith Jones to Betty Anderson, July 10, 1969, Harry Ransom Center, University of Texas at Austin.

118 *Judith put it into the hands of:* Judith Jones's Anne Tyler editorial file, Harry Ransom Center, University of Texas at Austin.

119 *less delicate; "Miss Tyler still exhibits":* "A Slipping-Down Life," *Kirkus Reviews*, March 1, 1970, https://www.kirkusreviews.com/book-reviews/anne -tyler/a-slipping-down-life/.

119 *"flawed." Still, it "represented":* Anne Tyler, in Willrich, "Watching Through Windows."

119 *"I'm afraid it is a novel that is not getting its due":* Judith Jones to Nora Ephron, April 26, 1972, Harry Ransom Center, University of Texas at Austin.

119 *"We are into a third printing":* Judith Jones to Anne Tyler, June 29, 1972, Harry Ransom Center, University of Texas at Austin.

119 *"a really good step forward for you":* Judith Jones to Anne Tyler, August 10, 1971, Harry Ransom Center, University of Texas at Austin.

119 *"I feel so good about this novel":* Judith Jones to Anne Tyler, July 18, 1971, Harry Ransom Center, University of Texas at Austin.

119 *"Rework and rework the drafts"; "the work of somebody":* Anne Tyler in Willrich, "Watching Through Windows."

120 *"This honest author":* Judith Jones to Anne Tyler, June 8, 1978, Harry Ransom Center, University of Texas at Austin.

120 *"I have been having a wonderful time":* Anne Tyler to Judith Jones, June 17, 1978, Knopf private files.

120 *"I've been meaning to tell you":* Judith Jones to Anne Tyler, November 19, 1978, Knopf private files.

120 *"Feminism, which one might have supposed":* Martha Weinman Lear, "The Second Feminist Wave: What Do These Women *Want?*," *New York Times*, March 10, 1968, https://timesmachine.nytimes.com/timesmachine /1968/03/10/90032407.html?pageNumber=323.

120 *had life-changing possibilities for women:* Betty Prashker, interview with author, April 4, 2019.

121 *"Judith was not a marcher":* Ann Close, interview with author, September 12, 2019.

121 *"needed [Judith] desperately":* Jane Friedman, interview with author, October 8, 2019.

121 *"There wasn't anything you could do with her":* Robert Gottlieb, interview with author, June 20, 2019.

121 *"Judith began telling me":* Betty Prashker, interview with author, April 4, 2019.

121 *For years, Dick had been urging Judith:* Chris Vandercook, interview with author, May 20, 2019. While there is no irrefutable proof or corroboration, Chris Vandercook said he believed Judith's salary plateaued at about $40,000 a year until Sonny Mehta became editor in chief of Knopf in 1986.

121 *"Dick would just go through the roof!":* Chris Vandercook, interview with author, May 20, 2019.

122 *"Everybody was always asking me":* Robert Gottlieb, interview with author, June 20, 2019.

122 *"In my entire career"*: Robert Gottlieb, interview with author, June 20, 2019.

122 *"Even I, who came along with the women's movement"*: Kathy Hourigan, interview with author, June 20, 2019.

122 *Judith never asked*: Bronwyn Dunne, interview with author, May 13, 2019.

CHAPTER 12

123 *She'd begun the bread dough*: Judith described this bread-baking routine in an interview for a piece by Jose Wilson in the *New York Post* (the article's title had been cut from clipping) published on November 15, 1978. Hard copy held in Judith Jones Private collection.

124 *Food Establishment; "His publisher, if he is lucky"*: Nora Ephron, "Critics in the World of the Rising Souffle (Or Is It the Rising Meringue?)," *New York*, September 30, 1968, 35.

124 *Judith had planned to print forty thousand*: Bob Spitz, *Dearie: The Remarkable Life of Julia Child* (New York: Alfred A. Knopf, 2012), 372.

124 *"Gottlieb upped the first run"*: Alex Prud'homme, *The French Chef in America: Julia Child's Second Act* (New York: Alfred A. Knopf, 2016), 54–55.

124 *"Liberated men and women, who used to brag"*: Ephron, "Critics in the World of the Rising Souffle," 35.

125 *Julia worked obsessively*: Spitz, *Dearie*, 383.

125 *"The revolt against plasticized bread"*: Judith Jones to John Hess at *New York Times*, October 10, 1973, Harry Ransom Center, University of Texas at Austin.

125 *"without rival, the finest"*: "Queen of Chefs," *Newsweek*, November 9, 1970, 94.

125 *"ambitious, inventive"*: Gael Greene, "Julia's Moon Walk with French Bread," *Life*, October 23, 1970, 8.

125 *"I want to be a publisher"*: Jane Friedman, interview with author, October 18, 2019.

127 *"sped up I-89"*: Joe Sherman, "Naked in the Moonlight," *Fast Lane on a Dirt Road: Vermont Transformed 1945–1990* (Woodstock, VT: Countryman Press, 1991), 82.

127 *"In 1917, the U.S. and Mexican governments"*: Philip Martin, "Mexican Braceros and US Farm Workers," Wilson Center, July 10, 2020, https://www.wilsoncenter.org/article/mexican-braceros-and-us-farm-workers.

128 *"There is a tremendous surge of interest"*: Judith Jones to Jane Grigson, September 1, 1971, Harry Ransom Center, University of Texas at Austin.

128 *"Dear Kit, I was just browsing"*: Judith Jones to Catharine Osgood Foster, November 24, 1970, Harry Ransom Center, University of Texas at Austin.

128 *"How good to hear from you":* Catharine Osgood Foster to Judith Jones, December 2, 1970, Harry Ransom Center, University of Texas at Austin.

128 *"When it is a question of restaurants":* Craig Claiborne, "Restaurant on Review: Vietnamese Cuisine Is Inexpensive," *New York Times,* August 15, 1961, https://timesmachine.nytimes.com/timesmachine/1961/08/15/97614866 .html?pageNumber=21.

128 *To rate his picks, Claiborne adapted:* Pete Wells, "When He Dined Out, the Stars Came Out," *New York Times,* May 8, 2012, https://www.nytimes .com/2012/05/09/dining/craig-claiborne-set-the-standard-for-restaurant -reviews.html.

129 *"small, poorly air-conditioned":* Craig Claiborne, "Restaurant on Review: Vietnamese Cuisine Is Inexpensive."

129 *When he premiered his weekly review column:* Craig Claiborne's first of his weekly restaurant columns for the *New York Times* was a group of five short write-ups of Manhattan eateries that ran on Friday, May 18, 1962, as "Directory To Dining," http://graphics8.nytimes.com/images/blogs/dinersjour nal/claiborne-62.pdf.

129 *Roden was born into a Syrian Jewish family:* Beth Schenker, "Claudia Roden," *The Shalvi/Hyman Encyclopedia of Jewish Women,* https://jwa.org/encyclope dia/article/roden-claudia.

129 *"The dishes that Claudia associated":* Judith Jones, interview by Linda Kulman, "Judith Jones Toasts a Culinary Life in 'Tenth Muse,'" Book Tour, NPR, January 8, 2008, https://www.npr.org/2008/01/08/17809903/judith-jones -toasts-a-culinary-life-in-tenth-muse.

130 *"not for myself and all the Egyptian Jews":* "Claudia Roden: The Woman Who Defined Our Diets," Penguin, November 4, 2021, https://www.pen guin.co.uk/articles/2021/november/claudia-roden-med-interview-recipes .html.

130 *"had to take people by the hand":* Judith Jones, interview by Linda Kulman, "Judith Jones Toasts a Culinary Life in 'Tenth Muse.'"

130 *"We didn't know what Middle Eastern food was":* Judith Jones, interview by Linda Kulman, "Judith Jones Toasts a Culinary Life in 'Tenth Muse.'"

130 *Jill Norman, Roden's British editor at Penguin:* Jill Norman published Elizabeth David, as well as many of the best-selling cookbook authors of the 1970s and 1980s; after working together on Roden, Jill and Judith formed a friendly and productive relationship, often tipping each other off to promising new talent and practically swapping rights.

131 *"I can't tell you how pleased I am":* Judith Jones to Claudia Roden, December 18, 1970, Harry Ransom Center, University of Texas at Austin.

131 *("Mostly a pleasure trip"):* Judith Jones to Catharine Osgood Foster, December 17, 1970, Harry Ransom Center, University of Texas at Austin.

132 *"An adherence to vegetarian diets":* Judith Jones to Jane Grigson, September 1, 1971, Harry Ransom Center, University of Texas at Austin.

132 *Thomas often invited her fellow film students:* Anna Thomas, email correspondence to author, October 20, 2022.

132 *Thomas, with nothing much to do besides:* Anna Thomas, interview with author, July 8, 2019.

132 *right at the nexus of expanding offerings and changing tastes:* See Warren J. Belasco, *Appetite for Change: How the Counterculture Took on the Food Industry,* 2nd ed. (Ithaca, NY: Cornell University Press, 2006), 62.

132 *"a certain joy":* Judith Jones to Anna Thomas, undated, on Knopf letterhead, Anna Thomas private collection.

132 *"the makings of an excellent book":* Judith Jones to Anna Thomas, undated, Knopf letterhead, Anna Thomas private collection.

132 *Despite plant-based diets' increasing popularity:* Belasco, *Appetite for Change,* 61–63.

132 *"The recipes themselves are so very good":* Judith Jones to Anna Thomas, undated, on Knopf letterhead, Anna Thomas private collection.

133 *"with no regret at all":* Anna Thomas to Judith Jones, June 7, 1971, Anna Thomas private collection.

133 *"a delight and a celebration of life":* Front cover of Anna Thomas, *The Vegetarian Epicure* (New York: Alfred A. Knopf, 1972).

133 *"I hope we can make it happen":* Anna Thomas to Judith Jones, June 7, 1971, Anna Thomas private collection.

133 *Next thing Thomas knew:* Anna Thomas, email to author, October 20, 2022.

133 *Thomas told Pryor she'd do the book:* Anna Thomas, interview with author, July 8, 2019, and Anna Thomas, email to author, October 20, 2022.

133 *"I'm eager to get it out":* Judith Jones to Anna Thomas, June 22, 1971, Anna Thomas private collection.

133 *"very fetching"; "just right"; "I made a vow":* Judith Jones to Anna Thomas, June 22, 1971.

134 *"Now that I have more distance":* Judith Jones to Catharine Osgood Foster, July 1, 1971, Harry Ransom Center, University of Texas at Austin.

134 *"We had a gorgeous weekend":* Judith Jones to Catharine Osgood Foster, July 8, 1971, Harry Ransom Center, University of Texas at Austin.

134 *"I was a completely unwashed newbie":* Anna Thomas, interview with author, July 8, 2019.

135 *"You have the ability":* Anna Thomas to Judith Jones, July 28, 1971, Anna Thomas private collection.

135 *She enclosed a note asking her editor:* Anna Thomas to Judith Jones, August 10, 1971, Anna Thomas private collection.

135 *"You must be feeling very pleased with yourself":* Judith Jones to Anna Thomas, August 13, 1971, Anna Thomas private collection.

135 *In November 1971 Elaine Markson:* Elaine Markson to Judith Jones, November 10, 1971, Harry Ransom Center, University of Texas at Austin.

135 *it was in London, at age nineteen, that Jaffrey began to cook:* Madhur Jaffrey, Voices from the Food Revolution: People Who Changed the Way Americans Eat—An oral history project conducted by Judith Weinraub, electronic record, MSS_309.ref 203.1, December 2, 2010, Fales Library and Special Collections, New York University.

135 *came to the States with Saeed Jaffrey:* Deborah Ross, "Saeed Jaffrey Interview: New Kid on the Street," *Independent*, January 25, 1999, https://www.independent.co.uk/arts-entertainment/saeed-jaffrey-interview-new-kid-on-the-street-1046303.html.

136 *"Indian Actress Is a Star":* Craig Claiborne, "Indian Actress Is a Star in the Kitchen, Too," *New York Times*, July 7, 1966, https://timesmachine.nytimes.com/timesmachine/1966/07/07/82474241.html?pageNumber=57.

136 *editors involved had since left the house:* Elaine Markson to Judith Jones, November 10, 1971, Harry Ransom Center, University of Texas at Austin.

136 *Indian chefs had been cooking food in New York:* Florence Fabricant, "The Origins of Indian Curry in New York," *New York Times*, July 31, 2017, https://www.nytimes.com/2017/07/31/dining/indian-food-nyc-curry-chef-j-ranji-smile.html.

136 *"There was no place":* Madhur Jaffrey, *An Invitation to Indian Cooking* (New York: Alfred A. Knopf, 1973), 3.

136 *Well into the 1960s, Indian food remained:* Laresh Jayasanker, "Indian Restaurants in America: A Case Study in Translating Diversity," in *Sameness in Diversity: Food and Globalization in Modern America* (Berkeley: University of California Press, 2020), 97–109.

137 *Proponents of immigration reform:* Lesley Kennedy, "How the Immigration Act of 1965 Changed the Face of America," History, August 12, 2019, https://www.history.com/news/immigration-act-1965-changes.

137 *"She seems so cooperative":* Judith Jones to Elaine Markson, January 24, 1972, Harry Ransom Center, University of Texas at Austin.

137 *"was there all the time":* Madhur Jaffrey, "Remembering Judith Jones, a Culinary Luminary," The New School, October 24, 2017.

138 *"a new way of doing cookbooks":* Raymond Sokolov, "Remembering Judith Jones, a Culinary Luminary," panel discussion with Joan Nathan, Ray Sokolov, Laura Shapiro, Anne Mendelson, Madhur Jaffrey, and Bronwyn Dunne; moderated by Andrew F. Smith, The New School, October 24, 2017. A video recording and transcript of the event is available on YouTube at https://www.youtube.com/watch?v=shHZywNaISU.

138 *"Thank heavens I am able":* Judith Jones to Mildred "Millie" Owens, February 24, 1972, Harry Ransom Center, University of Texas at Austin.

138 *"what needs to be done on Jaffrey's book":* Judith Jones to Mildred Owens, July 1972, Harry Ransom Center, University of Texas at Austin.

CHAPTER 13

141 *gifts poured in to room 905:* Details about date, room number, hospital, and gifts all come from Judith's 1972 datebook, Judith Jones Private Collection.

141 *His second wife, Helen:* "Alfred A. Knopf Weds Mrs. Helen E. Hedrick," *New York Times*, April 21, 1967, https://timesmachine.nytimes.com/timesmachine/1967/04/21/876867712.html?pageNumber=42.

141 *"she poured blood":* Nancy Nicholas, interview with author, July 9, 2019.

142 *while treatment options have improved:* "Endometriosis, World Health Organization, March 24, 2023, https://www.who.int/news-room/fact-sheets/detail/endometriosis.

142 *symptoms women suffering from the condition reported:* Nicky Hudson, "The Missed Disease? Endometriosis as an Example of 'Undone Science,'" *Reproductive Biomedicine and Society Online* 14 (March 2022): 20–27, https://www.sciencedirect.com/science/article/pii/S240566182100023X.

142 *"career women's disease":* Astrid C. H. Jaeger, "Endometriosis Disrupted My Work—but Opening Up to Colleagues Helped Me Cope," *Science* 375, no. 6587 (March 24, 2022), https://www.science.org/content/article/endometriosis-disrupted-my-work-opening-colleagues-helped-me-cope.

142 *In the two weeks between:* Details about dates come from Judith's 1972 datebook, Judith Jones Private Collection.

142 *Judith had kept her assistant in the dark:* Nancy Nicholas, interview with author, July 9, 2019.

143 *In 1968, Julia had been diagnosed:* Julia Child to Simone Beck, February 14, 1968, Arthur and Elizabeth Schlesinger Library on the History of Women in America, Radcliffe Institute for Advanced Study, Harvard University, Cambridge, MA.

143 *"a new woman"; "at least three more hours":* Judith Jones to A. J. Langguth, March 27, 1972, Harry Ransom Center, University of Texas at Austin.

143 *"I am at home recuperating":* Judith Jones to Mildred Owens, March 10, 1972, Harry Ransom Center, University of Texas at Austin.

144 *"believing my government represented me":* Frances Moore Lappé, *Diet for a Small Planet* (New York: Ballantine, 1971), 16.

145 *"Here is the masterpiece":* Judith Jones to Anna Thomas, October 8, 1971, and Judith Jones to Anna Thomas, April 27, 1972, Anna Thomas private collection.

145 *"lovely"; "comprehensive":* Nika Hazelton, "Cooking by the Book," *New York Times*, December 3, 1972, https://timesmachine.nytimes.com/timesmachine /1972/12/03/93422844.html?pageNumber=290.

145 *"a man, name of Battersby":* Judith Jones to Anna Thomas, March 19, 1973, Anna Thomas private collection.

145 *At first, all Judith's praise had little impact:* Anna Thomas, interview with author, July 9, 2019.

145 *"Your book seems to be doing so steadily well":* Judith Jones to Anna Thomas, April 27, 1972, Anna Thomas private collection.

145 *"gently forceful"; "wholesome as":* Joan Lee Faust, "Around the Garden," *New York Times*, July 30, 1972, 147, https://timesmachine.nytimes.com/times machine/1972/07/30/81928306.html?pageNumber=147.

146 *"I am happy to see I find the paperback":* Judith Jones to Catharine Osgood Foster, December 21, 1972, Harry Ransom Center, University of Texas at Austin.

146 *"At a time when food costs are soaring":* Letters, interoffice memos, flap copy drafts, and list of retailers for *A Book of Middle Eastern Food*, spanning from 1972 to 1973, are held in Judith Jones's Claudia Roden editorial file at the Harry Ransom Center, University of Texas at Austin.

147 *"A landmark in the field of cookery":* James Beard, quoted on "The New Book of Middle Eastern Food," Penguin Random House, https://www.penguin randomhouse.com/books/156488/the-new-book-of-middle-eastern-food -by-claudia-roden/.

147 *"Mimi Sheraton, who'd just written":* Alex Witchel, "At Lunch with Mimi Sheraton; Undisguised Pleasures of a Former Critic," *New York Times*, May 12, 2004, https://www.nytimes.com/2004/05/12/dining/at-lunch-with-mimi -sheraton-undisguised-pleasures-of-a-former-critic.html?searchResultPosi tion=10.

147 *"All this sounds terribly crass":* Judith Jones to Claudia Roden, May 4, 1972, Harry Ransom Center, University of Texas at Austin.

147 *the author wrote Judith saying she wanted to return again:* Claudia Roden to Judith Jones, August 28, 1973, Harry Ransom Center, University of Texas at Austin.

147 *"Your lovely Middle Eastern Food":* Judith Jones to Claudia Roden, May 7, 1973, Harry Ransom Center, University of Texas at Austin.

147 *she wrote to bookstores; reached out to specialty grocers:* Judith Jones to Leo Lerman, April 25, 1973; Judith Jones to Herman Bosboom, October 18, 1973; Judith Jones to Irv Mendelson, August 10, 1973, Harry Ransom Center, University of Texas at Austin.

148 *Judith got Jim Beard to let Jaffrey use:* Judith Jones, *The Tenth Muse: My Life in Food* (New York: Alfred A. Knopf, 2007), 98.

148 *"the most useful and interesting introduction to Indian food":* Raymond A. Sokolov, "Current Stars: Books on Indian, Italian, and Inexpensive Food." *New York Times*, April 19, 1973, https://timesmachine.nytimes.com/times machine/1973/04/19/99142468.html?pageNumber=54.

148 *"I understand you were hoping to have Jaffrey":* Judith Jones to Leo Lerman, April 25, 1973, Harry Ransom Center, University of Texas at Austin.

148 *"She was really making an author":* Madhur Jaffrey, "Remembering Judith Jones, a Culinary Luminary," panel discussion with Joan Nathan, Ray Sokolov, Laura Shapiro, Anne Mendelson, Madhur Jaffrey, and Bronwyn Dunne; moderated by Andrew F. Smith, The New School, October 24, 2017. A video recording and transcript of the event is available on YouTube at https://www.youtube.com/watch?v=shHZywNaISU.

148 *"I have tried to begin each chapter":* Madhur Jaffrey, *An Invitation to Indian Cooking* (New York: Alfred A. Knopf, 1973), 12.

148 *Two decades into the twenty-first century:* John Maher, "New Lee and Low Survey Shows No Progress on Diversity in Publishing," *Publishers Weekly*, January 29, 2020, https://www.publishersweekly.com/pw/by-topic/industry -news/publisher-news/article/82284-new-lee-and-low-survey-shows-no -progress-on-diversity-in-publishing.html; Jim Milliot, "The PW Publishing Industry Survey, 2019," *Publishers Weekly*, November 15, 2019, https:// www.publishersweekly.com/pw/by-topic/industry-news/publisher-news /article/81718-the-pw-publishing-industry-salary-survey-2019.html; Lyndsey Claro, "Women in the Gentlemen's Career of Publishing," Princeton University Press, March 6, 2020, https://press.princeton.edu/ideas /women-in-the-gentlemans-career-of-publishing#_ftn16.

CHAPTER 14

151 *"I grew up in Freetown, Virginia"*: Edna Lewis, introduction to *The Taste of Country Cooking* (New York: Alfred A. Knopf, 1976), xix.

152 *It had started back in September of 1971:* Judith Jones, preface to *The Taste of Country Cooking* by Edna Lewis, xv.

152 *Café Nicholson quickly earned a reputation:* William Grimes, "Johnny Nicholson, Whose Midtown Café Drew the 'New Bohemian,' Dies at 99," *New York Times,* August 8, 2016, https://www.nytimes.com/2016/08/09 /dining/johnny-nicholson-whose-manhattan-cafe-attracted-new-bohemian -crowd-dies-at-99.html.

152 *superb, French-inflected fare:* Clementine Paddleford, "New Discovery in Restaurants: Nicholson's, in E. 58th St, Only Seats 30 and Has a Standard Menu, but It Has Fine Points," *New York Herald Tribune,* March 24, 1951.

152 *"I was flattered of course":* Edna Lewis quoted at the website for *Edna Lewis: Photographs by John T. Hill,* Crook's Corner, Chapel Hill, North Carolina, April 7–May 7, 2018, http://annstewartfineart.com/news/2018/3/25/edna -lewis-photographs-by-john-t-hill-on-exhibit-at-crooks-corner-april-7 -to-may-7.

153 *With no high school diploma and few job options:* Lewis's return to domestic work is undocumented and a glaring omission from most biographical accounts of her life, including all of them in the collection I edited, *Edna Lewis: At the Table with an American Original* (Chapel Hill: University of North Carolina Press, 2018). It was during a book signing at the Union Square Greenmarket in the summer of 2018 that a white woman, who looked to be in her late sixties, came up to me and told me Edna Lewis had worked for her family as a maid during the 1960s. When, shocked, I pressed her, questioning whether Lewis wasn't a caterer brought in for special occasions—the version I'd always heard of how Lewis came to develop the reputation that led to her eventually working for, and writing *The Edna Lewis Cookbook* with Evangeline Peterson—she insisted: Lewis was her family's maid.

153 *At a time when more and more white women:* Janet L. Yellen, "The History of Women's Work and Wages and How it Has Created Success for Us all." Brookings, May 2020, https://www.brookings.edu/essay/the-history -of-womens-work-and-wages-and-how-it-has-created-success-for-us -all/. All other stats on women's employment rates by year and race cited here come from Cecilia A. Conrad, "Racial Trends in Labor Market Access and Wages: Women," in *America Becoming: Racial Trends and Their Consequences,* vol. 2, Neil J. Smelser, William Julius Wilson, and Faith Mitchell,

eds. (Washington, DC: National Academy Press, 2001), https://nap.national academies.org/read/9719/chapter/7#125.

154 *The* Edna Lewis Cookbook *marked Lewis's unwillingness:* Caroline Randall Williams, "How to Talk About Miss Lewis? Home Cook, Writer, Icon. One Young Black Woman's Act of Remembering," in *Edna Lewis*, 80.

154 *"knee-slapping, cornpone image":* Eric Asimov and Kim Severson, "Edna Lewis, 89, Dies; Wrote Cookbooks that Revived Refined Southern Cuisine," *New York Times*, February 14, 2006, https://www.nytimes.com/2006/02/14 /us/edna-lewis-89-dies-wrote-cookbooks-that-revived-refined-southern -cuisine.html.

154 *Peterson promptly wrote to Judith:* Evangeline Peterson to Judith Jones, September 28, 1971, Knopf private files.

154 *Education was a top priority:* Gracie Hart Brooks, "Educators and Students Gather to Celebrate Lightfoot Elementary," *Daily Progress*, August 5, 2020, https://dailyprogress.com/educators-and-students-gather-to-celebrate -lightfoot-elementary/article_414fc8b6-4574-505c-b82e-965e27619719 .html.

154 *"What money they had came mostly":* Ruth Lewis Smith in conversation with author, April 2018.

154 *"What began as hard work":* Edna Lewis's now iconic essay, "What Is Southern?," was published posthumously in *Gourmet* in January 2008, in an issue built around its discovery, http://www.gourmet.com.s3-website-us-east-1 .amazonaws.com/magazine/2000s/2008/01/whatissouthern_lewis.html.

154 *"It's not our intention to write":* Evangeline Peterson to Judith Jones, September 28, 1971, Knopf private files.

155 *"Attached are some of Edna's reminiscences":* Evangeline Peterson to Judith Jones, November 10, 1971, Knopf private files.

155 *"The material is so interesting":* Judith Jones to Evangeline Peterson, December 20, 1971, Knopf private files.

155 *"according to what aspect of the book":* Evangeline Peterson to Judith Jones, February 20, 1972, Knopf private files.

155 *"I was immediately struck":* Judith Jones, "Preface," *The Taste of Country Cooking*, xv.

156 *On April 4, the pair signed:* The original contract was dated April 4, 1972. It specified Knopf pay an advance of $2,500 for "a non-fiction cookbook UNTITLED (on country cooking southern style) . . . 100 recipes . . . to be delivered no later than July 31, 1973," Knopf private files.

156 *in April 1973, when Judith read the pages:* On April 30, 1973, Evangeline Peterson wrote to Judith Jones: "I would so like to learn your reaction and

criticisms of these pages—and of course I'll be glad to re-work them," Knopf private files.

156 *In February 1974, more than six months after:* The agreement, dated February 15, 1974, reads: "The parties have heretofore entered into an agreement dated April 4, 1972, for the publication of a work presently provisionally titled *Southern Cookbook*, which agreement they have decided to amend as follows . . . hereby terminated with respect to the services of Evangeline Rugoff," Knopf private files.

156 *"We decided that we would try to talk":* Judith Jones, "The Personal Touch," *Saveur*, April 1, 2008, https://www.saveur.com/article/Kitchen/The-Personal -Touch/.

156 *Black American women had been resourcefully:* The evolution of specific food-ways in the American South is thoroughly documented. See, for example, Jessica Harris, *High on the Hog: A Culinary Journey from Africa to America* (New York: Bloomsbury, 2011); John Egerton, *Southern Food: At Home, on the Road, in History* (New York: Alfred A. Knopf, 1987); Marcie Cohen Ferris, *The Edible South: The Power of Food and the Making of an American Region* (Chapel Hill: University of North Carolina Press, 2016); and Edna Lewis, "What Is Southern?," *Gourmet*, January 2008.

156 *Of the estimated one hundred thousand collections of recipes:* John Egerton, Foreword: "A Gallery of Great Cooks" to *The Jemima Code: Two Centuries of African American Cookbooks*, by Toni Tipton-Martin (Austin: University of Texas Press, 2015), ix.

156 *"poignant absence":* Marcie Cohen Ferris, *Matzoh Ball Gumbo: Culinary Tales of the Jewish South* (Chapel Hill: University of North Carolina Press, 2005), 17.

156 *Black food traditions with roots in the South:* See, for example, Adrian Miller, *Soul Food: The Surprising Story of an American Cuisine, One Plate at a Time* (Chapel Hill: University of North Carolina Press, 2013).

157 *In 1970 . . . Smart-Grosvenor . . . Helen Mendes:* Vertamae Smart-Grosvenor: *Vibration Cooking, or, The Travel Notes of a Geechee Girl* was published by Doubleday in 1970 (reprinted by the University of Georgia Press in 2011), and Macmillan published Mendes's *The African Heritage Cookbook* in 1971.

157 *"culture, emotional flexibility, and strength":* Alice Walker coined the term "womanism" in her 1979 story, "Coming Apart," and further articulated it in her 1983 *In Search of Our Mothers' Gardens.*

157 *"a lens through which":* Kimberlé Crenshaw coined the term "intersectionality" in 1989; her quote here is taken from "Kimberlé Crenshaw on Intersectionality, More than Two Decades Later," a write-up of an interview she

gave at Columbia Law School, published June 8, 2017, available at https://
www.law.columbia.edu/news/archive/kimberle-crenshaw-intersectional
ity-more-two-decades-later.

157 *She was picking wild blackberries:* Edna Lewis to Judith Jones, July 25, 1974,
Knopf private files.

157 *searching for records that named Freetown's first settlers:* Zora Neale Hurston
documented another such community—Africatown, Alabama, via oral history interviews conducted in the late 1920s, but her account remained unpublished until 2018 when *Barracoon: The Story of the Last "Black Cargo"* was
finally published by Amistad Press.

157 *"The book is rooted in tradition":* Judith Jones to Edna Lewis, August 2, 1974,
Knopf private files.

158 *her niece Nina:* Nina's married name, at the time of writing, is Nina
Williams-Mbengue.

158 *"I'm sending you a lovely book":* Judith Jones to Anna Thomas, May 14, 1976,
Anna Thomas private collection.

158 *"Galloped through"; "dignified" and "reticent":* Mary Frances Kennedy Fisher to
Judith Jones, November 21, 1975, Knopf private files.

159 *"It is such a beautiful expression":* Judith Jones to Craig Claiborne, January 16,
1976, Knopf private files.

159 *"most readable" cookbooks:* David Willis McCullough to Judith Jones, May 12,
1976, Knopf private files.

159 *"a rare combination":* Mimi Sheraton, "Two Cookbooks: Simple, and Sophisticated, Too," *New York Times,* June 2, 1976, https://timesmachine.nytimes
.com/timesmachine/1976/06/02/75606017.html?pageNumber=24.

159 *"contested, fought over, fought for":* Toni Morrison, "Literature and Public
Life," in *The Source of Self-Regard: Selected Essays, Speeches, and Meditations*
(New York: Alfred A. Knopf, 2019), 96–97.

159 *"Blacks in increasing numbers":* Paul Gray, "Yoknapatawpha Blues," *Time,*
September 20, 1976, 104–5.

160 *"beguiling—and authoritative":* Michael Demarest, "A Home-Grown Elegance," *Time,* September 20, 1976, 75.

160 *"It seems to me, too, that Edna Lewis says":* Judith Jones to Robert Manning,
October 30, 1975, Knopf private files.

160 *"Everyone I meet talks about the book":* Edna Lewis to Judith Jones and Richard Evan Jones, August 17, 1976, Knopf private files.

160 *"Now that the hardcover edition":* Judith Jones, interoffice memo to Dick Liebermann, November 15, 1976, Knopf private files.

160 *"inordinate wealth"; "single most beguiling cookbook":* Mimi Sheraton, "Cook-

ing," *New York Times Book Review*, December 5, 1976, https://times machine.nytimes.com/timesmachine/1976/12/05/355594212.html.

161 *"Many people think Blacks were only"*: Edna Lewis to Judith Jones, August 26, 1976, Knopf private files.

161 *"I had never thought of the people of Freetown"*: Edna Lewis to Judith Jones, August 26, 1976.

162 *grande dames of American home cookery:* "Conversations on Home Cooking," *San Francisco Chronicle*, July 15, 1987, Judith Jones Private Collection, Date and authorship ripped.

162 *"Everything gave one the feeling"*: Edna Lewis to Judith Jones, October 13, 1977, Knopf private files.

CHAPTER 15

164 *"significant contribution"*: Judith Jones to Phyllis Hanes, May 12, 1975, Judith Jones Private Collection.

164 *"whether we could honestly"*: Phyllis C. Richman, "Authors Work Bread Making into Busy Lifestyle," *Arizona Republic*, February 2, 1983, Judith Jones Private Collection.

165 *As it turned out, synthetic hormones had been linked:* Janet E. Lane-Claypon, *A Further Report on Cancer of the Breast, with Special Reference to Its Antecedent Conditions* (London: His Majesty's Stationery Office, 1926); J. M. Wainwright, "A Comparison of Conditions Associated with Breast Cancer in Great Britain and America," *American Journal of Cancer* 15 (1931): 2610–45.

165 *selling prolonged youth and sex appeal with hormone replacement therapy:* It would later come to be known that Dr. Robert A. Wilson, author of *Feminine Forever*, had been receiving payment from Wyeth pharmaceuticals, which held the patent on Premarin, to support his claim that HRT was safe. The funding skewed both his research and his work. But it wouldn't be until 2002, when the Women's Health Initiative released the results of a massive longitudinal study launched in 1991, that a conclusive link between HRT and breast cancer was finally made. After decades of surging breast cancer rates in the United States, use of HRT dropped dramatically, and the incidence of breast cancer finally began to come down.

165 *she relied on the pranayama techniques:* Ann Close, interview with author, September 12, 2019.

166 *"It wasn't so much* had *you published"*: Jonathan Morey, interview with author, August 5, 2019.

166 *It was Jane who spotted the advertisement:* Jane Gunther, interview with author, January 17, 2019.

167 *"As you know, we are much taken":* Judith Jones and Dick Jones to John Akin, August 20, 1980, Judith Jones Private Collection.

167 *For a couple of extra thousand dollars, Montoya said he'd include:* mortgage contract with Caledonia National Bank of Danville, VT, on October 13, 1980, Judith Jones Private Collection.

168 *Montoya's calico cat:* Dick Jones and Judith Jones to Carlos Montoya, September 9, 1980, Judith Jones Private Collection.

168 *By the end of the holiday weekend, they'd reached a deal:* Peter D. Watson to Dick Jones and Judith Jones, September 4, 1980, Judith Jones Private Collection.

168 *They bought boxes of nails:* A manila folder in Judith Jones's private collection, stuffed with faded receipts from the spring of 1981, shows the purchases the Joneses made for Bryn Teg in those early months of the year.

168 *another thousand dollars to purchase two more acres:* Shireen Avis Fisher to Dick Jones and Judith Jones, January 6, 1981, Judith Jones Private Collection.

168 *"We didn't know how rich":* Judith Jones in Rux Martin, "An American Way of Cooking," *Burlington Free Press*, September 3, 1984, Judith Jones Private Collection.

169 *"I'm back—in flesh":* Judith Jones to Anne Tyler, September 15, 1981, Knopf private files.

169 *"He is suspicious of intelligent women":* John Leonard, "'Rabbit Is Rich,'" *New York Times*, September 22, 1981, https://www.nytimes.com/1981/09/22/books/rabbit-is-rich.html.

169 *"To judge by the current outpouring":* Mimi Sheraton, Cooking, *New York Times*, December 6, 1981, https://timesmachine.nytimes.com/timesmachine/1981/12/06/119555.html?pageNumber=152.

169 *"[I]n recent years her narratives":* Benjamin De Mott, "Funny, Wise, and True," *New York Times Book Review*, March 14, 1982, https://archive.nytimes.com/www.nytimes.com/books/98/04/19/specials/tyler-dinner.html.

169 Homesick *became a finalist:* Patricia Rowe Willrich, "Watching Through Windows: A Perspective on Anne Tyler," *Virginia Quarterly Review* 68, no. 3 (Summer 1992), https://www.vqronline.org/essay/watching-through-windows-perspective-anne-tyler.

170 *"new spurts of selling":* Judith Jones to Anne Tyler, January 5, 1983, Knopf private files.

170 *"a classic, ludic and comprehensive":* Barbara Kafka, *"What's Cookin'? Good Readin'!,"* *Vogue*, December 1982, 190, Judith Jones Private Collection.

170 *"interesting history of bread baking":* Mimi Sheraton, Cookbooks, *New York*

Times, December 5, 1982, https://www.nytimes.com/1982/12/05/books/cookbooks.html.

170 *"She would be known as Julia Child's editor":* Phyllis C. Richman, "Authors Work Bread Making into Busy Lifestyle," *Arizona Republic*, February 2, 1983, Judith Jones Private Collection.

170 *"You need that sense of person":* Judith Jones, quoted in Richman, "Authors Work Bread Making into Busy Lifestyle."

170 *"Darling, you try to make the book say something":* Dick Jones, quoted in Richman, "Authors Work Bread Making into Busy Lifestyle."

171 *"This book is the result of a collaboration":* Marian Burros, "Christmas Books," Cooking, *New York Times*, December 11, 1983, https://timesmachine.nytimes.com/timesmachine/1983/12/11/081804.html?pageNumber=141.

171 *"relaxed, pluralistic vision":* Rux Martin, "An American Way of Cooking," *Burlington Free Press*, September 3, 1984, Judith Jones Private Collection.

171 *"When people say, 'Oh'":* Judith Jones, quoted in Rux Martin, "An American Way of Cooking."

171 *openly asserted her own strong opinions and tastes:* Kim Severson, "Remembering Judith Jones and Her Recipe for Food Writing," *New York Times*, August 2, 2017, https://www.nytimes.com/2017/08/02/dining/judith-jones-food-editor.html.

CHAPTER 16

173 *The year before, Dick had had it made as a gift:* Marion Cunningham wrote to Dick (who, by then, was more often going by Evan) on July 30, 1985, saying, "I know you are thriving in your corner of Vermont—Judith loves your pond. I think of you both often. Love, Marion"; Judith Jones Private Collection.

174 *In 1958, she'd become the first "woman's editor":* Along with Primrose Boyd, Gray wrote the cookbook *Plats du Jour*, published in 1957. The book became a bestseller.

174 *"from people who have never read a book":* Edward Behr, "Patience Gray: Appreciating One of the Finest of All Writers About Food," *The Art of Eating*, no. 69 (2005), https://artofeating.com/patience-gray/.

174 *"We plucked the birds":* Gray, *Honey from a Weed: Fasting and Feasting in Tuscany, Catalonia, the Cyclades and Apulia* (1987; repr., New York: North Point Press, 1990), 20.

174 *In 1987, when Barnes & Noble purchased:* "History," Barnes & Noble, https://www.barnesandnobleinc.com/about-bn/history/.

174 *"I feel frustrated"*: Judith Jones to Claudia Roden, February 23, 1978, Harry Ransom Center, University of Texas at Austin.

175 *"small treasures"*: Judith Jones to Alan Davidson, November 4, 1986, courtesy of Adam Federman.

175 *"I have been neurotic"*: Judith Jones to Alan Davidson, November 4, 1986.

176 *When word of who Knopf's new editor in chief; "learn how things functioned over here"; "I was totally intimidated"; "People associate Judith"; "She was extremely kind"; Mehta asked Judith:* Sonny Mehta, interview with author, September 23, 2019.

177 *by 1994, Anne Tyler's book advances:* Knopf bought Tyler's *Ladder of Years* for $1,750,000 in 1994; contract held in Knopf private files.

177 *In 2002, the median income:* Jim Milliot, "The PW Publishing Industry Salary Survey 2022," *Publishers Weekly*, December 16, 2002, https://www.publishersweekly.com/pw/by-topic/industry-news/publisher-news/article/91157-the-pw-publishing-industry-salary-survey-2022.html.

177 *her salary was $115,020.54:* Judith Jones 2002 tax return, Judith Jones Private Collection.

177 *"Basically she reported to me":* Sonny Mehta, interview with author, September 23, 2019.

177 *her radicalizing politics:* Mary Rourke cited Lewis's assertion in a November 2001 article in *Bon Appétit*, where she said, "I was a radical"; "Edna Lewis, 89; Chef Drew on Family's History in Reviving Southern Cuisine," *Los Angeles Times*, February 14, 2006, https://www.latimes.com/archives/la-xpm-2006-feb-14-me-lewis14-story.html.

177 *"After looking over my grandfather's life":* Edna Lewis to Judith Jones, October 13, 1977, Knopf private files.

178 *In March 1982, they signed a contract:* Contract for what became *In Pursuit of Flavor* is dated March 2, 1982, Knopf private files.

178 *hadn't provided much in the way of actual financial gain:* Nathalie Dupree, interview with author, April 14, 2016.

178 *"When you and I last talked"; "because I think they should know":* Judith Jones to Marilou Vaughan, November 5, 1979, Knopf private files.

178 *"When Mr. Beard and Mrs. Child":* Marilou Vaughan to Judith Jones, November 16, 1979, Knopf private files.

178 *In 1983, Fearrington House:* Evan Jones, "Southern Hospitality at the Fearrington House," *Gourmet*, April 1984, 58–62, 158–164.

179 *When Edna sought legal counsel:* Correspondence between Edna Lewis, R. B. Fitch, Judith Jones, and Dick Jones in 1983 and 1984 is held in Judith Jones Private Collection.

179 *"I could only guess at"*: Judith Jones to R. B. Fitch, April 19, 1984, Judith Jones Private Collection.

180 *Judith found a cowriter:* It's now a common formula in the cookbook world—restaurant chefs, of which Lewis had become one, are, Judith loved to remind me, notoriously bad writers of recipes for home cooks, and so cowriters are hired to help articulate and organize their recipes and stories—but at the time, it was still fairly unusual.

180 *Judith hoped Mehta's Knopf:* Judith wrote to Jane Friedman on September 13, 1982, urging her to help push Lewis further into the limelight; of *Taste*, she wrote, "as you know [the book] has been a real sleeper and continues to sell steadily more as she is becoming better known." Jane Friedman wrote to Mike Pratt and Ellen C. of Random House, July 12, 1978: "The world at large really believes in Edna Lewis and her book, but I'm afraid that copies are just not available in bookstores. . . . Wouldn't it be nice to have this book represented in B. Dalton and Walden stores? What can I do to help? Jane"; both from Knopf private files.

180 *"People aren't just looking":* Knopf internal memo, Knopf private files.

180 *No author was better positioned:* Judith Jones to Jane Friedman, September 13, 1982, Knopf private files.

180 *"I am not able to understand":* Judith Jones to Sonny Mehta, July 20, 1988, Knopf private files.

180 *Cookbooks were no longer the powerful shapers:* In Dorothy Kalins's words, Judith Jones's era is encapsulated by a time in which "food books could be culture shapers and not just party favors for TV chefs"; Dorothy Kalins, "Taste Maker," *New York Times*, November 4, 2007, https://www.nytimes.com/2007/11/04/books/review/Kalins-t.html.

181 *"What makes American food so different":* Judith Jones, undated, Knopf internal memo, Knopf private files.

181 *"One of the discouraging aspects":* Judith Jones, Knopf internal memo, undated, Knopf private files.

182 *Neal had trained:* Craig Claiborne, "For a Carolina Chef, Helpings of History," *New York Times*, July 10, 1985, https://www.nytimes.com/1985/07/10/garden/for-a-carolina-chef-helpings-of-history.html.

182 Biscuits *was not a nostalgic book:* Phyllis C. Richman, "Authors Work Bread Making into Busy Lifestyle," *Arizona Republic*, February 2, 1983, Judith Jones private collection.

182 *There was* Hot Links: Aidells's book, which was coauthored by Denis Kelly, and Voltz's first title in the KCA series were both published by Knopf in 1990.

183 *"There were places in the city"*: Kathy Zuckerman, interview with author, July 15, 2019.

184 *"an astonishing testimony"*: Anne Mendelson, "Remembering Judith Jones, a Culinary Luminary," panel discussion with Joan Nathan, Ray Sokolov, Laura Shapiro, Anne Mendelson, Madhur Jaffrey, and Bronwyn Dunne; moderated by Andrew F. Smith, The New School, October 24, 2017. A video recording and transcript of the event is available on YouTube at https://www .youtube.com/watch?v=shHZywNaISU.

184 *"The mere fact that she was eager"; "Judith's finest and bravest project"*: Anne Mendelson, "Remembering Judith Jones, a Culinary Luminary."

185 *"Each would require days of work"*: Chris Vandercook, interview with author, May 22, 2019.

185 *As cooking shows proliferated:* Michael Pollan, "Out of the Kitchen, Onto the Couch," *New York Times Magazine*, July 29, 2009, https://www.nytimes .com/2009/08/02/magazine/02cooking-t.html.

185 *By the end of 1993:* NPR Staff, "Exclusive First Read: 'From Scratch: Inside the Food Network,'" September 19, 2013, https://www.npr .org/2013/09/19/223173797/exclusive-first-read-from-scratch-inside-the -food-network.

185 *It wouldn't be until the early twenty-first century:* Sara B. Franklin, "She brought Us France with Julia Child, but Judith Jones's Culinary Legacy Also Tells an American Story," *Washington Post*, May 22, 2019, https:// www.washingtonpost.com/lifestyle/food/she-brought-us-france-with-julia -child-but-judith-joness-culinary-legacy-also-tells-an-american-story /2019/05/22/9a261560-773f-11e9-b7ae-390de4259661_story.html.

CHAPTER 17

187 *"Except for two or three general pieces"*: Judith Jones to Robert Gottlieb, March 2, 1971, Harry Ransom Center, University of Texas at Austin.

188 *"I am very much out of step"*: Judith Jones to Besmilr Brigham, September 21, 1971, Harry Ransom Center, University of Texas at Austin.

188 *"I've become increasingly disenchanted"*: Judith Jones to Besmilr Brigham, February 15, 1977, Harry Ransom Center, University of Texas at Austin.

188 *"The fact that she had fostered"*: Alice Quinn, interview with author, January 16, 2020.

188 *"Judith responded to Satan Says"*: Alice Quinn, interview with author, January 16, 2020.

188 *"willingness to take on"*: Alice Quinn, quoted in John Freeman, "Sharon Olds:

America's Brave Poet of the Body," *Literary Hub*, March 8, 2017, https://lithub.com/sharon-olds-americas-brave-poet-of-the-body/.

188 *Quinn wrote to Olds apologetically:* Alice Quinn, interview with author, January 9, 2020.

189 *Helen Vendler, one of America's most prominent:* David Firestone, "Public Lives; Physical Imagery from a Self-Effacing Poet," *New York Times*, March 6, 1998, https://www.nytimes.com/1998/03/06/nyregion/public-lives-physical-imagery-from-a-self-effacing-poet.html.

189 *"Sharon's compass for the kind of poem":* Alice Quinn, quoted in Freeman, "Sharon Olds."

189 *"shockingly intimate":* Sam Anderson, "Sex, Death, Family: Sharon Olds Is Still Shockingly Intimate," *New York Times Magazine*, October 12, 2022, https://www.nytimes.com/2022/10/12/magazine/sharon-olds-poetry.html.

189 *"I knew when I left":* Alice Quinn, interview with author, January 9, 2020.

189 *"a little intimidated":* Sharon Olds, interview with author, November 11, 2019.

189 *"an aura of restraint":* Alice Quinn, interview with author, January 9, 2020.

189 *"reserved, formal, and proper":* Bobbie Bristol, interview with author, August 5, 2019.

190 *"unbearable"; "unmistakable power":* Bobbie Bristol to Judith Jones, February 14, 1991, Knopf private files.

190 *She acquired Sharon Olds's* The Father: The contract, held in Knopf's private files, is dated July 16, 1991, for an advance of $5,000.

190 *"I hadn't expected to ever be there"; "Her sympathetic nature":* Sharon Olds, interview with author, November 11, 2019.

190 *"Praise* The Father. *Praise Sharon Olds":* Adam Mars-Jones. "Tomb for Two," *London Review of Books* 16, no. 3 (February 10, 1994), https://www.lrb.co.uk/the-paper/v16/n03/adam-mars-jones/tomb-for-two.

191 *"She knew a lot about feelings":* Sharon Olds, interview with author, November 11, 2019.

191 *"For Judith—Wise guide":* Signed broadside of "The Protester" by Sharon Olds, hung, framed, in Judith Jones's Manhattan apartment until after her death.

191 *their relationship deepened:* Bobbie Bristol, interview with author, August 5, 2019; Sharon Olds, interview with author, November 11, 2019.

191 *"Judith was not intimidatible":* Sharon Olds, interview with author, November 11, 2019.

191 *"pure fire in the hands":* Michael Ondaatje blurb on back jacket of Sharon Olds, *The Wellspring* (New York: Alfred A. Knopf, 1996).

192 *Judith moves like a dancer:* "The Scattering of Evan Jones' Ashes" was published in Galway Kinnell's collection, *Strong Is Your Hold* (Boston: Houghton Mifflin, 2006).

192 *Late one evening, she left Greensboro:* Story recounted by Sona Iyengar, "72-year-old survives washout," *Burlington Free Press*, July 6, 1996, Judith Jones Private Collection.

193 *"doing okay":* Judith Jones, quoted in Maggie Maurice, *Vermont Times*, July 10, 1996, 1.

193 *"Unforgettable"; "Only Judith would":* Rux Martin, quoted in Sona Iyengar, "72-year-old survives washout," 1 .

193 *"I felt a lot of fight in me":* Judith Jones, quoted in Sona Iyengar, "72-year-old survives washout," 1.

193 *"Hello You Guys!":* Nina Simonds, fax to Judith Jones, December 15, 1997, Judith Jones Private Collection.

193 *Schneider, who had:* Ken Schneider, interview with author, November 22, 2019.

193 *"She didn't necessarily want to live":* Bobbie Bristol, interview with author, August 5, 2019.

194 *"If you want to come":* Nina Simonds, fax to Judith Jones, December 15, 1997, Judith Jones Private Collection.

194 *"We had a lovely talk":* Judith Jones's notebook, Judith Jones Private Collection.

194 *She'd dreamed about Dick:* Judith Jones's notebook, Judith Jones Private Collection.

194 *"walked all the way back home":* Judith Jones's notebook, Judith Jones Private Collection.

194 *"that we have been sold to Bertelsmann":* Judith Jones's notebook, Judith Jones Private Collection.

196 *In the end, the advance:* Judith Jones to Geoffrey Drummond, January 15, 1997, Knopf private files.

196 *"Above all, the book should be":* Judith Jones to Geoffrey Drummond, January 15, 1997.

196 *In mid-February 1998, Judith had hired David Nussbaum:* David Nussbaum wrote to Judith on February 1, 1998, to accept the job offer. "Dear Judith Jones, I am still wonderfully excited that you called me about the Jacques and Julia project. I believe you have received from Rux Martin the letter I wrote her, in which I expressed my desire to work with culinary talents, seeking to elicit and articulate their most compelling ideas and useful knowledge. Could I possibly ask for a more thrilling assignment than the one you describe?," Knopf private files.

196 *"Your presence . . . was really helpful":* David Nussbaum to Judith Jones, May 1, 1998, Knopf private files.

197 *"tell the life story of food":* Kat Craddock, "A Note From Our Editor: *Saveur*'s New Chapter," *Saveur*, April 10, 2023, https://www.saveur.com/culture /saveur-new-chapter/. *Saveur*'s founding editors were Dorothy Kalins, Christopher Hirsheimer, Michael Grossman, and Colman Andrews.

197–98 *"I saw your photographs"; "I didn't give it any thought"; "It looked like a movie set"; "that wasn't me"; "Judith wasn't a visual person"; "She was so meticulous":* Christopher Hirsheimer, interview with author, June 20, 2023.

199 *"[I]t now reminds me":* Julia Child with Alex Prud'homme, *My Life In France* (New York: Knopf, 2006), 302.

199 *"I believe that some of us":* Judith Jones, "Le Cercle du Cirque," *Saveur*, April 2001, 27.

200 *"The experience opened up a new world":* Jones, "Le Cercle du Cirque."

200 *"I was simply delighted to read your piece":* Angus Cameron to Judith Jones, November 1, 2001, Judith Jones Private Collection.

200 *"You should write a big general book":* Angus Cameron to Judith Jones, November 24, 2001, Judith Jones Private Collection.

200 *"I am now more than ever convinced":* Angus Cameron to Judith Jones, undated, Judith Jones Private Collection.

CHAPTER 18

202 *After* Saveur *published Judith's essay about Paris:* Christopher Hirsheimer, interview with author, June 20, 2023.

202 *Judith wrote an essay on sorrel and gooseberries:* Judith Jones, "The Lemons of the North," *Saveur*, July 10, 2001, https://www.saveur.com/article/Kitchen /The-Lemons-of-the-North/.

202 *she told Hirsheimer about the beaver:* Christopher Hirsheimer, interview with author, June 20, 2023; Judith Jones, *The Tenth Muse: My Life in Food* (New York: Alfred A. Knopf, 2007), 168–70.

203 *Hirsheimer told Judith the story was too good:* Christopher Hirsheimer, interview with author, June 20, 2023.

204 *"I was afraid it wasn't good enough":* Lidia Bastianich, interview with author, September 9, 2019.

204 *"Here in America, the respect":* Lidia Bastianich, interview with author, September 9, 2019.

204 *"We live in a society that disparages age":* Judith Jones, "A Recipe for Life: A Ripe Old Age," *Vogue*, August 2005, 110, 115.

206 *Julia Child had called Peter Kump:* "About Us," James Beard Foundation https://www.jamesbeard.org/about.

207 *"I doubted that I would ever find pleasure":* Jones, *The Tenth Muse,* 181.

207 *"Ms. Jones may not be the mother":* Julia Moskin, "An Editing Life, a Book of Her Own," *New York Times,* October 24, 2007, https://www.nytimes.com/2007/10/24/dining/24jone.html.

207 *"If we had in our libraries only":* Dorothy Kalins, "Taste Maker," *New York Times,* November 4, 2007, https://www.nytimes.com/2007/11/04/books/review/Kalins-t.html.

208 *"added to that whole sense":* Judith Jones, interview by Linda Kulman, "Judith Jones Toasts a Culinary Life in 'Tenth Muse,'" Book Tour, NPR, January 8, 2008, https://www.npr.org/2008/01/08/17809903/judith-jones-toasts-a-culinary-life-in-tenth-muse.

208 *"I first heard about it when [Powell] had her blog":* Judith Jones, interview by Linda Kulman, "Judith Jones Toasts a Culinary Life in 'Tenth Muse.'"

209 *In 2012, Anne Tyler, who rarely gave interviews:* Anne Tyler, quoted in Hillel Italie, "Judith Jones Dies at 93; Changed American Cuisine by Publishing Julia Child," *Los Angeles Times,* August 2, 2017, https://www.latimes.com/local/obituaries/la-me-judith-jones-20170802-story.html.

209 *shoestring budget:* Christopher Hirsheimer, interview with author.

209 *Judith's advance from her employer of nearly fifty years was $25,000:* The contract for *The Pleasures of Cooking for One* is held in Judith Jones Private Collection.

209 *In early 2009, Judith had taken the bus:* Christopher Hirsheimer, interview with author, June 20, 2023.

209 *"I looked up and the light"; "It was such a special moment"; "I like to walk into a kitchen":* Christopher Hirsheimer, interview with author, June 20, 2023.

210 *"just panting by the time":* Charlotte Druckman, "Judith Jones, In Her Own Words," Eater, September 23, 2015, https://www.eater.com/2015/9/23/9355183/judith-jones.

210 *"This is apt to be a messy-looking pancake":* Judith Jones, *The Pleasures of Cooking for One* (New York: Alfred A. Knopf, 2009), 180.

210 *"Cooking is a sensual experience":* Jones, *The Pleasures of Cooking for One,* 12.

210 *"She was slowing down":* Ken Schneider, interview with author, November 22, 2019.

211–13 *On the morning of January 1, 2015; Bill Needelman, a close friend of Jane Gunther; Meri Zeinklishvili-Dubrova had been born; The family settled in Orlando; Judith was skeptical at first; "She had a very big wish to live"; Judith wasn't as steady on her feet; In the evenings, Judith would put on music; "She filled up her life a different way"; "She was able to do it"; Judith offered the guest bedroom; Meri accepted, and settled into, the small room:* Meri Zeinklishvili-Dubrova, interview with author, October 3, 2019.

214 *"Meri was the last great love":* Bobbie Bristol, email correspondence to author, June 7, 2023.

214 *"For Meri—From whom I've learned":* Inscription shared with author by Meri Zeinklishvili-Dubrova on October 3, 2019.

CODA

215 *"Judith, it's Christopher Hirsheimer":* Christopher Hirsheimer, interview with author, June 20, 2023.

216 *"Authors and publishing colleagues":* Robert D. McFadden, "Judith Jones, Editor of Literature and Culinary Delight, Dies at 93," *New York Times,* August 2, 2017, https://www.nytimes.com/2017/08/02/us/judith-jones-dead.html.

217 *"the legendary editor":* Joe Yonan, "Judith Jones, Cookbook Editor Who Brought Julia Child and Others to the Table, Dies at 93," *Washington Post,* August 2, 2017, https://www.washingtonpost.com/local/obituaries/judith -jones-cookbook-author-who-brought-julia-child-and-others-to-the-table -dies-at-93/2017/08/02/611b527c-7781-11e7-8f39-eeb7d3a2d304_story .html.

217 *"both as a person and as an editor"; "Few better embodied":* Hillel Italie, "Judith Jones Dies at 93; Changed American Cuisine by Publishing Julia Child," *Los Angeles Times,* August 2, 2017, https://www.latimes.com/local/obituaries /la-me-judith-jones-20170802-story.html.

218 *"I think a lot about how extraordinary":* Sharon Olds, interview with author, November 11, 2019.

INDEX

ABOUT THE AUTHOR

Sara B. Franklin is a writer, teacher, and oral historian. She received a 2020–2021 National Endowment for the Humanities (NEH) Public Scholars grant for her research on Judith Jones and teaches courses on food, writing, and oral history at New York University's Gallatin School of Individualized Study. She is the editor of *Edna Lewis: At the Table with an American Original* and coauthor of *The Phoenicia Diner Cookbook*. She holds a PhD in food studies from NYU and studied documentary storytelling at both the Duke Center for Documentary Studies and the Salt Institute for Documentary Studies. She lives with her children in Kingston, New York. Find out more at SaraBFranklin.com.